The University in Exception

Education for Critical Consciousness, Paulo Freire
Pedagogy of Hope, Paulo Freire
Marx's Concept of Man, Erich Fromm and Karl Marx
To Have or To Be?, Erich Fromm
Truth and Method, Hans Georg Gadamer
All Men Are Brothers, Mohandas K. Gandhi
Violence and the Sacred, René Girard
Among the Dead Cities, A. C. Grayling
Towards the Light, A. C. Grayling
The Three Ecologies, Félix Guattari
The Essence of Truth, Martin Heidegger
The Odyssey, Homer
Eclipse of Reason, Max Horkheimer
Language of the Third Reich, Victor Klemperer
Rhythmanalysis, Henri Lefebvre
After Virtue, Alasdair MacIntyre
Time for Revolution, Antonio Negri
Apologia Pro Vita Sua, John Henry Newman
The Politics of Aesthetics, Jacques Rancière
Course in General Linguistics, Ferdinand de Saussure
An Actor Prepares, Constantin Stanislavski
Building A Character, Constantin Stanislavski
Creating A Role, Constantin Stanislavski
Interrogating the Real, Slavoj Žižek

Some titles are not available in North America.

The Universal Exception

By Slavoj Žižek

Edited by Rex Butler and Scott Stephens

BLOOMSBURY

LONDON · NEW DELHI · NEW YORK · SYDNEY

Bloomsbury Academic

An imprint of Bloomsbury Publishing Plc

50 Bedford Square	1385 Broadway
London	New York
WC1B 3DP	NY 10018
UK	USA

www.bloomsbury.com

Bloomsbury is a registered trade mark of Bloomsbury Publishing Plc

First published 2006

British Library Cataloguing-in-Publication Data
A catalogue record for this book is available from the British Library.

ISBN: PB: 978-1-4725-7007-9
ePDF: 978-1-4725-7009-3
ePub: 978-1-4725-7008-6

Library of Congress Cataloging-in-Publication Data
A catalogue record for this book is available from the Library of Congress.

Typeset by Newgen Knowledge Works (P) Ltd., Chennai, India
Printed and bound in India

Contents

Section Three Really existing capitalism 169

Section Four What is (not) to be done 289

Acknowledgments

The editors would like to thank Sarah Douglas for her consistent enthusiasm and patience throughout the preparation of this and the preceding volume.

In particular, Scott Stephens would like to acknowledge the support of the Australian Research Theological Foundation, whose generosity at the early stages of this project was indispensable.

Preface to the paperback edition

The big Other between violence and civility

Slavoj Žižek

The 'universal exception', according to Lacan, is the fundamental feature of the symbolic order (the 'big Other') as the order of universality: each universality is grounded in its constitutive exception. This feature is to be supplemented with its no less paradoxical obverse, the so-called 'not-All [*pas tout*]': an order (or rather, a field, a signifying space) with no exception that is *eo ipso* not-all, and cannot be totalized. These two features – formalized by Lacan in his 'formulae of sexuation' – are the two aspects of the *inconsistency* of the big Other: the symbolic order is by definition antagonistic, thwarted, non-identical-with-itself, marked by a constitutive lack, virtual – or, as Lacan put it, 'there is no big Other'.

And since the second volume of my selected writings focuses on ethico-political topics, it seemed appropriate to add a new text to the paperback edition that would deploy the different modes in which this inconsistency of the big Other affects the functioning of the symbolic order in the ethico-political sphere: the ironic status of the big Other; the tension in every normative field between its explicit and implicit rules; the key role of civility (rules we are expected to obey without being ordered to do so); the unique figure of an individual who can directly stand in for the big Other; and, last but not least, different strategies for subverting the big Other, of suspending its efficiency.

Orwell's Lesson

In the introduction to my book on Krysztof Kieślowski, *The Fright of Real Tears*, I invoked an experience of mine in order to exemplify the sad state of cultural studies today:

> Some months before writing this, at an art round table, I was asked to comment on a painting I had seen there for the first time. I did not have *any* idea about it, and so I engaged in a total bluff, which went something like this: the frame of the painting in front of us is not its true frame; there is another, invisible, frame, implied by the structure of the painting, which frames our perception of the painting, and these two frames do not overlap – there is an invisible gap separating the two. The pivotal content of the painting is not rendered in its visible part, but is located in this dislocation of the two frames, in the gap that separates them. Are we, today, in our postmodern madness, still able to discern the traces of this gap? Perhaps more than the reading of a painting hinges on it; perhaps the decisive dimension of humanity will be lost when we lose the capacity to discern this gap . . . To my surprise, this brief intervention was a huge success, and many following participants referred to the dimension in-between-the-two-frames, elevating it into a term. This very success made me sad, really sad. What I encountered here was not only the efficiency of a bluff, but a much more radical apathy at the very heart of today's cultural studies.[1]

However, later on in the same book, I reused the example of 'between-the-two-frames', but this time without irony, as a straightforward theoretical concept:

> One of the minimal definitions of a modernist painting concerns the function of its frame. The frame of the painting in front of us is not its true frame; there is another, invisible frame, the frame implied by the structure of the painting, which frames our perception of the painting, and these two frames by definition never overlap – there is an invisible gap separating them. The pivotal content of the painting is not rendered in its visible part, but is located in this dislocation of the two frames, in the gap that separates them.[2]

What further saddened me is the way that even some of my friends and close readers missed the point: most of those who noticed the repetition read it either as a self-parodying indication of the fact that I don't take my own theories seriously, or else as a sign of my growing senility (that I simply forgot toward the end of the book that I mocked the same notion in the introduction). It should not have been that difficult to perceive that my gesture here perfectly illustrates the point I repeatedly try to make apropos of today's predominant attitude of cynicism and of not-taking-oneself-seriously: even if the subject mocks a certain belief, this in no way undermines this belief's symbolic efficiency – it continues to determine the subject's activity. When we make fun of an attitude, the truth most often lies in the attitude itself, not in our professed distance toward it: I will mock it in order to conceal from myself the fact that this attitude effectively determines my behaviour. In *The Road to Wigan Pier*, George Orwell identified, with remarkable precision, that our predominant attitude is one of ironic distance toward our true beliefs:

> The left-wing opinions of the average 'intellectual' are mainly spurious. From pure imitativeness he jeers at things which in fact he believes in. As one example out of many, take the public-school code of honour, with its 'team spirit' and 'Don't hit a man when he's down', and all the rest of that familiar bunkum. Who has not laughed at it? Who, calling himself an 'intellectual', would dare *not* to laugh at it? But it is a bit different when you meet somebody who laughs at it *from the outside*; just as we spend our lives in abusing England but grow very angry when we hear a foreigner saying exactly the same things . . . It is only when you meet someone of a different culture from yourself that you begin to realize what your own beliefs really are.[3]

For Orwell, there is nothing 'interior' about this true ideological identity of mine – my innermost beliefs are all 'out there', embodied in practices that go right up to the immediate materiality of my body: 'my notions – notions of good and evil, of pleasant and unpleasant, of funny and serious, of ugly and beautiful – are essentially *middle-class* notions; my taste in books and food and clothes, my sense of honour, my table manners, my turns of speech, my accent, even the characteristic movements of my body . . .'[4] One should definitely add to this list *smell*: perhaps the key difference between lower class and middle class concerns the way they relate to smell. For the middle class, lower classes smell: their members do not wash regularly – or, to quote the proverbial answer of a middle-class Parisian to the question of why he prefers to ride the first-class cars in the metro: 'I wouldn't mind riding with workers in the second class – it is only that they smell!' This brings us to one of the possible definitions of what 'neighbour' means today: a neighbour is the one who, by definition, *smells*. This is why deodorants and soaps are crucial – they make neighbours at least minimally tolerable: I am ready to love my neighbours . . . provided they don't smell too bad. According to a recent report, scientists in a laboratory in Venezuela added a further item to the above series: through genetic manipulation, they have succeeded in growing beans which, when eaten, do not generate bad-smelling and socially embarrassing flatulence! So now, along with decaffeinated coffee, fat-free pastries, diet cola and alcohol-free beer, we get wind-free beans![5] It is at this level that class antagonism is inscribed into our everyday habits. Exemplary here is the ambiguity of the predominant Leftist intellectual attitude toward class distinction – Orwell's description holds today more than ever:

> We all rail against class-distinctions, but very few people seriously want to abolish them. Here you come upon the important fact that every revolutionary opinion draws part of its strength from a secret conviction that nothing can be changed . . . Take the question of imperialism, for instance. Every left-wing 'intellectual' is, as a matter of course, an anti-imperialist. He claims to be outside the empire-racket as automatically and self-righteously as he claims to be outside the class-racket. Even the right-wing 'intellectual', who is definitely not in revolt against British imperialism, pretends to regard it with a sort of amused detachment . . . The fact that has got to be faced is that to abolish class-distinctions means abolishing a part of yourself. Here am I, a typical member of the middle class. It is easy for me to say that I want to get rid of class-distinctions, but nearly everything I think and do is a result of class-distinctions . . . When I grasp this I grasp that it is no use clapping a proletarian on the back and telling him that he is as good a man as I am; if I want real

contact with him, I have got to make an effort for which very likely I am unprepared.

Orwell's point is that radicals invoke the need for revolutionary change as a kind of superstitious token that is intended to achieve the opposite, to *prevent* that very change from actually occurring – and so today's academic Leftist who criticizes capitalist cultural imperialism is, in reality, terrified by the prospect that their field of study would break down. There is, however, a limit to this strategy: Orwell's insight holds only for a certain kind of 'bourgeois' Leftist: there are Leftists who *do have* the courage of their convictions, who do not only want 'revolution without revolution', as Robespierre put it – Jacobins and Bolsheviks, among others. The starting point of these true revolutionaries may in fact be the position of the 'bourgeois' Leftists. What happens is that, in the middle of their pseudo-radical posturing, they get caught up in their own game and are prepared to call into question their subjective position. It is difficult to imagine a more trenchant political example of the weight of Lacan's distinction between the 'subject of the enunciated' and the 'subject of the enunciation': first, in a direct negation, you start by wanting to 'change the world' without endangering the subjective position from which you are ready to enforce the change; then, in the 'negation of negation', the subject enacting the change is ready to pay the subjective price for it, to change himself, or, to quote Gandhi's nice formula, to *be* himself the change he wants to see in the world.

This substance of our being, which is so difficult to change, is *civility*. In a scene from the film *Break Up*, a nervous Vince Vaughn angrily reproaches Jennifer Aniston: 'You wanted me to wash the dishes, and I'll wash the dishes – what's the problem?' She replies: 'I don't want you to wash the dishes – I want you to *want* to wash the dishes!' This is the minimal reflexivity of desire, its 'terrorist' demand: I want you not only to do what I want, but I want you to do it as if you really want to do it – I want to regulate not only what you do, but also your desires. The worst thing you can do, even worse than not doing what I want you to do, is to do what I want you to do without wanting to do it . . . The mask of civility is precisely a way of feigning that I want to do what the other asks me to do, so that my compliance with the other's demand does not exert pressure on him or her.

The Shibboleth of Civility

In a wonderful short essay on civility,[6] Robert Pippin elaborates the enigmatic in-between status of this notion which designates all those acts that display the basic subjective stance of respect for others as free and autonomous agents, the benevolent attitude of making the step beyond any strictly utilitarian or 'rational' calculation of interpersonal costs and benefits, being willing to engage with others from a position of trust, and so on. Although measured by the degree of its obligatory character, it is more than kindness or generosity (one cannot oblige people to be generous), but distinctly less than a moral or legal obligation. And it is precisely this that is wrong with politically correct attempts to moralize or even directly penalize modes of behaviour which pertain to civility (such as hurting others with the vulgar obscenities of one's language): they potentially undermine the precious 'middle ground' of civility, which mediates between uncontrolled private fantasies and the strictly regulated forms of intersubjective behaviour. In more Hegelian terms, what gets lost in the penalization of un-civility is 'ethical substance [*Sittlichkeit*]' as such: in contrast to laws and explicit normative regulations, civility is by definition 'substantial', something experienced as always already given and never imposed as such. This is why civility participates in all the paradoxes of those 'states-that-are-essentially-by-products': it, by definition, cannot be purposefully enacted – if it is, we have the right to say that it is a false civility, not a true one. Pippin is therefore correct to link the crucial role of civility in modern societies to the rise of the autonomous free individual – not only in the sense that civility is the practice of treating others as equal, free and autonomous subjects, but, in a much more refined way, the fragile web of civility is the 'social substance' of free independent individuals, it is their very mode of (inter) dependence. If this substance disintegrates, then the social space of individual freedom is foreclosed.

The theoretical point of civility is thus that free subjectivity has to be sustained by an act of feigning. However, against our expectations, it is feigning to do freely what one is under pressure or obligation to do (the most elementary form, of course, is the ritual of 'potlatch', the exchange of gifts in primitive societies). How, then, does civility relate to the set of unwritten rules which *de facto* constrain my freedom while sustaining its appearance? Let us imagine a scene in which, in order to be polite and not to humiliate another, I phrase my order (since I am in the position of authority) as a kind request: 'Would you be so kind as to . . .' (Along the same lines, when powerful or famous people receive an insignificant individual, one of the common forms of politeness is to pretend that the individual is doing them a favour by visiting – 'Thank you for being so kind as to pay me this visit . . .') This, however, is not true civility: civility is not an obligation-feigned-as-a-free-act, but rather its exact opposite: *a free act feigned as an obligation*. Back to our example: the true act of civility from someone in power would have been to feign that he is just fulfilling his obligation, when, in reality, his is an act of generosity.

Freedom is thus sustained by a paradox that inverts the Spinozan definition of freedom as conceived necessity: *freedom is feigned necessity*. To put it in Hegelian terms, freedom is sustained by the ethical substance of our being. In a given society, certain features, attitudes and mores are no longer perceived as ideological but as 'neutral', as a non-ideological or common-sense way of life. Ideology is the explicitly posited (or 'marked' in the semiotic sense) position that stands out against this neutral background (like extreme religious zeal, or dedication to some political orientation). The Hegelian point here would have been that it is precisely this neutralization of some features into the spontaneously accepted background which today is ideology at its purest (and its most effective) – this is the dialectical 'coincidence of the opposites': the actualization of a notion (ideology, in this case) at its purest coincides with (or, more precisely, appears as) its opposite (as non-ideology). And, *mutatis mutandis*, the same goes for violence: social-symbolic violence appears as its opposite, as the spontaneity of the milieu in which we dwell, the air that we breathe.

One can also deduce the status of habits in a more formal way: every legal order (or every order of explicit normativity) must rely on a complex 'reflexive' network of informal rules that tell us how we are to apply its explicit norms: the extent to which we are to take them literally, how and when we are allowed, solicited even, to disregard them – this is the function of habit. To know the habits of a society, therefore, is *to know the meta-rules of how to practise its explicit norms*: when to apply or not to apply them; when to violate them; when not to take up a choice when offered; when we are implicitly obliged to do something but must pretend we are doing it freely. Recall the notorious offer-meant-to-be-refused: it is a 'habit' to refuse such an offer, and anyone who naïvely accepts it commits an unforgivable blunder. The same goes for those political situations in which a free choice is given *with the proviso that we make the right choice*: we are solemnly reminded that we can refuse, but we are expected to reject the offer and enthusiastically say 'Yes'. With many sexual prohibitions, the rules are the opposite: the explicit 'No' acts like an implicit injunction, 'Yes, do it – but in a discreet way!'

One of the more conspicuous strategies of 'totalitarian' régimes was to have criminal laws so severe that, if taken literally, *everyone* would be guilty of something, but then to hold back from their full enforcement. In this way, the régime could appear merciful ('You see, if we wanted, we could have all of you arrested and condemned, but don't be afraid, we will be lenient . . .') and, at the same time, wield a permanent threat over its subjects ('Do not play too much with us, remember that at any moment we can . . .'). In the former Yugoslavia, there was the infamous Article 133 of the penal code which could always be invoked to prosecute writers and journalists – it declared criminal any text that falsely presented the achievements of the socialist revolution or that *could arouse tension and discontent among the public* for the way it dealt with political, social, or other issues. This last category, obviously, was not only infinitely plastic but also conveniently self-relating: does not the very fact that you are accused by those in power confirm the fact that you 'aroused tension and discontent among the public'? In those years, I remember asking a Slovene politician how did he justify this article; he just smiled and, with a wink, told me: 'Well, we have to have some way of disciplining those who irritate us at our disposal.' This overlapping of potential total culpability (whatever you are doing *may* be a crime) and mercy (the fact that you are allowed to lead your life in peace is not a proof or consequence of your innocence, but of the mercy and benevolence of those in power) is a fundamental trait of totalitarian régimes, rendering them, by definition, as benevolent régimes that mercifully tolerate violations of the law.

The problem during the chaotic post-Soviet years under Yeltsin was precisely at this level: although the official laws were known (and largely the same as under the Soviet Union), what disintegrated was the complex network of implicit unwritten rules that sustained the entire social edifice. For example, if, in the Soviet Union, you wanted to get better hospital treatment, a new apartment, if you had some complaint against the authorities, if you were summoned to court, if you wanted your child to be admitted into a top school, if a factory manager needed raw materials delivered on time by the state contractors, everyone knew what you had to do, whom you had to bribe, what you could and couldn't do. After the collapse of Soviet power, one of the most frustrating aspects of the daily existence of ordinary people was that these unwritten rules themselves got blurred: people simply did not now know what to do. (One of the functions of organized crime was to provide a kind of *ersatz* legality: if you owned a small business and a customer owed you money, you turned to your mafia-protector who dealt with the problem because the state legal system was so inefficient). The stabilization under Putin amounts to the newly established transparency of these unwritten rules: now, once again, people mostly know what to do within the complex cobweb of social interactions.

This is also why at the most elementary level of symbolic exchange are the so-called 'empty gestures' – those offers made or meant to be rejected. It was Brecht who gave a poignant expression to this feature in his learning plays, particularly in *Jasager*, in which a young boy is asked freely to accept what will in any case be his fate (to be thrown into the valley); as his teacher explains it to him, it is customary to ask the victim if he agrees with his fate, but it is also customary for the victim to say 'Yes'. Belonging to society involves a paradoxical point at which each of us is ordered to embrace freely, as the result of our choice, what is imposed on us anyway (we all *must* love our country, our parents and so on). This paradox of choosing freely what is already necessary, of pretending (or maintaining the appearance) that there is a free choice, while effectively there is not, is a strict correlate of the notion of an empty symbolic gesture, a gesture that is meant to be rejected.

And is not a similar process at the heart of our everyday norms? In Japan, workers have the right to 40 days of leave each year – but they are expected not to take advantage of it. In John Irving's *A Prayer for Owen Meany*, after Owen, as a child, accidentally kills the mother of his best friend (John), he is, of course, terribly upset. To show how sorry he is, he discreetly delivers to John a gift of a complete collection of baseball cards, his most precious possession. However, Dan, John's delicate stepfather, tells him that the proper thing to do is to return the gift. Let us imagine a more down-to-earth situation: when, after being engaged in fierce competition for a promotion with my closest friend, I am successful, the proper thing to do is to offer to withdraw so that he gets the promotion, and the proper thing for my friend to do is to reject my offer – only in this way, perhaps, can our friendship be saved. What we have here is symbolic exchange at its purest: a gesture that is made to be rejected. The magic of symbolic exchange is that, although we end up back where we started, there is a palpable gain for both parties in their pact of solidarity. A similar logic is at work in the process of apologizing: if I hurt someone with a rude comment, the proper thing for me to do is to offer a sincere apology, and the proper thing for them to do is to say something like, 'Thanks, I appreciate it, but I wasn't offended. I knew you didn't mean it . . .' The point, of course, is that the declaration that no apology was needed can only be made after one has already apologized.

In politics proper, suffice it to recall the relationship between the great Western powers and Russia throughout the 1990s: in accordance with the silent pact regulating this relationship, Western states must treat Russia as a world power on condition that Russia doesn't act like one. In principle, it is possible for Russia effectively to behave as a world power, but if Russia wishes to retain its symbolic status as a world power, this possibility must not be taken advantage of.

The problem, of course, is this: what if the person to whom the offer is made actually accepts it? What if, upon being beaten in the competition for a promotion, I accept my friend's offer to take the promotion in his place? What if Russia really had behaved like a world power? This sort of situation is catastrophic: it causes the disintegration of the semblance (of freedom) that pertains to social order, which constitutes the dissolution of social substance itself. In this precise sense, those revolutionary-egalitarian figures, from Robespierre to John Brown, were (potentially, at least) *figures without habits*: they refused to take into account the habits that qualify the functioning of a universal rule. If all humans are equal, then all humans are to be treated as such; if blacks are also human, they should be immediately treated as such.

In another instance, during the early 1980s, a dissident student weekly newspaper in the former Yugoslavia wanted to protest against the so-called 'free' state elections. Fully aware of the limitations of the slogan, 'speak truth to power' (as Moustapha Safouan wrote, 'the trouble with this slogan is that it ignores the fact that power will not listen and that the people already know the truth as they make clear in their jokes'), rather than directly denouncing the elections as fixed, they decided to report them as if they really were free, as if their results really were uncertain. So, on the eve of the elections, they printed an extra edition of the newspaper with a large headline: 'Latest election results: it looks like the Communists will remain in power!' This simple intervention contravened the unwritten 'habit' (we all knew the elections weren't free, we just couldn't talk publicly about it): by treating the elections as free, it reminded the people of their non-freedom.

In the second season of *Nip-Tuck*, Sean learns that the real father of his adolescent son, Matt, is Christian, his partner. His first reaction is an angry outburst; then, in the aftermath of a failed operation to separate Siamese twins, he accepts Chris as a partner once again, with a moving speech around the operating table: 'I will never forgive you for what you did. But Matt is too precious, the best result of our partnership, so we should not lose this . . .' This resolution was obvious, too obvious – a much more elegant solution would have been for Sean simply to say: 'I will never forgive you for what you did'. The subjective position of this statement is already one of acceptance. The problem is that Sean *says too much* – so why does he go on? This is the interesting question. Is the American public that stupid? No. Why, then, this excess? What if a bald sign of true acceptance would already have been too much, too intense? Perhaps, since *Nip-Tuck* is an American series, this excess can be accounted for in terms of another difference between Europe and the USA. In Europe, the ground floor in a building is counted as '0', and the next floor up is the 'first floor'. In the USA, the 'first floor' is on the street level. In short, Americans start to count at '1', while Europeans know that '1' is already a stand-in for '0'. Or, to put it in more historical terms, Europeans are aware that, before one begins counting, there must be a 'ground' of tradition, which is always already given and, as such, cannot be counted. While in the USA – a land with no pre-modern historical tradition proper, and thus lacking such a 'ground' – things begin directly with self-legislated freedom, and the past is erased (or transposed on to Europe).[7] This lack of ground thus has to be supplemented by excessive speech: Sean cannot rely on the symbolic ground that would guarantee that Christian will get the message without explicitly stating it.

This also indicates how one should respond to the popular and seemingly convincing reply to all those worrying about the torture of prisoners suspected of terrorist acts: 'What's all the fuss about? The Americans are now openly admitting what they and other states were doing all along!' One should respond with a simple counter-question: 'If the representatives of the US government are only meaning this, *then why are they telling us this now?* Why didn't they just silently continue what they were doing before?' The proper dimension of human speech is the irreducible gap between the enunciated content and its act of enunciation: 'You tell me this, but why are you saying it openly now?' Let us imagine a wife and husband who coexist with a tacit agreement that they can carry on discreet extra-marital affairs. If, however, all of a sudden the husband openly tells his wife about an ongoing affair, she will have good reasons to panic: 'If it is just an affair, why are you telling me this? It must be something more!' The act of publicly reporting something is never neutral – it affects the reported content itself. The same goes for the recent open admission of torture: when we hear people like Dick Cheney making their obscene statements about the necessity of torture, we should ask them: 'If you just wanted secretly to torture some suspected terrorists, then why are you saying it publicly?' That is to say, what additional content is there in this statement that made the speaker enunciate it? The status of such sub- or meta-rules telling us how to deal with the explicit laws that regulate society is that of a *shibboleth*: the unannounced sign of some distinction known only to those who are already 'in', a sign whose very existence is invisible to those who are outside. This is why the first rule of egalitarian-emancipatory politics is, 'No shibboleths, please!'

Habits are thus the very stuff our identities are made of: in them, we enact and thus define what we effectively are as social beings, often in contrast with our perception of what we are – in their very transparency, they are the medium of social violence. We reach thereby the 'heart of darkness' of habits. Recall numerous cases of paedophilia that shatter the Catholic Church: when its representatives insist that these cases, deplorable as they are, are the Church's internal problem, and display great reluctance to collaborate with police in their investigation, they are, in a way, right – the paedophilia of Catholic priests is not something that concerns merely those persons who, because of accidental reasons of private history with no relation to the Church as an institution, happened to choose the profession of a priest; it is a phenomenon that concerns the Catholic Church as such, that is inscribed into its very functioning as a socio-symbolic institution. It does not concern the 'private' unconscious of individuals, but the 'unconscious' of the institution itself: it is not something that happens because the institution has to accommodate itself to the pathological realities of libidinal life in order to survive, but something that the institution itself needs in order to reproduce itself. One can well imagine a 'straight' (not paedophiliac) priest who, after years of service, gets involved in paedophilia because the very logic of the institution seduces him into it. Such an *institutional Unconscious* designates the obscene disavowed underside that, precisely as disavowed, sustains the public institution. (In the army, this underside consists of the obscene sexualized rituals of fragging, etc., that sustain group solidarity.) In other words, it is not simply that, for conformist reasons, the Church tries to hush up these embarrassing paedophilic scandals; in defending itself, the Church defends its innermost obscene secret. What this means is that identifying oneself with this secret side is a key constituent of the very identity of a Christian priest: if a priest seriously (not just rhetorically) denounces these scandals, he thereby excludes himself from the ecclesiastic community, he is no longer 'one of us' (in exactly the same way that a citizen of a town in the American South in the 1920s, if they denounced the Ku Klux Klan to the police, excluded themselves from their community, i.e., betrayed its fundamental solidarity). Consequently, the answer to the Church's reluctance should be not only that we are dealing with criminal cases and that, if the Church does not participate fully in their investigation, it is an accomplice after the fact; the Church *as such*, as an institution, should be investigated with regard to the way it systematically creates conditions for such crimes.

Save the appearances!

It may sound strange to characterize Stalinism as a régime of extreme civility, but, in a sense, this is precisely what it was. In what sense? The standard condemnation of Stalin is comprised of two propositions: (1) he was a cynic who knew very well how things were (for instance, that the accused at the show trials were really innocent);

and (2) he knew exactly what he was doing (he had complete control over events). But documents from the recently accessible Kremlin archives point to a rather opposite view: Stalin essentially *did* believe (in the official ideology, in his role as an honest leader, in the guilt of the accused and so on), and he did *not* in actuality control events (the results of his own actions frequently shocked him).[8] Lars T. Lih has proposed a distressing conclusion: 'The people of the Soviet Union would probably have been better off if Stalin had been more cynical than he was.'[9] There is, however, a different way of reading Stalin's 'belief': it was not that he 'personally' believed, but *he wanted the big Other to believe*. Lih himself points in this direction when he condones Robert Tucker's amazement at

> how much pain and suffering went into the mass production of confessions during 1937. These confessions served no earthly purpose; they were promptly filed away and forgotten. Tucker speculates that Stalin insisted on these confessions as proof to posterity that his vision of a world filled with enemies was basically correct.[10]

What if, however, we take the statement that the extorted confessions 'served no earthly purpose' more literally: they were 'filed away and forgotten' because their actual addressee was not the people who were to come but the virtual 'big Other' – the same big Other that can only account for the well-known incident concerning the *Great Soviet Encyclopaedia*, which occurred in 1954, immediately after the fall of Beria. When Soviet subscribers received the volume of the *Encyclopaedia* that contained entries under the letter 'B', there was, of course, a double-page article on Beria, praising him as the great hero of the Soviet Union. But after his fall and denunciation as a traitor, all subscribers received a letter from the publishing house requesting that they cut out and return the page on Beria, in exchange for which they were sent a double-page entry (with photos) on the Bering pass, so that, when they inserted it into the volume, its wholeness was re-established and there was no blank to bear witness to this sudden rewriting of history. The mystery here is: *for whom* was this (semblance of) wholeness maintained, if every subscriber *knew* about the manipulation (since he had to perform it *themselves*)? The only answer is, of course: it was for the innocent gaze of the big Other. This is why the structure of Stalinism is inherently theological, and why Stalinism so desperately sought to maintain appearances. This solution to the enigma also allows us to reject the dilemma over whether 'Stalin was a believer or a cynic'. He was both at the same time. Personally, of course, he was often aware of the falsity of the official discourse, but he was simultaneously quite sincere in his effort to safeguard the innocence and sincerity of the 'big Other'.

This brings us to the paradoxical figure of an individual who stands for the big Other. One should not think primarily of those leader-figures who directly embody their community (the king, president or master), but rather of the more mysterious figures of the *protectors of appearances* – such as a child whose otherwise corrupt parents and relatives try desperately to keep him ignorant of their depraved lives, or the leader for whom Potemkin's villages are raised.

Today, it seems that appearances no longer need to be protected. We all know of the innocent child from Andersen's 'The Emperor's New Clothes', who publicly proclaims the fact that the emperor is naked. Today, in our cynical era, such a strategy no longer works, it has lost its disruptive power, since everyone constantly states that the emperor is naked (that Western democracies are torturing terrorist suspects, that wars are fought for profit and so on) but nothing happens, and the system just goes on functioning.

When the lovers meet for the last time at the abandoned train station in David Lean's *Brief Encounter*, their solitude is immediately disturbed by Celia Johnson's noisy and inquisitive friend who, unaware of the underlying tension between the couple, goes on prattling about ridiculously insignificant everyday incidents. Unable directly to communicate, the couple can only desperately stare straight ahead. This common prattler is the 'big Other' at its purest: while it appears to be an accidental unfortunate intruder, its role is structurally necessary.[11] When, toward the film's end, we see this scene for the second time, accompanied now by Celia Johnson's voice-over, she tells us that she did not listen to what her friend was saying, not understanding even a word of it – however, precisely as such, this prattling provided the necessary background, a kind of safety-cushion, to the lovers' last meeting, preventing its self-destructive explosion or, even worse, its turn into banality: the insignificant prattling had to go on in order to prevent catastrophe, so the intruding friend arrived at exactly the right moment. That is to say, on the one hand, it is this very presence of the naïve prattler who 'understands nothing' of the true tension of the situation that enables the lovers to maintain a minimum of control over their predicament, since they feel compelled to 'maintain the proper appearances' in front of this gaze. On the other hand, one should recall that, in the few words the lovers manage to exchange privately prior to their interruption, they are confronted by an unpleasant question: if they really love each other so passionately that they cannot live without each other, why don't they simply divorce their spouses? The prattler arrives just in time, enabling the lovers to maintain the tragic grandeur of their predicament – without this third intruder, they would have to confront the banality and compromised nature of their predicament. The shift to be made in a properly dialectical analysis is thus from the condition of impossibility to the condition of possibility: what appears initially as the 'condition of impossibility', as an obstacle, becomes the enabling condition of what then transpires.[12]

When a person is experiencing some traumatic shock, possessed by the wish to disappear, to fall into the void, a superficial external intrusion – such as the incessant prattle of a bystander – is the only thing that stands between them and the abyss of self-destruction: what appears as a ridiculous intrusion is, in fact, the means of saving their life. So when, alone with her companion in a carriage compartment, Celia Johnson complains about the inane prattle and even expresses the desire to kill the intruder ('I wish you would stop talking . . . I wish you were dead now . . . no, that was silly and unkind . . . but I wish you would stop talking'), we can well imagine what would have happened if the intruder were actually to stop talking: either Celia Johnson would immediately have collapsed, or she would be compelled to utter a humiliating plea: 'Please, just go on talking, no matter what you are saying.' Is this unfortunate intruder not a kind of envoy of (a stand-in for) the absent husband, his representative (in the sense of Lacan's paradoxical statement that woman is one of the Names-of-the-Father)? She intervenes at just the right moment to prevent the drift into self-annihilation (as in the famous scene in *Vertigo* when the phone rings, thus arresting the dangerous drift of Scottie and Madeleine into too erotic an encounter). The husband and the prattler are effectively two aspects of one and the same entity, the 'big Other', the addressee of Celia Johnson's confession. The husband is the ideal confessor, dependable, open, understanding, but the one who should not know about what is to be confessed and thus cannot be told the truth – he should be protected from the truth, he is the subject supposed *not* to know: 'Dear Fred. There's so much that I want to say to you. You're the only one in the world with the wisdom and gentleness to understand it . . . As it is, you are the only one in the world that I can never tell. Never, never . . . I don't want you to be hurt.' The prattler as the unreliable gossiping acquaintance is the wrong person at the right time and place: Celia Johnson wants to confess to her, but cannot: 'I wish I could trust you. I wish you were a wise, kind friend instead of a gossiping acquaintance I've known casually for years and never particularly cared for.'

The 'big Other' between the Two Frames

This brings us to our final question: how are we to disturb the 'big Other' *qua* the order of appearances? A direct step outside, a brutal violation of the order of appearances, is not enough: it ruins the appearance without undermining it from within. There is, however, another way to be found – among others – in the films of Alfred Hitchcock, *the* master of appearances.

In pre-digital times, when I was in my teens, I remember seeing a bad copy of *Vertigo* – its last seconds were simply missing, so that the movie appeared to have a happy ending: Scottie reconciled with Judy, forgiving her and accepting her as a partner, the two of them passionately embracing. My point is that such an ending is not as artificial as it may seem: it is rather in the actual ending that the sudden appearance of the Mother Superior from the staircase below functions as a kind of negative *deus ex machina*, a sudden intrusion in no way properly grounded in the narrative logic, which prevents the happy ending. From where does the nun appear? From the same pre-ontological realm of shadows from which Scottie himself secretly observes Madeleine in the florist. And it is here that we should locate the hidden continuity between *Vertigo* and *Psycho*: the Mother Superior appears out of the same void from which, 'out of nowhere', Norman appears in the shower murder sequence of *Psycho*, brutally attacking Marion, interrupting the reconciliatory ritual of cleansing.

And we should follow this trajectory to its end: in an unexpected structural homology with the between-two-frames dimension of a painting, many of Hitchcock's films seem to rely on a between-two-stories dimension. What if *Vertigo* were to end after Madeleine's suicide, with the devastated Scottie listening to Mozart in the sanatorium? What if *Psycho* were to end moments before the murder in the shower, with Marion staring into the falling water, purifying herself? In each case, we would get a consistent short film. In the case of *Vertigo*, it would be a drama of the destruction caused by violent-obsessive male desire: it is the very excessive nature of male desire that makes it destroy or mortify its object – (male) love is murder, as Otto Weininger knew long ago. In the case of *Psycho*, it would be a morality tale about a catastrophe prevented at the last minute: Marion commits a minor crime, escaping with the stolen money to rejoin her lover; on the way, she meets Norman who is like a figure of moral warning, rendering visible to Marion what awaits her at the end of the line if she follows the path taken; this terrifying vision sobers her, and she withdraws to her room, plans her return and then takes a shower, as if to cleanse herself of moral dirt. In both cases, it is thus as if what we are at first lured into taking as the full story is all of a sudden displaced, re-framed, transposed into another story – something along the lines of the idea envisaged by Borges in the opening story of his *Ficciones*, which culminates in the claim: '*Un libro que no encierra su contra-libro es considerado incompleto* [A book which does not contain its counter-book is considered incomplete]'. In his 2005–2006 seminar, Jacques-Alain Miller elaborated this idea, with reference to the Argentine writer Ricardo Piglia. As an example of Borges' claim, Miller refers to Piglia's reading of a tale by Chekhov, whose nucleus is distilled as: 'A man goes to the casino at Monte Carlo, wins a million, returns to his place and commits suicide':

> If this is the nucleus of a story, one must, in order to tell it, divide the twisted story in two: on the one hand, the story of the game; on the other, that of the suicide. Thus Piglia's first thesis: that a story

always has a double characteristic and always tells two stories at the same time, which provides the opportunity to distinguish the story which is on the first plane from the number 2 story which is encoded in the interstices of story number 1. We should note that story number 2 only appears when the story is concluded, and it has the effect of surprise. What joins these two stories is that the elements, the events, are inscribed in two narrative registers which are at the same time distinct, simultaneous and antagonistic, and the construction itself of the story is supported by the junction between the two stories. The inversions which seem superfluous in the development of story number 1 become, on the contrary, essential in the plot of story number 2 . . .

There is a modern form of the story which transforms this structure by omitting the surprise finale without closing the structure of the story, which leaves a trace of a narrative, and the tension of the two stories is never resolved. This is what one considers as being properly modern: the subtraction of the final anchoring point which allows the two stories to continue in an unresolved tension.

This is the case, says Piglia, with Hemingway, who pushed the ellipse to its highest point in such a way that the secret story remains hermetic. One perceives simply that there is another story which needs to be told, but which remains absent. There is a hole. If one modified Chekhov's note in Hemingway's style, it would not narrate the suicide, but rather the text would be assembled in such a way that one might think that the reader already knew it.

Kafka constitutes another of these variants. He narrates very simply, in his novels, the most secret story, a secret story which appears on the first plane, told as if coming from itself, and he encodes the story which should be visible but which becomes, on the contrary, enigmatic and hidden.[13]

Back to Hitchcock's *Vertigo* and *Psycho*, is this not precisely the structure of the narrative twist/cut in both films? In each case, story number 2 (the shift to Judy and to Norman) only appears when the story appears to conclude and comes as something of a surprise; in each case, the two narrative registers are at once 'distinct, simultaneous and antagonistic, and the construction itself of the story is supported by the junction between the two stories'. The inversions which seem accidental to the plot of story number 1 (like the totally contingent intrusion of the murderous monster in *Psycho*) become essential to the plot of story number 2.

One can thus well imagine, along these lines, *Psycho* remade by Hemingway or Kafka. In Hemingway's version, Norman's story would remain hermetic: the spectator would simply perceive that there is another (Norman's) story which needs to be told, but which remains absent – there is a hole. In Kafka's version, Norman's story would appear in the first plane, told as if coming from itself: Norman's weird universe would have been narrated directly, in the first person, as something normal, while Marion's story would have been encoded/enframed within Norman's horizon, told as enigmatic and hidden.

This is how, from a proper Hegelian-Lacanian perspective, one should subvert the standard self-enclosed linear narrative: not by means of a postmodern dispersal into a multitude of local narratives, but by means of its redoubling in a hidden counter-narrative. (This is why the classic detective 'whodunit' is so similar to the psychoanalytic process: in it, also, the two narrative registers – the visible story of the discovery of crime and its investigation by the detective, and the hidden story of what really happened – are 'at the same time distinct, simultaneous and antagonistic, and the construction itself of the story is supported by the junction between the two stories'.)

Christ's Supplement

The same logic of a hidden counter-narrative is at work in Christianity: insofar as this Book-to-be-supplemented is ultimately the Old Testament, is the counter-Book not simply the New Testament itself? This would be the way to account for the strange coexistence of both sacred books in Christianity: the Old Testament, *the* Book shared by all three 'religions of the book', and the New Testament, the counter-Book that defines Christianity and (from within its perspective, of course) completes the Book, so that we can effectively say that 'the construction itself of the Bible is supported by the junction between the two Testaments . . .' This ambiguous supplement-completion is best encapsulated in Jesus' famous radicalization of the commandments (Matthew 5.17–48) – for example (quoting from the NRSV):

> Do not think that I have come to abolish the law or the prophets; I have come not to abolish but to fulfil. For truly I tell you, until heaven and earth pass away, not one letter, not one stroke of a letter, will pass from the law until all is accomplished . . . You have heard that it was said to those of ancient times, 'You shall not murder'; and 'whoever murders shall be liable to judgment'. But I say to you that if you are angry with a brother or sister, you will be liable to judgment . . . You have heard that it was said, 'You shall not commit adultery'. But I say to you that everyone who looks at a woman with lust has already committed adultery with her in his heart.

The official Catholic interpretation of this series of supplements is the so-called 'double standard view', which divides these teachings of Jesus into general precepts and specific counsels: obedience to the general precepts is essential for salvation, but obedience to the counsels is necessary only for perfection; or, as Aquinas put it: 'For if you are able to bear the entire yoke of the Lord, you will be perfect; but if you are not able to do this, do what you are able.'[14] Martin Luther notoriously rejected this Catholic stance and proposed a different two-level system, the so-called 'two realms view', which divides the world into the religious and secular realms, claiming that these teachings apply only to the spiritual: in the temporal world, obligations to family, employers, and country force believers to compromise; thus a judge should follow his secular obligations in sentencing a criminal, but, inwardly, should mourn for the fate of the criminal.

Clearly, both of these versions resolve the tension between Jesus' teachings and the Law by introducing a split between the two domains and restricting the more severe injunctions to the second. Predictably, in the case of Catholicism, this split is externalized into two kinds of people, the ordinary and the perfect (saints, monks, nuns); while in Protestantism, it is internalized as the split between the way I interact with others in the secular sphere and the way I inwardly regard others. Are these, however, the only options? A (perhaps surprising) reference to Richard Wagner might be of some help here: specifically, to his draft of the play *Jesus of Nazareth*, written somewhere between late 1848 and early 1849. Together with the libretto, *The Saracen Woman* (written in 1843, between *The Flying Dutchman* and *Tannhäuser*), these two drafts are key elements in Wagner's development: each of them indicates a path that might have been taken, but was abandoned; in other words, it points toward the 'what-if' scenario of an alternate Wagner, and thus reminds us of the open character of history. *The Saracen Woman* is, after Wagner found his voice in the *Dutchman*, the last counter-offensive of the Grand Opera, a repetition of *Rienzi* – if Wagner had been able to set the play to music, and if the opera had become a triumph like *Rienzi*, it is possible that Wagner would have succumbed to this last Meyerbeerian temptation and would have developed into an entirely different composer. Similarly, a couple of years later, after Wagner exhausted his potential for romantic operas with *Lohengrin* and was searching for a new way, *Jesus of Nazareth* again represented a path which was completely different from that of the music-dramas and their 'pagan' universe – *Jesus of Nazareth* is something like *Parsifal* written directly, without the long detour through the *Ring*. There, Wagner attributes to Jesus a series of alternate supplements to the commandments:

> The commandment saith: Thou shalt not commit adultery! But I say unto you: Ye shall not marry without love. A marriage without love is broken as soon as entered into, and who so hath wooed without love, already hath broken the wedding. If ye follow my commandment, how can ye ever break it, since it bids you to do what your own heart and soul desire? – But where ye marry without love, ye bind yourselves at variance with God's love, and in your wedding ye sin against God; and this sin avengeth itself by your striving next against the law of man, in that ye break the marriage-vow.[15]

The shift away from Jesus' actual words is crucial here: Jesus 'internalizes' the prohibition, rendering it much more severe (the Law says no actual adultery, while Jesus says that if you only covet the other's wife in your mind, it is the same as if you already had committed adultery); Wagner also internalizes it, but in a different way – the inner dimension he evokes is not that of one's intention, but that of the love that should accompany the Law (marriage). The true adultery is not to copulate outside of marriage, but to copulate within marriage but without love: simple adultery merely violates the Law from outside, while marriage without love destroys it from within, turning the letter of the Law against its spirit. So, to paraphrase Brecht yet again: what is simple adultery compared to (the adultery that is a loveless) marriage! It is not by chance that Wagner's underlying formula, 'marriage is adultery', recalls Proudhon's 'property is theft' – amid the stormy events of 1848, Wagner was not only a Feuerbachian celebrating sexual love, but also a Proudhonian revolutionary demanding the abolition of private property; so no wonder that, later on the same page, Wagner attributes to Jesus a Proudhonian supplement to 'Thou shalt not steal!':

> This also is a good law: Thou shalt not steal, nor covet another man's goods. Who goeth against it, sinneth: but I preserve you from that sin, inasmuch as I teach you: Love thy neighbour as thyself; which also meaneth: Lay not up for thyself treasures, whereby thou stealest from thy neighbour and makest him to starve: for when thou hast thy goods safeguarded by the law of man, thou provokest thy neighbour to sin against the law.[16]

This is how the Christian 'supplement' of the Book should be conceptualized: as a properly Hegelian 'negation of negation', which resides in the decisive shift from the *distortion of a notion* to a *distortion constitutive of this notion* – to this notion as a distortion-in-itself. Recall once again Proudhon's old dialectical motto, 'property is theft': the 'negation of negation' is here the shift from theft as a distortion (or violation) of property to the dimension of theft inscribed into the very notion of property (nobody has the right fully to own the means of production; human nature is inherently collective, so every claim that 'this is mine' is illegitimate). The same goes for crime and Law: the passage from crime as a distortion (negation) of the Law to crime as sustaining Law itself – that is, to the idea of the Law itself as universalized crime. One should note that, in this notion of the 'negation of negation', the encompassing unity of the two opposed terms is the lowest, 'transgressive' one: it is not crime which is a moment of Law's self-mediation (or theft which is a moment of property's self-mediation); the opposition of crime and Law is inherent to crime, and Law is thus a subspecies of crime, crime's self-relating negation (in the same way that property is theft's self-relating negation). And, ultimately, does the same not apply to nature itself? Here, the 'negation of negation' is the shift from the idea that we are violating some natural balanced order to the idea that imposing on the Real such a notion of order is itself the greatest violation – which is why the premise, the first axiom even, of every radical ecology must be 'there is no Nature'.

These lines cannot but evoke the famous passages from *The Communist Manifesto*, in which Marx and Engels respond to the bourgeois reproach that Communists wanted to abolish freedom, private property and the family: it is capitalist freedom itself which effectively is the freedom to buy and sell on the market and thus the very form of un-freedom for those who have nothing but their own labour to sell; it is capitalist property itself which represents the 'abolition' of property for those that own no means of production; it is bourgeois marriage itself which is universalized prostitution.[17] In each of these cases, the external opposition is internalized, so that one opposite becomes the form of appearance of the other (for example, bourgeois freedom is the form of appearance of the un-freedom of the majority). However, for Marx, at least in the case of freedom, this means that Communism will not abolish freedom but, by way of abolishing capitalist servitude, bring about actual freedom, which will no longer be the form of appearance of its opposite. It is thus not freedom as such that appears in the form of its opposite, but only false freedom, freedom distorted by the relations of domination. But is there not the danger that, underlying this 'negation of negation', a Habermasian 'normative' approach might immediately impose itself: how can we speak of crime if there is no prior notion of legal order violated by the criminal transgression? In other words, is the notion of Law as universalized crime not self-destructive? This, precisely, is what a properly dialectical approach rejects: before transgression, before good and evil, there is just the neutral, undifferentiated state of things; but when the balance of this state of things is disrupted, the positive norm (whether Law or property) arises as a secondary condition, an attempt to counteract and contain the transgression. With regard to the dialectic of freedom, this means that it is the very 'false', alienated, bourgeois freedom which creates the condition and opens up the space for 'actual' freedom.

This logic is also at work in Wagner, exemplarily in *Parsifal*, whose final message is a profoundly Hegelian one: 'The wound can be healed only by the spear that smote it [*Die Wunde schliesst der*

Speer nür der Sie schlug].' Hegel makes the same point, but with the accent on the opposite direction: the Spirit is itself the wound it tries to heal. That is to say, 'Spirit', at its most elementary, is the 'wound' of nature: the subject is the immense – absolute – power of negativity, the introduction of a gap or cut into immediate substantial unity, the power of *differentiation*, of 'abstraction', of tearing apart and treating as self-standing that which, in reality, is part of an organic whole. This is why the notion of the 'self-alienation' of Spirit (of Spirit losing itself in its otherness, in its objectivization) is more paradoxical than it may appear: it should be read together with Hegel's assertion of the thoroughly non-substantial character of Spirit: there is no *res cogitans*, no Thing which also (as its property) thinks; Spirit is nothing but the process of overcoming natural immediacy, of the cultivation of this immediacy, of withdrawing-into-itself or 'taking off' from it, of – why not – alienating itself from it.[18] The paradox is thus that there is no Self that precedes the Spirit's 'self-alienation': the very process of alienation generates the 'Self' from which Spirit is alienated and to which it then returns. (Hegel here inverts the standard notion that a failed version of X presupposes this X as its norm or measure: rather, for Hegel, X is created, its space is outlined, only through those repeated failures to achieve it.) Spirit's self-alienation is the same as its alienation from its Other (nature), because it constitutes itself through its 'return-to-itself' from its immersion in the objectivity of the Other. In other words, Spirit's return-to-itself creates the very dimension to which it returns. This means that the 'negation of negation', the 'return-to-oneself' from alienation, does not occur where it seems to: in the 'negation of negation', Spirit's negativity is not relativized, subsumed under an encompassing positivity; it is, on the contrary, the 'simple negation' which remains attached to the presupposed positivity it negated, the presupposed Otherness from which it alienates itself. The 'negation of negation' is thus nothing but the negation of the substantial character of this Otherness itself, the full acceptance of the abyss of Spirit's self-relating which retroactively posits its presuppositions. In other words, once we are within negativity, we never depart and regain the lost innocence of Origins; it is, on the contrary, only in the 'negation of negation' that these Origins are truly lost. The Spirit heals its wound, not by directly healing it, but by getting rid of the very Body into which the wound was cut.

In Christian theology, Christ's supplement (this repeated 'But I say to you . . .') is often designated as the 'antithesis' to the Law – the irony here is that, within the properly Hegelian perspective, this antithesis is synthesis itself at its purest. In other words, is what Christ does in his 'fulfilment' of the Law not the Law's *Aufhebung* in the strictest Hegelian sense of the term? In its very supplement, the Law is both negated and maintained by way of being transposed on to another (higher) level.

Notes

1 Slavoj Žižek, *The Fright of Real Tears: Krysztof Kielowśki between Theory and Post-Theory*, London, British Film Institute, 2001, pp. 5–6. [eds]

2 Žižek, *The Fright of Real Tears*, p. 130. [eds]

3 George Orwell, *The Road to Wigan Pier*, Harmondsworth, Penguin, 1962, pp. 144–5. [eds]

4 Ibid, p. 141. [eds]

5 Although, even here, the benevolent welfare state attempts to balance the annoyance of a bad-smelling neighbour with health concerns: a couple of years ago, the Dutch health ministry advised its citizens to break wind at least fifteen times per day, in order to avoid unhealthy tensions and pressures in the body.

6 Robert B. Pippin, 'The Ethical Status of Civility' in *The Persistence of Subjectivity: On the Kantian Aftermath*, Cambridge, Cambridge University Press, 2005, pp. 223–38.

7 Perhaps this feature accounts for another strange phenomenon: in (almost) all American buildings comprised of more than twelve floors, there is no 'thirteenth' floor (avoiding bad luck, of course); one jumps directly from the 'twelfth' to the 'fourteenth' floor. For a European, such a procedure is meaningless: who are we trying to fool? As if God doesn't know that what we designated as the 'fourteenth' floor is really the 'thirteenth' floor? Americans can play this game precisely because their God is merely a prolongation of our individual egos, not perceived as a true ground of being.

8 See Lars T. Lih's outstanding 'Introduction' to *Stalin's Letters to Molotov: 1925–1936*, ed. Lars T. Lih, Oleg V. Naumov and Oleg Khlevniuk, New Haven, Yale University Press, 1995, pp. 60–64.

9 Lih, 'Introduction', p. 48.

10 Lih, 'Introduction', p. 48.

11   A similar case of a person who stands in for the 'big Other' is found in *Casino Royale*, in the guise of the confused, excessively friendly and comically punctual Swiss banker who organizes the bank transfers for the poker players: toward the end of the film, when, in the lush garden of a Montenegro villa, the recuperating Bond and Vesper Lynd decide to stay together and start to embrace, the Swiss banker enters, embarrassed but intrusive, and, with a stupid smile, asks Bond to type in the password in order to get the money he won – the proverbial *Liebesstö*.

12   There are two further 'what ifs' in *Brief Encounter*. First (in a kind of Roald-Dahl style): what if Celia Johnson were all of a sudden to discover that Trevor Howard is a bachelor who concocted the story of his marriage and two children in order to add a melodramatic-tragic flavour to the affair, and to avoid the prospect of long-term commitment? Then (in a *Bridges-of-Madison-County* style): what if, at the end, Celia Johnson were to discover that her husband knew all along about the ongoing affair and just pretended not to know anything in order to safeguard appearances and not hurt his wife?

13   Jacques-Alain Miller, 'Profane Illuminations', *lacanian ink* 28 (2006), pp. 11–12.

14   Aquinas is citing here the early Christian treatise *The Didache*. For an English translation, see *The Didache in Context*, ed. Clayton N. Jefford, Leiden/New York, F.J. Brill, 1995. [eds]

15   Richard Wagner, *Jesus of Nazareth and Other Writings*, trans. William Ashton Ellis, Lincoln, University of Nebraska Press, 1995, p. 303.

16   Wagner, *Jesus of Nazareth*, pp. 303–4.

17   Karl Marx and Friedrich Engels, 'Manifesto of the Communist Party', in *The Revolutions of 1848: Political Writings, Volume 1*, ed. David Fernbach, London, Penguin/New Left Review, 1973, pp. 81–3. [eds]

18   G.W.F. Hegel, *Phenomenology of Spirit*, trans. A.V. Miller, Oxford, Oxford University Press, 1977, pp. 283–94. [eds]

Editors' introduction
Slavoj Žižek's 'third way'

Rex Butler and Scott Stephens

Let us begin here by noting an odd coincidence. After the terrorist strikes of 11 September 2001, both Slavoj Žižek and Jean Baudrillard leapt immediately into print. The two authors were, of course, already well known for their interventions in world political events, often writing responses in newspapers or on the internet mere days after momentous events or at the height of major public debates (the role of NATO in Yugoslavia, the attempted genocide in Rwanda, the fall of the Berlin Wall, the issues surrounding genetic cloning and manipulation). But, paradoxically, for all of their usual haste in making their views known and amid calls from both sides of politics for swift retaliation, they both urged a kind of caution or delay. Baudrillard, for his part, wrote in 'The Spirit of Terrorism':

> The whole play of history and power is disrupted by this event, but so, too, are the conditions of analysis. You have to take your time. While events were stagnating, you had to anticipate and move more quickly than they did. But when they speed up this much, you have to move more slowly – though without allowing yourself to be buried beneath a welter of words, or the gathering clouds of war, and preserving intact the unforgettable incandescence of the images.[1]

While Žižek, for his part, in the essay 'Welcome to the desert of the Real',[2] stated that any immediate reaction would be little more than an impotent *passage à l'acte*, whose sole purpose would be 'to *avoid* confronting the true dimension of what occurred on 11 September'.

To draw out what is going on here more precisely, it is crucial to realize that it is not simply a matter of these two highly 'engaged' thinkers suddenly losing their nerve in the face of an almost overwhelming disaster, as did so many others on the Left. Rather, what is astonishing is how quickly they formulated their responses and distributed them via the internet around the world. And yet, at the same time, what they advise is a form of inaction, a pause, time for reflection. This would, however, not be to do nothing, but to take the opportunity to *think*. It is through the minimal delay introduced by thinking that we might somehow avoid those hysterical calls for action that would merely reproduce the existing ideological coordinates (of which even the claim that everything is different following 11 September is only a variant, a 'hollow attempt to say something "deep" without really knowing what to say'). As Žižek writes in his essay 'The prospects of radical politics today',[3] in a surprising inversion of Marx's famous thesis 11 ('The philosophers have only *interpreted* the world in various ways; the point is to *change* it'):

> The first task today is precisely *not* to succumb to the temptation to act, to intervene directly and change things (which then inevitably ends in a cul-de-sac of debilitating impossibility: 'What can one do against global Capital?'), but to question the hegemonic ideological coordinates.

Indeed, once identified, this stress on thinking – on thinking as such – can be seen to form the basis of all of Žižek's specific political commitments. We might just speak here of three instances that occur in this book. In his response to NATO's endorsement of some minimal standard of 'human rights' in Kosovo,[4] Žižek insists that the transparent evocation of non-political 'humanitarianism' is little more than a ruse to prevent us from thinking 'the shady world of international Capital and its strategic interests'. In the aftermath of the collapse of the WTC Towers, Žižek unexpectedly endorses the plea of Mullah Omar, the leader of the Taliban, that Americans should exercise their own judgement when responding to 11 September: 'Don't you have your own thinking?' And, finally, in the months following the United States' invasion of Iraq, Žižek,[5] while rejecting the combined French and German opposition as a kind of appeasement 'reminiscent of the impotence of the League of Nations against Germany in the 1930s', nevertheless asserts that the very awareness of their failure to provide a substantive alternative itself constitutes a positive sign.

But is there a logical form, a consistent structural principle, behind Žižek's various positions with regard to these events? Might they not be seen – like France and Germany whom he condemns – as merely the hysterical rejection of existing alternatives without being able to suggest anything of his own? In a split between form and content, might we not say that on the level of *form* Žižek wants to see himself as an 'engaged' intellectual, but on the level of *content* he is struck by a kind of paralysis, unable to propose any meaningful action? In fact, this exact criticism, often coming from the perspective of a pseudo-ethical, pragmatic *Realpolitik*, has frequently been made against Žižek. It has been put forward by the English deconstructionist Simon Critchley,[6] and by Žižek himself (which shows that he is not entirely unaware of its pertinence);[7] but undoubtedly the exemplary instance is that of Žižek's early ally and critic of postmodern 'identity' politics Ernesto Laclau. As Laclau writes in the exchange between him, Žižek and Judith Butler, *Contingency, Hegemony, Universality*:

In his previous essay ['Class struggle or postmodernism? Yes, please!'], Žižek had told us that he wanted to overthrow capitalism; now we are served notice that he also wants to do away with liberal democratic regimes – to be replaced, it is true, by a thoroughly different régime about which he does not have the courtesy of letting us know anything . . . Žižek *does* actually know a third type of sociopolitical arrangement: the Communist bureaucratic régimes of Eastern Europe under which he lived. Is that what he has in mind? . . . And if what he has in mind is something entirely different, he has the elementary intellectual and political duty to let us know what it is . . . Only if that explanation is made available will we be able to start talking politics, and abandon the theological terrain. Before that, I cannot even know what Žižek is talking about – and the more this exchange progresses, the more suspicious I become that Žižek himself does not know either.[8]

Ironically, with surprising clarity, Laclau here identifies what actually *is* at stake in Žižek's work, the fundamental wager on which his various interventions depend: the possibility of some 'third type' of sociopolitical organization not covered by either the existing liberal democratic régimes or their socialist alternatives. Again, let us pursue this idea through those three representative examples discussed above. With regard to the NATO intervention in Kosovo, Žižek seeks to avoid what he calls the 'double blackmail' of having to choose between sides, the argument that, 'if you are against the NATO bombings, you are for Milošević's proto-fascist régime of ethnic cleansing; if you are against Milošević, you support the global capitalist New World Order'. Instead, his point is that 'phenomena like Milošević's regime are not the opposite of the New World Order, but rather its *symptom*, the place from which the hidden *truth* of the New World Order emerges'. With regard to the terrorist attacks on the WTC, Žižek rejects the argument that would have it that, 'if one simply, only and unconditionally condemns the attacks, one cannot but appear to endorse the blatantly ideological position of American innocence under threat from Third World Evil; if one draws attention to the deeper socio-political causes of Arab extremism, one cannot but appear to blame the victims who ultimately got what they deserved'. Instead, the 'only solution is to reject this very opposition and to adopt both positions simultaneously, which can be done only if one resorts to the dialectical category of *totality*'. And, finally, with regard to the American invasion of Iraq, Žižek refuses both proposed alternatives, arguing both for and against military intervention: 'Abstract pacifism is intellectually stupid and morally wrong – one must oppose a threat. Of course the fall of Saddam's régime would have been a relief to a large majority of the Iraqi people. Of course militant Islam is a horrifying ideology.' Nevertheless, although 'there is something hypocritical about objections to the war . . . there is something terribly wrong with *this* war'.

Now, in a conventional political discourse, the elaboration of wrong alternatives would merely be a preliminary to the eventual laying out of the correct one. Or, in some pseudo-Hegelian manner, it would be a matter of somehow finding a compromise between them, picking out the best elements of both. But this is not what Žižek means by 'third type of socio-political arrangement': it is not any balance or negotiation that he is interested in. Rather, if Žižek seeks to make a choice at all between these two alternatives, it is precisely to *maintain the choice*. If there is a solution to the problem he sets out, it is not to be found by deciding between alternatives or proposing some middle-path between them, but by thinking both together. Or if, within the current political situation, Žižek is forced to choose between them, he nevertheless wants to think what precedes that choice, what both choices exclude and stand in for. In a manner consistent with his analysis of how a subject is formed within the symbolic order by means of a certain 'forced choice' as to whether to enter society or not – which, although it appears free, is in fact forced because the only alternative to it is psychosis – so in his political pronouncements Žižek wants to think a situation before what we might call our political 'forced choice', as though we did not have to make it.[9]

However, Žižek does not stop there, which would again indicate a certain paralysis of thinking before the event. Instead, what he seeks to render through the identification of those two false choices we are confronted with is their *speculative identity*. Upon what is this identity founded? Why are all choices within our given ideological coordinates fundamentally the same choice? As Hegel would have it, the speculative identity of opposites is founded on the 'dark, shapeless abyss' of abstract universality, which like the Lacanian Real is 'always in the same place'. And Žižek will translate this in his work as the undifferentiated domain of global Capital. That is to say, for Žižek, as for Hegel, thinking is the withholding of the forced choice in thinking the totality that precedes and conditions it. But, in thinking this totality, in immersing it in the medium of representational thinking (*Vorstellung*), Žižek, following Hegel, also introduces a kind of delay into it, makes it pass from Substance to Subject.[10] In so doing – this is Marx's point that the only alternative to Capital is Capital itself – Žižek shows that Capital is 'remarked' from somewhere else, is only possible because from the beginning it stands in for its own opposite. To the very extent that it can be *thought* – this is Hegel's point about immersing abstract universality in the medium of representational thinking – it is not a true universality, it is not abstract enough. It is only its own exception. Or, to put it another way, it is revealed as exception by a still greater universality, which is Žižek's point concerning universality: it is nothing else but what makes every particular particular.

But to go back to that passage from Substance to Subject, which is the power of dialectical thinking, we might say that – in a literal way – all Žižek does here is to 'humanize' Capital (but then, from this perspective, what is the 'human'?). And this cannot but remind us of that 'Third Way' alternative Žižek so vehemently rejects throughout his work. However, are the reasons for this rejection – and let us even suggest, as he does with regard to Blair and Haider,[11] a certain clinching of Žižek and Blair – not to be explained as arising out of Žižek's own uncomfortable proximity to Blair, as indeed is hinted at by Laclau's suggestion that what is implicit in Žižek is some kind of impossible 'third way'?[12] But let us be more exact here. At stake in Žižek's 'third way' is a necessary distinction between form and content. With regard to content, he is absolutely in agreement with the Third Way and its desire to institute progressive social programmes in the face of conservative opposition. There is simply no alternative to capitalism (at this moment). But with regard to form, Žižek absolutely rejects the Third Way's concession to this fact in advance. For Žižek, the conclusion that there is no alternative to capitalism can only be reached via the thinking of the alternative that, precisely through its exclusion (this again is Hegel's point concerning the distinction between concrete and abstract universalities), ensures that there is only capitalism. In other words, as opposed to the Third Way in which we always *begin* with capitalism, for Žižek capitalism is only the *result* of a more abstract universality (capitalism and its other).

And this allows us to account for Žižek's much-criticized political practice in the former Yugoslavia in terms consistent with his current political theory. His actions then, from the perspective of what is now assumed to be his radical leftism, are usually represented as a liberal compromise, something he would wish to leave behind. (Žižek ran as a pro-reform candidate for the presidency in the first free elections in Slovenia.) However, our point would be that, far from having to be disavowed in the light of his later political theory, these early actions only make sense in light of it. For what Žižek can be seen to be doing at that time is – while acknowledging the necessity of having to make a choice within the newly 'liberated' (i.e., capitalist) Yugoslavia – attempting to maintain the fundamental choice, to avoid foreclosing the possibility of some utopian social transformation. (And it is crucial to note that at no point in his work has Žižek ever repudiated the implicit utopian dimension of democracy or a shared civic space, just that platform on which he ran in the election: this may even have analogies to his support for the 'inner greatness' of Stalinist bureaucracy.) It is for this reason – and the comparison is intended – that Žižek will call those transitional social movements in the newly ex-Communist countries, such as East Germany's *Neues Forum*, a 'third way'. Once more, with regard to their content, these movements were probably no different from those Third Way movements that subsequently broke out in the West. (Were they in fact their inspiration?) But, with regard to their form, they were absolutely different. While on the surface appearing to adapt to the new capitalist exigencies, they did, for a brief moment, embody a true alternative to both capitalism and Communism (exactly what Laclau demands of Žižek).

But perhaps this last statement – that is was only for 'a brief moment' that those new movements of ex-Communism opened up an alternative – is a little too 'pathetic'. By this we mean that absolutely – and we insist on this point – Žižek approves of someone like Blair's instrumentalization of the 'progressive' policies of the Third Way, his willingness to 'get his hands dirty' as Žižek says approvingly of all 'conservatives'.[13] What he in fact admires about the 'third way' alternative at the breaking down of Communism was not so much its momentary utopianism as its readiness to embody a new liberal bureaucratic state, in short, its desire *not to fail*, unlike so much typical leftism, including even *Neues Forum* itself, whose tragic character was that it came to embrace its own inevitable failure. (This is also the tragedy of a figure like Václav Havel: that he was not always a pathetic, liberal 'fool', who knew very well his own impotence, but for a moment was a conservative 'knave', who was prepared to do what it took to seize and maintain power.) We might say here that, in the exact sense that Žižek gives to an authentic conservatism, the Third Way is *conservative*: a way of 'maintaining the Old' (that is, maintaining the excluded alternative to capitalism) within the new conditions of multinational capitalism. This is for Žižek the most radical gesture of all – and it might apply even to Žižek himself. His new, seemingly extreme radical Leftism might ultimately only be a way of maintaining his original liberal 'conservatism' within the new conditions of the Left's theoretical perversion and decline.

At this point, we return for the last time to those three examples of Žižek's specific political commitments with which we began. With regard to their content, we would say that Žižek's actual position does not much differ from our contemporary 'Really Existing' Third

Way. But as to their form, there is an absolute difference. And what we mean by this is that the 'third way' alternative – this is the very 'speculative identity' with its opposite that makes it possible – can only be arrived at by considering its opposite, or more exactly by comparing its own rule to itself. To put this more simply, Žižek by and large agrees with the actions of democratic liberalism in each of those situations, but each time – and this is the very time of thinking – suggests not merely that they have to apply their own standards to themselves, but that they are only possible because they have *already* applied their own standard to themselves, are already in a speculative relationship with their opposite. We can only arrive at these decisions in the first place because they stand in for, take the place of, that 'dark, shapeless abyss' they imply from the beginning. It is this abstract universality – which in effect makes these decisions always exceptions – that pushes these decisions into realization, precipitates them, makes them pass over from Substance to Subject, a subject that is nothing else but that decision or action within a determined situation. (And, not coincidentally, it is just this kind of Hegelian speculative identity of opposites, of actions not only leading to but only being possible because of their opposites, that Baudrillard means by the 'symbolic exchange' between the West and its other in his analysis of 11 September.)

In each of these examples, therefore, there is a certain 'infinite justice' implied, which we might define here simply as the Third Way being taken more seriously than it does itself, the Third Way applying its own ruthless pragmatism and lack of excuses first of all to itself. Again, it would not at all be an apology for inaction or indicate any moral equivocation, but on the contrary point to the necessity of always *doing more*, of always acting *on time*. Thus, with regard to Yugoslavia, Žižek (in a statement significantly elided from the 'official' version of the text published in the *New Left Review*) suggests as a 'solution' to the problem of NATO intervention: 'Precisely as a Leftist, my answer to the dilemma, "Bomb or not?", is: "*Not yet enough* bombs and they are already *too late*".' With regard to 11 September, Žižek speaks of the way that, to the extent that the 'coalition' forces seek their enemy outside of themselves, they would always miss their target; that they would obtain 'infinite justice' only insofar as they also struck *at themselves*: 'The justice exerted must be truly infinite in the strict Hegelian sense, i.e., that, in relating to others, it has to relate to itself – in short, that it has to ask the question of how we ourselves, who enforce justice, are involved in what we are fighting against.' Finally, with regard to the American invasion of Iraq, Žižek is not opposed to it – those reasons he put forward earlier against its pacifist condemnation still hold – but he objects to *who* does it, for what *reasons* it is done: 'It is *who does it* that makes it wrong. The reproach should thus be: *who are you to do this?*' And this is why, in an essay published after this collection was put together, Žižek argues for the 'justice' of Bush's re-election: not for the typical Leftist reason that his excesses will somehow hasten the collapse of capitalism, but in order to ensure that he will be held accountable for his actions. As he writes: 'If Kerry had won, it would have forced the liberals to face the consequences of the Iraq War, allowing Bush to blame the Democrats for the results of his own catastrophic actions.'[14]

It is, in conclusion, worthwhile noting that, for all of the abstraction of which Žižek might be accused, the essays in this volume are full of the details of specific leaders' names, particular events, concrete and nuanced political opinions. Again, we would simply say two things about this. First, we mustn't think of these details and the abstract form of Žižek's argument as opposed. As we have tried to make clear, Žižek's invariable method is to think the excluded 'third' option in any political situation, which can never be grasped as such but only as its own exception. However, the details of Žižek's writing – *contra* Laclau – only come to light because of this abstraction, are only this exception. Secondly, these details – considered political opinions, the smallest accuracies of fact (Žižek is fond of quoting Lenin's aphorism that the 'fate of the entire working-class movement for long years can be decided by a word or two in the Party programme') – are precisely themselves a way of *maintaining the fundamental choice*. The patient, meticulous elaboration of the facts is the very time of thinking itself, the refusal to act in such a way that merely confirms the existing ideological coordinates. And yet, of course, these facts are never neutral: they can only be seen from a particular symbolic perspective. The details in Žižek are always only an exception, one of two sides, and thus miss what they are aiming at. Indeed, Žižek's entire work – even his so-called theoretical arguments – is merely a series of details understood in this way. It both attempts to think the forced choice (and thus seeks to overcome it) and only repeats it, misses it yet again. It at once is the thinking of the exception and merely itself another exception. And it is in this complicated sense that we might conceive of that split in appearance that is the exception: a split not simply between the world and some transcendental realm for which it stands in, but between the world and what allows it to be re-marked as detail – the world itself as exception. True thinking is based not on something outside the world, producing a split between the *ought* and the *is*, but only on the world itself, producing a split between the *is* and the *is*. It is a split that is the very time and place of thought itself.

And this perhaps is the point at which to rehabilitate Hegel's critique of Spinoza, now infamously characterized by Žižek as 'the ideologue of late capitalism'[15] who was unable to contemplate this 'Capital-Substance':

On the side of content, the defect of Spinoza's philosophy consists precisely in the fact that the form is not known to be immanent to that content, and for that reason it supervenes upon it only as an external, subjective form. Substance, as it is apprehended immediately by Spinoza without preceding dialectical mediation – being the universal might of negation – is only the dark, shapeless abyss, so to speak, in which all determinate content is swallowed up as radically null and void, and which produces nothing out of itself that has a positive subsistence of it own.[16]

Notes

1   Jean Baudrillard, *The Spirit of Terrorism*, trans. Chris Turner, London and New York, Verso, 2002, p. 4.

2   Žižek's paper, 'Welcome to the desert of the Real' (reprinted as Chapter 15 of this volume), was first circulated on the internet from 7 October 2001, An abbreviated version appeared in *South Atlantic Quarterly* 101, 2002, pp. 385–9, until it reached its final, book-length version, *Welcome to the Desert of the Real*, London and New York, Verso, 2002.

3   Slavoj Žižek, 'The prospects of radical politics today', in *Democracy Unrealized: Documenta 11 – Platform 1*, ed. Okwui Enwezor *et al.*, Kassel, Documenta, 2002, pp. 67–85 (reprinted as Chapter 13 of this volume).

4   Slavoj Žižek, 'Against the double blackmail', *New Left Review* 234, 1999, pp. 76–82 (reprinted as Chapter 14 of this volume).

5 Žižek's paper, 'The Iraq War – where is the true danger?' (reprinted as Chapter 16 of this volume), was first circulated on the internet from 23 April 2003, and then was published in an expanded form as *Iraq: The Borrowed Kettle*, London and New York, Verso, 2004.

6 Simon Critchley, 'The problem of hegemony', a paper presented at the 2004 *Albert Schweitzer Series on Ethics and Politics*, at New York University, p. 5 [www.politicaltheory.info/essays/critchley.html].

7 See, for example, Žižek's comments that his recent book on Iraq represents little more than 'a *bric-à-brac* of the author's immediate impressions and reactions to the unfolding story of the US attack on Iraq' (*Iraq: The Borrowed Kettle*, p. 7).

8 Ernesto Laclau, 'Constructing universality', in *Contingency, Hegemony, Universality: Contemporary Dialogues on the Left*, London and New York, Verso, 2000, p. 289.

9 For Žižek's analysis of the 'forced choice', see 'Why is every act a repetition?', in *Enjoy Your Symptom! Jacques Lacan In Hollywood and Out*, London and New York, Routledge, 1992, pp. 69–105.

10 We might also compare this to the 'choice' proposed by Jacques Lacan between 'Being (the subject)' and 'Meaning (for the other)' in *The Seminar of Jacques Lacan XI: The Four Fundamental Concepts of Psychoanalysis*, ed. Jacques-Alain Miller, trans. Alan Sheridan, New York and London, W.W. Norton, 1977, pp. 210–13.

11 Slavoj Žižek, 'Why we all love to hate Haider', *New Left Review* 2, 2000, p. 45 (reprinted as Chapter 2 of this volume).

12 In fact, we would argue that, in the same way that the conciliatory tone of Hegel's claim that his critique of Schelling in *The Phenomenology of Spirit*, directed not at Schelling himself, but rather at the 'shallowness' of those Schellingians who 'make so much mischief with your forms in particular and degrade your science into a bare formalism' (Letter to Schelling, 1 May 1807, in *Hegel: The Letters*, trans. Clark Butler and Christiane Seiler, Bloomington, Indiana University Press, 1984, p. 80), revealed how grave the philosophical rift between the two of them was, so Žižek's admission that he is 'not actually arguing against [Laclau's or Butler's] position but against a watered-down popular version they would also oppose' (*Contingency, Hegemony, Universality*, p. 91) functions as an internal reflection of the irreducible difference between Žižek and Butler and Laclau, the 'invisible frontier' that forever separates them. By contrast, we would say that Žižek's most publicly declared antipathies often mask an undeclared affinity. This, we would suggest, is the case with Blair and the Third Way. Indeed, could we not even propose that Žižek sees in Blair something of that great 'critique' of bureaucracy he also finds in Stalin, the idea that a revolution without its corresponding form of bureaucracy is ultimately a revolution without a revolution? Or, more exactly, do not events regarding the agreed handing-over of power after the recent election in Britain lead us to think that Blair is like Lenin, who understood he was to be thrown away after his usefulness was over, while his deputy, Gordon Brown, the Chancellor the Exchequer, is more like Stalin? That Blair's true greatness – for all of the accusations of the lack of ideals of the Third Way – will ultimately lie in his sacrificing himself for the Cause? To this extent, we would contrast the profound, 'inhuman' self-instrumentalization of Blair with the 'objective beauty' of someone like Havel, who remains 'human, all too human'.

13 Hence the long list of 'conservatives' that Žižek has gone on the record as praising: not just the well-known likes of Pascal, Chesterton, C. S. Lewis and W. B. Yeats, but also Pope John Paul II, Christopher Hitchens, Stalin, Hegel, even Lacan himself . . .

14 Slavoj Žižek, 'Hooray for Bush!', *London Review of Books* 26, 2 December 2004.

15 Slavoj Žižek, *Tarrying with the Negative: Kant, Hegel, and the Critique of Ideology*, Durham, Duke University Press, 1993, pp. 216–19.

16 G. W. F. Hegel, *The Encyclopedia Logic: Part 1 of the Encyclopedia of Philosophical Sciences (with the Zusätze)*, trans. T. F. Geraets, W. A. Suchting and H. S. Harris, Indianapolis, Hackett, 1991, p. 227.

SECTION ONE

The absent 'second way'

Chapter 1
Eastern European liberalism and its discontents

In good old deconstructionist manner, I would like to begin by calling into question the hidden implications behind the request made of me to give a report on recent ethnic conflicts in the exotic place I come from, Slovenia. In an article for *New Left Review*,[1] I endeavoured to describe why, a year or two ago, the West was so fascinated by events in Eastern Europe: the true object of fascination was the supposed gaze of the East, fascinated by Western democracy, still naïvely believing in it, a kind of 'subject supposed to believe' – in the East, the West found a sucker that still has faith in its values. The leftist demand to give a report on what is 'really going on' in Eastern Europe functions as a kind of mirror-image and reversal of this demand: we are expected to confirm suspicions, to say that people are already disappointed in 'bourgeois' democracy, that they are slowly perceiving, not only what they have gained, but also what they have lost (social security, etc.). In my article, I consciously walked into this trap and gave the Left what it wanted: a vengeful vision of the way that now things are even worse, how the effective result of democratic enthusiasm is nationalist corporatism – in short, it serves us right for betraying socialism! Yet, in accordance with the great guiding principle of socialism – that self-criticism is the impetus of progress – this criticism of the demand, as I perceive it, is actually a criticism of myself as a member of the Slovenian liberal-democratic party and its candidate in the recent elections. Let me take as my starting point the liberal-democratic vision according to which, after the breakdown of 'Really Existing Socialism', we would have a flourishing market economy and pluralist democracy in Eastern Europe, if it were not for two stains that mar the picture: on the one hand, the remainders of old totalitarian forces that, although losing the battle, continue their underground machinations; and, on the other hand, national corporatism, the obsession with national unity and some imagined 'threat to the nation'.

If, in the recent disintegration of 'Really Existing Socialism' in Slovenia, there was a political agent whose rule fully deserved the designation 'tragic', it was the Slovenian Communists who lived up to their promise to make possible the peaceful, non-violent transition to pluralist democracy. From the very beginning they were caught in the Freudian paradox of the superego: the more they gave way to the demands of the (then) opposition and accepted the democratic rules of the game, the more violent were the opposition's accusations of their 'totalitarianism', the more they were suspected of accepting democracy 'in word' only, while actually engaged in demonic plots against it. The paradox of this accusation emerged in its purest form when, finally, after a long period of accusations that their democratic commitments were not to be taken seriously, it became clear that they 'meant it': far from being perplexed, the opposition simply altered its charge and accused the Communists of 'unprincipled behaviour' – how can you trust someone who shamelessly betrays his old revolutionary past and accepts democratic reform?

The demand of the opposition that can be detected through this paradox is an ironic repetition of the Stalinist demand at work in the political monster trials, where the accused were forced to admit their guilt and claim supreme punishment for themselves: for the anti-Communist opposition, the only good Communist would be the one who first organized free multi-party elections, and then voluntarily assumed the role of scapegoat within them, a representative of totalitarian horrors who must be beaten. In short, Communists were expected to assume the impossible position of pure metalanguage, saying, 'We confess, we are totalitarian, we deserve to lose the election!' – just like the victims of the Stalinist trials. The shift in public perception of Slovenian democratic Communists was truly enigmatic: up to the 'point of no return' on the way to democracy, the public trembled on account of them, counting on them to endure the pressure of the truly anti-democratic forces (the Yugoslav army, Serbian populism, old hard-liners) and to organize free elections; yet, once it became clear that free elections would in fact take place, they suddenly became the enemy.

The logic of this shift from the 'open' condition before elections to its closure afterwards is illuminated by Jameson's concept of the 'vanishing mediator'.[2] A system reaches its equilibrium, that is, establishes itself as a synchronous totality, when – in Hegelese – it 'posits' its external presuppositions as its own inherent moments and thus obliterates the traces of its traumatic origins. What we have here is the tension between the open situation when a new social pact is generated and its subsequent closure – in Kierkegaard's terms, the tension between possibility and necessity: the circle is closed when the new social pact establishes itself in its necessity and renders invisible its 'possibility', the open, undecided process that engendered it.[3] In between, when the socialist régime was already in a state of disintegration, but before the new régime had stabilized itself, we witnessed a kind of opening; things that were for a moment visible immediately became invisible. To put it bluntly, those who triggered the process of democratization and fought the greatest battles are not those who today enjoy its fruits, not because of a simple usurpation and deception on the part of the present winners, but because of a deeper structural logic. Once the process of democratization reached its peak, it buried its catalysts.

Who effectively triggered this process? New social movements, punk, the New Left – after the victory of democracy, all these impulses suddenly and enigmatically lost ground and more or less disappeared from the scene. Culture itself, the set of cultural preferences, changed radically: from punk and Hollywood to national poems and quasi-folkloric commercial music (in contrast to the usual overshadowing of authentic national roots by universal American-Western culture). What we had was a genuine 'primitive accumulation' of democracy,[4] a chaotic story of punkers, students with their sit-ins, committees for human rights, and so on, which literally became invisible the moment the new system established itself – and with it, its own myth of origin was likewise extinguished. The same people who, a few years previously, abused 'new social movements' from their position as party hard-liners, now, as members of the ruling anti-Communist coalition, accused their representatives of 'proto-Communism'.

This dialectics is especially interesting in its theoretical aspect. Roughly, we could say that in the last two decades, two philosophical orientations dominated intellectual life in Slovenia: Heideggerianism among the opposition, and Frankfurt School Marxism among 'official' party circles. So, one would expect the main theoretical fight to take place between those two orientations, with the third block – us, Lacanians and Althusserians – playing the role of innocent bystanders. Yet, as soon as polemics broke out, both orientations ferociously attacked the same author, Althusser. And, even more surprisingly, the two main proponents of these polemics, a Heideggerian and a (then) Frankfurt School Marxist, are now both ruling members of the ruling anti-Communist coalition.

In the 1970s, Althusser actually functioned as a kind of symptomatic point, a name apropos of which all of the 'official' adversaries – Heideggerians and Frankfurt School Marxists in Slovenia, praxis philosophers and central committee ideologues in Zagreb and Belgrade – *suddenly started speaking the same language*, pronouncing the same accusations. From the very beginning, our starting point was this experience of the way that the name 'Althusser' triggered an enigmatic uneasiness in all camps. One is even tempted to suggest that the unfortunate event in Althusser's private life (his strangling of his wife) played the role of a welcome pretext, a 'little piece of reality' enabling his theoretical adversaries to repress the real trauma represented by his theory ('How can a theory of someone who strangled his wife be taken seriously?').

It is perhaps more than a mere curiosity that, in Yugoslavia, Althusserians (and, more generally, the structuralist and poststructuralist orientations) were the only ones who remained 'pure' in the fight for democracy; all other philosophical schools at some point or other sold themselves to the régime. The analytic philosophers were sending the régime the message: 'True, we're not Marxists, but we are also not dangerous; our thought is pure apolitical professional apparatus, so not only do you not have to be afraid of us, but by leaving us alone you can even gain a reputation for allowing non-Marxism without risking your hold on political power.' The message was received, and they were left alone.

In the Republic of Bosnia, it was the Frankfurt School that enjoyed a semi-official status in the 1970s, whereas in Croatia and partly in Serbia there were 'official' Heideggerians, especially in army circles. There were cases in which, in university purges, someone lost his job for not understanding the subtleties of negative dialectics (as it was put in the justification after the fact), and cases in which the apology for socialist armed forces was written in the purest Heideggerian style ('the essence of the self-defence of our society is the self-defence of the essence of our society', etc.).

The resistance to Althusser indicated that it was precisely Althusserian theory – often defamed as proto-Stalinist – that functioned as a kind of 'spontaneous' theoretical tool for effectively undermining the Communist totalitarian régimes: his theory of ideological state apparatuses assigned the crucial role in the reproduction of an ideology to 'external' rituals and practices with regard to which 'inner' beliefs and convictions are strictly secondary.[5] And is it necessary to call attention to the central place of such rituals in 'Really Existing Socialism'? What counted was external obedience, not 'inner' conviction; that is, obedience coincided with the *semblance of obedience*, which is why the only way to be truly 'subversive' was to act 'naïvely', to make the system 'eat its own words', to undermine the *appearance* of its ideological consistency.

This disappearance of the 'vanishing mediator', of course, is not peculiar to Slovenia. Is not the most spectacular case of this the role of *Neues Forum* in East Germany? There is an inherently tragic ethical dimension in its fate: it presents a point at which an ideology takes itself literally and ceases to function as an 'objectively cynical' legitimation of existing power relations. *Neues Forum* consisted of groups of passionate intellectuals who took socialism seriously and were prepared to put everything at stake in order to destroy the compromised system and replace it with a utopian 'third way' beyond capitalism and 'Really Existing Socialism'. Their sincere belief and insistence that they were not working for the restoration of Western capitalism, of course, proved to be nothing but an illusion; however, we could say that precisely this (a thorough illusion without substance) made it *stricto sensu* non-ideological: it did not 'reflect' in an inverted-ideological form any actual relations of power.

At this point, I should correct the Marxist vulgate: contrary to the commonplace according to which an ideology becomes 'cynical' (accepts the gap between words and deeds, no longer 'believes in itself', and is no longer experienced as truth but treats itself as a purely instrumental means of legitimating power) in the period of the 'decadence' of a social formation, it could be said that precisely such a period opens up the possibility of 'taking itself seriously' to the ruling ideology, and effectively opposes its own social basis (with Protestantism, the Christian religion opposes feudalism as its social basis; the same with *Neues Forum*, which opposes 'Really Existing Socialism' in the name of a 'true' socialism). In this way, unknowingly, it unleashes the forces of its own final destruction: once their job is done, they are 'overrun by history' (*Neues Forum* obtained three per cent of the vote in the elections). A new 'scoundrel time' sets in; people are in power who were mostly silent during the Communist repression and nonetheless now accuse *Neues Forum* of being 'crypto-Communist'.

The general theoretical lesson to be drawn from this illustration is that the concept of ideology must be disengaged from the 'representationalist' problematic: *ideology has nothing to do with 'illusion'*, with a false, distorted representation of its social content. To put it another way: a political standpoint can be quite accurate ('true') as to its objective content and yet thoroughly ideological, and vice versa: the idea it presents of its social content can prove totally wrong, and yet there is absolutely nothing 'ideological' about it. With regard to 'factual truth', the position of *Neues Forum* – conceiving of the disintegration of the Communist régime as the opening up of a possibility to invent some new form of social space that would reach beyond the confines of capitalism – was doubtless illusory. *Neues Forum* was opposed by the forces who put their bets on the quickest possible annexation to West Germany, that is, on the inclusion of their country in the world capitalist system; for them, the people around *Neues Forum* were nothing but a bunch of heroic daydreamers. This position proved accurate, *yet it is nonetheless thoroughly ideological*. Why?

The conformist adoption of the West German model implied an ideological belief in the unproblematic, non-antagonistic functioning of the late-capitalist 'social State', whereas the first stance, although illusory as to its factual ('enunciated') content, by means of its scandalous and exorbitant position of enunciation attested to an awareness of the antagonism that pertains to late capitalism. This is one way to conceive of the Lacanian thesis according to which truth has the structure of fiction: in those confused months along the passage from 'Really Existing Socialism' to capitalism, *the fiction of a 'third way' was the only point at which social antagonism was not obliterated*. Therein resides one of the tasks of the 'postmodern' criticism of ideology: to designate those elements within an existing social order that – in the guise of 'fiction', that is, of the utopian narratives of possible but failed alternative histories – point towards its antagonistic character and thus 'estrange' us from the self-evidence of its established identity.

The other monster that haunts liberal democracy, the stain that disturbs the idyllic image of pluralist democracy, is nationalism. One usually states with regret that, even after the fall of Communism, we cannot begin to live in peace and true pluralist democracy because the disintegration of Communism opened up space for the emergence of nationalist obsessions, provincialism, anti-Semitism, xenophobia, ideologies about national security, anti-feminism, a post-socialist Moral Majority inclusive of the pro-life movement – in short, *enjoyment* in its entire 'irrationality'. At this point, the implicit demand made to a critical intellectual from Eastern Europe is at its strongest: he or she is expected to decry this dark reverse of Eastern European democracy, to depict all the dirty details that belie the image of Eastern Europe's nations bathing in freedom and democracy . . . and I in no way intend to disown such a demand, and yet what is deeply suspicious about this attitude, about the attitude of an anti-nationalist liberal Eastern European intellectual, is the obvious fascination that nationalism exerts upon him: liberal intellectuals refuse it, mock it, yet at the same time stare at it with powerless fascination. The intellectual pleasure procured by the denunciation of nationalism is uncannily close to the satisfaction of successfully explaining one's own impotence and failure (which was always the speciality of Western Marxism).

The Western gaze upon the East encounters here its own uncanny reversal, usually qualified (and by the same token disqualified) as 'fundamentalism': the end of cosmopolitanism, liberal democracy's impotence in the face of this return to tribalism, and so on. It is precisely here that, for the sake of democracy itself, one has to gather the strength to repeat the exemplary heroic gesture of Freud who answered the threat of fascist anti-Semitism by targeting Jews themselves and depriving them of their founding father: *Moses and Monotheism* is Freud's answer to Nazism. In a similar move, one has to detect the flaw of liberal democracy, which opens up the space for 'fundamentalism'. That is to say, there is ultimately only one question that confronts political philosophy today: is liberal democracy the ultimate horizon of our political practice, or is it possible effectively to institute its inherent limitation?

The standard neo-conservative answer here is to bemoan the 'lack of roots' that allegedly pertains to liberal democracy, to this kingdom of Nietzsche's 'last man', in which there is no place left for ethical heroism, in which we are more and more submerged in the idiotic routine of everyday life regulated by the pleasure principle, and so on: within this perspective, fundamentalism is simply a reaction to this loss of roots, a perverted yet desperate search for new roots in an organic community. Yet this neo-conservative answer falls short in its failure to demonstrate the way that the very project of formal democracy, conceived in its philosophical founding gesture, opens up the space for fundamentalism itself.

The structural homology between Kantian formalism and formal democracy is a classical *topos*: in both cases, the starting point, the founding gesture, consists in an act of radical emptying, an evacuation. With Kant, what is evacuated is the locus of the Supreme Good: every positive object destined to occupy this place is by definition 'pathological', marked by moral contingency; this is why the moral Law must be reduced to pure Form, which would then bestow upon our acts the character of universality. The elementary operation of democracy is also the evacuation of the locus of Power: every pretender to this place is by definition a 'pathological' usurper – 'nobody can rule innocently', to quote Saint-Just. The crucial point is that 'nationalism', as a specifically modern, post-Kantian phenomenon, designates the moment when the Nation, the national Thing, usurps, fills out the empty place of the Thing opened up by Kantian formalism, by its reduction of every 'pathological' content. The Kantian term for this filling out of the void, of course, is the fanaticism of *Schwärmerei*: does not nationalism epitomize fanaticism in politics?

This paradox of filling out the empty place of the Supreme Good defines the modern notion of Nation. The ambiguous and contradictory nature of the modern Nation is the same as that of the vampires and other living dead:[6] they are wrongly perceived as 'leftovers from the past' – their place is constituted by the very break from modernity. On the one hand, 'Nation' of course designates the modern community delivered of traditional 'organic' ties, a community in which the pre-modern links that connect the individual to a particular estate, family, religious group, and so on, are broken: the traditional corporate community is replaced by the modern nation-state whose constituents are 'citizens', that is, people as abstract members, not as members of particular estates, for example. On the other hand, 'Nation' can never be reduced to a network of purely symbolic ties: there is always a kind of 'surplus of the Real' that sticks to it; to define itself, 'national identity' must appeal to the contingent materiality of 'common roots', of *Blut und Boden*. In short, 'Nation' designates both the instance by means of which traditional 'organic' links are dissolved *and* the 'remainder of the pre-modern in modernity', the form 'organic inveteracy' acquires within the modern post-traditional universe, the form 'organic substance' acquires within the universe of substanceless Cartesian subjectivity. The crucial point is again to conceive of both aspects in their interconnectedness: it is the new 'suture' brought about by the Nation that renders possible the 'desuturing', the disengagement from traditional organic ties. 'Nation' is a pre-modern leftover that functions as the inner condition of modernity itself, as an inherent impetus to its progress.

This pathological 'stain' also determines the deadlocks of liberal democracy today. The problem with liberal democracy is that – for structural reasons – it cannot be universalized *a priori*. Hegel said that the moment of victory of a political force is the very moment of its splitting: the triumphant liberal-democratic 'New World Order' is more and more marked by a frontier separating its 'inside' from its 'outside', a frontier between those who succeeded in remaining 'within' (the 'developed', those to whom the rules of human rights, social security, etc., still apply) and the others, the excluded (the main concern of the 'developed' with regard to them is how to contain their explosive potential, even if the price to be paid is the neglect of elementary democratic principles).

This opposition – and not the one between capitalist and socialist 'blocs' – defines the contemporary constellation: the 'socialist' bloc was the true 'third way', a desperate attempt at modernization outside the constraints of capitalism. What is effectively at stake in the present crisis of post-socialist states is the struggle for one's place, now that the illusion of this 'third way' has evaporated: who will be admitted 'inside', integrated into the developed capitalist order, and who will remain excluded from it? Ex-Yugoslavia is perhaps the exemplary case: every actor in the blood-play of its disintegration endeavours to legitimize its place inside by presenting itself as the last bastion of European civilization (the current ideological designation for the capitalist 'inside') in the face of oriental barbarism. For the right-wing nationalist Austrians, this imaginary frontier is Karavanke, the mountain chain between Austria and Slovenia: beyond it, the rule of Slavic hordes begins. For the nationalist Slovenes, this frontier is the river Kolpa, separating Slovenia from Croatia: we Slovenians are *Mitteleuropa*, while Croatians are already Balkan, involved in irrational ethnic feuds that do not really concern us. We are on their side, we sympathize with them, yet in the same way that one sympathizes with a third world victim of aggression. For Croatians, of course, the crucial frontier is the one between them and the Serbians, that is, between Western Catholic civilization and the Eastern Orthodox collective spirit, which cannot grasp the values of Western individualism. Serbians, finally, conceive of themselves as the last line of defence of Christian Europe against the fundamentalist danger embodied in Muslim Albanians and Bosnians. (It should now be clear who, within ex-Yugoslavia, effectively behaves in the civilized 'European' way: those at the very bottom of this ladder, excluded from all other groups – Albanians and Muslim Bosnians.) Thus, the traditional liberal opposition between 'open' pluralist societies and 'closed' nationalist-corporatist societies founded on the exclusion of the Other must be brought to its point of self-reference: the liberal gaze itself functions according to the same logic, insofar as it is founded upon the exclusion of the Other to whom one attributes fundamentalist nationalism, and so on.

This antagonistic splitting inherent to capitalism as a world-system opens up the field for the Khmer Rouge, Sendero Luminoso and other similar movements that seem to personify the 'radical Evil' in politics today: if 'fundamentalism' functions as a kind of 'negative judgement' on liberal capitalism, as an inherent negation of the universalist claim of liberal capitalism, then movements like Sendero Luminoso enact an 'infinite judgement' on liberal capitalism. In his *Philosophy of Right*, Hegel conceives of the 'rabble [*Pöbel*]' as a necessary product of modern society: a segment not integrated into the legal order, prevented from participating in its benefits, and for this very reason delivered from responsibility towards it – a necessary structural surplus excluded from the closed circuit of the social edifice.[7] It seems as if it is only today, with the advent of late capitalism, that this notion of the 'rabble' has achieved its adequate realization in social reality, with the political forces that paradoxically unite the most radical indigenist anti-modernism (the refusal of everything that defines modernity: market, money, individualism) with the eminently modern project of effacing the entire symbolic tradition and beginning from a zero point (in the case of Khmer Rouge, the abolition of the entire system of education and the physical liquidation of intellectuals). In what precisely does the 'shining path' of the Senderistas consist? In the idea of reinscribing the construction of socialism within the frame of the return to the ancient Incan empire (much as Khmer Rouge saw their régime as the return to the lost grandeur of the old Khmer kingdom).

The result of this desperate endeavour to surmount the antagonism between tradition and modernity is a double negation: a radically anti-capitalist movement (the refusal of integration into the world market) coupled with a systematic dissolution of all traditional hierarchical social links, beginning with the family (at the level of 'micropower', the Khmer Rouge régime incited adolescents to denounce their parents: an anti-Oedipal régime at its purest). The truth articulated in an inverted form in the paradox of this double negation is that capitalism cannot reproduce itself without the support of pre-capitalist forms of the social link. In other words, far from presenting a case of exotic barbarism, the 'radical Evil' of Khmer Rouge and the Senderistas is conceivable only against the background of the constitutive antagonism of capitalism today. There is more than a contingent idiosyncrasy in the fact that, in both cases, the leader of the movement is an intellectual, well-skilled in the subtleties of Western culture (prior to becoming a revolutionary, Pol Pot was a teacher at a French lycée in Phnom Penh, known for his subtle readings of Rimbaud and Mallarmé; Antonio Guzman, 'presidente Gonzalo', the leader of the Senderistas, is a philosophy professor whose favourite authors are Heidegger and Jaspers). For that reason, it is too simple to conceive of these movements as the last embodiments of the millenarian radicalism that structures the social space as the exclusive antagonism between 'us' and 'them', allowing for no possible forms of mediation: rather, they represent a desperate attempt to break out of the vicious circle of the constitutive imbalance of capitalism, without seeking support in some previous tradition supposed to enable us to master this imbalance (Islamic fundamentalism, within this logic, is, for that reason, ultimately a perverted instrument of modernization). In other words, behind Sendero Luminoso's attempt to erase the entire tradition and to begin again 'from scratch', in an act of creative sublimation, is the correct insight into the complementary relationship of modernity and tradition: any true return to tradition today is *a priori* impossible; its role is simply to serve as a shock absorber for the process of modernization. Khmer Rouge and the Senderistas as the 'infinite judgement' on late capitalism are, therefore, in Hegelese, an integral part of its notion: if one wants to constitute capitalism as a world system, one must take into account its inherent negation, 'fundamentalism', as well as its absolute negation – the infinite judgement on it.

The exotic story of Eastern Europe's nineteenth-century nationalism thus changes into a story about the West itself: for Western liberal intellectuals, the affirmation of their own autochthonous tradition is a redneck horror, a site of populist proto-fascism (for example, in the United States, the 'backwardness' of Polish, Italian and other communities, the alleged brood of 'authoritarian personalities' and similar liberal scarecrows), whereas they are always ready to hail the autochthonous ethnic communities of the other (blacks, Puerto Ricans, native Americans). Enjoyment is good, on the condition that it is not too close to us, that it remains the *other's* enjoyment.

The positive expression of this ambivalence toward the other's enjoyment is the obsessive attitude that one can easily detect in what is usually referred to as 'PC', Political Correctness: the compulsive effort to uncover ever new, ever more refined forms of racial and/or sexual domination and violence (it is not PC to say that the President 'smoked a peace pipe', because this patronizes native Americans, etc.). The problem here is simple: how can one be a white heterosexual male and still retain a clear conscience? All other positions can affirm their specificity, their specific mode of enjoyment, and only the white-heterosexual-male position must remain empty, must sacrifice its enjoyment.

The weak point of the PC position is thus the weak point of the neurotic compulsion: the problem is not that it is too severe, too fanatical, but quite the contrary: that *it is not severe enough*. At first glance, the PC attitude seems to involve extreme self-sacrifice, the renunciation of everything reminiscent of sexism and racism, the unending effort to unearth traces of it in oneself, an effort not unworthy of the early Christian saint who dedicated his life to discovering in himself ever new layers of sin. Yet all this effort should not deceive us; it is ultimately a stratagem whose function is to conceal the fact that the PC type is not ready to renounce what really matters: 'I'm prepared to sacrifice everything *but that*' – but what? The very gesture of self-sacrifice. In other words, the PC attitude implies the same antagonism between the enunciated content and the position of enunciation that Hegel denounced apropos of ascetic self-humiliation: it conceals a patronizing elevation over those whose discriminations are allegedly compensated. In the very act of emptying the white-male-heterosexual position of all positive content, it retains it as a universal form of subjectivity. Or, to put it in straightforward, old-fashioned political terms: far from being a disguised expression of the extreme Left, the PC attitude is the primary ideological protective shield of bourgeois liberalism against a genuine Leftist alternative.[8]

What truly disturbs liberals is therefore *enjoyment* organized in the form of self-sufficient ethnic communities. Against this background, we should conceive of the ambiguous consequences of the politics of school bussing in the United States, for example. Its principal aim, of course, was to surmount racist barriers: children from black communities will widen their cultural horizons by partaking in the white way of life; children from white communities will experience the nullity of racial prejudices by way of contact with blacks. Yet inextricably intermixed with this was another logic, especially where bussing was externally imposed by the 'enlightened' liberal state bureaucracy: to destroy the enjoyment of the closed ethnic communities by abrogating their boundaries. For that reason, bussing – insofar as it was experienced by the affected communities as imposed from the outside – reinforced or to some extent even generated racism where previously an ethnic community maintained a relative closure in its way of life, a phenomenon that is *not* in itself 'racist' (as liberals themselves admit through their fascination with exotic 'modes of life' of others).[9]

What one should do here is call into question the entire theoretical apparatus that sustains this liberal attitude, up to its Frankfurt School psychoanalytic *pièce de résistance*, the theory of the so-called authoritarian personality, which ultimately designates the form of subjectivity that 'irrationally' insists on its specific way of life and, in the name of its own enjoyment, resists liberal evidence of what are its supposed 'true interests'. The theory of 'authoritarian personality' is nothing but an expression of the *ressentiment* of the leftist-liberal intellectuals apropos of the fact that the 'unenlightened' working classes were not prepared to accept their guidance: an expression of their incapability of offering a positive theory of this resistance.[10]

The impasses around bussing enable us also to delineate the inherent limitation of the liberal political ethic as articulated in John Rawls's theory of distributive justice.[11] That is to say, bussing fully meets the conditions of distributive justice (it stands the trial of what Rawls calls the 'veil of ignorance'): it procures a more just distribution of social goods, it equalizes the chances of success of individuals from different social strata, etc. Yet the paradox is that everyone, including those deemed to profit most by it, somehow felt cheated and wronged. Why? The dimension infringed upon was precisely that of *fantasy*. The Rawlsian liberal-democratic idea of distributive justice ultimately relies on a 'rational' individual who is able to abstract a particular position of enunciation, to look upon him- or herself and all others from a neutral position of pure 'metalanguage', and thus perceive all of their 'true interests'. This individual is the supposed subject of the social contract that establishes the coordinates of justice. What is thereby *a priori* left out of consideration is the realm of fantasy in which a community organizes its 'way of life' (its mode of enjoyment). Within this space, what 'we' desire is inextricably linked to (what we perceive as) the other's desire, so that what 'we' desire may turn out to be the very destruction of our object of desire (if, in this way, we deal a blow to the other's desire). In other words, human desire, insofar as it is always already mediated by fantasy, can never be grounded in (or translated back into) our 'true interests': the ultimate assertion of our desire – sometimes the only way to assert its autonomy in the face of a 'benevolent' other providing for our Good – is to act *against* our Good.[12]

Every 'enlightened' political action legitimized by reference to some form of 'true interests' encounters sooner or later the resistance of a particular fantasy space: in the guise of the logic of 'envy', the 'theft of enjoyment'. Even such a clear-cut issue as that of the Moral Majority pro-life movement is, in this respect, more ambiguous than it may seem: one aspect of it is *also* the reaction to the attempt of upper-middle-class ideology to pervade lower-class community life. On another level, was not the same attitude at work in the uneasiness of a wide circle of English leftist-liberal intellectuals apropos of the long and traumatic miners' strike in 1988? Many were quick to denounce it as 'irrational', the 'expression of an outdated working-class fundamentalism', and while all this was undoubtedly true, the fact remains that this strike was also the desperate form of resistance of a certain traditional working-class way of life. As such it was perhaps more 'postmodern', on account of the very features that its critics perceived as 'regressive', than the usual 'enlightened' leftist-liberal criticism of it.[13]

The liberal horror of 'fundamentalist' overidentification thus epitomizes the current spontaneous ideological perception of threats to the existing world order: today, with the disintegration of Really Existing Socialism, the neutral, universal medium, the presupposed measure of the 'normal' state of things, is organized around the notion of capitalist democracy (media, market, pluralism, etc.), whereas those who oppose it are more and more reduced to 'irrational' marginal positions ('terrorists', 'fundamentalist fanatics'). As soon as some political force threatens the circulation of Capital too much – even if it is, for example, a benign ecological protest against the destruction of old-growth forests – it is instantly labelled 'terrorist', 'irrational', and so on. Perhaps our very survival depends on our capacity to perform a kind of dialectical reversal and to locate the true source of madness in the allegedly neutral measure of 'normality', which enables us to perceive all opposition to it as 'irrational'. Today, when the media bombard us with shocking revelations about different versions of madness that threaten the normal course of our everyday lives, from serial killers to religious fundamentalists, from Saddam Hussein to narco-cartels, one has to rely more than ever on Hegel's dictum that *the true source of Evil is the very neutral gaze that perceives Evil all around*.[14]

The fear of 'excessive' identification is therefore the fundamental feature of late-capitalist ideology: the Enemy is the 'fanatic' who 'overidentifies', instead of maintaining a proper distance from the dispersed plurality of subject-positions. In short: the elated 'deconstructivist' logomachy focused on 'essentialism' and 'fixed identities' ultimately fights a straw-man. Far from containing any kind of subversive potential, the subject hailed by postmodern theories – the dispersed, plural, constructed subject, the subject who undermines every performative mandate by way of its parodic repetition, the subject prone to particular, inconsistent modes of enjoyment – simply designates *the form of subjectivity that corresponds to late capitalism*. Perhaps the time has come to resuscitate the Marxian insight concerning Capital as the ultimate power of 'deterritorialization' that undermines every fixed social identity, and to see 'late capitalism' as the epoch in which the traditional fixity of ideological positions (patriarchal authority, fixed sex roles, etc.) becomes an obstacle to the unbridled commodification of everyday life.

Where then are we to look for the way out of this vicious circle? Needless to stress, I am here far from advocating fundamentalist overidentification as 'anti-capitalist': the point is precisely that the contemporary forms of 'paranoiac' overidentification are the inherent reverse of Capital's universalism, an inherent reaction to it. *The more the logic of Capital becomes universal, the more its opposite will assume features of 'irrational fundamentalism'*. In other words, there is no way out as long as the universal dimension of our social formation remains defined in terms of Capital. The way to break out of this vicious circle is not to fight 'irrational' ethnic particularism but to invent forms of political practice that contain a dimension of universality beyond Capital: the exemplary case today, of course, is ecology.

And where does this leave us with regard to Eastern Europe? The liberal point of view, which opposes liberal-democratic 'openness' to nationalist-organic 'closure' – the view sustained by the hope that 'true' liberal-democratic society will arise once we get rid of proto-Fascist nationalistic constraints – falls short, since it fails to take into account their interconnection, that is, the way the supposedly neutral liberal-democratic framework produces nationalist closure as its inherent opposite.[15] The only way to prevent the emergence of proto-Fascist nationalist hegemony is to call into question the very standard of 'normality', the universal framework of liberal-democratic capitalism – as was done, for a brief moment, by the 'vanishing mediators' in the passage from socialism into capitalism.

The general theoretical lesson to be drawn from this second part is that a cynical non-identification with the ruling ideology's explicit content is a positive condition of its functioning: the ideological apparatuses 'run smoothly' precisely when subjects experience their innermost desire as 'oppositional', as 'transgressive', as the desire for a moment when one is, so to speak, allowed to break the Law in the name of the Law itself. What we encounter here is perversion as a socially constructive attitude: one can indulge in illicit drives, torture and kill for the protection of law and order. This perversion relies on the split of the field of Law into Law *qua* 'Ego-Ideal', that is, the symbolic order that regulates social life and maintains peace, and its obscene, superegoic reverse. As numerous analyses from Bakhtin onward have shown, periodic transgressions are inherent to the social order; they function as a condition of the latter's stability. (The mistake of Bakhtin – or, rather, of some of his followers – was to present an idealized image of these 'transgressions', to pass in silence over lynching parties, and so forth, as the crucial form of the 'carnivalesque suspension of social hierarchy'.) The deepest identification that holds a community together is not so much an identification with the Law that regulates its 'normal' everyday rhythms, but rather identification with the specific form of transgression of the Law, of its suspension (in psychoanalytic terms, with the specific form of *enjoyment*).

Let us return to those rural white communities in the American South of the 1920s, where the rule of the official, public Law was accompanied by its shadowy double, the nightly terror of Ku Klux Klan, with its lynchings of helpless blacks: a (white) man could easily be forgiven minor infractions of the Law, especially when they could be justified by a 'code of honour' – the community still recognizes him as 'one of us'. But he would be effectively excommunicated, perceived as 'not one of us', the moment that he disowned the specific form of *transgression* that pertains to this community – say, the moment he refused to partake in ritual lynchings by the Klan, or even reported them to the Law (which, of course, did not want to hear about them since they represented its own hidden underside). The Nazi community relied on the same solidarity-in-guilt adduced by participation in a common transgression: it ostracized those who were not ready to assume the dark side of the idyllic *Volksgemeinschaft*, the night pogroms, the beatings of political opponents – in short, all that 'everybody knew, yet did not want to speak about aloud'.

The truly subversive gesture is therefore to undermine the fundamental identification with the 'transgressive' mode of enjoyment that holds a community together, to contaminate the stuff of which the ideological dream effectively consists. The same holds for Really Existing Socialism: nationalism, the attachment to the national Thing, was from the very beginning its fantasy-support, its inherent transgression, so that what we are left with now, once the symbolic network intertwined around this Thing dissolved, is simply the always already present fantasy-support in its nakedness, devoid of its symbolic clothing. Nationalism is what one obtains after the public proclamation that the socialist emperor is naked, that is, after one assumes the nullity of the socialist ideological fabric.

In this way, the final question is already answered: Wherein consists the link between the two surpluses that disturb the liberal-democratic gaze? On the one hand, the democratic Communists and new social movements in general present the moment of the 'vanishing mediator', of what must disappear, must become invisible, for the new order to establish its identity-with-itself. The agent who actually triggered the process must be perceived as its main impediment, or, to use the terms of Propp's structural analysis of fairy tales, the Donor must appear as the Malefactor, like Lady Catherine de Bourgh in Jane Austen's *Pride and Prejudice* who, under her mask as the evil impediment to Darcy and Elizabeth's marriage, is effectively the hand of Destiny that enables the happy outcome. 'Nation' as the substantial support is, on the other hand, what the new ruling ideology *sees* so that it can *not see, overlook*, the 'vanishing mediator': 'Nation' is a fantasy entity that fills the void of the vanishing mediator. Here one must learn the materialist lesson of anti-evolutionist creationism, which resolves the contradiction between the literal meaning of Scripture (according to which the universe was created about 5,000 years ago) and irrefutable proofs of its greater age (million-year-old fossils and the like) not via the usual indulging in the delicacies of the allegorical reading of Scripture ('Adam and Eve were not really the first couple but a metaphor for the early stages of humanity') but by sticking to the literal truth: the universe was created recently, only 5,000 years ago, *but with built-in false traces of the past* (God created fossils to give humans a false perspective of infinite openness).[16] The past is always strictly synchronous; it is *the way a synchronous universe thinks its antagonism*. It suffices to recall the infamous role of the 'remnants of the past' in accounting for the difficulties of the 'construction of socialism'. In this sense, the tale of ethnic roots is from the very beginning a 'myth of origins': what is 'national heritage' if not a kind of ideological fossil created retroactively by the ruling ideology in order to blur its *present* antagonism?

In other words, instead of marvelling in a state of traumatic disorientation at the shocking swiftness of the emergence of nationalism in Eastern Europe, it would perhaps be more appropriate to accomplish a kind of Hegelian reversal and to transpose this shock into the 'thing itself', to conceive of this traumatic disorientation not as a problem but as a key to the solution: the recourse to nationalism itself emerged in order to protect us from the traumatic disorientation, from the loss of the ground under our feet caused by the disintegration of the social order, of the Lacanian 'big Other' epitomized by Really Existing Socialism.

Notes

This text is an abbreviated version of a paper presented on Saturday, 25 April 1992, at a conference on 'The re-emergence of nationalism and xenophobia in Germany and Central Europe', Deutsches Haus, Columbia University, New York. A longer version was subsequently published in *New German Critique* 57, 1992, pp. 25–49. [eds]

1 Slavoj Žižek, 'Eastern Europe's Republics of Gilead', *New Left Review* 183, 1990, pp. 50–62.

2 Fredric Jameson, 'The vanishing mediator; or, Max Weber as storyteller', in *The Ideologies of Theory, Essays 1971–1986: Volume 2, Syntax of History*, Minneapolis, University of Minnesota Press, 1988, pp. 3–34.

3 As to this problematic, see Slavoj Žižek, *For They Know Not What They Do: Enjoyment as a Political Factor*, London and New York, Verso, 1991, pp. 182–8.

4 Karl Marx, *Capital: A Critique of Political Economy, Volume 1*, London, Penguin/New Left Review, 1976, pp. 873–4. [eds]

5 Louis Althusser, 'Ideology and ideological state apparatuses (notes towards an investigation)', in *Lenin and Philosophy and Other Essays*, trans. Ben Brewster, London, New Left Books, 1971, pp. 166–8. [eds]

6 For a further development of this point, see Slavoj Žižek, 'A hair of the dog that bit you', in *Interrogating the Real: Selected Writings, Volume 1*, ed. Rex Butler and Scott Stephens, London, Continuum, 2005, pp. 167–70. [eds]

7 G. W. F. Hegel, *Elements of the Philosophy of Right*, ed. Allen W. Wood, trans. H. B. Nisbet, Cambridge, Cambridge University Press, 1991, pp. 349–55. [eds]

8 The hysterical counterpoint to this American obsessional attitude is the position of the traditional European 'critical intellectual' tormented by the question: Which is the legitimate power that I would be allowed to obey with a clear conscience? In other words, the traditional European Left is – even more than Jane Eyre, the classic example of the female hysteric – *in search of a Good Master*: he wants a master, but a master whom he would dominate, who would follow his advice. This attitude provokes a hysterical reaction, the reaction of 'This is not *that!*' whenever his side comes to power: a desperate search for reasons that would legitimate his continuing disobedience. (An exemplary case is that of French Leftist intellectuals after the electoral victory of Mitterand's socialists in 1981: they were quick to discover in the socialist government features that made it even worse than the preceding liberal-conservative government, up to the signs of proto-fascist nationalism!)

9 See the success of Peter Weir's thriller *Witness*, which takes place mostly in an Amish community: are not the Amish an exemplary case of a closed community that persists in its way of life, yet without falling prey to a paranoiac logic of the 'theft of enjoyment'? In other words, the paradox of the Amish is that, while they live according to the highest standards of the Moral Majority, they have absolutely nothing to do with the Moral Majority *qua* politico-ideological movement, that is, they are as far as possible from the Moral Majority's paranoiac logic of envy, of aggressive imposition of its standards upon others. And, incidentally, the fact that the most affecting scene of the film is the collective building of a new barn testifies again to what Fredric Jameson calls the 'utopian' potential of contemporary mass culture. See, particularly, his 'Reification and utopia in mass culture', in *Signatures of the Visible*, New York and London, Routledge, 1990, pp. 9–34.

10 As already noted by numerous critics, the theory of 'authoritarian personality' is actually a foreign body within the Frankfurt School theoretical edifice: it is based on suppositions undermined by Adorno–Horkheimer's theory of late-capitalist subjectivity.

11 John Rawls, *A Theory of Justice*, Cambridge, Harvard University Press, 1971.

12 The notion of fantasy thus designates the inherent limitation of distributive justice: although the other's interests are taken into account, the other's fantasy is wronged. In other words, when the trial by 'veil of ignorance' tells me that, even if I were to occupy the lowest place in the community, I would still accept my ethical choice, I move within my own fantasy-frame – what if the other judges within the frame of an absolutely incompatible fantasy? For a more detailed Lacanian critique of Rawls's theory of justice, see Slavoj Žižek, *Enjoy Your Symptom! Jacques Lacan in Hollywood and Out*, New York and London, Routledge, 1992, pp. 70–105.

13 The reverse of this resistance is a desire to maintain the 'other' in its specific, limited form of (what our gaze perceives as) 'authenticity'. In the recent case of Peter Handke, who expressed doubts about Slovene independence, he also claimed that the notion of Slovenia as an independent state is something imposed on Slovenes from outside, not part of the inherent logic of their national development. Handke's mother was Slovene and, within his artistic universe, Slovenia functions as a mythical point of reference, a kind of maternal paradise, a country where words still refer directly to objects, somehow miraculously by-passing commodification, where people are still organically rooted in their landscape, and so on. (See Peter Handke, *Repetition*, trans. Ralph Manheim, London and New York, Farrar, Straus and Giroux, 1988.) What ultimately bothers him is therefore simply the fact that the actual Slovenia does not conform to his private myth and hence disturbs the balance of his artistic universe.

14 G. W. F. Hegel, *Phenomenology of Spirit*, trans. A. V. Miller, Oxford, Oxford University Press, 1977, pp. 401–2. [eds]

15 Thereby it repeats the mistake of the classic liberal opposition of the 'open' liberal and the 'closed' authoritarian personalities: here, also, the liberal perspective fails to notice that the authoritarian personality is not an external opposite to the 'open' tolerant liberal personality, a simple distortion of it, but its hidden 'truth' and presupposition.

16 Stephen Jay Gould, 'Adam's navel', in *The Flamingo's Smile: Reflections on Natural History*, New York and London, W. W. Norton, 1985, pp. 99–113.

Chapter 2
Why we all love to hate Haider

The entry of Jörg Haider's Freedom Party into a coalition government in Austria has been greeted with expressions of horror from the entire spectrum of the 'legitimate' democratic political bloc in the Western world. From the social-democratic Third Way to the Christian conservatives, from Chirac to Clinton – not to mention, of course, the Israeli régime – all voiced 'dismay' and announced a diplomatic quarantine of Austria until the plague should disappear. Establishment commentators naturally hailed this demonstrative reaction as evidence that the antifascist consensus of post-war European democracy holds firm. But are things really so unequivocal?

Plain to see, in fact, is the structural role of the populist Right in the legitimation of the current liberal-democratic hegemony. For what this Right – e.g., Buchanan, Le Pen, Haider – supplies is the negative common denominator of the entire established political spectrum. These are the excluded ones who, by their very exclusion (their 'unacceptability' for governmental office), furnish the proof of the benevolence of the official system. Their existence displaces the focus of political struggle – whose true object is the stifling of any radical alternative to the Left – to the 'solidarity' of the entire 'democratic' bloc against the Rightist danger. The *Neue Mitte* manipulates the rightist scare in order better to hegemonize the 'democratic' field, i.e., to define the terrain and discipline its real adversary, the radical Left. Therein resides the ultimate rationale of the Third Way: that is, a social democracy purged of its minimal subversive sting, extinguishing even the faintest memory of anti-capitalism and class struggle.

The result is what one would expect. The populist Right moves to occupy the terrain evacuated by the Left, as the only 'serious' political force that still employs an anti-capitalist rhetoric – even if thickly coated with a nationalist/racist/religious veneer (international corporations are 'betraying' the decent working people of our nation, etc.). At the congress of the National Front a couple of years ago, Jean-Marie Le Pen brought on stage an Algerian, an African and a Jew, embraced them all, and told his audience: 'They are no less French than I am – it is the representatives of big multinational Capital, ignoring their duty to France, who are the true danger to our identity!' In New York, Pat Buchanan and black activist Leonora Fulani can proclaim a common hostility to unrestricted free trade, and both (pretend to) speak on behalf of the legendary *desaparecidos* of our time, the proverbially vanished proletariat. While multicultural tolerance becomes the motto of the new and privileged 'symbolic' classes, the far Right seeks to address and mobilize whatever remains of the mainstream 'working class' in our Western societies.

The consensual form of politics in our time is a bi-polar system that offers the appearance of a choice where essentially there is none, since today poles converge on a single economic stance – the 'tight fiscal policy' that Clinton and Blair declare to be the key tenet of the modern Left, that sustains economic growth, that allows us to improve social security, education and health. In this uniform spectrum, political differences are more and more reduced to merely cultural attitudes: multicultural/sexual (etc.) 'openness' versus traditional/natural (etc.) 'family values'. This choice – between Social Democrat or Christian Democrat in Germany, Democrat or Republican in the States – recalls nothing so much as the predicament of someone who wants an artificial sweetener in an American cafeteria, where the omnipresent alternatives are *Nutra-Sweet* or *Sweet & Low*, small bags of red and blue, and most consumers have a habitual preference (avoid the red ones, they contain cancerous substances, or vice versa), whose ridiculous persistence merely highlights the meaninglessness of the options themselves.

Does the same not go for late-night talk shows, where 'freedom of channels' comes down to a choice between Jay Leno and David Letterman? Or for the soda drinks: Coke or Pepsi? It is a well-known fact that the 'Close the Door' button in most elevators is a totally inoperative placebo, placed there just to give people the impression they are somehow contributing to the speed of the elevator journey – whereas in fact, when we push this button, the door closes in exactly the same time as when we simply pressed the floor button. This extreme case of fake participation is an appropriate metaphor for the role accorded citizens in our 'postmodern' political process. Postmoderns, of course, will calmly reply that antagonisms are radical only so long as society is still – anachronistically – perceived as a totality. After all, did not Adorno admit that contradiction is difference under the aspect of identity?[1] So today, as society loses any identity, no antagonism can any longer cut through the social body.

Postmodern politics thus logically accepts the claim that 'the working class has disappeared' and its corollary, the growing irrelevance of class antagonisms *tout court*. As its proponents like to put it, class antagonisms should not be 'essentialized' into an ultimate point of hermeneutic reference to whose 'expression' all other antagonisms can be reduced. Today we witness a thriving of new multiple political subjectivities (class, ethnic, gay, ecological, feminist, religious), alliances between which are the outcome of open, thoroughly contingent struggles for hegemony. However, as thinkers as different as Alain Badiou and Fredric Jameson have pointed out, today's multiculturalist celebration of the diversity of lifestyles and thriving of differences relies on an underlying One – that is, a radical obliteration of Difference, of the antagonistic gap.[2] (Of course, the same goes for the standard postmodern critique of sexual difference as a 'binary opposition' to be deconstructed: 'there are not two sexes but a multitude of sexes and sexual identities.' The truth of these multiple sexes is Unisex, the erasing of Difference in a boringly repetitive, perverse Sameness that is the container of this multitude.) In all these cases, the moment we introduce the 'thriving multitude' what we effectively assert is its exact opposite, an underlying all-pervasive Sameness – a non-antagonistic society in which there is room for all manner of cultural communities, lifestyles, religions, sexual orientations. The reply of a materialist theory is to show that this very One already relies on certain exclusions: the common field in which plural identities disport is from the start sustained by an invisible antagonistic split.

Memory traces of Labour

Of course, even to mention terms like 'class' or 'labour' is enough to invite the reproach of 'economic essentialism' from the postmodernists of the Third Way. My first reaction to the charge is: *why not?* If we look around the world today, we soon see how handy a dose of this out-of-date way of thinking can be. The lands of former 'socialism', which the ideology of the moment still finds so hard to assign to their place in its scheme of things, offer particularly rich examples. How else should we conceive the connection between the two mega-powers, the United States and China, for example? They relate to each other more and more as Capital and Labour. The United States is turning into a country of managerial planning, banking, servicing, etc., while its 'disappearing working class' (except for migrant Chicanos and others who mainly toil in the service economy) is reappearing in China, where a large proportion of American goods, from toys to electronic hardware, is manufactured in ideal conditions for capitalist exploitation: no strikes, little safety, tied labour, miserable wages. Far from being merely antagonistic, the relationship between China and the United States is actually also symbiotic. The irony of history is that China is coming to deserve the title of a 'working-class state': it is turning into the state of the working class for American Capital.

Meanwhile, the failed 'Real Socialist' venture has left another legacy in Europe. There, the idea of labour (material, industrial production) as the privileged site of community and solidarity was especially strong in East Germany. Not only was engagement in the collective effort of production in the GDR supposed to bring individual satisfaction, but the problems of private life (from divorce to illness) were held to be put in their proper perspective by discussion in the workplace. This notion is the focus of what is arguably the ultimate GDR novel, Christa Wolf's *Divided Heaven*. It is to be confused neither with the pre-modern idea of work as a ritualized communal activity, nor with the romantic celebration of older industrial forms of production (say, elegies for the authenticity of the Welsh miners' lives in the manner of *How Green Was My Valley*), still less with any proto-fascist cult of craft work (along the lines of *Die Meistersinger*). The production group is a collective of modern individuals who rationally discuss their problems, not an archaic organic community.

Therein perhaps resides the ultimate cause of *Ostalgie*, a continuing sentimental attachment to the defunct 'Real Socialism' of the former GDR – the sense that, in spite of all its failures and horrors, something precious was lost with its collapse, which now has been repressed once again into a criminal underground. For in the ideological sensibility of the West today, is it not work itself – manual labour as opposed to 'symbolic' activity – rather than sex, that has become the site of obscene indecency to be concealed from the public eye? The tradition, which goes back to Wagner's *Rhinegold* and Lang's *Metropolis*, in which the working process takes place in dark caves underground, now culminates in the millions of anonymous workers sweating in Third World factories, from Chinese gulags to Indonesian or Brazilian assembly lines. Due to the invisibility of all these, the West can afford to babble on about the 'disappearance of the working class'. Crucial to this tradition is a tacit equation of labour with crime: the idea that hard work is a felonious activity to be hidden from public view.

Thus the only place in Hollywood films where we see a production process in all its amplitude is in the genre of the thriller where the hero penetrates the master criminal's secret domain, and sees a hidden installation of furiously concentrated labour (distilling and packaging drugs, constructing a rocket that will destroy New York, etc.). When the arch-villain, after capturing Bond or his like, typically takes the hero on a tour of his monstrous enterprise, is not this vision of some vast, illegal production-complex the nearest American equivalent to the proud socialist-realist images of the Soviet epoch? Bond's role, of course, is to escape and blow up the whole assemblage in a spectacular fireball that returns us to the daily semblance of our life in a world cleansed of the working class. What is abolished in the final orgy of such violence is a certain utopian moment in Western history, when participation in a collective process of material labour was perceived as the ground of an authentic sense of community and solidarity. The dream was not to get rid of physical labour, but to find fulfilment in it, reversing its biblical meaning as a curse for Adam's Fall.

In his short book on Solzhenitsyn, one of his last works, Georg Lukács offered an enthusiastic appraisal of *One Day in the Life of Ivan Denisovich*, a novella that depicted for the first time in Soviet literature daily life in a gulag (its publication had to be cleared by Nikita Khrushchev in person). Lukács singled out the scene in which, towards the end of the long working day, Ivan Denisovich rushes to complete the section of wall he has been building; when he hears the guard's call for all the prisoners to re-group for the march back to the camp, he cannot resist the temptation of quickly inserting a final couple of bricks into it, although he thereby risks the guard's wrath. Lukács read this impulse to finish the job as a sign of how, even in the brutal conditions of the gulag, the specifically socialist notion of material production as the locus of creative fulfilment survived; when, in the evening, Ivan Denisovich takes mental stock of the day, he notes with satisfaction that he has built a wall and enjoyed doing so. Lukács was right to make the paradoxical claim that this seminal dissident text perfectly fits the most stringent definition of socialist realism.[3]

Perduring in the place

Yugoslavia offers another variant of postmodern misconceptions of post-communism which casts more light on the West than on the former East. 'Enlightened' liberal states seem baffled by the reaction of rulers like Slobodan Milošević and Saddam Hussein to the campaigns against them. They appear to be impervious to all external pressures: the West bombards them, chips off parts of their territory, isolates them from their neighbours, imposes tough boycotts on them, humiliates them in every way possible, and yet they survive with their glory intact, maintaining the semblance of courageous leaders who dare to defy the New World Order. It is not so much that they turn defeat into triumph; it is rather that, like some version of a Buddhist sage, they sit in their palaces and perdure, occasionally defying expectations with eccentric gestures of almost Bataillean expenditure, like Milošević's son opening a local version of Disneyland in the midst of the NATO bombing of Yugoslavia, or Saddam completing a large amusement park for his elite *nomenklatura*. Sticks (threats and bombings) achieve nothing, and neither do carrots. So where have Western perceptions gone wrong?

Our theorists, projecting on to these régimes a stereotyped opposition of the rational hedonistic pursuit of happiness and ideological fanaticism, fail to take note of a more apposite couple: apathy and obscenity. The apathy that pervades daily life in Serbia today expresses not only popular disillusion in the 'democratic opposition' to Milošević, but also a deeper indifference towards 'sacred' nationalist goals themselves. How was it that Serbs did not rally against Milošević when he lost Kosovo? Every ordinary Serb knows the answer – it's an open secret in Yugoslavia. They really don't care about Kosovo. So when the region was lost, the secret reaction was a sigh of relief: 'Finally, we are rid of that overrated piece of soil which caused us so much trouble!' The key to the readiness of 'ordinary' Serbs to tolerate Milošević lies in the combination of this kind of apathy with its apparent opposite, an obscene permissivity. Here is how Aleksandar Tijanić, a leading Serb columnist who was even for a brief period Milošević's minister for information and public media, describes 'the strange symbiosis between Milošević and the Serbs':

> Milošević generally suits the Serbs. Under his rule, Serbs have abolished working hours. No one does anything. He has allowed the black market and smuggling to flourish. You can appear on state TV and insult Blair, Clinton, or any other 'international dignitary' of your choice. Milošević gave us the right to carry weapons, and to solve all our problems with weapons. He gave us the right to drive stolen cars . . . Milošević changed the life of Serbs into one long holiday, making us all feel like high-school pupils on a graduation trip – which means that nothing, but really nothing, of what you do is punishable.[4]

Marx long ago emphasized that the critical test of any historico-materialist analysis is not its ability to reduce ideological or political phenomena to their 'actual' economic foundations, but to cover the same path in the opposite direction – that is, to show why these material interests articulate themselves in just such an ideal form.[5] The true problem is not so much to identify the economic interests that sustain Milošević, as to explain how the rule of obscene permissivity can serve as an effective ideological social bond in today's Yugoslavia. Of course, Milošević's rule also yields an unexpected bonus for the nationalist 'democratic opposition' in the country, because for the

Western powers he is a pariah who embodies all that is wrong in Yugoslavia. The opposition is therefore counting on his death as the moment when, like Christ, he will take upon himself all their sins. His demise will be hailed as the chance of a new democratic beginning, and Yugoslavia will be accepted again into the 'international community'. This is the scenario that has already taken place with the death of Franjo Tudjman in Croatia. Ignoring the ominous pomp of his funeral, Western commentators dwelt on the way his personal obstinacy had been the main obstacle to the democratization of Croatia, opening up a fair prospect for the future of the nation – as if all the skeletons of independent Croatia, from corruption to ethnic cleansing, had now magically vanished, interred forever with Tudjman's corpse. Will this be Milošević's last service to his nation, too?

Expelling the material realities of sweat-shop labour, collective production and anomic licence from its visions of the East, the official imaginary naturally has no time for traces of the working class in the West. In today's political discourse, the very term 'workers' tends to have disappeared from sight, substituted or obliterated by 'immigrants' – Algerians in France, Turks in Germany, Mexicans in the United States, etc. In this new vocabulary, the class problematic of exploitation is transformed into the multiculturalist problematic of 'intolerance of the Other', and the investment of liberals in the particular rights of ethnic minorities draws much of its energy from the repression of the general category of the collective labourer. The 'disappearance' of the working class then fatally unleashes its reappearance in the guise of aggressive nativism. Liberals and populists meet on common ground; all they talk about is identity. Is not Haider himself the best Hegelian example of the 'speculative identity' of the tolerant multiculturalist and the postmodern racist? Now that his party has reached office, he takes pains to stress the affinity between New Labour and the Austrian Free Democrats, which renders the old oppositions of Left/ Right irrelevant. Both forces, he notes, have jettisoned old ideological ballast, and now combine a flexible market economics, determined to dismantle statist controls and free entrepreneurial energies, with a politics of care and solidarity concerned to protect children and help the elderly and disadvantaged, without reverting to dogmas of the welfare state. As for immigration, Haider contends that his policies are more liberal than those of Blair.[6]

There is both truth and falsehood in such claims. Once in power, Haider – blatantly an opportunist rather than a genuine 'extremist' – would no doubt perform quite conventionally. After all, in Italy his homologue Fini, until recently a fervent admirer of Mussolini, is now the most respectable of democratic statesmen, whose reputation the whole Italian establishment – from President Ciampi and Prime Minister D'Alema downwards – has rushed to defend against 'anachronistic' slurs from Schröder. But for the moment, Haider is still a demagogue whose attraction in Austria is based on remaining an outsider. His self-comparisons with New Labour are to that extent deliberately misleading, designed to cover up the xenophobic kernel of his populism. They belong to the same series as attempts by Afrikaans politicians of old to present apartheid as just another version of identity politics, devoted to safeguarding the rich variety of cultures in South Africa. Ernesto Laclau has taught us the distinction between the elements of an ideological construct and the articulation that gives them their meaning. Thus fascism was not characterized simply by a series of features like economic corporatism, populism, xenophobic racism, militarism and so on, for these could also be included in other ideological configurations; what made these features 'fascist' was their specific articulation within an overall political project (for example, large public works did not play the same role in Nazi Germany and New Deal America). Along the same lines, it would be easy to show that Haider's manipulation of a menu of free-market and social-liberal dishes is not to be confused with the Third Way: even if Haider and Blair do propose a set of identical measures, these are inscribed in different ideological enterprises.

This, however, is not the whole story. There is also a sense in which Haider is indeed a kind of uncanny double of Blair, his obscene sneer accompanying New Labour's big smile like a shadow. For New Right populism is the necessary supplement of the multiculturalist tolerance of global Capital, as the return of the repressed. The 'truth' of Haider's claim does not lie in the identity of New Labour and the New Right, but in the generation of his populism by the zombification of European social democracy as a whole. In Haider's clinching to Blair – I use the term in the precise sense, of the boxing-ring – the Third Way gets its own message back in inverted form. Participation by the far Right in government is not punishment for 'sectarianism' or a failure to 'come to terms with postmodern conditions'. It is the price the Left pays for renouncing any radical political project, and accepting market capitalism as 'the only game in town'.

Notes

This paper was originally published in *New Left Review* 2, 2000, pp. 37–45. [eds]

1 Theodor W. Adorno, *Negative Dialectics*, trans. E. B. Ashton, London and New York, Routledge, 1973, pp. 149–52. [eds]

2 Alain Badiou, *Deleuze: The Clamour of Being*, trans. Louise Burchill, Minneapolis, University of Minnesota Press, 2000, p. 56; Fredric Jameson, 'Notes on globalization as a political issue', in *The Cultures of Globalization*, ed. Fredric Jameson and Masao Miyoshi, Durham, Duke University Press, 1998, p. 71. [eds]

3 Georg Lukács, *Solzhenitsyn*, trans. William David Graf, London, Merlin, 1970, pp. 17–23. [eds]

4 Aleksandar Tijanić, 'The remote day of change', *Mladina*, 6 August 1999, p. 33.

5 Karl Marx, *Capital: A Critique of Political Economy, Volume 1*, trans. Ben Fowkes, London, Penguin, 1976, pp. 164–5. [eds]

6 Jörg Haider, 'Blair and me versus the forces of conservatism', *The Daily Telegraph*, 22 February 2000.

Chapter 3
Heiner Müller out of joint

The documentary on Heiner Müller and his 1989 staging of *Hamlet*, 'Zeit aus den Fügen', deploys the entire scope of his reticence to embrace German unification and the simple direct transposition of the BRD model on to the GDR. What distinguishes Müller is that he went much further than those who merely complained that the unique chance of developing a 'third way' beyond State socialism and global capitalism had been missed: Müller questioned the *a priori* legitimacy of free elections themselves, proposing a risky comparison with 1933 ('free elections also brought Hitler to power'). Was this just an arrogant display of a fake dissident whose narcissism was injured when the masses rejected the alternative of democratic socialism? Was Müller himself thrown out of joint, or can his stance be defended? Now that the tenth anniversary of Müller's death is approaching, it is perhaps time to revisit this question. My aim here is to take Müller's stance seriously as a *theoretico-political* position, not just as pseudo-radical chic tolerated and excused in advance as belonging to an eccentric artist.

To begin with, the case against Müller seems clear. One can immediately reproach him with succumbing to the temptation of catastrophism, of perceiving the situation (in 1989) as one of utter despair – recall his statements from those years that he just wants to drown himself in alcohol and drugs. Most of today's claims that the twentieth century was the most catastrophic in human history, the lowest point of nihilism, a situation of extreme danger, etc., forget the elementary lesson of dialectics: the twentieth century appears as such because the criteria themselves changed – today, we simply have much higher standards of what constitutes a violation of human rights, and so on. The fact that the situation *appears* catastrophic is thus in itself a positive sign, a sign of (some kind of) progress: we are today much more sensitive to things that were also occurring in previous epochs. Take the example of feminism: only in the last 200 years was the situation of women progressively perceived as unjust, although it was 'objectively' getting better. Or recall the treatment of disabled individuals: even a couple of decades ago, the special entrances that enable them access to restaurants, theatres, etc., would have been unthinkable.

More specifically, is Müller's stance not emblematic of privileged 'official dissidents' with visas for travelling freely to the West, angry at the stupid crowd for betraying their dreams? Along the same lines, there is the hypocrisy of pro-Castro Western leftists who despise what Cubans themselves call '*gusanos* [worms]', those who emigrated from Cuba. With all sympathy for the Cuban revolution, what right does a typical middle-class Western leftist have to despise Cubans who decided to leave Cuba, not only because of political disenchantment, but also because of poverty (so severe as to involve genuine hunger)? I myself remember how, in the early 1990s, dozens of Western leftists proudly declared that, as far as they were concerned, Yugoslavia still existed, and reproached me for betraying a unique chance to maintain Yugoslavia – to which I have always answered that I am not yet ready to lead my life so that it will not disappoint the dreams of Western leftists. There are few things more worthy of contempt, few attitudes more *ideological* (if this word has any meaning today, it should be applied here), than a tenured Western academic leftist arrogantly dismissing (or, even worse, 'understanding' in a patronizing way) an Eastern European from a Communist country who longs for Western liberal democracy and a few consumer goods.

It is here that the Frankfurt School miserably failed: one cannot but be struck by the almost total absence of theoretical confrontation with Stalinism in the Frankfurt School, in clear contrast to its permanent obsession with fascist anti-Semitism. The very exceptions to this rule are telling: Franz Neumann's *Behemoth*, a study of National Socialism which, in the typical fashionable style of the late 1930s and early

1940s, suggested that the three great world systems – the emerging New Deal capitalism, fascism and Stalinism – tend towards the same bureaucratic, globally organized, 'administered' society; Herbert Marcuse's *Soviet Marxism*, his least passionate and arguably worst book, a strangely neutral analysis of the Soviet ideology with no clear commitments; and, finally, attempts by some Habermasians who, reflecting upon the emerging dissident phenomenon, have endeavoured to elaborate the notion of civil society as a site of resistance to the Communist régime – a position that is interesting politically, but far from offering a satisfactory global theory of the specificity of Stalinist 'totalitarianism'.

The standard excuse (authors in the Frankfurt School did not want to oppose Communism too openly because, in so doing, they would play into the hands of their domestic Cold Warriors) is obviously insufficient – the point is not that this fear of being placed in the service of official anti-Communism proves how they were secretly pro-Communist, but rather the opposite: if they were *really* cornered as to where they stood with respect to the Cold War, they would have chosen Western liberal democracy (as Max Horkheimer explicitly did in some of his late writings). 'Stalinism' (that is, Really Existing Socialism) was thus, for the Frankfurt School, a traumatic topic apropos of which it *had* to remain silent – this silence was the only way for them to retain the inconsistency of their position of underlying solidarity with Western liberal democracy, without losing their official guise of 'radical' leftist critique. Openly acknowledging this solidarity would have deprived them of their 'radical' aura, changing them into yet another version of Cold War anti-Communist leftist liberals, while showing too much sympathy for the Really Existing Socialism would have forced them to betray their unacknowledged basic commitment to Western liberal democracy.

This ultimate solidarity with the Western system when the latter was genuinely threatened displays a clear symmetry with the stance of the 'democratic socialist opposition' in the German Democratic Republic. While its members criticized Communist Party rule, they endorsed the basic premise of the GDR régime: the thesis that the Federal Republic of Germany is a neo-Nazi State, the direct heir of Nazism and, therefore, that the existence of the GDR as an anti-Fascist bulwark must be protected at any cost. For that reason, as soon as the situation got really serious and the socialist system was effectively threatened, they publicly supported the system (like Brecht apropos of East Berlin workers' demonstrations in 1953, and Christa Wolf apropos of the Prague Spring in 1968). They sustained a belief in the inherent reformability of the system – but for this true democratic reform to take place, time and patience were needed: a too rapid disintegration of socialism would return Germany to the capitalist-fascist régime and thus strangle the utopia of that 'Other Germany' which, in spite of all its horrors and failures, the GDR continued to represent. Hence the deep distrust of these intellectuals for 'people' as opposed to Power: in 1989, they openly opposed free elections, well aware that, if free elections were to be held, the majority would have chosen despised capitalist consumerism. Heiner Müller was thus quite consequent when, in 1989, he claimed that free elections also brought Hitler to power . . . (Many Western social democrats played the same game, feeling much closer to 'reform-minded' Communists than to dissidents – the latter somehow embarrassed them as an obstacle to the process of *détente*.) Along the same lines, it was also clear to perceptive dissidents like Václav Havel that Soviet intervention in a way saved the myth of the Prague Spring of 1968, i.e., the utopian notion that, if the Czechs were left alone, they would effectively give birth to a 'socialism with a human face', to an authentic alternative to both Real Socialism and Real Capitalism. That is to say, what would have happened if the Warsaw Pact forces had *not* intervened in August of 1968? Either the Czech Communist leadership would have imposed restraint and Czechoslovakia would remain a (more liberal, true) Communist régime, or it would have turned into a 'normal' Western capitalist society (maybe with a stronger Scandinavian social-democratic flavour).

One should thus fully admit the falsity of what I am tempted to call the 'interpassive socialism' of the Western academic Left: what these leftists displace on to the Other is not a specific kind of activity, but their passive authentic experience. They allow themselves to pursue their well-paid academic careers in the West, while using an idealized Other (like Cuba, Nicaragua, Tito's Yugoslavia) as the stuff of their ideological fantasy: they dream through the Other, and rage against it if it in any way disturbs their complacency (by abandoning socialism and opting for liberal capitalism). What is of particular interest here is the basic misunderstanding, the lack of communication, between the Western Left and dissidents in late socialism – it is as if it was forever impossible for them to find a common language. Although sensing that they should be on the same side, an elusive gap seemed forever to separate them: for Western Leftists, Eastern dissidents were all too naïve in their belief in democracy (in their rejection of socialism, they unknowingly threw out the baby with the bath water); in the eyes of the dissidents, the Western Left played the patronizing game of disavowing the true harshness of the totalitarian régime (the accusation that dissidents were somehow guilty of not seizing the unique opportunity amid the disintegration of socialism and inventing an authentic alternative to capitalism was hypocrisy at its purest). However, what if this *lack of communication* was, in fact, an example of successful communication in the precise Lacanian sense? What if each of the two positions received from its other its own repressed message in an inverted and true form?

However, the constellation is not as simple as it may appear. As Alain Badiou pointed out, in spite of its horrors and failures, Really Existing Socialism was the only political force that – for some decades, at least – seemed to pose a serious threat to the global rule of capitalism, genuinely scaring its representatives, driving them into paranoiac reaction.[1] But now that, today, capitalism defines and structures the totality of human civilization, every 'Communist' territory was and is – again, in spite of its horrors and failures – a kind of 'liberated territory', as Fredric Jameson put it apropos of Cuba.[2] What we are dealing with here is the old structural notion of the gap between a space and the positive content that fills it: although, as to their positive content, Communist régimes were mostly a dismal failure, generating terror and misery, *at the same time* they opened up a certain space, the space of utopian expectations which, among other things, enabled us to measure the failure of Really Existing Socialism itself. What anti-Communist dissidents as a rule tend to overlook is that the very space from which they themselves criticized and denounced the everyday misery of the régimes *was opened and sustained by the Communist breakthrough, by its attempt to escape the logic of Capital*. In short, when dissidents like Havel denounced the existing Communist régime from the standpoint of authentic human solidarity, they (unknowingly, for the most part) spoke from the space opened up by Communism itself – which is why they tended to be so disappointed when 'really existing capitalism' failed to meet the high expectations of their anti-Communist struggle. Perhaps Václav Klaus, Havel's pragmatic double, was right when he dismissed Havel as a 'socialist' . . .

This externality to capitalism also compelled dissidents to question the incessant drive towards productivity shared by capitalism and State socialism. The obverse of this drive is the growing piles of useless waste, mountains of used cars, computers, etc. (like the famous airplanes' 'resting place' in the Mojave desert); in these ever-growing piles of inert, dysfunctional 'stuff', which cannot but impress us with their useless, bare presence, one can, as it were, perceive the capitalist drive at rest. Therein resides the interest of Andrei Tarkovsky's masterpiece *Stalker*, with its post-industrial wasteland of wild vegetation growing over abandoned factories, concrete tunnels and railroads full of stale water, a terrain of wild overgrowth in which stray dogs and cats wander. Here, nature and industrial civilization again overlap, but through their common decay – a decaying civilization is in the process of being reclaimed (not by an idealized harmonious Nature, but) by nature in its decomposition. The ultimate irony is that an author from the Communist East displayed the greatest sensitivity for this obverse of the drive to produce-and-consume. Perhaps, however, this irony displays a deeper necessity which hinges on what Heiner Müller called the 'waiting-room mentality' of Communist Eastern Europe:

> There would be an announcement: The train will arrive at 18:15 and depart at 18:20 – and it never did arrive at 18:15. Then came the next announcement: The train will arrive at 20:10. And so on. You went on sitting there in the waiting room, thinking, it's bound to come at 20:15. That was the situation. Basically, a state of Messianic anticipation. There are constant announcements of the Messiah's impending arrival, and you know perfectly well that he won't be coming. And yet somehow, it's good to hear him announced all over again.[3]

The point of this Messianic attitude was not that hope was maintained, but that, because the Messiah did *not* arrive, people began to look around and take note of the inert materiality of their surroundings, in contrast to the West, where people, engaged in permanent frenetic activity, fail properly to notice what goes on all around them. Because of the lack of acceleration, people could enjoy greater contact with the earth on which the waiting room was built; caught in this delay, they deeply experienced the idiosyncrasies of their world, all of its topographical and historical details . . .

There are, therefore, good reasons to take Müller's reticence seriously. There are four motifs, four topics, around which his political stance is crystallized: (a) the rejection of the unconditional drive towards productivity, (b) the distrust of democracy, (c) the theatralization of politics and (d) the inevitability of violence. These four imperatives directly contradict the four dogmas of today's post-politics: (a) the focus on economic growth, (b) liberal democracy, (c) non-theatrical pragmatism and (d) non-violent tolerance.

Let us begin with the key role of theatralization. Recall the staged performance of the 'Storming of the Winter Palace' in Petrograd on the third anniversary of the October Revolution (7 November 1920). This event (directed by Nikolai Evreinov who, in 1925, immigrated to France) involved 8,000 direct participants and an audience of 100,000 (a quarter of the city's population) in spite of heavy rain. The underlying idea was formulated by Anatoli Lunatcharsky, People's Commisar for Enlightenment, in the spring of 1920: 'In order to acquire a sense of self the masses must outwardly manifest themselves, and this is possible only when, in Robespierre's words, they become a spectacle unto themselves.'[4] Thousands of workers, soldiers, students and artists worked round the clock, living on *kasha* (tasteless wheat porridge), tea and frozen apples, preparing the performance at the very place where the event 'really took place' three years earlier. Their work was coordinated by Army officers, as well as by avant-garde artists, musicians and directors, from Malevich to Meyerhold. Although this was acting and not 'reality', the soldiers and sailors were playing *themselves* – many of them not only actually participated in the event of 1917, but also were simultaneously involved in the real battles of the civil war that was raging in the nearby vicinity of Petrograd, a city under siege and suffering from severe shortages of food. A contemporary commented on the performance: 'The future historian will record how, throughout one of the bloodiest and most brutal revolutions, all of Russia was acting.'[5] The formalist theoretician Viktor Shklovski further noted that, 'some kind of elemental process is taking place where the living fabric of life is being transformed into the theatrical.'[6]

We all remember the infamous, self-celebratory 'First of May' parades that were one of the supreme signs of recognition of the Stalinist régime. If one needs proof of how Leninism functioned in an entirely different way, are such performances as the 'Storming of the Winter Palace' not the ultimate proof that the October Revolution was definitely *not* a simple *coup d'état* by a small group of Bolsheviks, but an event that unleashed a tremendous emancipatory potential? Does the 'Storming of the Winter Palace' performance not display the force of a sacred (pagan?) pageant, the magic act of founding a new community? It is here that, perhaps, one should look for the realization of Wagner's *Gesamtkunstwerk*, of what he aimed at with the designation of his *Parsifal* as *Bühnenweihfestspiel* ('sacred festival drama'): it was in the Petrograd of 1920, much more than in Ancient Greece, that, 'in intimate connection with its history, the people itself that stood facing itself in the work of art, becoming conscious of itself, and, in the space of a few hours, rapturously devouring, as it were, its own essence'.[7] This aestheticization, in which the people quite literally 'plays itself', certainly does not fall under Benjamin's indictment of the Fascist 'aestheticization of the political' – instead of abandoning this aestheticization to the political Right, instead of a blanket dismissal of every mass political spectacle as 'proto-fascist', one should perceive in this minimal, purely formal, difference of the people from itself the unique case of 'real life' differentiated from art by nothing more than an invisible formal gap. The very fact that, in historical documentaries, footage from the performance (as well as from Eisenstein's *October* of 1927) of the 'Storming of the Winter Palace' is often presented as though in the form of a documentary, is to be taken as an indication of this deeper identity of people playing themselves.

The archetypal Eisensteinian cinematic scene rendering the exuberant orgy of revolutionary destructive violence (what Eisenstein himself called 'a veritable bacchanalia of destruction') belongs to the same series: when, in *October*, the victorious revolutionaries penetrate the wine cellars of the Winter Palace, they indulge in an ecstatic orgy of smashing thousands of expensive wine bottles. In *Behzin Meadow*, the village pioneers force their way into the local church and desecrate it, robbing it of its relics, squabbling over an icon, sacrilegiously trying on vestments, heretically laughing at the statuary. In this suspension of goal-orientated instrumental activity, we effectively get a kind of Bataillean 'unrestrained expenditure'. Recall the classic reproach of Robespierre to the Dantonist opportunists: 'What you want is a revolution without revolution!' – the pious desire to deprive the revolution of this excess is simply the desire to have a revolution without revolution.

However, this 'unrestrained expenditure' is not enough: in a revolution proper, such a display of what Hegel would have called 'abstract negativity' merely, as it were, wipes the slate clean for the second act, the imposition of a New Order. The tautology 'revolution *with* revolution' thus has another aspect: it also signals the urge to repeat the negation, to relate it to itself – in its course, a true revolution revolutionizes its own starting presuppositions. This is what Mao Zedong called the 'Cultural Revolution' as the condition of successful social revolution. What, exactly, does this mean? The problem with hitherto revolutionary attempts was not that they were 'too extreme', but that they were *not radical enough*, that they did not question their own presuppositions. In a wonderful essay on *Chevengur*, Andrei Platonov's great peasant utopia written between 1927 and 1928 (just prior to forced collectivization), Fredric Jameson describes the two moments of the revolutionary process. It begins with the gesture of radical negativity:

This first moment of world-reduction, of the destruction of the idols and the sweeping away of an old world in violence and pain, is itself the precondition for the reconstruction of something else. A first moment of absolute immanence is necessary, the blank slate of absolute peasant immanence or ignorance, before new and undreamed-of sensations and feelings can come into being.[8]

There then follows a second stage, the invention of a new life – not only the construction of a new social reality within which our utopian dreams would be realized, but the (re)construction of these dreams themselves:

a process that it would be too simple and misleading to call reconstruction or Utopian construction, since in effect it involves the very effort to find a way to begin imagining Utopia to begin with.

Perhaps in a more Western kind of psychoanalytic language . . . we might think of the new onset of the Utopian process as a kind of desiring to desire, a learning to desire, the invention of the desire called Utopia in the first place, along with new rules for the fantasizing or daydreaming of such a thing – a set of narrative protocols with no precedent in our previous literary institutions.[9]

The reference to psychoanalysis here is crucial and very precise: in a radical revolution, people not only 'realize their old (emancipatory, etc.) dreams'; rather, they have to reinvent their very modes of dreaming.[10] Is this not the exact formula of the link between death drive and sublimation? It is *only* this reference to what happens *after* the revolution, the proverbial 'morning after', that allows us to distinguish between libertarian pathetic outbursts and true revolutionary upheavals: these upheavals lose their energy when one has to approach the prosaic work of social reconstruction – at this point, lethargy begins to set in. By contrast, recall the immense creativity of the Jacobins just prior to their fall: the numerous proposals about new civic religion, about how to sustain the dignity of old people, and so on. Therein also resides the interest in reading reports about daily life in the Soviet Union in the early 1920s, with its enthusiastic urge to invent new rules for quotidian existence: How does one get married? What are the new rules of courting? How does one celebrate a birthday? How is one to be buried? It is precisely with regard to *this* dimension that revolution proper is to be opposed to carnivalesque reversal as temporary respite, the exception stabilizing the hold of power.

And this brings us to the key question: how are we to construct a social space within which revolution can stabilize itself? Perhaps, one of the options is to pursue the trend of self-organized collectives in areas outside the law. Arguably the greatest literary monument to such a utopia comes from an unexpected source – Mario Vargas Llosa's *The War of the End of the World*, a novel about Canudos, an outlaw community deep in the Brazilian backlands, which was home to prostitutes, freaks, beggars, bandits and the most wretched of the poor.[11] Canudos, led by an apocalyptic prophet, was a utopian space without money, property, taxes and marriage. In 1897, it was destroyed by the military forces of the Brazilian government.

Echoes of Canudos are clearly discernible in today's *favelas* in Latin American megalopolises: in some sense, are they not the first 'liberated territories', cells of future self-organized societies? Are institutions like community kitchens not a model of 'socialized' communal local life? The Canudos' liberated territory in Bahia will remain forever the model of a liberated space, an alternative community, which thoroughly negates the existing space of State. Everything is to be endorsed here, right up to religious 'fanaticism'. It is as if, in such communities, *the Benjaminian other side of historical progress, the defeated ones, acquires a space of their own*. Utopia *existed* here for a brief period of time – this is the only way to account for the 'irrational', excessive violence of the destruction of these communities (in Brazil in 1897, *all* inhabitants of Canudos, children and women included, were slaughtered, as if the very memory of the possibility of freedom had to be erased – and this by a government that presented itself as 'progressive' liberal-democratic-republican . . .). Until now, such communities irrupted from time to time as passing phenomena, sites of eternity that interrupted the flow of temporal progress – one should have the courage to recognize them in the wide span from the Jesuit *reduciones* in the eighteenth century in Paraguay (brutally destroyed by the joint action of Spanish and Portuguese armies) up to the settlements controlled by Sendero Luminoso in Peru in the 1990s. Can one imagine a point at which this subterranean dimension of the utopian 'Other Space' could unite with the positive space of 'normal' social life?

The key political question here is: in our 'postmodern' time, does a space for such communities still exist? Are they limited to the undeveloped outskirts (*favelas*, ghettos, etc.), or is a space for them emerging in the very heart of the 'post-industrial' landscape? Can one make a wild wager that the dynamics of 'postmodern' capitalism, with its rise of new eccentric geek communities, provide a unique opportunity? That, perhaps for the first time in history, the logic of alternative communities can be grafted on to the latest state of technology?

The primary form of such alternative communities in the twentieth century were so-called councils ('soviets') – (almost) everybody in the West loved them, up to liberals like Hannah Arendt who perceived in them echoes of the ancient Greek social form of the *polis*. Throughout the era of Really Existing Socialism, the secret hope of 'democratic socialists' was the direct democracy of the 'soviets', local councils as the form of self-organization of the people; and it is deeply symptomatic that, with the decline of Really Existing Socialism, this emancipatory shadow which accompanied it constantly also disappeared. (Is this not the ultimate confirmation of the fact that the council-version of 'democratic socialism' was just a spectral double of 'bureaucratic' Really Existing Socialism, its inherent transgression with no substantial positive content of its own – i.e., unable to serve as the permanent basic organizing principle of a society?) What both Really Existing Socialism and council-democracy shared is the belief in the possibility of a self-transparent organization of society that would preclude political 'alienation' (state apparatuses, institutionalized rules of political life, legal order, police, etc.) – and is the basic experience of the end of Really Existing Socialism not precisely the rejection of this *shared* feature, the resigned 'postmodern' acceptance of the fact that society is a complex network of 'sub-systems', which is why a certain level of 'alienation' is constitutive of social life, so that a completely self-transparent society is deemed a utopia with totalitarian potentials?[12] (In this sense, it is Habermas who is 'postmodern', in contrast to Adorno who, in spite of all his political compromises, remained attached to a radically utopian vision of revolutionary redemption to the end.)

But, apropos of democracy, are things really so simple? First, direct democracy is not only still alive in many places (like *favelas*), it is even being 'reinvented' and given a new impetus by the rise of 'post-industrial' digital culture – do the descriptions of new 'tribal' communities of computer-hackers not often evoke the logic of 'council-democracy'? Second, the awareness that politics is a complex game in which a certain level of institutional alienation is irreducible should not lead us to ignore the fact that there nevertheless remains a line of separation that divides those who are 'in' from those who are 'out', excluded from the space of the *polis* – there are citizens, and there is the spectre of *homo sacer* haunting them all. In other words, even 'complex' contemporary societies still rely on the basic divide between inclusion and exclusion. The now fashionable notion of 'multitude' is insufficient precisely insofar as it cuts across this divide: there is a multitude *within* the system and a multitude of those *excluded*, and simply to encompass them within the scope of a single notion amounts to the same obscenity as equating starvation with dieting to lose weight. Those who are excluded do not simply dwell in a psychotic non-structured Outside – they have (and are forced into) their own self-organization, one of names (and practices) that are precisely those of 'council-democracy'.

But should it still be called 'democracy'? It seems politically more productive and theoretically more adequate to limit 'democracy' to the translation of *antagonism* into *agonism*: while democracy acknowledges an irreducible plurality of interests, ideologies, narratives, etc., it excludes those who, as we put it, reject the democratic rules of the game – liberal democrats are quite right to claim that populism is inherently 'anti-democratic'. 'Democracy' is not merely the 'power of, by and for the people'; it is not enough simply to claim that, in democracy, the will and interests (the two in no way automatically coincide) of the majority determine decisions of State. Democracy – in the way the term is used today – concerns, above all, *formal legality*: its minimal definition is the unconditional adherence to a certain set of formal rules which guarantee that antagonisms are fully absorbed into the agonistic game. 'Democracy' means that, whatever electoral manipulation takes place, every political agent will unconditionally respect the results. In this sense, the American presidential elections of 2000 were effectively 'democratic': despite obvious electoral manoeuvrings, and the patent meaninglessness of the fact that a few hundred Floridian voices decided who would be President, the Democratic candidate accepted his defeat. In the weeks of uncertainty following the elections, Bill Clinton made an appropriately acerbic comment: 'The American people have spoken; we just don't know what they said.' This comment should be taken more seriously than it was intended: even now, we don't know what the American people said – and, maybe, it is because there was no substantial 'message' behind the result at all.

At this point, it is crucial to avoid the 'democratic' trap. Many 'radical' leftists accept the legalistic logic of 'transcendental guarantee': they refer to 'democracy' as the ultimate guarantee of those who are aware that there is no guarantee. That is to say, because no political act can claim direct foundation in some transcendent figure of the big Other (of the 'we are just instruments of a higher Necessity or Will' type), because every such act involves the risk of a contingent decision, nobody has the right to impose a choice on others – which means that every collective choice must be democratically legitimized. From this perspective, democracy is not so much a guarantee of the correct choice as a kind of opportunistic 'insurance' against possible failure: if things turn out wrong, one can always say we are all responsible . . . Consequently, this last refuge must be abandoned; one should fully assume the risk of one's decision. The only adequate position is the one advocated already by Lukács in *History and Class Consciousness*: democratic struggle should not be fetishized; it is merely one of many forms of struggle, and its choice should be determined by a global strategic assessment of circumstances, not by its ostensibly superior intrinsic value. Like the Lacanian analyst, a political agent has to commit acts that can only be authorized by themselves, for which there is no external guarantee. An authentic political act can be, as to its form, democratic as well as non-democratic. There are some elections or referendums in which 'the impossible happens' – recall, decades ago in Italy, a referendum on divorce where, to the great surprise of the Left (which distrusted the people), the pro-divorce side convincingly won, so that even the Left, while privately sceptical, was ashamed of its distrust. (There were elements of the event even in the unexpected initial electoral victory of François Mitterand.) It is only in *such* cases that one is justified in saying that, over and above mere numerical majority, the people effectively *have spoken* in the substantial sense of the term. On the other hand, an authentic act of popular will can *also* occur in the form of a violent revolution, of a progressive military dictatorship, etc.

Interestingly enough, there is at least one scenario in which formal democrats themselves (or, at least, a substantial portion of them) would tolerate the suspension of democracy: what if a 'free election' was won by an anti-democratic party whose platform promised the abolition of formal democracy? (This did happen, among other places, in Algeria a couple of years ago.) In such a case, many a democrat would concede that the people were not yet 'mature enough' to be entrusted with democracy, and that some kind of enlightened despotism, whose aim will be to educate the majority into proper democrats, is preferable. Every old leftist remembers Marx's reply in *The Communist Manifesto* to critics who reproached the Communists that they aim at undermining family, property, etc.: it is the capitalist order itself whose economic dynamics are destroying the traditional family order (incidentally, a fact more true today than in Marx's time), as well as expropriating a large majority of the population.[13] In the same vein, is it not precisely that those who pose today as global defenders of democracy are effectively undermining it? This gradual limitation of democracy is clearly perceptible in the attempts to 'rethink' the present situation – of course, one is for democracy and human rights, but one should 'rethink' them . . . A series of recent interventions in public debate give a clear sense of the direction of this 'rethinking'. More than a year ago, Jonathan Alter and Alan Derschowitz proposed to 'rethink' human rights so that they include torture (of suspected terrorists). In *The Future of Freedom*, Fareed Zakaria, Bush's favourite columnist, already drew a more general conclusion: he located the threat to freedom in 'overdoing democracy', i.e., in the rise of 'illiberal democracy at home and abroad'.[14]

In a recent television interview, Ralf Dahrendorf linked the growing distrust in democracy to the fact that, after every revolutionary change, the road to new prosperity leads through a 'valley of tears': after the breakdown of socialism, one cannot pass directly to the abundance of a successful market economy – the limited, but real, social welfare and security had to be dismantled, and these first steps are necessarily painful; the same goes for Western Europe, where the passage from the post-World War II welfare State to a new global economy involved painful renunciations, less security, less guaranteed social care. For Dahrendorf, the problem is best encapsulated in the simple fact that this passage through the 'valley of tears' lasts longer than the average period between (democratic) elections, so that the temptation to postpone such difficult changes for short-term electoral gains is considerable. For him, the paradigmatic constellation is the disappointment of the large strata of post-Communist nations over the economic results of the new democratic order: in the glorious days of 1989, they equated democracy with the abundance of Western consumerist societies; now, ten years later, when that abundance is still missing, they blame democracy itself. Unfortunately, Dahrendorf avoids discussing the opposite temptation: if the majority resists necessary structural changes in the economy, would not (one of) the logical conclusion(s) be that, for a decade or so, an enlightened élite should seize power, even by non-democratic means, in order to enforce the necessary measures and thus lay the foundations for a truly stable democracy? Along these lines, Zakaria points out that democracy can only 'catch on' in economically developed countries: if developing countries are 'prematurely democratized', the result is a populism that will end in economic catastrophe and political despotism – it is no wonder that today's most economically successful Third World countries (Taiwan, South Korea and Chile) embraced full democracy only after a period of authoritarian rule. And does the predicament of Germany not point in the same direction? In the Federal Republic of Germany, the welfare State remained more or less intact, rendering its economy less competitive and flexible; the necessary 'restructuring' of the economy (the dismantling of the welfare State) met with strong opposition from the majority of voters (workers, retirees, etc.), so it could only be implemented by *non-democratic* means.

The exemplary economic strategy of today's capitalism is outsourcing – to subcontract the 'dirty' process of material production (but also publicity, design, accountancy, etc.) to another company. In this way, one easily avoids ecological and health regulations: production is done in, say, Indonesia where regulations are much lower than in the West, and the Western international corporation that owns the logo then claims that it is not responsible for violations in another company. Are we not seeing something homologous with regard to torture? Is torture also not being 'out-sourced' to Third World allies of the United States who can do it without worrying about legal problems or public protest? Was such out-sourcing not explicitly advocated by Jonathan Alter in *Newsweek* immediately after 11 September? After stating, 'We can't legalize torture; it's contrary to American values', he nevertheless concludes, 'we'll have to think about transferring some suspects to our less squeamish allies, even if that's hypocritical. Nobody said this was going to be pretty.'[15] This is how, today, First World democracy increasingly functions: by way of 'out-sourcing' its dirty underside to other countries . . .

This inherent crisis of democracy is also the reason for the renewed popularity of Leo Strauss. The key feature that makes his political thought relevant today is its élitist notion of democracy, i.e., the idea of a 'necessary lie', of how the élites should rule: though they are aware of the actual state of things (driven by the brutal materialist logic of power, etc.), they feed the people with fables designed to keep them satisfied in their blessed ignorance. For Strauss, the lesson of the trial and execution of Socrates is that *Socrates was guilty as charged*: philosophy *is*, in fact, a threat to society. By questioning the gods and the *ethos* of the city, philosophy undermined the citizens' loyalty, and thus the basis of normal social life. Yet philosophy is also the highest, the worthiest, of all human endeavours. Strauss' resolution of this conflict is that the philosophers should, and in fact did, keep their teachings secret, passing them on by the esoteric art of writing 'between the lines'. The true, hidden message contained in the 'Great Tradition' of philosophy from Plato to Hobbes and Locke is that there are no gods, that morality is ungrounded prejudice, and that society is not grounded in nature.[16]

This is the sense in which one should render democracy problematic: why should the Left always and unconditionally respect the formal democratic 'rules of the game'? Why should it not, in some circumstances at least, call into question the legitimacy of the outcome of a formal democratic procedure? All democratic leftists venerate Rosa Luxemburg's famous dictum, 'Freedom is freedom for those who think differently'. Perhaps, the time has come to shift the accent from 'differently' to 'think': 'Freedom is freedom for those who *think* differently' – i.e., *only* for those who *really think*, not for those who blindly (unthinkingly) act out their opinions. What this means is that one should gather the courage radically to question today's predominant attitude of anti-authoritarian tolerance. It was, surprisingly, Bernard Williams who, in his perspicacious reading of David Mamet's *Oleanna*, outlined the limits of this attitude:

> A complaint constantly made by the female character is that she has made sacrifices to come to college, in order to learn something, to be told things that she did not know, but that she has been offered only a feeble permissiveness. She complains that her teacher . . . does not control or direct her enough: he does not tell her what to believe, or even, perhaps, what to ask. He does not exercise authority. At the same time, she complains that he exercises power over her. This might seem to be a muddle on her part, or the playwright's, but it is not. The male character has power over her (he can decide what grade she gets), but just because he lacks authority, this power is mere power, in part gender power.[17]

Power appears (is experienced) 'as such' at the very point where it is no longer covered by 'authority'. There are, however, further complications to Williams' view. First, 'authority' is not simply a direct property of the master-figure, but an effect of the social relation between the master and his subjects: even if the master remains the same, it may happen, because of the change in the socio-symbolic field, that his position is no longer perceived as legitimate authority, but as mere illegitimate power. (Is such a shift not the most elementary gesture of feminism: male authority is all of a sudden unmasked as mere power?) The lesson of every revolution from 1789 to 1989 is that such a disintegration of authority, its transformation into arbitrary power, always precedes the revolutionary irruption. Where Williams is correct is in his emphasis on how the very permissiveness of the power-figure, his restraint from exercising authority by directing, controlling, his subject makes that authority appear as illegitimate power. Therein resides the vicious cycle of today's academia: the more professors renounce 'authoritarian' active teaching, the imposition of knowledge and values, the more they are experienced as figures of power. And, as every parent knows, the same goes for parental education: a father who exerts true transferential authority will never be experienced as 'oppressive' – it is, on the contrary, a father who tries to be permissive, who does not want to impose his views and values on his children, but allows them to discover their own way, who is denounced as exerting power, as being 'oppressive' . . .

The paradox to be fully endorsed here is that the only way effectively to abolish power relations is through freely accepting relations of authority: the model of the free collective is not a group of libertines indulging their pleasures, but an extremely disciplined revolutionary collective. The injunction that holds together such a collective is best encapsulated in the logical form of double negation (prohibition), which, precisely, is *not* the same as direct positive assertion. Towards the end of Brecht's *Die Massnahme*, the Four Agitators declare:

> It is a terrible thing to kill.
> But not only others would we kill, but ourselves too if need be
> Since only force can alter this
> Murderous world, as
> Every living creature knows.
> It is still, we said
> Not given to us not to kill.[18]

Notice, the text does *not* say, 'we are allowed to kill', but, 'it is still not permitted (an adequate paraphrase of *vergönnen*) for us not to kill' – or, simply, it is still *prohibited* for us not to kill. Brecht's precision is here admirable. 'It is allowed to kill' would have amounted to simple immoral permissivity; 'it is ordered to kill' would have transformed killing into an obscene-perverse superego injunction, which is the truth of the first version (as Lacan put it, the permitted *jouissance* inexorably turns into a prescribed one). The only correct way is thus the reversal of the biblical prohibition, the prohibition *not* to kill, which obtains all the way to the anti-Antigonean prohibition to provide a proper funeral ritual: the young comrade has to 'vanish, and vanish entirely', i.e., his disappearance (death) itself should disappear, not leaving any (symbolic) traces.

Bernard Williams can again be of some help here, when he elaborates the distance that separates *must* from *ought: 'Ought* is related to *must* as *best* is related to *only*.'[19] We arrive at what we must do after a long and anxious consideration of alternatives, and we can even retain 'that belief while remaining uncertain about it, and still very clearly seeing the powerful merits of alternative courses.'[20] This difference between 'must' and 'ought' also relies on temporality: we can reproach somebody for not having done what he 'ought to have done', but we cannot say to someone, 'you must have done it' if he did not do it – we use the expression, 'you must have done it' when consoling somebody who *did* a thing that he found distasteful (such as, 'Do not blame yourself. Even if you loved him, you must have punished him!'), while the standard use of the expression, 'you ought to have done it' implies, on the contrary, that you did *not* do it.

This reference to 'must' creates the space of manipulation, like when a bargaining partner or outright blackmailer says that, 'regrettably', this leaves him with no alternative but to take an unpleasant course of action – and, we may add, like the ruthless Stalinist who 'cannot but' engage in terror. The falsity of this position resides in the fact that, when we 'must' do something, it is not simply that we 'cannot do otherwise than this' within the limits of our situation: the character of a person is not just revealed in that he does what he must, but also 'in the location of those limits, and in the very fact that one can determine, sometimes through deliberation itself, that one cannot do certain things, and must do others.'[21] One *is* thus responsible for one's character, i.e., for the choice of coordinates which prevent me from doing some things and impel me to do others. This brings us to the Lacanian notion of *l'acte*: in an act, I redefine the very coordinates of what I *cannot* and *must* do.

'Must' and 'Ought' thus correspond to Real and Symbolic: the Real of a drive whose injunction cannot be avoided (which is why Lacan says that the status of a drive is ethical); the Ought as a symbolic ideal caught in the dialectic of desire (if you ought not do something, this very prohibition generates the desire to do it). When you 'must' do something, it means you have no choice *but* to do it, even if it is terrible: in Wagner's *Die Walküre*, Wotan is confronted by Fricka and he 'must' ('cannot but') allow the murder of Siegmund, even though his heart bleeds for him; he 'must' ('cannot but') punish Brünnhilde, his dearest child, the embodiment of his own innermost striving. And, incidentally, the same goes for Wagner's *Tristan und Isolde*, the Bayreuth staging of which was Müller's last great theatrical achievement: they 'must' ('cannot but') indulge their passion, even if this goes against their *Sollen*, their social obligations.

In Wotan's forced act of punishment, Wagner encounters here the paradox of 'killing with *pietà*' at work from the Talmud (which calls us to dispense Justice with Love) to Brecht's two key *Lehrstücke, Der Jasager* and *Die Massnahme*, in which the young comrade is killed by his companions with loving tenderness. And although Müller disagreed with *Die Massnahme*, proposing, in his *Mauser*, a critique of its political logic, his critique is strictly internal: he reproaches Brecht precisely for not drawing all consequences from the stance of 'killing with *pietà*', of killing without dehumanizing the enemy. And this is why, today, in our time in which the abstract humanitarian rejection of violence is accompanied by its obscene double, we need just this anonymous killing '*without pietà*' more than ever.

Notes

1   Alain Badiou, *Le siècle*, Paris, Éditions du Seuil, 2005, pp. 10–13, 89–90. [eds]

2   Fredric Jameson, 'Actually existing Marxism', in *Marxism Beyond Marxism*, ed. Saree Makdisi, Cesare Casarino and Rebecca E. Karl, New York and London, Routledge, 1996, p. 15. [eds]

3   Heiner Müller and Jan Höt, 'Insights into the Process of Production: A Conversation', *documenta* 9, 1992, pp. 96–7.

4   Quoted in Richard Taylor, *October*, London, British Film Institute, 2002, p. 8.

5   Quoted in Susan Buck-Morss, *Dreamworld and Catastrophe: The Passing of Mass Utopia in East and West*, Cambridge, Harvard University Press, 2001, p. 144.

6   Quoted in Buck-Morss, ibid.

7   Taylor, *October*, pp. 8–9. [eds]

8   Fredric Jameson, 'Utopia, modernism and death', in *The Seeds of Time*, New York, Columbia University Press, 1994, p. 89. [*Editorial note*: Jameson provides his most cogent description of this 'moment of world-reduction' in an early essay on Ursula Le Guin's *The Left Hand of Darkness* ('World-Reduction in Le Guin: The emergence of utopian narrative', *Science-Fiction Studies* 2, 1975, p. 223): 'a principle of systematic exclusion, a kind of surgical excision of empirical reality, something like a process of ontological attenuation in which the sheer teeming multiplicity of what exists, of what we call reality, is deliberately thinned and weeded out through an operation of radical abstraction and simplification.']

9   Jameson, ibid., p. 90.

10   Fredric Jameson, 'Progress versus utopia; or, Can we imagine the future', *Science-Fiction Studies* 9, 1982, pp. 147–58. [eds]

11   Mario Vargas Llosa, *The War of the End of the World*, trans. Helen R. Lane, London, Penguin, 1981. [eds]

12   For a clear articulation of this stance, see Martin Jay, 'No power to the Soviets,' in *Cultural Semantics: Keywords of Our Time*, Amherst, University of Massachusetts Press, 1998, pp. 79–84.

13   Karl Marx and Friedrich Engels, 'Manifesto of the Communist Party', in *The Revolutions of 1848: Political Writings, Volume I*, ed. David Fernbach, London, Penguin, 1973, pp. 82–4. [eds]

14   Fareed Zakaria, *The Future of Freedom: Illiberal Democracy at Home and Abroad*, New York and London, W. W. Norton, 2003.

15   Jonathan Alter, 'Time to think about torture', *Newsweek*, November 2001, p. 45. [eds]

16   Furthermore, does Strauss' notion of esoteric knowledge not confuse two different phenomena: the cynicism of power, its unreadiness to admit publicly its own true foundations, and the subversive insights of those who aim at undermining the power system itself? For instance, in Really Existing Socialism there is a difference between a critical intellectual who, in order to convey his message, has to conceal it in the terms of official ideology, and the cynical top member of *nomenklatura* who is aware of the falsity of the basic claims of the ruling ideology – equating the two is, again, like equating starvation and dieting.

17 Bernard Williams, *Truth and Truthfulness*, Princeton, Princeton University Press, 2002, pp. 7–8.

18 Bertolt Brecht, *The Collected Plays: Volume III, Part Two*, ed. John Willett and Ralph Mannheim, trans. John Willett *et al.*, London, Methuen, 1997, p. 87.

19 Williams, *Truth and Truthfulness*, p. 125.

20 Williams, *Truth and Truthfulness*, p. 126.

21 Williams, *Truth and Truthfulness*, p. 130.

Really existing socialism

Chapter 4

Why are Laibach and the *Neue Slowenische Kunst* not Fascists?

Superego is the obscene 'nightly' law that necessarily redoubles and accompanies, as its shadow, the 'public' Law. This inherent and constitutive splitting in the Law is the subject of Rob Reiner's film, *A Few Good Men*, a court-martial drama about two United States marines accused of murdering one of their fellow soldiers. The military prosecutor claims that the two marines' act was deliberate murder, whereas the defence successfully proves that the defendants were merely obeying a so-called 'Code Red', which authorizes the clandestine night-time beating of a fellow soldier who, in the opinion of his peers or superior officer, has broken the ethical code of the marines. The function of this 'Code Red' is extremely interesting: it condones an act of transgression – illegal punishment of a fellow soldier – and yet at the same time reaffirms the cohesion of the group, i.e., it calls for an act of absolute identification with group values. Such a code must remain under the cover of night, unacknowledged, unuttered – in public everybody pretends to know nothing about it, or even actively denies its very existence. It represents *l'ésprit du corps* in its purest form, exerting strong pressure on the individual to comply with its mandate of group identification. Yet, simultaneously, it violates the explicit rules of community life. (The plight of the two accused soldiers is that they are unable to grasp this exclusion of 'Code Red' from the 'Big Other', the domain of public Law: they desperately ask themselves, 'What did we do wrong?', because they just followed the orders of their superior officer.) Where does this splitting of Law into the written public Law and its underside, the 'unwritten', obscene secret code, come from? The answer is from the incomplete, 'not-all' character of public Law itself: explicit, public rules do not suffice, so they must be supplemented by a clandestine, 'unwritten' code aimed at those who, although they violate no public rules, maintain a kind of inner distance and do not truly identify with *l'ésprit du corps*.

The field of Law is thus split into Law *qua* 'Ego-Ideal', i.e., a symbolic order that regulates social life and maintains harmony, and its obscene, superegoic inverse. As has been shown by numerous analyses from Mikhail Bakhtin onwards, periodic transgressions of the public Law are inherent to social order, they function as a condition of the latter's stability. (The mistake of Bakhtin – or, rather, of some of his followers – was to present an idealized image of these 'transgressions', while passing over in silence lynching parties, etc., as a crucial form of the 'carnivalesque suspension of social hierarchy'.) What most deeply 'holds together' a community is not so much identification with the Law that regulates the community's 'normal' everyday rhythms, but rather *identification with a specific form of transgression of the Law, of the Law's suspension* (in psychoanalytic terms, with a specific form of enjoyment). Let us return to those rural white communities in the American South of the 1920s, where the rule of the official, public Law was accompanied by its shadowy double, the nightly terror of the Ku Klux Klan, with its lynchings of helpless blacks: a (white) man could easily be forgiven minor infractions of the Law, especially when they could be justified by a 'code of honour' – the community still recognizes him as 'one of us'. But he would be effectively excommunicated, perceived as 'not one of us', the moment that he disowned the specific form of transgression that pertains to this community – say, the moment he refused to partake in ritual lynchings by the Klan, or even reported them to the Law (which, of course, did not want to hear about them since they represented its own hidden underside). The Nazi community relied on the same solidarity-in-guilt adduced by participation in a common transgression: it ostracized those who were not ready to assume the dark side of the idyllic *Volksgemeinschaft*, the night pogroms, the beatings of political opponents – in short, all that 'everybody knew, yet did not want to speak about aloud'.

It is against the background of this constitutive tension within the Law between public-written Law and obscene superego that one should comprehend the extraordinary critical-ideological impact of the *Neue Slowenische Kunst*, especially of the group Laibach. In the process of the disintegration of socialism in Slovenia, they staged an aggressive, inconsistent mixture of Stalinism, Nazism and *Blut und Boden* ideology. The first reaction of enlightened leftist critics was to conceive of Laibach as the ironic imitation of totalitarian rituals; however, their support for Laibach was always accompanied by an uneasy feeling: 'What if they really mean it? What if they truly identify with totalitarian rituals?' – or, in a more cunning version of the same thing, transferring one's own doubt on to the other: 'What if Laibach overestimates their public? What if the public takes seriously what Laibach mockingly imitates, so that Laibach actually strengthens what it purports to undermine?' This uneasy feeling feeds on the assumption that ironic distance is automatically a subversive attitude. What if, on the contrary, the dominant attitude of the contemporary 'post-ideological' universe is precisely cynical distance towards public values? What if this distance, far from posing any threat to the system, designates the supreme form of conformism, since the normal function of the system *requires* cynical distance? In this sense, the strategy of Laibach appears in a new light: *it 'frustrates' the system (the ruling ideology) precisely insofar as it is not its ironic imitation, but represents an over-identification with it* – by bringing to light the obscene superego underside of the system, over-identification suspends its efficiency. (In order to clarify the way this baring, this public staging of the obscene fantasmatic kernel of an ideological edifice, suspends its normal functioning, let us recall a somewhat homologous phenomenon in the sphere of individual experience: each of us has some private ritual, phrases [like nicknames, etc.] or a gesture, used only within the most intimate circle of closest friends or relatives; when these rituals are rendered public, their effect is necessarily one of extreme embarrassment and shame – one wishes to be swallowed by the earth.)

The ultimate expedient of Laibach is its deft manipulation of transference: its public (especially intellectuals) is obsessed with the 'desire of the Other' – what is Laibach's actual position, is it really totalitarian or not? – i.e., they address Laibach with a question and expect from it an answer, failing to notice that Laibach itself *does not function as an answer but a question*. By means of the elusive character of its desire, of the undecidability as to 'where it actually stands', Laibach compels us to take up our own position and decide upon our desire. Laibach here actually accomplishes the reversal that defines the end of the psychoanalytic cure. At the outset of the cure is transference: the transferential relationship is put in force as soon as the analyst appears in the guise of the 'subject supposed to know [*sujet supposé savoir*]' – the one who knows the truth about the analysand's desire. When, in the course of analysis, the analysand complains that he doesn't know what he wants, all this moaning and groaning is addressed to the analyst, with the implicit supposition that the analyst *does* know what he wants. In other words, insofar as the analyst stands for the Big Other, the analysand's illusion lies in the reduction of his ignorance to an 'epistemological' *incapacity*: the truth about his desire already exists, it is registered somewhere in the Big Other, one has only to bring it to light and his desiring will run smoothly. The end of psychoanalysis, the dissolution of transference, occurs when this 'epistemological' incapacity shifts into 'ontological' *impossibility*: the analysand has to experience the fact that the Big Other does not possess the truth about his desire as well, that his desire is without guarantee, groundless, authorized only in itself. In this precise sense, the dissolution of transference designates the moment when the arrow of the question that the analysand pointed at the analyst turns back towards the analysand himself: first, the analysand's (hysterical) question is addressed to the analyst supposed to possess the answer; then, the analysand is forced to acknowledge that the analyst himself is nothing but a big question mark addressed to the analysand. Here one can clarify Lacan's thesis that an analyst is authorized only by himself: an analysand becomes analyst upon assuming that his desire has no support in the Other, that the authorization of his desire can come only from himself. And insofar as this same reversal of the direction of the arrow defines drive, we could say (as Lacan does) that what takes place at the end of psychoanalysis is the shift from desire to drive.

Note

This paper was published in *Primary Documents: A Sourcebook for Eastern and Central European Art since the 1950s*, ed. Laura Hoptman and Tomás Pospiszyl, New York, MoMA, 2002, pp. 285–8. It was originally written in 1993 and first appeared in *M'ARS*, Ljubljana, Moderna Galerija, 1993, Volume 3/4. [eds]

Chapter 5
The fetish of the party

The totalitarian body

In his speech 'On the death of Lenin' in 1924, Stalin made the following pronouncement: 'We Communists are people of a special mould. We are made of a special stuff.'[1] Here we immediately recognize that the Lacanian name for this 'special stuff' is *objet petit a*. The weight of Stalin's sentence comes from the basic fetishist functioning of the Stalinist Party: that the Party functions as the miraculous immediate incarnation of an objective, neutral Knowledge, which in turn serves as a point of reference to legitimate the activity of the Party (the so-called 'knowledge of objective laws'). Similarly, Marx determines money in its relation to other commodities as a paradoxical element that immediately incarnates, through its very singularity, the generality of 'all', that is to say, as a 'singular reality, that includes in itself all the really existing species of the same thing':

> It is as if, next to and other than lions, tigers, hares, and all the other real animals that constitute in a group different races, species, sub-species, families, etc., of the animal kingdom, existed, furthermore, *the animal*, the individual incarnation of the animal kingdom.[2]

This is precisely the logic of the Party: it is as if, next to and other than classes, social strata, social groups and subgroups, and their economic, political and ideological organizations, that constitute in a group the different parts of the socio-historical universe ruled by the objectives of social development, existed, furthermore, *the Party* – the immediate and individual incarnation of these objective laws, the short circuit, the paradoxical intersection between the subjective will and objective laws. Therefore, the 'special stuff' of the Communists is precisely the incarnation of the 'objective reason of history'. Because the stuff from which they are made is, after all, their body, this body undergoes a true transubstantiation; it becomes the carrier of *another* body, the *sublime* body.

It is interesting to read the letters of Lenin to Maxim Gorky from the standpoint of the logic of the Communists' sublime body, especially a series of letters from 1913, concerning the debate on the 'Construction of God [*bogograditel 'stvo*]', of which Gorky was an advocate. The first obvious thing to notice is an apparently unimportant trait, lacking much theoretical weight: Lenin is literally obsessed by Gorky's health. Here are excerpts from a few letters:

I wish you all the very best, and above all health![3]

Write and tell me about your health. / Yours, *Lenin*.[4]

How are you getting on? Has your health improved since the spring? I wish you with all my heart to get better and have a good rest. / Yours, *Lenin*.[5]

Joking apart. *Keep well*. Send me a couple of words. *Rest* as well as you can. / Yours, *Lenin*.[6]

When, in the autumn of 1913, Lenin hears of Gorky's pulmonary illness, he writes to him immediately:

What you write about your illness worries me terribly. Are you doing the right thing in living without treatment at Capri? The Germans have excellent sanatoria . . . where they treat and *completely* cure lung diseases, achieve *complete* healing . . .

While you, after Capri, and in winter, want to go to Russia???? I am terribly afraid that this will injure your health and undermine your work capacity. Are there *first-class* doctors in that Italy of yours?

Really, go and visit some first-class doctors in Switzerland or Germany, and set about a couple of months of *serious* treatment in a *good* sanatorium. Because to squander official property, i.e., to go on being ill and undermining your work capacity, is something quite intolerable in every respect.[7]

What is important here is to establish the *field of meaning* of Lenin's concern for Gorky's health. At first glance, the question is clear and quite innocent: Gorky was a valuable ally and thus worthy of care. But the very next letter sheds a different light on the matter. Lenin is alarmed by Gorky's positive attitude towards the 'construction of God' – that it should be, according to Gorky, merely 'postponed' and set aside for the moment, but not entirely rejected. Such sentiments are, for Lenin, incomprehensible, an extremely unpleasant surprise. Here are the beginning and end of his letter written in November 1913:

> Whatever are you doing? This is simply terrible, it really is . . .
> Why do you do this?
> It's damnably disappointing. / Yours, *V.I.*

And here is the postscript:

> Get as good *medical* treatment as you can, please, so that you can travel in the winter, *without colds* (it's dangerous in the winter).[8]

The true stakes are even more clearly noticeable at the end of the following letter, sent together with the preceding letter:

> I enclose my letter from yesterday: do not hold it against me if I got carried away. Perhaps I did not understand you *correctly*? Perhaps *you* were *joking* in writing 'for the moment'? Concerning the 'construction of God', perhaps you were not serious? For heaven's sake, take care of yourself a little better. Yours, *Lenin*.

Here, it is stated in an explicit and formal manner that, in the last resort at least, Lenin takes Gorky's fluctuations and ideological confusion for an effect of his physical exhaustion and illness. He thus refuses to take Gorky's arguments seriously. In the end, his response consists in saying: 'Rest, take care of yourself a little better . . .' Lenin's procedure, however, was not based on some vulgar materialism or on the immediate reduction of ideas to bodily processes. Quite the contrary, his presupposition and implications are precisely that a Communist is a man of a 'special stuff'. When the Communist speaks and acts as a Communist, it is the objective necessity of history itself that speaks and acts through him. In other words, the spirit of a true Communist cannot deviate, because this spirit is immediately the self-awareness of historical necessity. Consequently, the only thing that can disturb or introduce disorder and deviation is his body – this fragile materiality serving to support another body, the sublime body, 'made of a special stuff'.

Phallus and fetish

Is it also possible to maintain the proposition of the fetishist character of the Party, in the analytic use of this term? The fetish is, as we well know, the *ersatz* of the maternal phallus: it is a question of the repudiation of castration. Thus, we should approach fetishism from the phallic signifier.

One of the elements in Lacan's 'The signification of the phallus' had already been developed by Saint Augustine.[9] The phallic organ incarnates the revolt of the human body against mastery by man; as such, it represents divine punishment for the arrogance of man who wanted to be God's equal and become the master of the world. The phallus is thus the organ whose pulsation and erection mostly escape man, his will and his power. All the parts of the human body are, in principle, at the disposal of the will; their unavailability is always *de facto*, with the exception of the phallus, whose erection is unavailable 'in principle'. However, we must relate this aspect to another, indicated by this witticism: 'What is the lightest object in the world? The phallus, because it is the only thing that can be raised by a mere thought.'

This witticism, according to Lacan, grasps the 'signification of the phallus': the short-circuit at which point the 'inside' and the 'outside' intersect, the point at which the pure exteriority of the body unavailable to the subjective will passes, without mediation, into the interiority of 'pure thought'.[10] At this point, we could almost recall the Hegelian critique of Kant's *Ding an sich*: this transcendental *Ding an sich*, inaccessible to human thought, is revealed to be simply the interiority of pure thought brought about by the abstraction of each objective content. Such is precisely the 'contradiction' that could be described as the 'phallic experience': I can do nothing (the Augustinian moment) although everything depends on me (the moment of the above mentioned witticism). The 'signification of the phallus' is the very pulsation between the *everything* and the *nothing*. Potentially, it is 'all meanings' or the very universality of meaning (in other words: 'in the last instance, we only talk about this'), and for this reason the 'signification of the phallus' is effectively without any determined meaning; it is the signifier-without-signified. Naturally, this is one of the commonplaces of the Lacanian theory. As soon as we try to grasp 'all' of the signifiers of a structure, as soon as we try to 'fill' its universality by its particular components, we must add a paradoxical signifier that has no particular-determined signified, but that incarnates in a way 'all meanings' or the very universality of this structure, while at the same time being 'the signifier without signified'.

A passage from Marx's 'Class struggle in France' is of special interest to us here because it develops the logic of the phallic signifier precisely in relation to the political party. It is a question of the role of the 'party of Order' during the revolutionary events in the middle of the nineteenth century:

> The *party of Order* was formed immediately following the days of June; only after 10 December had it allowed it to get rid of the *National* coterie, the bourgeois republicans, was the secret of its existence revealed: the *coalition of the Orleanists* and *Legitimists* in *one party* . . . Bourbon was the royal name for the dominance of the interests of one fraction; Orleans was the royal name for the dominance of the interests of the other. The *nameless realm of the republic* was the only form of rule under which both fractions were able to maintain their common class interest with equal power and without giving up their mutual rivalry.[11]

According to this logic, the republican is a species inside the genus of royalism. Within (the species of) this genus, the republican stands for the genus itself. This paradoxical element, the specific point at which the universal *genus falls on itself* among its particular species, is this very phallic signifier. Its paradoxical place, the point of intersection between the 'outside' and the 'inside', is crucial for grasping fetishism: it is precisely this place that is lost. In other words, the *castrative* dimension of the phallic signifier is disavowed with the fetish, the 'nothing' that necessarily accompanies its 'all', the radical heterogeneity of this element relative to the *universality* that it is meant to incarnate (the fact that the phallic signifier can allow the potential universality of meaning only as a signifier-without-signified, that we can be royalist in general only in the form of being republicans). The fetish is the master signifier (S_1) that, by its position of exception, immediately incarnates its Universality, the Particular that is immediately 'merged' with its Universal.

This is the logic of the Stalinist Party, which appears as the immediate incarnation of the Universality of the masses or the working class. The Stalinist Party would be, to use Marx's terms, something like royalism in general in the very form of royalism – which is precisely the fetishist illusion. In fetishism, the phallic signifier, the *intersection* of the two species ('Orleanists' and 'Legitimists'), is immediately established as *All*, 'the general line', and the two species whose intersection it is become two 'deviations' (that of the 'right' and that of the 'left') of the 'general line'.

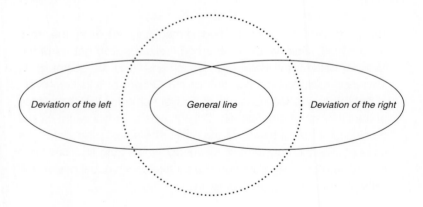

In the 'short-circuit' between the Universal (the masses, class) and the Particular (the Party), the relation between the Party and the masses is not dialectized, such that if there is any conflict between the Party and the rest of the working class (as today in Poland), this does not mean that the Party is 'alienated' from the working class but that, on the contrary, elements of the working class itself have become estranged from their own Universality ('the true interests of the working class') incarnated in the Party. It is because of this fetishist character of the Party that there is, for the Stalinist, no contradiction between the demand that the Party should be open to the masses and merged with the masses, and the Party in the position of Exception, the authoritarian Party, concentrating power in itself. Let us, for example, take up this passage from *Foundations of Leninism*:

> Wherein lies the strength of the Soviets as compared with the old forms of organization?
>
> In that the Soviets are the most *all-embracing* mass organizations of the proletariat, for they and they alone embrace all workers without exception . . .
>
> In that the Soviets are the *most powerful organs* of the revolutionary struggle of the masses, of the political actions of the masses, of the uprising of the masses – organs capable of breaking the omnipotence of finance Capital and its political appendages.
>
> In that the Soviets are the *immediate* organizations of the masses themselves, i.e., they are the *most democratic* and therefore the most authoritative organizations of the masses, which facilitate to the utmost their participation in the work of building up the new state and in its administration, and which bring into full play the revolutionary energy, initiative and creative abilities of the masses in the struggle for the destruction of the old order, in the struggle for the new, proletarian order.[12]

But then, later in the same document, he writes:

> The Party must be, first of all, the *advanced* detachment of the working class . . . But in order that it may really be the advanced detachment, the Party must be armed with revolutionary theory, with a knowledge of the laws of movement, with a knowledge of the laws of revolution . . . The Party cannot be a real party if it limits itself to registering what the masses of the working class feel and think . . . if it is unable to raise the masses to the level of understanding the class interests of the proletariat.[13]

Here, the authoritarian character of the Party is directly accentuated. Stalin presents this exclusive and authoritarian power *immediately* as a truly democratic power, as an effective power of the people. From this point, a certain naïveté of the so-called 'dissident' critiques ensues. The Stalinist discursive field is organized in such a way that the critique misses its aim; *one can guess in advance* what the critique is trying to demonstrate (the authoritarian character of power, etc.) when it presents Stalinism from another perspective, in taking it precisely as proof of the effective power of the people. In short, to speak in the usual way: the critique tries to attack Stalinism at the level of facts within a presupposed common code that plays on the contradiction between effectiveness and ideological legitimation ('in principle, the USSR is supposed to be a democratic society, but effectively . . .'), while displacing in advance the conflict at the level of the code itself.

Here is the impossible position of the fetish: a singular that immediately 'incarnates' the general, without signifying this with castration. It is an element that occupies the position of metalanguage while being part of the 'thing itself'; it is at the same time an 'objective' gaze and an 'involved party'. In *Bananas*, Woody Allen's political comedy, there is a scene that perfectly illustrates this point. The protagonist, who is from an unidentified dictatorship in Central America, is invited to dinner by the ruling general, an invitation that is delivered to him in his hotel room. As soon as the messenger is gone, the protagonist throws himself on the bed in joy, turns his eyes towards the celestial heights as we hear the sound of a harp. As spectators, we perceive this sound, of course, as a musical accompaniment and not as real music within the story-line itself. Suddenly, however, the protagonist sobers up, rises, opens the armoire and discovers a 'typical' Latin American, who is playing the harp. The paradox of this scene lies in this passage from outside to inside: what we had perceived as an 'external' musical accompaniment is affirmed as 'internal' to the reality of the scene. The comical effect comes from the position of the impossible knowledge of the protagonist. He behaves as if he is in a position from which he could hear, at the same time, what is both in the realm of cinematographic 'reality' and its 'external' musical accompaniment.

It is not surprising that we find this same 'short-circuit', this same ambiguous position of the fetish in totalitarian discourse, and precisely at the point when it is necessary to affirm, at the same time, both the ideological 'neutrality' and the 'professional' character of the regions of culture (art, science), and their submission to the ruling doctrine and to the people. Let us take up a passage from the famous letter of Joseph Göbbels to Wilhelm Furtwängler of 11 April 1933:

It is not sufficient that art be excellent, it should also present itself as the expression of the people. In other words, only an art that takes inspiration from the people can at the end be considered as excellent and mean something for the people it addresses.

Here is the pure form of the logic that is in question: it is *not only* excellent *but also* an expression of the people, because to *tell the truth*, it can be excellent only in being an expression of the people. In replacing art by science, we obtain one of the topics of the Stalinist ideology: 'scientificity alone does not suffice, we also need a just ideological orientation, a dialectic-materialistic vision of the world, because it is only through a just ideological orientation that we can achieve true scientific results.'

Stalinist discourse

The fetishist functioning of the Party guarantees the position of a neutral knowledge (knowledge that is *décapitonné*) that belongs to the agent of Stalinist discourse. Stalinist discourse is presented as a pure metalanguage, as the knowledge of 'objective laws', as a descriptive [*constatif*] discourse that applies to a pure object (S_2). The very engagement of theory with the proletariat, its hold over the Party, is thus not 'internal' – Marxism does not speak from the position of the proletariat; it is orientated to the proletariat from an external, neutral, 'objective' position:

In the eighties of the past century, in the period of the struggle between the Marxists and the Narodniks, the proletariat in Russia constituted an insignificant minority of the population, whereas the individual peasants constituted the vast majority of the population. But the proletariat was developing as a class, whereas the peasantry as a class was disintegrating. And just because the proletariat was developing as a class the Marxists based their orientation on the proletariat. And they were not mistaken, for, as we know, the proletariat subsequently grew from an insignificant force into a first-rate historical and political force.[14]

At the time of their struggle against the populists, *where did the Marxists speak from* to be susceptible to mistake in their choice of the proletariat as the basis of their orientation? They could, of course, speak from an external place where the historical process extends as a field of objective forces, where one must be careful not to be mistaken and be guided by just forces – those forces that will win. In short, one must 'bet on the right horse'. From this external position, we can approach the famous 'theory of reflection': one must ask the question of who occupies the neutral-objective position from which this 'objective reality', reflected yet external to reflection, can be judged, from which the reflection can be compared to the objective reality and judged as to whether the reflection corresponds to it or not.

We have already touched on the secret behind the functioning of this 'objective knowledge': this very point of pure objectivity to which Stalinist discourse is related and by which it is legitimized (the 'objective meaning' of facts) is already constituted by the performative. It is even the point of the pure performative, the tautology of pure self-reference. It is precisely there, the point at which, in words, the discourse refers to a pure reality outside language, that 'in (its own) act' it refers only to itself. Here, once again, the Hegelian critique of Kant's *Ding an sich* is most pertinent: this supposedly transcendental entity, independent of subjectivity, is revealed to be merely the interiority of pure thought, the necessary abstraction of every objective content. In classical terminology, propositions of validity (just-unjust) take the form of propositions of being. When the Stalinist pronounces a judgement, he pretends to describe or 'observe' an objective state. In short, in Stalinist discourse the performative functions as the *repressed truth* of the descriptive [*constatif*], as it is pushed 'under the bar'. Consequently, we could write the relation between S_1 and S_2 in this way: S_2/S_1. This means that Stalinist discourse presents a neutral-objective knowledge as its agent, while the repressed truth of this knowledge remains S_1, the performative of the master. This is the paradoxical point at which the

Stalinist discourse locates the victim of the political process. If I insist on the descriptive [*constatif*] falsity of the judgement of the Party ('You are a traitor!'), *in reality* I act against the Party and effectively break its unity. The only way to affirm my adherence to the Party by my activity, at the performative level, is, of course, to confess – what? – precisely my exclusion, that I am in fact a 'traitor'.

What, then, takes the place of the *other*? At first the answer appears rather simple. The other of 'objective knowledge' is obviously subjective knowledge, a knowledge that is only a semblance of knowledge, something like 'metaphysics' or 'idealism', relative to which Stalinist objective knowledge is defined. The paradoxical nature of this opposing pole appears as soon as we look more closely at the Stalinist divisive procedure. We can thus read the four famous 'Fundamental Traits of the Marxist Dialectic Method' in opposition to the traits of metaphysics as a process of differentiation, of disjunction, as follows:

1 *either* we view nature as an accidental accumulation of objects *or* we view it as a unified, coherent All;

2 *either* we view the unified All as a state of rest and immobility *or* we view it as a process of development;

3 *either* we view the process of development as a circular movement *or* we view it as a development from the inferior to the superior;

4 *either* we view the development from the inferior to the superior as a harmonious evolution *or* we view it as a struggle between opposites.

At first glance, we are dealing here with a classic case of exhaustive disjunction: at each level, the genus is divided in two species. However, if we look at things more closely, we immediately perceive the paradoxical character of this division. There is basically an implicit affirmation that all the variants of metaphysics are 'by their essence' objectively the same thing. We can verify this by reading the scheme backwards. Harmonious development, essentially, objectively, is in no way a development from the inferior to the superior, but a circular movement pure and simple. The circular movement, essentially, is not at all a movement but the conservation of a state of immobility.

This means that, in the end, there is *only one choice*: the choice between *dialectics* and *metaphysics*. In other words, the diagonal that separates dialectics from metaphysics must be read as a vertical line. If we choose harmonious evolution, we lose not only the struggle of opposites but also the very common genus, the development from the inferior to the superior, because, 'objectively', we fall into a circular movement.

This vertical reading of the diagonal thus unifies the 'enemy'. Thereby, we can evade the fact that it is a question of a gradual differentiation. Initially, it was Bukharin who, together with Stalin, got rid of Trotsky. The conflict with Bukharin emerged only later – in the same way that it was first the circular movement that, in connection with evolution as a whole, was opposed to immobility and became its opposite only after the 'expulsion' of immobility. With all of these oppositions, we can construct a *single* 'Bukharin–Trotskyist plot': the 'short-circuit' of such a unification is, of course, a particular perversion of the primacy of synchrony over diachrony. We project backwards the present distinction, the opposition that determines the present concrete situation. Thus, for instance, the implicit presupposition of official historians of East Germany is that it was West Germany that initiated World War II.

What is the secret behind this process of division? The *History of the Communist Party of the Soviet Union* characterizes the 'united Trotsky–Bukharin gang of fascist hirelings' as 'remnants' or 'scraps' of the defeated classes.[15] This distinction is to be taken literally and must be applied to the very process of differentiation. In this process, each genus has only one true and *proper* species; any other species is only a *scrap* of the genus, the non-genus in the guise of a species of the genus. The development from the inferior to the superior has only one species, the struggle of opposites; harmonious evolution is only the scrap of this genus.

From there, unexpectedly, we fall into the scheme of the division encountered in the process of Hegelian dialectics: each genus has only one species, the other species is the paradoxical negative of the genus itself. Just as in the instance of the 'limit case' of the logic of the signifier, the All is divided into its Part and a remainder that is not nothing but a paradoxical, impossible, contradictory entity. Metaphysics pretends, at one and the same time, that (1) nature is an accidental accumulation and not an All and that (2) nature as All is a state of immobility and not a movement. Unlike the Hegelian division, however, instead of *including* through its specification/determination, the genus *excludes* its own absence and 'negativity'. The development from the inferior to the superior as a concretization of the process of development in general is not a 'synthesis' of initial abstract universality and its negation (of circular movement) but precisely the exclusion of circular movement from the process of development in general. Through its specification, the genus is purified of its scraps. Far from particularizing it, the division consolidates the All as All. If we subtract the scrap from the All of the genus, we subtract nothing and the All remains All. The 'development from the inferior to the superior' is no less 'all' than the process of development in general. From this point we can grasp the logic of this apparently absurd formulation: 'In its immense majority the Party wholeheartedly rejected the platform of the bloc.' The 'immense majority' is equivalent to 'wholeheartedly'; the rest (the minority) does not even count. In other words, we are dealing with a fusion between the Universal and the Particular, between the genus and the species. This is why, in reality, one does not choose between Nothing and the *Party*. Each Particular is immediately fused with the Universal and, thus, we are thrown towards the choice, *'ou bien ou bien absolu'*, between the *Nothing* and the *All*. Thus, the Stalinist disjunction is precisely the contrary of the habitual disjunction between two particulars in which we can never 'catch up with the turtle' (to be understood on account of the movement of enunciation itself), of the division between a part and a remainder that would not be nothing, that would stand in the place of the enunciation itself (this division functions as an inaccessible asymptotic point). In the Stalinist disjunction, the problem is rather how to escape the *'ou bien ou bien absolu'*: the inaccessible is a division between particulars, a division in which one of the terms would not evaporate into a 'nothing' of pure semblance.

Metaphysics consequently functions as a paradoxical object that 'is not nothing', an irrational surplus, a purely contradictory element, non-symbolizable, that is the other of oneself; a lack where nothing is missing, precisely the *objet petit a* of *desire* or the pure seeming that is always added to S_2 and forces us in this way to continue with the differentiation. Or, in terms of the order of classification and articulation of genuses and species, metaphysics functions as a surplus that disturbs the symmetrical articulation, as a paradoxical species that does not want to be limited merely to being a species or the unilaterally accentuated partial object (the 'absolutization of a determined moment', as Lenin used to write). Thus, we can write the relation between the agent of Stalinist discourse, 'objective knowledge' (S_2), and its other in the following way: $(S_2/S_1) \rightarrow a$. The arrow indicates the repetitive differentiation by which knowledge tries to penetrate its 'positive' object and grasp it by demarcating it from the surplus of the metaphysical seeming-object that always prevents the accomplishment of the objective knowledge of reality. In other words, the object of Stalinist discourse, in the sense of 'positive object', is of course so-called objective reality. It is, nevertheless, far from occupying the place of the object-cause of desire. The *plus-de-jouir* that pushes forward its process of differentiation is to be sought rather in the pure seeming of metaphysics.

The Stalinist political process functions precisely as a hallucinatory '*mise-en-scène*' of this desire, which the Stalinist renounces and with which he refuses to be identified. The condemned (the 'victim') is the one who acknowledges desire (his own desire and thereby, in accord with the hysteric's formula of desire, the desire of the Stalinist other). This function of the victim in Stalinist discourse is not at all comparable to the function of the same in Fascist discourse. For the Fascist, the Jew is sacrificed as the object of desire. The logic of this sacrifice is: '*I love you, but, because inexplicably I love in you something more than you – the* objet petit a *– I mutilate you.*'[16] The Stalinist 'traitor' does not in any way occupy the position of the object of desire; the Stalinist is not at all 'in love' with it. He is, rather, $: the desiring divided *subject*. This division indicates the very confession that is unthinkable in Fascism.

In Fascism, the universal medium – that the accuser and the guilty would have in common and by which he could 'convince' the guilty of his fault – is missing. One of the fundamental mechanisms of the Stalinist trials consisted in the displacement of the split between the neutral place of objective knowledge and the hold of the particularity of the 'scraps' over the victim. The victim is guilty, but at the same time capable of reaching the 'universal-objective' point of view, from which he can recognize his fault. This fundamental mechanism of *self-criticism* is unthinkable in fascism. In its pure form, we can find it in the self-accusations of Slansky and Rajk during their well-known trials. To the question of how he became a traitor, Slansky responded very clearly, in the style of a positivist observation or of pure metalanguage, that it was because of his bourgeois milieu and education that he could never be part of the working class. This is the moment at which Stalinist discourse is the heir of the Lumières. They share the same presupposition of a universal and uniform reason that even the most abject Trotskyist scrap has the capacity of 'comprehending', and then confessing.

The Real of 'class struggle'

At this point, we can link all of the moments we have so far developed. Stalinist discourse is presented as a neutral objective knowledge (S_2), whose other is a pure seeming of subjective (metaphysical) knowledge (*a*). The reality of this neutral knowledge is the performative gesture of the master (S_1), who addresses the hystericized, split subject of desire ($\$$). This result, as disenchanting as this is, is Lacan's formulae of the discourse of the University:[17]

$$\frac{S_2}{S_1} \rightarrow \frac{a}{\$}$$

Stalinist discourse is perhaps the purest form of the discourse of the University in the position of the master – a possibility already envisioned by Alain Grosrichard.

We can add a series of additional distinctions between fascism and Stalinism by examining, for example, *the* book of fascism and *the* book of Stalinism. On the one hand, in *Mein Kampf*, the immediate speech of the master presents his vision 'in person' with a quasi-existential passion; on the other, *The History of the Communist Party of the Soviet Union (Bolsheviks): Short Course (b)* is an anonymous objective summary whose academic character is already revealed in its subtitle. The latter book is not the immediate word of the master but a commentary. On the other hand, the Fascist discourse's medium par excellence is the living *speech* that hypnotizes by its very performative strength, without taking into account its signified content. To cite Hitler himself: 'All great events that have shaken the world have been provoked by speech and not writing.' By contrast, the medium par excellence of Stalinist discourse is *writing*. The Stalinist is almost obliged to read his very discourses in a monotonous voice, clearly attesting the fact that we are dealing with the reproduction of a prior writing.

In Lacanian theory, the Real has two principal sides. One is the Real as a remainder that is impossible to symbolize, a scrap, the refuse of the symbolic, a hole in the Other (in other words, the Real aspect of *objet a*, the voice, the gaze . . .); the other is the Real as writing, construct, number and mathème. These two sides perfectly correspond to the opposition fascism/Stalinism. The hypnotic power of Fascist discourse is supported by the 'gaze' and especially the 'voice' of the leader. The support of Stalinist discourse is, in turn, the writing. Which writing? We must consider the decisive difference between the 'classical' texts and their commentaries and applications. The impossible-Real is the institution of the 'classics of Marxism–Leninism' as the sacred Text, approachable only through the proper-just commentary that gives it its meaning, and vice versa. It is precisely the reference to the nonsense of the classical text (the famous 'citation') that 'gives sense' to the commentary–application (to take up again the distinction between sense and meaning: sense = meaning + nonsense).

We could prolong this *ad infinitum*, but instead let us remain at a general level. By linking the preceding discussion to the fact that Capitalist discourse is that of the Hysteric,[18] we can read the scheme of the four discourses as providing a schema for the three types of today's political discourses: the Capitalist discourse of the Hysteric; the attempt to suppress it by a return to the discourse of the Master in fascism; and the discourse of the University of post-revolutionary society, that is to say, Stalinist discourse.

$$\textit{Hysteric} \qquad \textit{Master} \qquad \textit{University}$$

$$\frac{\$}{a} \to \frac{S_1}{S_2} \qquad \frac{S_1}{\$} \to \frac{S_2}{a} \qquad \frac{S_2}{S_1} \to \frac{a}{\$}$$

To the notion that capitalist discourse is the discourse of the Hysteric, we should add the proposition that I have suggested elsewhere: it was Marx who discovered the symptom.[19] What does the hysteric-capitalism 'produce' as its symptom? The answer is, of course, the proletariat as its 'own gravedigger' (as Marx put it), the irrational element of the given totality, the class whose very existence is the negation of the rationality of the existing order (S_2), the place of a knowledge ('class consciousness') that later (after the revolution) will take the place of the agent. Lacan links this precisely to the Marxian discovery of the symptom: the existence of the proletariat as pure subjectivity, freed from the particular ties of the Middle Ages. We also recall the connection established by Lacan between *plus-de-jouir* and Marxian surplus value.[20] Capitalism, the true common ground of historical materialism, is different from preceding formations in that an internal condition of its reproduction is to surpass itself constantly, to revolutionize the given situation and to develop the productive forces. The reason should be sought in surplus value as a 'driving force' that pushes the mechanism of social reproduction. In short, in the place of the truth of the capitalist discourse we find the *plus-de-jouir*.

And the fourth moment, the discourse of the Analyst $((a/S_2) \rightarrow (\$/S_1))$? Is it really the destiny of the political field to wander between the three positions of the *Master*, who constitutes the new social contract (the 'new harmony') of the *Academic*, who elaborates it in a system, and of the *Hysteric*, who produces its symptom? Should the void in the place of the fourth discourse be read as an indication that we are already at the political level? We are tempted to suggest things work differently.

Marx writes in a letter that his *Capital* must conclude with class struggle as the 'dissolution of all this shit'. It is, of course, precisely this dissolution that 'does not cease from not being written', and that is lacking in the text itself. The third book of *Capital* is interrupted, as we know, at the beginning of the chapter on classes. In this way, we could say that class struggle functions in a strict sense as the 'object' of *Capital*, that which *cannot* become the 'positive object of research' and that which necessarily *falls* outside and thus makes of the totality of the three books of *Capital* a 'not-all'. This object never arrives at the end, as some 'subjective expression of objective economic processes'. Rather, it is an agent always at work at the very heart of the positive content of *Capital*. All of the categories of *Capital* are already coloured by class struggle, all objective determinations (labour value, the degree of surplus value, etc.) are already achieved by means of this struggle.

If we say that an aspect of class struggle is of the Real, we are only reiterating the Lacanian formula of the impossibility of the sexual relation: 'there is no class relation'. Classes are not 'classes' in the usual or logical-classificatory sense; there is no universal medium. The 'struggle' (the relation that is precisely a non-relation) between classes has a constitutive role for the classes themselves. In other words, class struggle functions as this Real because of which the socio-ideological discourse is never 'all'. Consequently, class struggle is not some objective fact, but rather the name (one of the names) for the impossibility of a discourse being 'objective', of remaining at an objective distance and of telling 'the truth about the truth', the name of the fact that each word on class struggle falls *into* class struggle.

From this logic it follows that Stalinist discourse dissimulates the essential dimension of class struggle. Objective knowledge is presented as a neutral discourse on society, stated from an excluded place, a place that is not in itself split or marked by the separating line of class struggle. That is why one could say that, for Stalinist discourse, 'all is politics', or 'politics is all', which is different from the Maoist discourse where, for example, politics is inscribed on to the feminine as 'not-all'. However, it is here that we must be most careful concerning the paradoxes of not-all. Precisely because 'all is politics', the Stalinist discourse always needs *exceptions*, neutral foundations in which politics is invested from the outside, such as the innocence of technology, language as the neutral-universal tool at the disposition of all classes and so forth. These traits are not at all indices of some 'de-Stalinizing' process, but precisely the internal condition of Stalinist totalitarianism.

Stalinism versus Fascism

Class struggle today seems, of course, like something outmoded. However, the reasoning by which we reach this conclusion is very much homologous to that which leads us to affirm (in the era of so-called 'permissive sexual morals') the obsolescence of the object of psychoanalysis (the repression of sexual desire). During the 'heroic' epoch of psychoanalysis, it was believed that the unleashing of sexual taboos would bring about or at least contribute to life without anxiety, without repression, a life full of free enjoyment. The experience of this so-called 'sexual liberation' helps us rather to recognize the dimension proper to the constitutive law of desire, of that 'crazy' law that inflicts *jouissance*. Likewise, during the 'heroic' epoch of the labour movement, it was believed that with the abolition of private ownership, classes and their struggles would be abolished and that we would arrive at a new solidarity. The experience of so-called 'Stalinism' helped us recognize, in 'Really Existing Socialism', the realization of the very concept of class struggle in its distilled form, no longer clouded by the difference between civil society and the State.

Here again Really Existing Socialism differs radically from fascism. Let us start with the latter: how can we link class struggle (insofar as it constitutes the core of an 'impossible' difference) to the fact that, in Fascist discourse, *objet a* is really the Jew? The answer is that the Jew functions as a *fetish* that masks class struggle and stands in its place. Fascism wrestles against capitalism and liberalism, which are supposed to destroy and corrupt the harmony of society as 'organic', where particular states have the function of members, that is to say, where each and everyone has his natural and determined place (head, hands, etc.). Fascism thus tries to restore a harmonious *relation* between the classes within the framework of an organic All, and the Jew incarnates the moment that introduces discord 'from outside'. The Jew is the surplus that disturbs the harmonious co-operation of the social 'head' and 'hands', of Capital and labour. 'Jew' nicely suits this disruption due to his historical and proverbial connotations: 'Jew' represents a condensation of the negative traits of the two poles of the social scale. On the one hand, he incarnates the exorbitant, non-harmonious behaviour of the ruling class (the financier who drains his workers) and, on the other, the dirt of the lower classes. Moreover, the Jew appears as the personification of mercantile Capital that is (according to the spontaneous ideological representation) the true place of exploitation and thereby reinforces the ideological fiction of capitalists and 'honest' workers, of the productive classes exploited by the Jewish merchant. In brief, the 'Jew', in playing the role of the disruptive element and introducing 'from outside' the surplus of class struggle, is really the positive repudiation of class struggle and of the notion 'there is no class relation'. It is for this reason that fascism, as distinct from socialism, is not a *sui generis* discourse, a global social contract, determining the whole social edifice. We could say that fascism, with its ideology of corporativism, of returning to the pre-bourgeois master, causes in some way an interference with Capitalist discourse without changing its fundamental nature – the proof being precisely the figure of the Jew as enemy.

To grasp this point, we should start from the decisive cut in the relation of domination that occurs with the passage from pre-bourgeois to bourgeois society. In the pre-bourgeois order, civil society is not yet liberated from organic ties; that is to say, we are dealing with 'the immediate relations of domination and servitude' (as Marx put it). The relation of the master to his subject is that of an interpersonal link, direct subjection, paternal concern on the part of the Master and veneration on the part of the subject. With the advent of bourgeois society, this rich network of 'affective' and 'organic' relations between the master and his subjects lies in tatters. The subject frees himself from his tutelage and stands as an autonomous and rational subject. Now, Marx's fundamental lesson is that the subject remains nevertheless subjected to a certain master, that the link to the master is only displaced. The fetishism of the personal master is replaced by the fetishism of merchandise. The will of the person of the master is replaced by the anonymous power of the market or the famous 'invisible hand' (Adam Smith) that decides the destiny of individuals behind their back.

It is within this framework that we must locate the fundamental wager of fascism. While preserving the fundamental relation of capitalism (between Capital and labour), fascism wants to abolish its organic, anonymous and savage character; that is to say, to make of it an organic relation of patriarchal domination between the 'hand' and the 'head', between the leader and his escort, and replace the anonymous 'invisible hand' by the will of the master. Now, insofar as we remain within the fundamental framework of capitalism, this operation does not work. There is always a surplus of the 'invisible hand' that contradicts the design of the master. The only way to recognize this surplus is (for the fascist whose epistemic field is that of the master), again, to personalize the 'invisible hand' and imagine another master, but now a hidden master who in reality pulls all the strings and whose clandestine activity is the true secret behind this anonymity of the market – i.e., the Jew.

As to socialism, it should be conceived of as a paradox of a *class society with only one class*. This is the solution to the question of whether Really Existing Socialism is a class society or not. The so-called 'ruling bureaucracy' is not just the new class; it comes to stand in the place of the ruling class. This must be taken literally, and certainly not in some evolutionist-teleological perspective (that the new class already has some traits of the ruling class and the future will show that it will be consolidated as a ruling class). This 'in the place of' is not at all to be regarded as the mark of an unfinished, partial character. In Really Existing Socialism, the ruling bureaucracy is found in the place of the ruling class, *which does not exist*, holding its place empty. In other words, Really Existing Socialism would be this paradoxical point at which class difference actually becomes differential. It is no longer a question of the difference between two positive entities, but rather a difference between the 'absent' class and the 'present' class, between the lacking (ruling) class and the existing (working) class. This lacking class can actually be the working class itself insofar as it is opposed to actual 'empirical' workers. In this manner, class difference coincides with the difference between the Universal (the working class) and the Particular (the empirical working class), with the ruling bureaucracy incarnating its own Universality over against the empirical working class. It is this split between the Class as Universal and its own particular-empirical existence that clarifies an apparent contradiction of the Stalinist text. The *History of the Communist Party of the Soviet Union* ends with a long quotation of Stalin against 'bureaucratic rust' that reveals for us the secret of the 'invincibility' of the Bolshevik Party:

> I think that the Bolsheviks remind us of the hero of Greek mythology, Antæus. They, like Antæus, are strong because they maintain connection with their mother, the masses, who gave birth to them, suckled them and reared them. And as long as they maintain connection with their mother, with the people, they have every chance of remaining invincible.[21]

The same allusion to Antæus is found at the beginning of Marx's 'Eighteenth Brumaire' as a metaphor of the class enemy in the face of proletarian revolutions that 'seem to throw their opponent to the ground only to see him draw new strength from the earth and rise again before them, more colossal than ever'.[22] We must read these lines in relation to the vow of Stalin with which this paper began: 'We Communists are people of a special mould. We are made of a special stuff.' At first glance, these two passages seem to be contradictory: on the one hand, it is a question of the fusion of the Bolsheviks with the masses as the source of their strength; on the other, they are 'people of a special mould'. We can resolve this paradox (how does the privileged *link* with the masses *separate* them from other people, precisely from the masses?) if we take into account the above-mentioned difference between the *Class* (the working masses) as All and *masses* as 'not-all', i.e., an 'empirical' collection. The Bolsheviks (the Party) are the only empirical representatives, the only incarnation of the true masses, of the Class as All.

From here, it is not difficult to determine the place of the Party in the economy of Stalinist discourse. This 'striking force of the working class', composed of 'people of a different making' and at the same time intimately attached to their mother or the masses, really takes the place of the 'maternal phallus', the fetish that rejects the Real of class difference, of the struggle, of the non-relation between All of the class and its own 'not-all'. While, in Fascist discourse, the role of the fetish is played by the Jew, or the enemy, the Stalinist fetish is the Party itself.

Although already in Lenin we find this logic of the Party, the incarnation of historical objectivity, the continuity between Leninism and Stalinism should not lead us to an immediate identification of their discursive positions. On the contrary, it is precisely on the basis of this continuity that we can highlight their difference, the decisive 'step forward' relative to Leninism accomplished by Stalin. In Lenin, we already find the fundamental position of neutral-objective knowledge and the 'objectivization' of our subjective intentions ('the important thing, is the objective meaning of your acts, regardless of your subjective intentions, sincere as they may be'). The 'objective meaning' is determined, of course, by the Leninist himself from his position of neutral-objective knowledge. Now, Stalin takes a step forward and again subjectifies this objective meaning, projecting it upon the subject himself as his secret desire: *what your act objectively means is what you in fact wanted*.

We can also deduce the different status of the political adversary: for Lenin, the adversary (of course, always the 'internal enemy', the Menshevik, the 'social revolutions of the Left', the 'opportunist', etc.) is, according to the rule, determined as the *Hysteric* who has lost contact with reality, who, unable to be his own master, reacts emotionally when reasoning is required, who does not know what he is talking about, and who is 'all talk and no action'. The elementary figures are Martov, Kamenev and Zinoviev at the time of October and Olga Spiridonovna (arrested after the failed coup attempt of the social revolutionaries of the Left in the summer of 1918 when, at the Bolshoi Theatre where the Constituent Assembly took place, she played the role of the hystericized speaker and was later admitted to a psychiatric hospital). The hidden truth of the Leninist is, of course, the fact that he, by his position as holder of the neutral-objective knowledge and a universal and uniform reason, *produces the Hysteric*. This position of objective knowledge implies that there is basically no dialogue, because it is impossible to have a discussion with someone who has access to reality itself, with the one who incarnates historical objectivity. Any different position is, in advance, defined as mere seeming, as nothing, and the dialogue is replaced by pedagogy, by the patient work of persuasion (the elegy of Lenin's great art of persuasion is, it is well known, a commonplace of Stalinist hagiography). In this climate of total blockage, the only option available to the one who thinks otherwise is the hysterical cry that announces a knowledge that escapes this universality. Now, with Stalin, we are done with the hysterical game: the Stalinist adversary, the 'traitor', is not the one who 'does not know what he is talking about' or 'what he is doing', but on the contrary, precisely the one who, to use a Stalinist turn of phrase par excellence, 'knows very well what he is doing'. With the menace implied by this syntagm, a conspirator is the one who plots consciously, with intention. In other words, while Leninism remains a 'normal' academic discourse (knowledge in the position of the agent produces as its result the barred-hystericized subject), Stalinism takes a step into 'madness': academic knowledge becomes that of paranoia and the adversary becomes the deliberate and literally 'divided' conspirator, the rubbish, the pure scrap, who nevertheless has access to neutral-objective knowledge, whence he can recognize the importance of his act and *confess*.

The totalitarian fantasy, the totalitarianism of the fantasy

What is essential here is not to reduce this Stalinist 'psychosis' to a simple excess, but to grasp it as an immanent possibility that brings out the truth of the fundamental position itself. This is already the truth of Marx. It allows a new approach to the passage from 'utopian' socialism to so-called 'scientific' socialism. Although Marx discovered the symptom and developed the logic of the social symptom (the moment when the fundamental blockage of the given social order emerges and it seems to call on its own revolutionary practical-dialectical dissolution), he underestimated the importance of *fantasy* in the historical process, and the importance of inertia that does not dissolve due to its dialectization and whose exemplary intrusion would be what is called the 'negative behaviour of the masses', who appear to be acting against their best interests and let themselves get entangled in diverse forms of the 'conservative revolution'. The enigmatic character of such a phenomenon is to be sought in the simple *jouissance* that is implied through their actions: social theory tries to get rid of what is worrisome in this *jouissance* by designating it as the 'delirium of the masses', their mindlessness, regression, their lack of conscience.

Where is the fantasy here? The fantasmatic scene aims at the realization of the sexual relation, blinding us with its fascinating presence to the impossibility of the sexual relation. Similarly, with the social fantasy, the fantasmatic construct supports an ideological field. We are always dealing with the fantasy of a *class relation*, with the utopia of a harmonious, organic and complementary relation between diverse parts of the social totality. The elementary image of the social fantasy is that of a *social body*, through which one eludes the impossible, the antagonism around which the social field is structured. The anti-liberal ideologies of the Right that serve as a foundation for the so-called 'regressive behaviour of the masses' are precisely distinguished by recourse to this organicist metaphor. Their *leitmotif* is that of society as a body, an organic totality of members corrupted later by the intrusion of a liberal atomism.

We already find this fantasmatic dimension in so-called 'utopian' socialism. Lacan determines the illusion specific to Sade's perverse fantasy as the 'utopia of desire'.[23] In the sadist scene, the split between desire and *jouissance* is suppressed (an impossible operation insofar as desire is supported by the interdiction of *jouissance*, that is to say, insofar as desire is the structural underside of *jouissance*), and at the same time the gap that separates *jouissance* from pleasure is removed. By way of pain, or the 'negative' of pleasure, an attempt is made to reach *jouissance* in the very field of pleasure. The word 'utopia' should also be taken in the political sense: the famous sadist 'One more effort . . .' (in *Philosophy in the Boudoir*) should be placed along the same lines as 'utopian socialism', as one of its most radical variants because utopian socialism always implies a 'utopia of desire'. In the utopian project from Campanella to Fourier, we are always dealing with a regulated and finally dominated fantasy of enjoyment.

With the passage to 'scientific socialism', Marx forecloses this fantasmatic dimension. We must give to the term 'foreclosure' all the weight it has in Lacanian theory: that is to say, not only the repression but also the exclusion and rejection of a moment outside the symbolic field. And whatever is foreclosed in the Symbolic, we well know that it returns in the Real, in our case, in *Really Existing Socialism*. Utopian, scientific and 'Really Existing' socialism thus form a sort of triad. The utopian dimension, excluded by its 'scientificization', returns in the Real, or in the 'Utopia in Power', to borrow the well-justified title of a book on the Soviet Union. Really Existing Socialism is the price paid in the flesh for the misrecognition of the fantasy dimension in scientific socialism.

To speak of the 'social fantasy' seems nevertheless to imply a fundamental theoretical error insofar as a fantasy is basically *non-universalizable*. The social fantasy is particular, 'pathological' in the Kantian sense, personal (the very foundation of the unity of the 'person' insofar as it is distinguished from the subject and the signifier), the unique way that each of us tries to come to terms with the Thing, the impossible *jouissance*. That is to say, the manner in which, with the help of an imaginary construct, we try to dissolve the primordial impasse in which the 'speaking-being [*parlêtre*]' is situated, the impasse of the inconsistent Other, the hole at the heart of the Other. The field of the Law, of rights and duties, on the contrary, is not only universalizable but universal in its very nature. It is the field of universal equality, of equalization effected by exchange through an equivalent principle. According to this perspective, we could designate the *objet a*, the *plus-de-jouir* as a surplus, and that is why the formula of fantasy, insofar as it is non-universalizable, is written $\$ \lozenge \alpha$, that is to say, the confrontation of the subject with this 'impossible', unexchangeable remainder. Here we have the link between *plus-de-jouir* and surplus value as a surplus that contradicts the equivalent exchange between capitalism and the proletariat, a surplus that the capitalist appropriates within the framework of the equivalent exchange of Capital for the labour force.

Now, there was no need to wait for Marx to experience the cul-de-sac of equivalent exchange. In its effort to enlarge the bourgeois form of the egalitarian and universal law, does not Sade's heroism rely precisely on universal exchange, on the rights and duties of man within the domain of *jouissance*? Its starting point is that the revolution stopped midway, because within the domain of *jouissance* it continued to be a prisoner of patriarchal and theological prejudices, that is to say, the revolution did not reach the end of its project of bourgeois emancipation. Now, as Lacan demonstrates in 'Kant with Sade', the formulation of a universal norm, of a 'categorical imperative' that would legislate enjoyment, necessarily fails and ends in an impasse. Thus, we cannot, according to the model of formal bourgeois rights, legislate the right to *jouissance* in the mode of 'To each his fantasy!' or 'Each has a right to his particular mode of enjoyment!' Sade's hypothetical universal law is reinstated by Lacan as: 'I have the right to enjoy your body, someone may say to me, and this right I shall exercise without any limit stopping me in the caprice of (whatever) exactions I have the fancy to gratify.'[24] Its impasse is glaring, the symmetry is false: to occupy the position of the torturer in a consistent manner is revealed as impossible because everyone in the final analysis is also a victim.

How can we, then, repudiate the reproach that speaking of a 'social fantasy' is equivalent to an *in adjecto* contradiction? Far from being simply epistemological, far from indicating a theoretical error, this impasse *defines the thing itself*. Is not the fundamental trait of the totalitarian social link precisely the loss of distance between the fantasy that gives the indicators of the enjoyment of the subject and the formal-universal Law that governs social exchange? The fantasy is 'socialized' in an immediate way insofar as the social Law coincides with the injunction, 'Enjoy!' It begins to function as a superego imperative. In other words, in totalitarianism, it is really the fantasy that is in power and this is what distinguishes totalitarianism *stricto sensu* (Germany in 1938–45, the Soviet Union in 1934–51, Italy in 1943–45) from the patriarchal-authoritarian régimes of law-and-order (Salazar, Franco, Bolfuss, Mussolini until 1943) or from 'normalized' socialism. Such pure totalitarianism is necessarily self-destructive; it cannot be stabilized; it cannot arrive at a minimal homeostasis that would allow it to reproduce in a circuit of equilibrium. It is constantly shaken by convulsions. An immanent logic pushes it to violence directed at an external (Nazism) or internal (the Stalinist purges) 'enemy'. The theme of the post-Stalinist 'normalization' in the Soviet Union was for good reason that of the 'return to the socialist *legality*'. The only way out of the vicious circle of the purges was perceived to be the reaffirmation of a Law supposed to introduce a minimal distance towards the fantasy, of a symbolic-formal system of rules that would not be immediately impregnated with *jouissance*.

This is why we can determine totalitarianism also as the social order where, although there is no law (no positive legality with universal validity, established in an explicit form), all that we do can at any moment pass for an illegal and forbidden thing. Positive legislation does not exist (or if it does, it has a totally arbitrary and non-obligatory character), but despite this we can at any moment find ourselves in the position of the infractor of an unknown and non-existent Law. If the paradox of the interdiction that founds the social order consists in forbidding something already impossible, totalitarianism reverses this paradox in putting us in the no less paradoxical position of the infractor who transgresses a non-existent Law. In the law-less state, although the law does not exist, we can nevertheless transgress against it, which is the supreme proof that, as Lacan emphasizes in his *Seminar II*, the famous proposition of Dostoevsky should be turned around: if God (the positive legality) does not exist, everything is forbidden.[25]

At this point, the difference between the fascist leader and the Stalinist leader is also explained. Let us start from the duality of power developed by Alain Grosrichard:[26] despot/vizier corresponds approximately to the Hegelian duality monarch/ministerial power. This means that despotism is not the fantasy of totalitarian power, which is defined precisely by a 'short-circuit' in the relation despot/vizier. If the fascist master wants to rule in his own name, if he does not want to part with effective power but wants to be his own vizier (at least in the domain of war as the only domain worthy of the master), he discovers that the impossibility of the operation of integrating knowledge (S_2) provokes the fantasmatic transposition of this knowledge on to the Jews, who effectively 'pull all the strings'. The Stalinist leader is, by contrast, the paradox of *the vizier without the despot-master*. He acts in the name of the working class itself and constitutes it as a master opposed to the 'empirical' class.

Notes

This paper was originally published in *Lacan, Politics, Aesthetics*, ed. Willy Apollon and Richard Feldstein, Albany, State University of New York Press, 1996, pp. 3–29, and was edited and translated by Aïda Der Hovanessian. We have revised the translation and made corrections to certain grammatical and terminological errors. [eds]

1 J. V. Stalin, 'On the death of Lenin', in *Works, Volume 6*, Moscow, Foreign Languages Publishing House, 1953, p. 47.

2 Cited in Paul-Dominque Dognin, *Les 'Sentiers Escarpes' de Karl Marx, Tome 1: Textes*, Paris, Éditions CERF, 1977, pp. 72–3.

3 V. I. Lenin, *Collected Works, Volume 35*, ed. Robert Daglish, trans. Andrew Rothstein, Moscow, Progress Publishers, 1966, p. 69. [eds]

4 Lenin, *Collected Works, Volume 35*, p. 85. [eds]

5 V. I. Lenin, *Collected Works, Volume 43*, trans. Martin Parker and Bernard Isaacs, Moscow, Progress Publishers, 1969, p. 356. [eds]

6 Lenin, *Collected Works, Volume 35*, p. 98. [eds]

7 Lenin, *Collected Works, Volume 35*, p. 112. [eds]

8 Lenin, *Collected Works, Volume 35*, pp. 121–4. [eds]

9 See Augustine, *Concerning the City of God against the Pagans*, trans. Henry Bettenson, Harmondsworth, Penguin, 1972, pp. 574–87. [eds]

10 Jacques Lacan, 'The signification of the phallus', in *Écrits*, trans. Bruce Fink, New York and London, W. W. Norton, 2002, pp. 274–5. [eds]

11 Karl Marx, 'Class struggles in France: 1848 to 1850', in *Surveys from Exile: Political Writings, Volume 2*, ed. David Fernbach, trans. Ben Fowkes *et al.*, London, Penguin/New Left Review, 1973, pp. 88–9.

12 J. V. Stalin, 'The foundations of Leninism', in *Works, Volume 6*, pp. 122–3.

13 Stalin, 'The foundations of Leninism', pp. 177–8.

14 *The History of the Communist Party of the Soviet Union (Bolsheviks): Short Course (b)*, Moscow, Foreign Languages Publishing House, 1939, pp. 110–11.

15 *The History of the Communist Party of the Soviet Union*, pp. 324–6. [eds]

16 Jacques Lacan, *The Seminar of Jacques Lacan XI: The Four Fundamental Concepts of Psychoanalysis*, ed. Jacques-Alain Miller, trans. Alan Sheridan, New York and London, W. W. Norton, 1977, p. 268. [eds]

17 Jacques Lacan, 'Radiophonie', in *Autres écrits*, ed. Jacques-Alain Miller, Paris, Éditions du Seuil, 2001, pp. 444–7. [eds]

18 Jacques Lacan, *Le Séminaire de Jacques Lacan XVII: L'envers de la psychanalyse, 1969–70*, ed. Jacques-Alain Miller, Paris, Éditions du Seuil, 1991, pp. 31–59. [eds]

19 Slavoj Žižek, *The Sublime Object of Ideology*, London and New York, Verso, 1989, pp. 11–53. [eds]

20 Lacan, *Séminaire XVII*, pp. 18–19, 123–4, 206–7. [eds]

21 *The History of the Communist Party of the Soviet Union (Bolsheviks): Short Course (b)*, p. 363.

22 Karl Marx, 'The Eighteenth Brumaire of Louis Bonaparte', in *Surveys from Exile*, p. 150. [eds]

23 Jacques Lacan, 'Kant avec Sade', in *Écrits II*, Paris, Éditions du Seuil, 1966, p. 253.

24 Lacan, 'Kant avec Sade', p. 247.

25 Jacques Lacan, *The Seminar of Jacques Lacan II: The Ego in Freud's Theory and in the Technique of Psychoanalysis*, ed. Jacques-Alain Miller, trans. Sylvana Tomaselli, New York and London, W. W. Norton, 1988, p. 128.

26 Alain Grosrichard, *The Sultan's Court: European Fantasies of the East*, trans. Liz Heron, London and New York, Verso, 1998.

Chapter 6
Georg Lukács as the philosopher of Leninism

Georg Lukács' *History and Class Consciousness* (1923) is one of the few authentic events in the history of Marxism.[1] Today, we cannot but experience the book as a strange remainder from a bygone era – it is difficult even to imagine properly the traumatic impact its appearance had on generations of Marxists, including the later Lukács himself who, in his Thermidorian phase, i.e., from the early 1930s onwards, desperately tried to distance himself from it, to confine it to a document of merely historical interest, and conceded to its reprint only in 1967, accompanied by a new, long, self-critical introduction. Until this 'official' reprint, the book led the kind of underground spectral existence of an 'undead' entity, circulating in pirated editions among German students in the 1960s, available in some rare translations (like the legendary French one from 1959). In my own country, the now defunct Yugoslavia, reference to *History and Class Consciousness* served as the ritualistic *signe de reconnaissance* of the entire critical Marxist circle around the journal *Praxis* – its attack on Engels' notion of the 'dialectics of nature' was crucial for the critical rejection of the 'reflection' theory of knowledge as the central tenet of 'dialectical materialism'. This impact was far from confined to Marxist circles: even Heidegger was obviously affected by *History and Class Consciousness*, since there are a couple of unmistakable hints at it in *Being and Time* – for instance, in the very last paragraph, Heidegger, in an obvious reaction to Lukács' critique of 'reification', asks the question: 'We have long known that ancient ontology deals with "reified concepts" and that the danger exists of "reifying consciousness." But what does reifying [*Verdinglichung*] mean? Where does it arise from? . . . Is the "distinction" between "consciousness" and "thing" sufficient at all for a primordial unfolding of the ontological problematic?'[2]

I

So how did *History and Class Consciousness* attain this cult status of a quasi-mythical forbidden book, comparable, perhaps, only to the no less traumatic impact of *For Marx*, written by Louis Althusser, Lukács' later great anti-Hegelian antipode? The answer that first comes to one's mind, of course, is that we are dealing with the founding text of the entire tradition of Western Hegelian Marxism, with a book that combines an engaged revolutionary stance with topics that were later developed by the different strands of so-called critical theory up to cultural studies today (the notion of 'commodity fetishism' as the structural feature of the entire social life, of 'reification' and 'instrumental reason', and so on). However, on a closer look, things appear in a slightly different light: there is a radical break between *History and Class Consciousness* – more precisely, between Lukács' writings from circa 1915 to circa 1930, inclusive of his *Lenin* from 1924, a series of his other short texts from this period not included in *History and Class Consciousness* and published in the 1960s under the title *Tactics and Ethics*, as well as the manuscript of *Tailism and the Dialectic* [*Chvostismus and Dialektik*], Lukács' answer to his Comintern critics[3] – and the later tradition of Western Marxism. The paradox (from our Western 'post-political' perspective) of *History and Class Consciousness* is that we have a philosophically extremely sophisticated book, one that can compete with the highest achievements of the non-Marxist thought of its period, and yet a book that is thoroughly engaged in the ongoing political struggle, a reflection of the author's own radically Leninist political experience (among other things, Lukács was a minister of cultural affairs in the short-lived Hungarian Communist government of Bela Kun in 1919).[4]

The paradox is thus that, with regard to 'standard' Frankfurt School Western Marxism, *History and Class Consciousness* is at the same time much more openly politically engaged *and* philosophically much more speculative-Hegelian in character (see the notion of proletariat as the subject-object of history, a notion towards which members of the Frankfurt School always retained an uneasy distance) – if there ever was a philosopher of Leninism, of the Leninist party, it is the early Marxist Lukács who went to the very limit in this direction, up to defending the 'undemocratic' features of the first year of the Soviet power against Rosa Luxemburg's famous criticism, accusing her of 'fetishizing' formal democracy, instead of treating it as one of the possible strategies to be endorsed or rejected with regard to the demands of a concrete revolutionary situation.[5] And what one should avoid today is precisely the temptation to obliterate this aspect, thereby reducing Lukács to a gentrified and depoliticized cultural critic, warning about 'reification' and 'instrumental reason', motifs long ago appropriated even by the conservative critics of 'consumer society'.

So, precisely as the originating text of Western Marxism, *History and Class Consciousness* occupies the position of an exception, confirming yet again Schelling's notion that 'the beginning is the negation of that which begins with it'.[6] In what is this exceptional state grounded? In the mid-1920s, what Alain Badiou calls the 'Event of 1917' began to exhaust its potential, and the process took a Thermidorian turn.[7] This term is to be conceived of not only in the usual Trotskyist way (the betrayal of the revolution by a new bureaucratic class), but also in the strict sense elaborated by Badiou: as the cessation of the Event, as the betrayal not of a certain social group and/or their interests, but of the fidelity to the (revolutionary) Event itself. From the Thermidorian perspective, the Event and its consequences became unreadable, 'irrational', dismissed as a bad dream of the collective plunge into madness – 'we were all caught in a strange destructive vortex . . .'

What then happened with the saturation of what Badiou calls the 'revolutionary sequence of 1917' is that a direct theoretico-political engagement like that of Lukács in *History and Class Consciousness* became impossible. The socialist movement definitively split into social-democratic parliamentary reformism and the new Stalinist orthodoxy, while Western Marxism, which abstained from openly endorsing either of these two poles, abandoned the stance of direct political engagement and turned into a part of the established academic machine whose tradition runs from the early Frankfurt School up to cultural studies today – therein resides the key difference that separates it from the Lukács of the 1920s. On the other hand, Soviet philosophy gradually assumed the form of 'dialectical materialism' as the legitimizing ideology of 'Really Existing Socialism' – one of the signs of the gradual rise of Thermidorian Soviet orthodoxy in philosophy is precisely the series of vicious attacks on Lukács and his theoretical colleague Karl Korsch, whose *Marxism and Philosophy* is a kind of companion piece to *History and Class Consciousness*, even to the extent of being published in the same year (1923).[8] The watershed for this development was the Fifth Congress of the Comintern in 1924, the first congress after Lenin's death, and simultaneously the first after it became clear that the era of revolutionary agitation in Europe was over and that socialism would have to survive in Russia on its own.[9] In his famous intervention at this Congress, Zinoviev afforded himself a rabble-rousing anti-intellectualist attack on the 'ultra-leftist' deviations of Lukács, Korsch and other 'professors', as he contemptuously referred to them, supporting Lukács' Hungarian Party companion László Rudas in the latter's critical rejection of Lukács' 'revisionism'. Afterwards, the main criticism of Lukács and Korsch originated in Abram Deborin and his philosophical school, at that time predominant in the Soviet Union (although later purged as 'idealist Hegelian'), who were the first systematically to develop the notion of Marxist philosophy as a universal dialectical method, elaborating general laws which can then be applied either to natural or to social phenomena – Marxist dialectics was thus deprived of its directly engaged, practical-revolutionary attitude, and turned into a general epistemological theory dealing with the universal laws of scientific knowledge.

As was noted already by Korsch in the aftermath of these debates, their crucial feature was that critiques from the Comintern and those from the 'revisionist' social-democratic circles, officially sworn enemies, basically repeated the *same* counter-arguments, being disturbed by the same theses in Lukács and Korsch, denouncing their 'subjectivism' (the practical-engaged character of Marxist theory, and so on). Such a position was no longer admissible at a time when Marxism was changing into a state ideology whose ultimate *raison d'être* was to provide the after-the-fact legitimation for the pragmatic political party decisions in the ahistorical ('universal') laws of dialectics. Symptomatic here was the sudden rehabilitation of the notion that dialectical materialism was the 'world-view [*Weltanschauung*] of the working class': for Lukács and Korsch, as well as for Marx, a 'world-view' by definition designates the 'contemplative' stance of ideology with which Marxist revolutionary engaged theory has to break.

Evert Van der Zweerde developed in detail the ideological functioning of the Soviet philosophy of dialectical materialism as the 'scientific world-view of the working class':[10] although it was a self-proclaimed ideology, the catch is that it was not the ideology it claimed to be – it did not motivate, but rather legitimated political acts; it was not to be believed in, but ritualistically enacted; the point of its claim to be 'scientific ideology' and thus the 'correct reflection' of social circumstances was to preclude the possibility that there could still be in Soviet society a 'normal' ideology which 'reflected' social reality in a 'wrong' way; and so on. We thus totally miss the point if we treat the infamous 'diamat' as a genuine philosophical system: it was an instrument of power legitimation to be enacted ritualistically and, as such, to be located in the context of the thick cobweb of power relations. Emblematic here are the different fates of I. Ilyenkov and P. Losev, two prototypes of Russian philosophy under socialism. Losev was the author of the last book published in the Soviet Union (in 1929) that openly rejected Marxism (discarding dialectical materialism as 'obvious nonsense'); however, after a short prison term, he was allowed to pursue his academic career and, during the Second World War, even started lecturing again – the 'formula' of his survival was that he withdrew into the history of philosophy (aesthetics) as a specialist scientific discipline, focusing on ancient Greek and Roman authors. Under the guise of reporting on and interpreting past thinkers, especially Plotinus and other neo-Platonists, he was thus able to smuggle in his own spiritualist mystical theses while, in the introductions to his books, paying lip service to the official ideology by a quote or two from Khrushchev or Brezhnev. In this way, Losev survived all of the vicissitudes of socialism and lived to see the end of Communism, hailed as the grand old man of the authentic Russian spiritual heritage! In contrast to Losev, the problem with Ilyenkov, a superb dialectician and expert on Hegel, was that he was the eerie figure of a sincere Marxist–Leninist; for that reason (i.e., because he wrote in a personally engaging way, endeavouring to elaborate Marxism as a serious philosophy, not merely as a legitimizing set of ritualistic formulae), he was gradually excommunicated and finally driven to suicide – was there ever a better lesson on how an ideology effectively functions?[11]

In the gesture of a personal Thermidor, Lukács himself, in the early 1930s, withdrew and turned to the more specialized areas of Marxist aesthetics and literary theory, justifying his public support of Stalinist politics in the terms of the Hegelian critique of the Beautiful Soul: the Soviet Union, including all its unexpected hardships, was the outcome of the October Revolution, so, instead of condemning it from the comfortable position of the Beautiful Soul keeping its hands clean, one should bravely 'recognize the heart in the cross of the present' – Adorno was fully justified in sarcastically designating this Lukács as someone who misread the clatter of his chains for the triumphant march forward of World Spirit, and, consequently, endorsed the 'extorted reconciliation' between the individual and society in the East European Communist countries.[12]

II

This fate of Lukács nonetheless confronts us with the difficult problem of the emergence of Stalinism: it is too easy to contrast the authentic revolutionary *élan* of the 'Event of 1917' with its later Stalinist Thermidor – the true problem is 'how did we get from there to here?' As Alain Badiou has emphasized, the great task today is to think the necessity of the passage from Leninism to Stalinism without denying the tremendous emancipatory potential of the Event of October, i.e., without falling into the old liberal babble of the 'totalitarian' potential of radical emancipatory politics, on account of which every revolution must end up in a repression worse than that of the old overthrown social order. The challenge to be faced here is the following one: while conceding that the rise of Stalinism was the inherent result of the Leninist revolutionary logic (not the result of some particular external corruptive influence, like the 'Russian backwardness' or the 'Asiatic' ideological stance of its masses), one should nonetheless stick to a concrete analysis of the logic of the political process and, at any price, avoid recourse to some immediate quasi-anthropological or philosophical general notion like 'instrumental reason'. The moment we endorse this gesture, Stalinism loses its specificity, its specific political dynamic, and turns into just another example of this general notion (the gesture exemplified by Heidegger's famous remark, from his *Introduction to Metaphysics*, that, from the epochal historical view, Russian communism and Americanism are 'metaphysically the same'[13]).

Within Western Marxism, it was, of course, Adorno and Horkheimer's *Dialectic of Enlightenment*, as well as Horkheimer's later numerous essays on the 'critique of instrumental reason', that accomplished this fateful shift from concrete socio-political analysis to philosophico-anthropological generalization, the shift by means of which the reifying 'instrumental reason' is no longer grounded in concrete capitalist social relations, but itself almost imperceptibly becomes their quasi-transcendental 'principle' or 'foundation'.[14] Strictly correlative to this shift is the almost total absence of theoretical confrontation with Stalinism in the Frankfurt School, in clear contrast to its permanent obsession with fascist anti-Semitism. The very exceptions to this rule are telling: Franz Neumann's *Behemoth*,[15] a study of National Socialism which, in the typical fashionable style of the late 1930s and early 1940s, suggested that the three great world systems – the emerging New Deal capitalism, fascism and Stalinism – tend towards the same bureaucratic, globally organized, 'administered' society; Herbert Marcuse's *Soviet Marxism*,[16] his least passionate and arguably worst book, a strangely neutral analysis of the Soviet ideology with no clear commitments; and, finally, attempts by some Habermasians who, reflecting upon the emerging dissident phenomenon, have endeavoured to elaborate the notion of civil society as a site of resistance to the Communist régime – a position that is interesting politically, but far from offering a satisfactory global theory of the specificity of Stalinist 'totalitarianism'. The standard excuse – that authors in the Frankfurt School did not want to oppose Communism too openly because, in so doing, they would play into the hands of their domestic Cold Warriors – is obviously insufficient: the point is not that this fear of being placed in the service of official anti-Communism proves how they were secretly pro-Communist, but rather the opposite: if they were *really* cornered as to where they stood with respect to the Cold War, they would have chosen Western liberal democracy (as Max Horkheimer explicitly did in some of his late writings). It was *this* ultimate solidarity with the Western system when it was really threatened that they were somehow ashamed to acknowledge publicly, in clear symmetry to the stance of the 'critical democratic socialist opposition' in the German Democratic Republic, whose members criticized Party rule, but, the moment the situation became really serious and the socialist system was threatened, publicly supported the system (Brecht apropos of East Berlin workers' demonstrations in 1953, and Christa Wolf apropos of the Prague Spring in 1968). 'Stalinism' (that is, Really Existing Socialism) was thus, for the Frankfurt School, a traumatic topic apropos of which it *had* to remain silent – this silence was the only way for them to retain the inconsistency of their position of underlying solidarity with Western liberal democracy, without losing their official guise of 'radical' leftist critique. Openly acknowledging this solidarity would have deprived them of their 'radical' aura, changing them into yet another version of Cold War anti-Communist leftist liberals, while showing too much sympathy for Really Existing Socialism would have forced them to betray their unacknowledged basic commitment.

It is difficult not to be surprised by the unconvincing, 'flat' character of the standard anti-Communist accounts of Stalinism with their references to the 'totalitarian' character of radical emancipatory politics, and so on – today, more than ever, one should insist that only a Marxist dialectical-materialist account can effectively explain the rise of Stalinism. While, of course, this task is far beyond the scope of the present essay, one is tempted to risk a brief preliminary remark. Every Marxist recalls Lenin's claim, from his *Philosophical Notebooks*, that no one who has not read and studied in detail Hegel's entire *Science of Logic* can really understand Marx's *Capital* – along the same lines, one is tempted to claim that no one who has not read and studied in detail the chapters on judgement and syllogism from Hegel's *Logic* can grasp the emergence of Stalinism. That is to say, the logic of this emergence can perhaps best be grasped as the succession of the three forms of syllogistic mediation, which vaguely fit the triad of Marxism–Leninism–Stalinism. The three mediated terms (Universal, Particular and Singular) are History (the global historical movement), the proletariat (the particular class with a privileged relationship to the Universal) and the Communist Party (the singular agent). In the first, classical Marxist form of their mediation, the Party mediates between History and proletariat: its action enables the 'empirical' working class to become aware of its historical mission inscribed into its very social position and to act accordingly, i.e., to become a revolutionary subject. The accent is here on the 'spontaneous' revolutionary stance of the proletariat: the Party only acts in a maieutic role, rendering possible the purely formal conversion of the proletariat from Class-in-Itself to Class-for-Itself.

However, as always in Hegel, the 'truth' of this mediation is that, in the course of its movement, its starting point, the presupposed identity, is falsified. In the first form, this presupposed identity is that between proletariat and History, i.e., the notion that the revolutionary mission of universal liberation is inscribed in the very objective social condition of the proletariat as the 'universal class', the class whose true particular interests overlap with the universal interests of humanity – the third term, the Party, is merely the operator of the actualization of this universal potential of the particular. What becomes palpable in the course of this mediation is that the proletariat can 'spontaneously' achieve only trade-unionist reformist awareness, so we come to the (supposedly) Leninist conclusion: the constitution of the revolutionary subject is possible only when (those who will become) Party intellectuals gain insight into the inner logic of the historical process and accordingly 'educate' the proletariat.[17] In this second form, the proletariat is thus diminished to the role of the mediator between History (global historical process) and the scientific knowledge about it embodied in the Party: after gaining insight into the logic of historical process, the Party 'educates' workers into being the willing instrument of the realization of the historical goal. The presupposed identity in this second form is that between Universal and Singular, between History and the Party, i.e., the notion that the Party as the 'collective intellectual' possesses effective knowledge of the historical process. This presupposition is best rendered by the overlapping of the 'subjective' and the 'objective' aspects: the notion of History as an objective process determined by necessary laws is strictly correlative to the notion of Party intellectuals as the Subject whose privileged knowledge of, and insight into, this process allows it to intervene and direct it. And, as one might expect, it is this presupposition that is falsified in the course of the second mediation, bringing us to the third, 'Stalinist', form of mediation, the 'truth' of the entire movement, in which the Universal (History itself) mediates between the proletariat and the Party: to put it in somewhat simplistic terms, the Party merely uses the reference to History – that is, its doctrine, 'dialectical and historical materialism', embodying its privileged access to the 'inexorable necessity of historical progress' – in order to legitimate its actual domination over and exploitation of the working class, that is, to provide opportunistic pragmatic Party decisions with a kind of 'ontological cover'.[18]

To put it in the terms of the speculative coincidence of the opposites, or of the 'infinite judgement' in which the highest coincides with the lowest, the fact that Soviet workers were awakened early in the morning by music from loudspeakers playing the first chords of the *Internationale*, whose words are, 'Arise, you prisoners of work!', is granted a deeper ironic meaning: the ultimate 'truth' of the pathetic original meaning of these words ('Resist, break the chains that constrain you and reach for freedom!') turns out to be its literal meaning, the call to tired workers, 'Get up, slaves, and start working for us, the Party *nomenklatura*!'

III

So, back to the triple syllogistic mediation of History, the proletariat and the Party: if each form of mediation is the 'truth' of the preceding one (the Party that instrumentalizes the working class as the means to realize its goal, founded on insight into the logic of historical progress, is the 'truth' of the notion that the Party merely enables the proletariat to become aware of its historical mission, that it only enables it to discover its 'true interest'; the Party ruthlessly exploiting working classes is the 'truth' of the notion that the Party just realizes through them its profound insight into the logic of History), does this mean that this movement is inexorable, that we are dealing with an iron logic on account of which, the moment we endorse the starting point – the premise that the proletariat is, as to its social position, potentially the 'universal class' – we are caught, with a diabolic compulsion, in a process that ends with the gulag? If this were the case, *History and Class Consciousness*, in spite of (or, rather, on account of) its intellectual brilliance, would be the founding text of Stalinism, and the standard postmodernist dismissal of this book as the ultimate manifestation of Hegelian essentialism, as well as Althusser's identification of Hegelianism as the secret philosophical core of Stalinism – the teleological necessity of the progress of History towards the proletarian revolution as its great turning point, in which the proletariat, as the historical Subject-Object, the 'universal class' enlightened by the Party about the mission inscribed into its very objective social position, accomplishes the self-transparent act of liberation – would be fully justified. The violent reaction of the partisans of 'dialectical materialism' against *History and Class Consciousness* would again be an example of Lucien Goldmann's rule of the way that the ruling ideology must necessarily disavow its true fundamental premises: in this perspective, the Lukácsian megalomaniac Hegelian notion of the Leninist Party as the embodiment of the historical Spirit, as the 'collective intellectual' of the proletariat *qua* absolute Subject-Object of History, would be the hidden 'truth' of the apparently more modest 'objectivist' Stalinist account of revolutionary activity as grounded in a global ontological process dominated by universal dialectical laws. And, of course, it would be easy to play against this Hegelian notion of Subject-Object the basic deconstructionist premise that the subject emerges precisely in/as the *gap* in Substance (objective Order of Things), that there is subjectivity only in so far as there is a 'crack in the edifice of Being', only in so far as the universe is in a way 'derailed', 'out of joint', in short, that not only does the full actualization of the subject always fail, but that what Lukács would have dismissed as a 'defective' mode of subjectivity, as a thwarted subject, is effectively the subject itself.

The Stalinist 'objectivist' account would thus also be the 'truth' of *History and Class Consciousness* for strictly inherent philosophical reasons: since the subject is failed by definition, its full actualization as the Subject-Object of History necessarily entails its self-cancellation, its self-objectivization as the instrument of History. And, furthermore, it would be easy to assert, against this Hegelian–Stalinist deadlock, the Laclauian postmodern assertion of radical contingency as the very terrain of (political) subjectivity: political universals are 'empty', the link between them and the particular content that hegemonizes them is what is at stake in an ideological struggle, which is thoroughly contingent; in other words, no political subject has its universal mission written into its 'objective' social condition.

Is, however, this actually the case with *History and Class Consciousness?* Can Lukács be dismissed as the advocate of such a pseudo-Hegelian assertion of the proletariat as the absolute Subject-Object of History? Let us return to the concrete political background of *History and Class Consciousness*, in which Lukács continues to speak as a fully engaged revolutionary. To put it in somewhat rough and simplified terms, the choice, for the revolutionary forces in the Russia of 1917, in the difficult situation in which the bourgeoisie was not able to bring to fruition the democratic revolution, was the following one.

On the one hand, the Menshevik stance was that of obedience to the logic of the 'objective stages of development': first the democratic revolution, then the proletarian revolution. In the whirlpool of 1917, instead of capitalizing on the gradual disintegration of state apparatuses and building on the widespread popular discontent and resistance against the provisional government, all radical parties must resist the temptation to push the movement too far and rather join forces with democratic bourgeois elements in order first to achieve the democratic revolution, waiting patiently for the 'mature' revolutionary situation. From this point, a socialist take-over in 1917, when the situation was not yet 'ripe', would trigger a regression to primitive terror. (Although this fear of the catastrophic terrorist consequences of a 'premature' uprising may seem to augur the shadow of Stalinism, the ideology of Stalinism effectively marks a *return* to this 'objectivist' logic of the necessary stages of development.)[19]

On the other hand, the Leninist stance was to take a leap, throwing oneself into the paradox of the situation, seizing the opportunity and intervening, even if the situation was 'premature', with a wager that this very 'premature' intervention would radically change the 'objective' relationship of forces itself, within which the initial situation appeared as 'premature', that is, that it would undermine the very standards with reference to which the situation was judged as 'premature'.

Here, one must be careful not to miss the point: it is not that, in contrast to Mensheviks and sceptics among the Bolsheviks themselves, Lenin thought that the complex situation of 1917 – that is, the growing dissatisfaction of the broad masses with the irresolute politics of the provisional government – offered a unique chance of 'jumping over' one phase (the democratic bourgeois revolution), of 'condensing' the two necessary consecutive stages (democratic bourgeois revolution and proletarian revolution) into one. Such a notion still accepts the fundamental underlying objectivist 'reified' logic of 'necessary stages of development'; it merely allows for the different rhythm of its course in different concrete circumstances (in other words, that in some countries, the second stage can immediately follow the first one). In contrast to this, Lenin's point is much stronger: ultimately, there is no objective logic of 'necessary stages of development', since 'complications' arising from the intricate texture of concrete situations and/or from the unanticipated results of 'subjective' interventions always derail the straight course of things. As Lenin was keen on observing, the fact of colonialism and of the super-exploited masses in Asia, Africa and Latin America radically affects and 'displaces' the 'straight' class struggle in developed capitalist countries – to speak about 'class struggle' without taking into account colonialism is an empty abstraction which, translated into practical politics, can result only in condoning the 'civilizing' role of colonialism and thus, by subordinating the anti-colonialist struggle of the Asian masses to the 'true' class struggle in developed Western states, *de facto* accepts that the bourgeoisie defines the terms of class struggle.[20] One is tempted to resort here to Lacanian terms: what is at stake in this alternative is the (in)existence of the 'big Other': the Mensheviks relied on the all-embracing foundation of the positive logic of historical development, while the Bolsheviks (Lenin, at least) were aware that 'the big Other doesn't exist' – a political intervention proper does not occur within the coordinates of some underlying global matrix, since what it achieves is precisely the 'reshuffling' of this very global matrix.

This, then, is the reason for Lukács' high admiration for Lenin: his Lenin was the one who, apropos of the split in Russian social democracy between Bolsheviks and Mensheviks, when the two factions fought over the precise formulation of who could be a Party member as defined by the Party Programme, wrote: 'Sometimes, the fate of the entire working-class movement for long years to come can be decided by a word or two in the party programme.' Or the Lenin who, when he saw the chance for the revolutionary take-over in late 1917, said: 'History will never forgive us if we miss this opportunity!' At a more general level, the history of capitalism is a long history of the way that the predominant ideologico-political framework was able to accommodate – and soften the subversive edge of – the movements and demands that seemed to threaten its very survival. For example, for a long time, sexual libertarians thought that monogamic sexual repression was necessary for the survival of capitalism – we now know that capitalism can not only tolerate, but even actively incite and exploit, forms of 'perverse' sexuality, not to mention promiscuous indulgence in sexual pleasures. However, the conclusion to be drawn from this is *not* that capitalism has the endless ability to integrate and thus cut off the subversive edge of all particular demands – the question of *timing*, of 'seizing the moment', is crucial here. A certain particular demand possesses, at a specific moment, a global detonating power; it functions as a metaphoric stand-in for the global revolution: if we unconditionally insist on it, the system will explode; if, however, we wait too long, the metaphorical short-circuit between this particular demand and the global overthrow is dissolved, and the system can, with sneering hypocritical satisfaction, reply in turn, 'You wanted this? Here, have it!', without anything truly radical happening. The art of what Lukács called *Augenblick* – the moment when, briefly, there is an opening for an act to intervene in a situation – is the art of seizing the right moment, of aggravating the conflict before the system can accommodate itself to our demand. So we have here a Lukács who is much more 'Gramscian' and conjuncturalist than is usually assumed – the Lukácsian *Augenblick* is unexpectedly close to what, today, Alain Badiou endeavours to formulate as the Event: an intervention that cannot be accounted for in terms of its pre-existing 'objective conditions'. The crux of Lukács' argumentation is to reject the reduction of the act to its 'historical circumstances': there are no neutral 'objective conditions', or, in Hegelese, all presuppositions are already minimally posited.

Exemplary here is, at the very beginning of *Tailism and the Dialectic*, Lukács' analysis of the 'objectivist' enumeration of the causes of the failure of the Hungarian revolutionary council-dictatorship in 1919: the treason of the officers in the army, the external blockade that caused hunger . . .[21] Although these are undoubtedly facts that played a crucial role in this revolutionary defeat, it is none the less methodologically wrong to evoke them as raw facts, without taking into account the way they were 'mediated' by the specific constellation of 'subjective' political forces. Take the blockade: why was it that, in contrast to the even stronger blockade of the Russian Soviet State, the latter did not succumb to the imperialist and counter-revolutionary onslaught? Because, in Russia, the Bolshevik Party made the masses aware of how this blockade was the result of foreign and domestic counter-revolutionary forces, while, in Hungary, the Party was ideologically not strong enough, so that the working masses succumbed to anti-Communist propaganda, which claimed that the blockade was the result of the 'anti-democratic' nature of the régime – the logic of 'let's return to "democracy" and foreign aid will start to flow in . . .'. What about the treason of the officers? Yes, but why did similar treason not lead to the same catastrophic consequences in Soviet Russia? And, when traitors were discovered, why was it not possible to replace them with reliable cadres? Because the Hungarian Communist Party was not strong and active enough, while the Russian Bolshevik Party mobilized properly the soldiers who were ready to fight to the end to defend the revolution. Of course, one can claim that the weakness of the Communist Party is again an 'objective' component of the social situation; however, behind this 'fact', there are again other subjective decisions and acts, so that we never reach the zero level of a purely 'objective' state of things – the ultimate point is not objectivity, but social 'totality' as the process of the global 'mediation' between the subjective and the objective aspects. In other words, the act cannot ever be reduced to an outcome of objective conditions.

To take an example from a different domain, the way an ideology involves 'positing its presuppositions' is also easily discernible in the standard (pseudo-) explanation for the growing acceptance of Nazi ideology in Germany in the 1920s: that the Nazis were deftly manipulating ordinary middle-class people's fears and anxieties generated by the economic crisis and rapid social changes. The problem with this explanation is that it overlooks the self-referential circularity at work here: yes, the Nazis certainly did deftly manipulate fears and anxieties – however, far from being simple pre-ideological facts, these fears and anxieties were already the product of a certain ideological perspective. In other words, Nazi ideology itself (co)generated the 'anxieties and fears' against which it then proposed itself as a solution.

IV

We can now return, once again, to our triple 'syllogism' and determine wherein, precisely, resides its mistake: in the very opposition between its first two forms. Lukács, of course, was opposed to the 'spontaneist' ideology of advocating the autonomous grass-roots self-organization of the working masses against the externally imposed 'dictatorship' of Party bureaucrats, as well as to the pseudo-Leninist (actually Kautsky's) notion that the 'empirical' working class can, on its own, only reach the level of trade-unionist reformism, and that the only way for it to become the revolutionary subject is that independent intellectuals gain neutral 'scientific' insight into the 'objective' necessity of the passage from capitalism to socialism, and then import this knowledge into the empirical working class, 'educating' them about the mission inscribed into their very objective social position. It is here that we encounter the opprobrious dialectical 'identity of opposites' at its purest: the problem with these oppositions is not that the two poles are too crudely opposed and that the truth is somewhere in between, in their 'dialectical mediation' (class consciousness emerges from the 'interaction' between the spontaneous self-awareness of the working class and the educational activity of the Party); the problem is rather that the very notion that the working class has the inner potential to reach adequate revolutionary class consciousness (and, consequently, that the Party merely plays a modest, self-erasing, maieutic role of enabling the empirical workers to actualize this potential) legitimizes the Party's exertion of dictatorial pressure over the 'empirical', actually existing workers and their confused, opportunistic self-awareness, in the name of (the Party's correct insight into) what their true inner potentials and/or their 'true long-term interests' in fact are. In short, Lukács is here simply applying the Hegelian speculative identification of the 'inner potential' of an individual with the external pressure exerted on him by his educators to the false opposition between 'spontaneism' and external Party domination: to say that an individual possesses 'inner potential' to be a great musician is strictly equivalent to the fact that this potential has to be already present in the educator who, through external pressure, will compel the individual to actualize it.

So the paradox is that the more we insist on the way that a revolutionary stance directly translates the true 'inner nature' of the working class, the more we are compelled to exert external pressure on the 'empirical' working class to actualize this inner possibility. In other words, the 'truth' of this immediate identity of opposites, of the first two forms, is, as we have seen, the third form, the Stalinist mediation – why? Because this immediate identity precludes any place for the *act* proper: if class consciousness arises 'spontaneously', as the actualization of inner potential inscribed into the very objective situation of the working class, then there is no real act at all, just the purely formal conversion from in-itself to for-itself, the gesture of bringing to light what was always-already there; if the proper revolutionary class consciousness is to be 'imported' via the Party, then we have, on the one hand, 'neutral' intellectuals who gain 'objective' insight into historical necessity (without engaged *intervention* into it), and then what is ultimately their instrumental-manipulative use of the working class as a tool to actualize the necessity already written into the situation – again, no place for an *act* proper.

This notion of the act also enables us to deal with the feature that seems fully to justify the critical dismissal of Lukács as a determinist 'Hegelian' Marxist: his ill-famed distinction between empirical, factual, class consciousness (a phenomenon of collective psychology to be established via positive sociological research) and 'attributed/ascribed/imputed [*zugerechnete*]' class consciousness (consciousness that it is 'objectively possible' for a certain class to achieve if it fully mobilizes its subjective resources). As Lukács emphasizes, this opposition is not simply the opposition between truth and falsity: in contrast to all other classes, it is 'objectively possible' for the proletariat to achieve the self-consciousness which allows it correct insight into the true logic of the historical totality – it depends on the mobilization of its subjective potential through the Party to what extent the factual working class will reach the level of this 'ascribed' class consciousness. In contrast to the proletariat, the 'imputed' consciousness of all other classes, although it also reaches beyond their factual consciousness, is not yet the true insight into historical totality, but remains an ideological distortion (Lukács refers here to Marx's well-known analysis of the French Revolution of 1848, in which the cause of Napoleon III's 'Eighteenth Brumaire' was that the radical bourgeoisie did not even fully actualize its own progressive political potential). The reproach imposes itself here almost automatically: does not Lukács himself implicitly regress to the Kantian opposition between ideal formal possibility and the empirical factual state of things that always lags behind this ideal? And is not implicit in this lag the justification for the domination of the Party over the working class: the Party is ultimately precisely the mediator between the 'imputed' and the factual consciousness – it knows the potential ideal consciousness and endeavours to 'educate' the empirical working class to reach this level? If this were all that Lukács meant by 'subjective mediation', by act and decision, then, of course, we would still remain within the confines of a 'reified' reliance on the 'objective stages of development': there is the prescribed ideal-typical limit of what is 'objectively possible', the limit of the 'ascribed' consciousness determined by the objective social position of a class, and the entire manoeuvring space that is left for historical agents is the gap between this 'objectively possible' maximum and the extent to which they effectively approach this maximum.

There, is, however, another possibility open to us: to read the gap between factual and 'imputed' class consciousness not as the standard opposition between the ideal type and its factual blurred actualization, but as the inner self-fissure (or 'out-of-jointness') of the historical subject. To be more precise, when one speaks of the proletariat as the 'universal class', one should bear in mind the strictly dialectical notion of universality which becomes actual, 'for itself', only in the guise of its opposite, in an agent who is out-of-place in any particular position within the existing global order and thus entertains towards it a negative relationship – let me quote here Ernesto Laclau's apposite formulation (thoroughly Hegelian notwithstanding Laclau's declared anti-Hegelianism):

> The universal is part of my identity in so far as I am penetrated by a constitutive lack – that is, in so far as my differential identity has failed in its process of constitution. The universal emerges out of the particular not as some principle underlying and explaining it, but as an incomplete horizon suturing a dislocated particular identity.[22]

In this precise sense, as he says in the same paper, 'the universal is the symbol of a missing fullness': I can relate to the Universal as such only in so far as my particular identity is thwarted, 'dislocated', only in so far as some impediment prevents me from 'becoming what I already am' (with regard to my particular social position). The claim that the proletariat is the 'universal class' is thus ultimately equivalent to the claim that, within the existing global order, the proletariat is the class that is radically dislocated (or, as Badiou would have put it, occupying the point of 'symptomal torsion') with regard to the social body: while other classes can still maintain the illusion that 'Society exists', and that they have their specific place within the global social body, the very existence of the proletariat repudiates the claim that 'Society exists'. In other words, the overlapping of the Universal and the Particular in the proletariat does not stand for their immediate identity (in the sense that the particular interests of the proletariat are at the same time the universal interests of humanity, so that proletarian liberation will be equivalent to the liberation of the entire humanity): the universal revolutionary potential is rather 'inscribed into the very being of the proletariat' as its inherent radical split. This split, again, is not the immediate split between the particular interests/positions of the proletariat and its universal historical mission – the 'universal mission' of the proletariat arises from the way that the very particular existence of the proletariat is 'barred', hindered, from the way that proletariat is *a priori* ('in its very notion', to put it in Hegelese) not able to realize its *particular* social identity. The split is thus the split between the particular positive identity and the barrier, inherent blockage, that prevents proletarians from actualizing this very particular positive identity (their 'place in society') – only if we conceive of the split in this way, is there a space for the act proper, not merely for actions that follow universal 'principles' or 'rules' given in advance – and thus providing the 'ontological cover' for our activity.

Therein resides the ultimate difference between, on the one hand, the authentic Leninist Party, and, on the other hand, the Kautskyist–Stalinist Party as embodying the non-engaged 'objective knowledge' that is to be imparted to the uneducated working class: the Kautskyist–Stalinist Party addresses the proletariat from a position of 'objective' knowledge intended to supplement the proletarian subjective (self-) experience of suffering and exploitation, i.e., the split here is the split between proletarian 'spontaneous' subjective self-experience and objective knowledge about one's social situation, while, in an authentic Leninist Party, the split is thoroughly subjective, i.e., the Party addresses the proletariat from a radically subjective, engaged position of the lack that prevents the proletarians from achieving their 'proper place' in the social edifice.[23] And, furthermore, it is this crucial difference that also explains why the Stalinist sublime body of the Leader (with mausoleums and all the accompanying theatrics) is unthinkable within the strict Leninist horizon: the Leader can be elevated into a figure of Sublime Beauty only when the 'people', whom he represents, is no longer the thoroughly dislocated proletariat, but the positively existing substantial entity, the 'working masses'.

To those whose reaction here is that what we are describing now is a hair-splitting philosophical distinction of no use to engaged fighters, let us recall a similar experience with Kant's practical philosophy: is it not that Kant's apparently 'difficult' propositions on the pure form of Law as the only legitimate motif of an ethical act, and so on, suddenly become clear if we directly relate them to our immediate ethical experience? The same goes for the above-mentioned distinction: the gap that separates reliance on 'objective logic' from the risk of an authentic act is 'intuitively' known to anyone engaged in a struggle.

V

At this point, a further possible misunderstanding must be clarified: Lukács' position is not, as it may appear to a superficial reader, that the whole of history hitherto was dominated by 'reified' objective necessity, and that it is only with the late capitalist crisis, and the concomitant strengthening of the revolutionary proletarian stance, that the 'objective possibility' arises for the all-encompassing chain of necessity to be broken. All human history is characterized by the dialectical tension and interdependence between necessity and contingency; what one should be careful about is to distinguish different historical shapes of this interdependence. In pre-modern society, it was, of course, not only possible – it effectively happened all the time – that totally meaningless contingencies (the madness or some other psychological peculiarity of the monarch) could lead to global catastrophic consequences (like the utter destruction of rich and highly civilized Arab cities by the Mongols); however, psychological idiosyncrasies could have such consequences only within certain well-defined power relations and relations of production in which so much authority is effectively invested in the leader. In modern capitalist society, contingency reigns in the guise of the 'unpredictable' interplay of market forces, which can, 'for no apparent reason at all', instantly ruin individuals who worked hard all their lives: as Marx and Engels already put it, the Market is the modern reincarnation of ancient capricious Fate;[24] in other words, this 'contingency' is the form of appearance of its dialectical obverse, the impenetrable blind necessity of the capitalist system. Finally, in the revolutionary process, the space is open, not for a metaphysical foundational 'act', but for a contingent, strictly 'conjunctural', intervention that can break the very chain of necessity dominating all history hitherto.

Exemplary here is Lukács' critique of the liberal sceptical attitude towards the October Revolution, which is regarded as an important, but risky, 'political experiment': the position is that of 'let's wait and patiently observe its final outcome . . .'. As Lukács was fully justified to retort, such an attitude transposes the experimental/observational stance of natural sciences on to human history: it is the exemplary case of observing a process from a safe distance, exempting oneself from it, not of the engaged stance of someone who – as always-already caught, embedded, in a situation – intervenes in it. Of course, Lukács' key point here is that we are not dealing with a simple opposition between the stance of impassive observation and that of practical intervention ('enough of words and empty theories, let's finally do something!'): Lukács advocates the dialectical unity/mediation of theory and practice, in which even the utmost contemplative stance is eminently 'practical' (in the sense of being embedded in the totality of social [re]production and thus expressing a certain 'practical' stance of how to survive within this totality), and, on the other hand, even the most 'practical' stance implies a certain 'theoretical' framework; it materializes a set of implicit ideological propositions.[25] For example, the resigned 'melancholic' stance of searching for the meaning of life in withdrawn contemplative wisdom is clearly embedded in the historical totality of a society in decay, in which public space no longer offers an outlet for creative self-affirmation; or, the stance of the external observer who treats social life as an object in which one 'intervenes' in an instrumental-manipulative way and 'makes experiments', is the very stance required for the participation in a market society.[26] On the other hand, the utmost individualistic stance of radical hedonism 'practises' the notion of man as a hedonistic being, that is, as Hegel would have put it, a person is never directly a hedonist, rather he relates himself to himself as one. In classical Marxist terms, not only is social consciousness a constitutive part of social being (of the actual process of social [re]production), but this 'being' itself (the actual process of social [re]production) can run its course only if mediated/sustained by an adequate form of 'consciousness': say, if, in a capitalist society, individuals are, in their daily practical lives, not prey to 'commodity fetishism', the very 'real' process of capitalist (re)production is perturbed. At this point we encounter the crucial Hegelian notion of (self-)consciousness, which designates the gaining of self-awareness as an inherently *practical act*, to be opposed to the contemplative notion of a scientific 'correct insight': self-consciousness is an insight that directly 'changes its object', affects its actual social status – when the proletariat becomes aware of its revolutionary potential, this very 'insight' transforms it into an *actual* revolutionary subject.

In so far as (self-)consciousness designates the way that things appear to the subject, this identity of thought and being in the practical act of self-consciousness can also be formulated as the dialectical identity of Essence and its Appearance. Lukács relies here on Hegel's analysis of the 'essentiality' of appearance: appearance is never 'mere' appearance, but belongs to essence itself. This means that consciousness (ideological appearance) is also an 'objective' social fact with an effectivity of its own: as we have already pointed out, bourgeois 'fetishistic' consciousness is not simply an 'illusion' masking actual social processes, but a mode of organization of the very social being, crucial to the actual process of social (re)production.[27]

Lukács here can be said to participate in the great 'paradigm shift' at work also in quantum physics, and whose main feature is not the dissolution of 'objective reality', its reduction to a 'subjective construction', but, on the contrary, the unheard-of assertion of the 'objective' status of appearance itself. It is not sufficient to oppose the way things 'objectively are' to the way they 'merely appear to us': the way they appear (to the observer) affects their very 'objective being'. This is what is so pathbreaking in quantum physics: the notion that the limited horizon of the observer (or of the mechanism that registers what goes on) determines what effectively goes on. We cannot say that self-awareness (or colour or material density or . . .) designate merely the way we experience reality, while 'objectively' there are only sub-atomic particles and their fluctuations: these 'appearances' have to be taken into account if we are to explain what 'effectively is going on'.[28] In a homologous way, the crux of Lukács' notion of class consciousness is that the way the working class 'appears to itself' determines its 'objective' being.[29]

It is of crucial importance not to misread Lukács' theses as another version of the standard hermeneutical opposition between *Erklären* (the explanatory procedure of the natural sciences) and *Verstehen* (the form of comprehension at work in the human sciences): when Lukács opposes the act of self-consciousness of a historical subject to the 'correct insight' of natural sciences, his point is not to establish an epistemological distinction between two different methodological procedures, but, precisely, to break up the very standpoint of formal 'methodology' and to assert that *knowledge itself is part of social reality*. All knowledge, of nature and of society, is a social process, mediated by society, an 'actual' part of the social structure, and, on account of this self-referential inclusion of knowledge into its own object, a revolutionary theory is ultimately (also) its own meta-theory. Although Lukács was adamantly opposed to psychoanalysis, the parallel with Freud is here striking: in the same way that psychoanalysis interprets the resistance against itself as the result of the very unconscious processes that are its topic, Marxism interprets the resistance against its insights as the 'result of class struggle in theory', as accounted for by its very object – in both cases, theory is caught in a self-referential loop; it is, in a way, the theory about the resistance to itself.

However, a further, even more fateful, misunderstanding would be to read this thesis on the social mediation of every form of knowledge in terms of the standard historicist assertion that each form of knowledge is a social phenomenon, 'a child of its age', dependent upon and expressing the social conditions of its emergence. Lukács' point is precisely to undermine this false alternative of historicist relativism (there is no neutral knowledge of 'objective reality', since all knowledge is biased, embedded in a specific 'social context') and the distinction between the socio-historical conditions and the inherent truth-value of a body of knowledge (even if a certain theory emerged within a specific social context, this context provides only external conditions, which in no way diminish or undermine the 'objective truth' of its propositions – for example, although, as everyone knows, Darwin elaborated his evolutionary theory under the stimulus of Malthus' economics, Darwinism is still acknowledged as true, while Malthus is deservedly half-forgotten). As he put it in *History and Class Consciousness*, the problem of historicism is that it is not 'historicist' enough: it still presupposes an empty external observer's point *for* which and *from* which all that happens is historically relativized.[30] Lukács overcomes this historicist relativization by bringing it to its conclusion, that is, by including in the historical process the observing subject itself, thus undermining the very exempted measure with regard to which everything is relativized: the attainment of self-consciousness of a revolutionary subject is *not* an insight into the ways its own stance is relativized, conditioned by specific historical circumstances, but a practical act of *intervening* into these 'circumstances'.[31] Marxist theory describes society from the engaged standpoint of its revolutionary change and thereby transforms its object (the working class) into a revolutionary subject – the neutral description of society is formally 'false', since it involves the acceptance of the existing order. Far from 'relativizing' the truth of an insight, the awareness of its own embeddedness in a concrete constellation – and thereby of its engaged, partial, character – is a positive condition of its truth.

And therein resides the great achievement of *Tailism and the Dialectic*: Lukács sets the record straight with regard to the possible misreadings of his basic position as articulated in *History and Class Consciousness*, not only against its obvious target, the emerging pseudo-Leninist Soviet orthodoxy that was later sanctified in the guise of Stalinist 'Marxism–Leninism', but – for us today even more importantly – against the already mentioned predominant Western reception of *History and Class Consciousness* focused on the fashionable motif of 'reification'. When, in *Tailism*, Lukács elaborates in detail the passing critical remarks on Engels' notion of the 'dialectics of nature' from *History and Class Consciousness*, he makes it clear that his critique of the 'dialectics of nature' is embedded in a more fundamental critique of the notion of the revolutionary process as determined by the 'objective' laws and stages of historical development. The point of Lukács' polemics against the 'dialectics of nature' is thus not the Kantian abstract-epistemological one (the idea that 'dialectics of nature' misrecognizes the 'subjective mediation' of what appears as natural reality, i.e., the subjective constitution of – what we perceive as – 'reality'), but ultimately a *political* one: the 'dialectics of nature' is problematic because it legitimizes the stance towards the revolutionary process as obeying 'objective laws', leaving no space for the radical contingency of *Augenblick*, for the *act* as a practical intervention irreducible to its 'objective conditions'.

And today, in the era of the worldwide triumph of democracy when (with some notable exceptions like Alain Badiou) no leftist dares to question the premises of democratic politics, it is more crucial than ever to bear in mind Lukács' reminder, in his polemics against Rosa Luxemburg's critique of Lenin, as to the way that the authentic revolutionary stance of endorsing the radical contingency of *Augenblick* should also not endorse the standard opposition between 'democracy' and 'dictatorship' or 'terror'. The first step to make, if we are to leave behind the opposition between liberal-democratic universalism and ethnic/religious fundamentalism on which even today's mass media focus, is to acknowledge the existence of what one is tempted to call 'democratic fundamentalism': the ontologicization of democracy into a depoliticized universal framework that is not itself to be (re)negotiated as the result of politico-ideological hegemonic struggles. Lukács is well aware that the qualification of the 'dictatorship of the proletariat' as the 'democratic rule of the wide working classes, directed only against the narrow circle of ex-ruling classes', is a simplistic sleight of hand: the Bolsheviks, of course, often *did* break the democratic 'rules of the game', we *did* experience the Bolshevik 'Red Terror'.

Democracy as the form of State politics is inherently 'Popperian': the ultimate criterion of democracy is that the régime is 'falsifiable', that is, that a clearly defined public procedure (the popular vote) can establish that the régime is no longer legitimate and must be replaced by another political force. The point is not that this procedure is 'just', but rather that all parties concerned agree in advance and unambiguously upon it irrespective of its 'justice'. In their standard procedure of ideological blackmail, defenders of State democracy claim that the moment we abandon this feature, we enter the 'totalitarian' sphere in which the régime is 'non-falsifiable', that is, it forever avoids the situation of unequivocal 'falsification': whatever happens, even if thousands demonstrate against the régime, the régime continues to maintain that it is legitimate, that it stands for the true interests of the people and that the 'true' people support it . . . Here, we should *reject* this blackmail (as Lukács does apropos of Rosa Luxemburg): there are no 'democratic (procedural) rules' that one is *a priori* prohibited to violate. Revolutionary politics is not a matter of 'opinions', but of the truth on behalf of which one often *is* compelled to disregard the 'opinion of the majority' and to impose the revolutionary will against it. In the difficult times of foreign intervention and civil war after the October Revolution, Trotsky openly admitted that the Bolshevik government was ready sometimes to act against the factual opinion of the majority – not on behalf of a privileged 'insight into objective truth', but on behalf of the very 'subjective' tension between fidelity to the Revolutionary Event and the opportunistic retreat from it, the tension that is inherent to the revolutionary process itself. (Significantly, although Stalinism was factually a much more violent dictatorship, it would never openly acknowledge acting against the opinion of the majority – it always clung to the fetish of the People whose true will the leadership expresses.) The political legacy of Lukács is thus the assertion of the unconditional, 'ruthless' revolutionary will, ready to 'go to the end', effectively to seize power and undermine the existing totality; its wager is that the alternative between authentic rebellion and its later 'ossification' in a New Order is not exhaustive, in other words, that revolutionary effervescence should take the risk of translating its outburst into a New Order. Lenin was right: after the Revolution, the anarchic disruptions of the disciplinary constraints of production should be replaced by an even stronger discipline. Such an assertion is thoroughly opposed to the 'postmodern' celebration of the good 'revolt' as opposed to bad 'revolution', or, in more fashionable terms, of the effervescence of the multitude of marginal 'sites of resistance' against any actual attempt to attack the totality itself (see the mass media's depoliticizing appropriation of May '68 as an 'outburst of spontaneous youthful creativity against the bureaucratized mass society').[32]

As Alain Badiou repeatedly emphasizes, an Event is fragile and rare – so instead of merely focusing on 'how did the October Revolution turn into a Stalinist Thermidor?', we should perhaps turn the question around: is it the Thermidorian forswearing of the Event, the passive following of the course of things, that appears as 'natural' to the human animal? The big question is rather the opposite one: how is it possible that, from time to time, the impossible miracle of an Event does take place at all and leaves traces in the patient work of those who remain faithful to it? So the point is not to 'develop further' Lukács in accordance with the 'demands of new times' (the great motto of all opportunist revisionism, up to New Labour), but to repeat the Event in new conditions. Are we still able to imagine ourselves a historical moment when terms like 'revisionist traitor' were not yet parts of the Stalinist mantra, but expressed an authentic engaged insight?

In other words, the question to be asked today apropos of the unique Event of the early Marxist Lukács is not: 'How does his work stand in relation to today's constellation? Is it still alive?', but, to paraphrase Adorno's well-known reversal of Croce's patronizing historicist question concerning, 'what is dead and what is alive in Hegel's dialectic' (the title of his main work):[33] how do we today stand in relation to – in the eyes of – Lukács? Are we still able to commit the *act* proper, described by Lukács? Which social agent is, on account of its radical dislocation, *today* able to accomplish it?

Notes

A longer version of this essay first appeared as the 'Postface' to Georg Lukács, *A Defence of 'History and Class Consciousness': Tailism and the Dialectic*, trans. Esther Leslie, London and New York: Verso, 2000, pp. 151–82. [eds]

1 See Georg Lukács, *History and Class Consciousness: Studies in Marxist Dialectics*, trans. Rodney Livingstone, Cambridge, MIT Press, 1971. [eds]

2 Martin Heidegger, *Being and Time*, trans. Joan Stambaugh, Albany, State University of New York Press, 1996, p. 397.

3 See Georg Lukács, *Lenin: A Study on the Unity of His Thought*, trans. Nicholas Jacobs, Cambridge, MIT Press, 1971; *Tactics and Ethics: Political Essays, 1919–1929*, trans. Michael McColgan, New York, Harper and Row, 1975; *A Defence of 'History and Class Consciousness': Tailism and the Dialectic*, trans. Esther Leslie, London and New York, Verso, 2000. [eds]

4 *History and Class Consciousness* thus also marks a radical break from the early pre-Marxist Lukács himself, whose main work, *A Theory of the Novel*, belongs to the Weberian tradition of socio-cultural criticism – no wonder that, in this book, he signed his name Georg von Lukács! [See Georg Lukács, *The Theory of the Novel: A Historico-Philosophical Essay*

on the Forms of Great Epic Literature, trans. Anna Bostock, Cambridge, MIT Press, 1971. (eds)]

5   Of course, if one is willing to play alternative history games, one can safely surmise that, if Lenin were to have read *History and Class Consciousness*, he would have rejected its philosophical premises as 'subjectivist' and contrary to 'dialectical materialism' with its 'reflection' theory of knowledge (it is already significant how, in order to maintain his Leninist credentials, Lukács has virtually to ignore Lenin's *Materialism and Empirio-criticism*). On the other hand, in Lenin's entire writings, there is only one mention of Lukács: in 1921, in a brief note for the journal *Kommunismus*, the organ of the Comintern for south-eastern Europe, Lenin intervenes in a debate between Lukács and Bela Kun, ferociously attacking Lukács' text as 'very leftist and very bad. In it, Marxism is present only at a purely verbal level' (see V. I. Lenin, *Complete Works, Volume 41*, Moscow, Progress Publishers, 1969, pp. 135–7). However, this is no way undermines the claim that Lukács is the ultimate philosopher of Leninism: it was rather Lenin himself who was not fully aware of the philosophical stance he 'practised' in his revolutionary work, and who only gradually (through reading Hegel during World War I) became aware of it. The other key question, of course, is: was this misrecognition of one's true philosophical stance necessary for one's political engagement? In other words, does the rule, established already by Lucien Goldmann, in his classic *The Hidden God*, apropos of Pascal and the Jansenists (who were also unacceptable for the ruling Catholic circles), of how the ruling ideology necessarily has to disavow its true fundamental premises, apply also to Leninism? If the answer is 'yes', if the Leninist misrecognition of its philosophical premises is structurally necessary, then Leninism is just another ideology and Lukács' account of it, even if true, is insufficient: it can penetrate to the true philosophical premises of Leninism, but what it cannot explain is the very gap between truth and appearance, i.e., the necessary disavowal of the truth in the false (objectivist, ontological, 'dialectical materialist') Leninist self-consciousness – as Lukács himself knew very well (this is one of the great Hegelian theses of *History and Class Consciousness*), appearance is never merely appearance, but is, precisely as appearance, essential.

6   F. W. J. Schelling, *Sämtliche Werke*, ed. K. F. A. Schelling, Stuttgart, Cotta, 1856–61, Volume 6, p. 600.

7   See Alain Badiou, 'Qu'est-ce qu'un thermidorien?', in *Abrégé de métapolitique*, Paris, Éditions du Seuil, 1998, pp. 139–54.

8   Karl Korsch, *Marxism and Philosophy*, trans. Fred Halliday, London, New Left Books, 1971. [eds]

9   Incidentally, the lesson of these early years of the October Revolution is ultimately the same as that of post-Maoist China: contrary to liberal ideologues, one has to assert that there is no necessary link between

market and democracy. Democracy and market go together only with stable property relations: the moment they are perturbed, we get either dictatorship *à la* Pinochet's Chile or a revolutionary explosion. That is to say, the paradox to be emphasized is that, in the hard years of 'war communism' prior to the application of the New Economic Policy (NEP) which opened up the space again for market 'liberalization', there was much more democracy in Soviet Russia than in the years of the NEP. The market liberalization of the NEP goes hand-in-hand with the emergence of a strong party of *apparatchiks* gaining control over society: this party arose precisely as a reaction to the autonomy of the market civil society, out of the need to establish a strong power structure in order to control these newly unleashed forces.

10 Evert van der Zweerde, *Soviet Historiography of Philosophy*, Dordrecht, Kluwer, 1997.

11 Paradigmatic here is the legendary story of Ilyenkov's failed participation at a world philosophy congress in the United States in the mid-1960s: Ilyenkov had already been granted a visa and was set to take a plane, when his trip was cancelled because his written intervention, 'From the Leninist point of view', which he had to present in advance to the Party ideologues, displeased them – not because of its (wholly acceptable) content, but simply because of its style, the engaged manner in which it was written; already the opening sentence ('It is my personal contention that . . .') struck a wrong chord.

12 Theodor W. Adorno, 'Extorted reconciliation: on Georg Lukács' *Realism in Our Time*', in *Notes to Literature, Volume One*, ed. Rolf Tiedemann, trans. Shierry Weber Nicholsen, New York, Columbia University Press, 1991, pp. 216–40.

13 Martin Heidegger, *Introduction to Metaphysics*, trans. Gregory Fried and Richard Polt, New Haven, Yale University Press, 2000, p. 48. [eds]

14 Max Horkheimer and Theodor Adorno, *Dialectic of Enlightenment: Philosophical Fragments*, ed. Gunzelin Schmid Nörr, trans. Edmund Jephcott, Stanford, Stanford University Press, 2002. [eds]

15 Franz Neumann, *Behemoth: The Structure and Practice of National Socialism, 1933–1944*, New York, Octagon, 1963. [eds]

16 Herbert Marcuse, *Soviet Marxism: A Critical Analysis*, New York, Columbia University Press, 1958. [eds]

17 See V. I. Lenin, *What Is To Be Done?*, trans. Joe Fineberg and George Hanna, Harmondsworth, Penguin, 1962, p. 98. [eds]

18 What makes Fidel Castro's famous statement – 'Within the Revolution, everything. Outside it, nothing!' – problematic and 'totalitarian' is the way its radicality covers up its total indeterminacy: what it leaves unsaid is who, and based on what criteria, will decide if a particular artistic work (the

statement was formulated to provide the guidelines for dealing with artistic freedom) effectively serves the revolution or undermines it. The way is thus open for the *nomenklatura* to enforce its arbitrary decisions. (There is, however, another possible reading that may redeem this slogan: revolution is not a process that follows predestined 'laws', so there are no *a priori* objective criteria that would allow us to draw a line of separation between the revolution and its betrayal – fidelity to the revolution does not reside in simply following and applying a set of norms and goals given in advance, but in the continuous struggle to redefine again and again the line of separation.)

19 Let us also not forget that, in the weeks before the October Revolution, when the debate was raging between Bolsheviks, Stalin did take sides against Lenin's proposal for an immediate Bolshevik take-over, arguing, along Menshevik lines, that the situation was not yet 'ripe', and that, instead of such dangerous 'adventurism', one should endorse a broad coalition of all anti-Tsarist forces!

20 Again, one can discern here an unexpected closeness to the Althusserian notion of 'overdetermination': there is no ultimate rule that allows one to measure 'exceptions' against it – in real history, there are, in a way, nothing but exceptions.

21 Lukács, *Tailism and the Dialectic*, pp. 51–3. [eds]

22 Ernesto Laclau, 'Universalism, Particularism, and the question of identity', *October* 61, 1992, p. 89.

23 Perhaps, a reference to Kierkegaard might be of some help here: this difference is the one between the positive Being of the Universal (the 'mute universality' of a species defined by what all members of the species have in common) and what Kierkegaard called the 'Universal-in-becoming', the Universal as the power of negativity that undermines the fixity of every particular constellation. For a closer elaboration of this distinction, see Slavoj Žižek, *The Ticklish Subject: The Absent Centre of Political Ontology*, London and New York, Verso, 1999, pp. 90–8.

24 See, for instance, Karl Marx and Friedrich Engels, 'Manifesto of the Communist Party', in *The Revolutions of 1848: Political Writings, Volume 1*, ed. David Fernbach, London, Penguin/New Left Review, 1973, pp. 70–1. [eds]

25 Lukács, *History and Class Consciousness*, pp. 97–100. [eds]

26 Žižek's description here condenses his early paper on 'pathological narcissism', published as a foreword to the Croatian edition of Christopher Lasch's *The Culture of Narcissism* (*Narcisistička kultura*, Zagreb, Naprijed, 1986). It was subsequently translated and published as '"Pathological Narcissus" as a socially mandatory form of subjectivity', in *Manifesta*, Ljubljana, European Biennial of Contemporary Art, 2000, pp. 234–55. [eds]

27 In a more detailed approach, one would have to elaborate here this key Hegelian notion of the essentiality of appearance. Hegel's point is not the standard platitude that 'an essence has to appear', that it is only as deep as it is wide – expressed – externalized, etc., but a much more precise one: essence is, in a way, its own appearance, it appears as essence in the domain of appearance, i.e., essence is *nothing but* the appearance of essence, the appearance that there is something behind which is the Essence.

28 For Žižek's further elaboration of this point, see 'Quantum physics with Lacan', in *The Indivisible Remainder: An Essay on Schelling and Related Matters*, London and New York, Verso, 1996, pp. 208–13. As Žižek notes, the so-called *qualia* or 'seemings' of consciousness take on the same status within cognitivism; see *Organs without Bodies: Deleuze and Consequences*, New York and London, Routledge, 2004, pp. 135–6. [eds]

29 Here also, it would be interesting to establish the connection between Lukács and Badiou, for whom 'appearance' is the domain of the consistency of positive 'hard reality', while the order of Being is inherently fragile, inconsistent, elusive, accessible only through mathematics, which deals with pure multitudes. See Alain Badiou, 'Being and appearance', in *Theoretical Writings*, ed. and trans. Ray Brassier and Alberto Toscano, London and New York, Continuum, 2004, pp. 163–75. Although Lukács and Badiou are far from deploying the same notion of appearance, what they do have in common is the way both turn around the standard metaphysical opposition between Appearance and Being, in which appearance is transitory; in contrast to the hard positivity of Being – with Lukács, 'appearance' stands for 'reified' objective reality, while the true 'actuality' is that of the transitory movement of subjective mediation. The homology with quantum physics again presents itself: in the latter, what we experience as 'reality' is also the order of consistent 'appearance' that emerges through the collapse of quantum fluctuation, while the order of Being is that of the transitory, substanceless quantum fluctuations.

30 Lukács, *History and Class Consciousness*, pp. 186–9. [eds]

31 The same criticism could also be made apropos of Richard Rorty's notion that there is no objective truth, just a multitude of (more or less effective) stories about ourselves that we narrate to ourselves: the problem with this notion is not that it is too relativistic, but that it is not 'relativistic' enough – in a typically liberal way, Rorty still presupposes a non-relative neutral universal framework of rules (respect for others' pain, etc.) that everyone should respect when indulging in their own idiosyncratic way of life, the framework that guarantees the tolerable co-existence of these ways of life.

32 See, as exemplary of this stance, Kristeva's statements: 'Today the word "revolt" has become assimilated to Revolution, to political action. The events of the twentieth century, however, have shown us that political "revolts" – Revolutions – ultimately betrayed revolt, especially the psychic sense of the term. Why? Because revolt, as I understand it – psychic revolt, analytic revolt, artistic revolt – refers to a state of permanent questioning, of transformation, change, an endless probing of appearances. If we look at the history of political revolts, we see that the process of questioning has ceased . . . in the case of the Russian Revolution, a revolution that became increasingly dogmatic as it stopped questioning its own ideals until it ultimately degenerated into totalitarianism.' (Julia Kristeva, 'The necessity of revolt', *Trans* 5, 1998, p. 125.) One is tempted to add sarcastically to this last thesis: were not the great Stalinist or the Khmer Rouge purges the most radical form of the political régime's 'permanent questioning'? More seriously, what is problematic with this position of depoliticizing the revolt is that it precludes any actual radical political change: the existing political régime is never effectively undermined or overturned, just endlessly 'questioned' from different marginal 'sites of resistance', because every actual radical change is in advance dismissed as inevitably ending up in some form of 'totalitarian' regression. So what this celebration of the 'revolt' effectively amounts to is the old reactionary thesis of the way that, from time to time, the existing order has to rejuvenate itself with some fresh blood in order to remain viable, like the vulgar conservative wisdom that every good conservative was in his youth briefly a radical leftist . . .

33 Theodor W. Adorno, *Drei Studien zu Hegel*, Frankfurt am Main, Suhrkamp, 1971, p. 13.

Chapter 7

Prolegomena to a theory of Kolkhoz musicals

The first thing one cannot but take note of apropos of Stalinist discourse is its contagious nature: the way (almost) everyone likes mockingly to imitate it, use its terms in various political contexts, in stark contrast to fascism. Stalinism is not prohibited in quite the same way: even if we are fully aware of its monstrous aspects, one nonetheless finds *Ostalgie* acceptable: 'Goodbye Lenin' is tolerated, 'Goodbye Hitler' is not – why?

John Berger recently made a salient point regarding a French publicity poster for Selftrade, an internet-based company for investment brokers: beneath an image of a hammer and sickle cast in solid gold and embedded with diamonds, the caption reads, 'And if the stock market profited everybody?' The strategy of this poster is obvious: today, the stock market fulfils the criteria of egalitarian Communism, which is that everybody can participate in it. Berger indulges in a simple mental experiment: 'Imagine a communications campaign today using an image of a swastika cast in solid gold and embedded with diamonds! It would of course not work. Why? The swastika addressed potential victors not the defeated. It invoked domination not justice.' By way of contrast, the hammer and sickle invoke the hope that 'history would eventually be on the side of those struggling for fraternal justice'. Or, to indulge in a similar mental experiment, in the last days of Really Existing Socialism, the protesting crowds often sang the official songs, including national anthems, reminding the powers of their unfulfilled promises. What better strategy for an East German crowd to undertake in 1989 than simply to sing the GDR national anthem? Because its words ('*Deutschland einig Vaterland* [Germany, the united Fatherland]') no longer fitted the emphasis on East Germany as a new socialist nation, it was *prohibited* to be sung in public from the late 1950s up until 1989: at official ceremonies, only the orchestral version was performed. (The GDR was thus a unique country in which singing the national anthem was a criminal act!) Can one imagine the same thing under Nazism?

Already at an anecdotal level, the difference between fascism and the Stalinist universe is obvious; say, in the Stalinist show trials, the accused has publicly to confess his crimes and give an account of how he came to commit them – in stark contrast to Nazism, in which it would be meaningless to demand from a Jew the confession that he was involved in a Jewish plot against the German nation. This difference points towards different attitudes to the Enlightenment: Stalinism still conceives of itself as part of the Enlightenment tradition, within which truth is accessible to any rational person, no matter how depraved he is, which is why he is subjectively responsible for his crimes, in contrast to the Nazis, for whom the guilt of the Jews is a direct fact of their very biological constitution – one does not have to prove that they are guilty, they are guilty solely by virtue of being Jews. For this same reason, on Stalin's birthday, prisoners sent telegrams to Stalin, wishing him all the best and the success of socialism, even from the darkest gulags like Norilsk or Vorkuta, while one cannot even imagine Jews sending Hitler a telegram from Auschwitz for his birthday.

It is against this background that one should approach Ernst Nolte's book on Heidegger,[1] which brought a breath of fresh air into the eternal debate on 'Heidegger and the political' – it did so on account of its very 'unacceptable' option: far from excusing Heidegger's infamous political choice in 1933, it justifies it – or, at least, it de-demonizes it, rendering it as a viable and meaningful choice. Against the standard defenders of Heidegger, whose mantra is that Heidegger's Nazi engagement was a personal mistake of no fundamental consequence for his thought, Nolte accepts the basic claim of Heidegger's critics that his Nazi choice is inscribed necessarily into his thought – but with a twist: instead of problematizing his thought, Nolte justifies his political choice as a viable option in the situation of late 1920s and early 1930s, with its looming economic chaos and the Communist threat:

> Insofar as Heidegger resisted the attempt at the [Communist] solution, he, like countless others, was historically right . . . In committing himself to the [National Socialist] solution perhaps he became a 'fascist'. But in no way did that make him historically wrong from the outset.[2]

Nolte also formulated the basic terms and topics of the 'revisionist' debate whose basic tenet is to 'objectively compare' fascism and Communism: fascism, and even Nazism, was ultimately a reaction to the Communist threat and a repetition of its worst practices (concentration camps, mass liquidations of political enemies):

> Could it be the case that the National Socialists and Hitler carried out an 'Asiatic' deed [i.e., the Holocaust] only because they considered themselves and their kind to be potential or actual victims of a [Bolshevik] 'Asiatic' deed? Did not the 'Gulag Archipelago' precede Auschwitz?[3]

The merit of Nolte's approach is to take seriously the task of grasping fascism – and even Nazism – as a feasible political project, which is a *sine qua non* of its effective criticism. It is here that one has to make the choice: the 'pure' liberal stance of equidistance toward leftist and rightist 'totalitarianism' (they are both dead, based on intolerance towards political and other differences, the rejection of democratic and humanist values, etc.) is *a priori* false – one *has* to take a side and proclaim one fundamentally 'worse' than the other. For this reason, the ongoing 'relativization' of fascism, the notion that one should rationally compare the two totalitarianisms, *always* involves the – explicit or implicit – thesis that fascism was 'better' than Communism, an understandable reaction to the Communist threat. When, in the summer of 2003, Silvio Berlusconi provoked a violent outcry with his statements that, while a dictator, Mussolini was not a political criminal and murderer like Hitler, Stalin or Saddam, one should bear in mind the true stakes of this scandal: far from deserving to be dismissed as Berlusconi's personal idiosyncrasies, his statements are part of a larger ongoing ideologico-political project of changing the terms of the post-World War II symbolic pact of European identity based on anti-Fascist unity.

This is why Nolte's 'revisionist' argument concerning the relationship between Nazism and (Soviet) Communism cannot be so easily dismissed. According to Nolte, reprehensible though it was, Nazism not only appeared after Communism, it was also, with regard to its content, an excessive *reaction* to the Communist threat. Furthermore, all of the horrors committed by Nazism were mere formal copies of the horrors already committed by Soviet Communism: the reign of secret police, concentration camps, genocidal terror, etc. But is this the form we are talking about? Is the idea that Communism and Nazism share the same totalitarian form, and that the difference concerns only the empirical agents that ill the same structural places ('Jews' instead of 'class enemy', etc.)? The usual liberal reaction to Nolte consists in a moralistic outcry: Nolte relativizes Nazism, reducing it to a secondary echo of Communist Evil – however, how can one even compare Communism, this thwarted attempt at liberation, with the radical Evil of Nazism? In contrast to this dismissal, one should fully concede Nolte's central point: yes, Nazism effectively was a reaction to the Communist threat; it effectively *just* replaced class struggle with the struggle between Aryans and Jews – the problem, however, resides in this 'just', which is by no means as innocent as it appears. We are dealing here with displacement [*Verschiebung*] in the Freudian sense of the term: Nazism displaces class struggle on to racial struggle and thereby obfuscates its true site. What changes in the passage from Communism to Nazism is the *form*, and it is in this change of the form that the Nazi ideological mystification resides: political struggle is naturalized into racial conflict, the (class) antagonism inherent to the social edifice is reduced to an invasion by a foreign (Jewish) body which disturbs the harmony of the Aryan community. The difference between fascism and Communism is thus 'formal-ontological', not simply ontic: it is not (as Nolte claims) that we have in both cases the same formal antagonistic structure, where only the place of the Enemy is filled in with a different positive element (class, race). In the case of race, we are dealing with a positive naturalized element (the presupposed organic unity of Society is perturbed by the intrusion of a foreign body), while class antagonism is absolutely inherent to and constitutive of the social field – fascism thus obfuscates antagonism, translating it into a conflict between positive opposed terms.

Correlative to this failure is the lack of any systematic and thorough confrontation with the phenomenon of Stalinism, which constitutes the absolute *scandal* of the Frankfurt School. How could a Marxist thought that claimed to focus on the conditions of the failure of the Marxist emancipatory project abstain from analysing the nightmare of Really Existing Socialism? Was not its focus on fascism *also* a displacement, a silent admission of its failure to confront the true trauma? To put it in a slightly simplified way: Nazism was enacted by a group of people who wanted to do very bad things, and they did them; Stalinism, on the contrary, emerged as the result of a radical emancipatory attempt. (Perhaps, therein resides the ultimate enigma of the tension between Adorno and Hannah Arendt: while they both shared the radical rejection of Stalinism, Arendt based her rejection on an explicit large-scale analysis of the 'origins of totalitarianism', as well as on the positive normative notion of *vis activa*, of the engaged political life; Adorno, on the other hand, rejected this step altogether.) It is no wonder, then, that Stalinism is often misplaced, sought and located where it is not to be found. For instance, in his famous short poem, 'The Solution' from 1953 (published in 1956), Brecht mocks the arrogance of the Communist *nomenklatura* when faced with the workers' revolt:

> After the uprising of the 17th June
> The Secretary of the Writers Union
> Had leaflets distributed in the *Stalinallee*
> Stating that the people
> Had forfeited the confidence of the government
> And could win it back only
> By redoubled efforts.
> Would it not be easier
> In that case for the government
> To dissolve the people
> And elect another?[4]

However, this poem is not only politically opportunistic, the obverse of his letter of solidarity with the East German Communist régime published in *Neues Deutschland* – to put it brutally, Brecht wanted to cover both his flanks, to profess his support for the régime as well as to hint at his solidarity with the workers, so that whoever won, he would be on the winning side – but it is also simply *wrong* in the theoretico-political sense: one should bravely admit that it effectively *is* a duty – *the* duty, even – of a revolutionary party to 'dissolve the people and elect another', i.e., to bring about the transubstantiation of the 'old' opportunistic people (the inert 'crowd') into a revolutionary body aware of its historical task. Far from being an easy task, to 'dissolve the people and elect another' is the most difficult of them all . . .

The proper task is thus to think the *tragedy* of the October Revolution: to perceive its greatness, its unique emancipatory potential, and, simultaneously, the *historical necessity* of its Stalinist outcome. One should oppose both temptations: the Trotskyite notion that Stalinism was ultimately a contingent deviation, as well as the notion that the Communist project is, in its very core, totalitarian. How are we to draw the line here? A revolutionary process is not a well-planned strategic activity, with no place in it for a full immersion into the Now, without regard for long-term consequences. Quite the contrary: the suspension of all strategic considerations based upon hope for a better future, the stance of *'On s'engage et puis . . . on voit'* (a Napoleonic slogan to which Lenin often referred),[5] is a key part of any revolutionary process. Recall the staged performance of the 'Storming of the Winter Palace' in Petrograd on the third anniversary of the October Revolution (7 November 1920). This event (directed by Nikolai Evreinov who, in 1925, immigrated to France) involved 8,000 direct participants and an audience of 100,000 (a quarter of the city's population) in spite of heavy rain. The underlying idea was formulated by Anatoli Lunatcharsky, People's Commisar for Enlightenment, in the spring of 1920: 'In order to acquire a sense of self the masses must outwardly manifest themselves, and this is possible only when, in Robespierre's words, they become a spectacle unto themselves.'[6] Thousands of workers, soldiers, students and artists worked round the clock, living on *kasha* (tasteless wheat porridge), tea and frozen apples, preparing the performance at the very place where the event 'really took place' three years earlier. Their work was co-ordinated by army officers, as well as by avant-garde artists, musicians and directors, from Malevich to Meyerhold. Although this was acting and not 'reality', the soldiers and sailors were playing themselves – many of them not only actually participated in the event of 1917, but also were simultaneously involved in the real battles of the Civil War that was raging in the nearby vicinity of Petrograd, a city under siege and suffering from severe shortages of food. A contemporary commented on the performance: 'The future historian will record how, throughout one of the bloodiest and most brutal revolutions, all of Russia was acting.'[7] The formalist theoretician Viktor Shklovski further noted that, 'some kind of elemental process is taking place where the living fabric of life is being transformed into the theatrical'.[8]

We all remember the infamous, self-celebratory 'First of May' parades that were one of the supreme signs of recognition of the Stalinist régime. If one needs proof of how Leninism functioned in an entirely different way, are such performances as the 'Storming of the Winter Palace' not the ultimate proof that the October Revolution was definitely *not* a simple *coup d'état* by a small group of Bolsheviks, but an event which unleashed a tremendous emancipatory potential? Does the 'Storming of the Winter Palace' performance not display the force of a sacred (pagan?) pageant, the magic act of founding a new community? It is *here* that Heidegger should have looked when writing about founding a State as the event of truth (and not to the Nazi rituals); it is, perhaps, *here* that there occurred the only meaningful 'return of the sacred'. In short, it is here that, perhaps, one should look for the realization of Wagner's *Gesamtkunstwerk*, of what he aimed at with the designation of his *Parsifal* as *Bühnenweihfestspiel* ('sacred festival drama'): it was in Petrograd of 1920, much more than in Ancient Greece, that, 'in intimate connection with its history, the people itself stood facing itself in the work of art, becoming conscious of itself, and, in the space of a few hours, rapturously devouring, as it were, its own essence.' This aestheticization, in which the people quite literally 'plays itself', certainly does not fall under Benjamin's indictment of the fascist 'aestheticization of the political' – instead of abandoning this aestheticization to the political Right, instead of a blanket dismissal of every mass political spectacle as 'proto-fascist', one should perceive in this minimal, purely formal, difference of the people from itself, the unique case of 'real life' differentiated from art by nothing more than an invisible formal gap. The very fact that, in historical documentaries, footage from the performance (as well as from Eisenstein's *October* of 1927) of the 'Storming of the Winter Palace' is often presented in the form of a documentary, is to be taken as an indication of this deeper identity of the people playing itself.

The archetypal Eisensteinian cinematic scene rendering the exuberant orgy of revolutionary destructive violence (what Eisenstein himself called 'a veritable bacchanalia of destruction') belongs to the same series: when, in *October*, the victorious revolutionaries penetrate the wine cellars of the Winter Palace, they indulge in an ecstatic orgy of smashing thousands of expensive wine bottles. In *Behzin Meadow*, the village pioneers force their way into the local church and desecrate it, robbing it of its relics, squabbling over an icon, sacrilegiously trying on vestments, heretically laughing at the statuary. In this suspension of goal-orientated instrumental activity, we effectively get a kind of Bataillean 'unrestrained expenditure'. Recall the classic reproach of Robespierre to the Dantonist opportunists: 'What you want is a revolution without revolution!' – the pious desire to deprive the revolution of this excess is simply the desire to have a revolution without revolution. However, this 'unrestrained expenditure' is not enough: in a revolution proper, such a display of what Hegel would have called 'abstract negativity' merely, as it were, wipes the slate clean for the second act, the imposition of a New Order.

It is this dimension that disappears in Stalinism. According to the standard leftist periodization (first proposed by Trotsky), the 'Thermidor' of the October Revolution occurred in the mid-1920s – in short, when Trotsky lost power, when the revolutionary *élan* changed into the rule of the new *nomenklatura* bent on constructing 'socialism in one country'. To this, one is tempted to oppose two alternatives: either the claim (advocated by Sylvain Lazarus and Alain Badiou[9]) that the proper revolutionary sequence ended precisely in October 1917, when the Bolsheviks took over State power and thereby began to function as a *State* party; or the claim (articulated and defended in detail by Sheila Fitzpatrick[10]) that the collectivization and rapid industrialization of the late 1920s was part of the inherent dynamic of the October Revolution, so that the revolutionary sequence proper ended only in 1937 – the true 'Thermidor' occurred only when the large-scale purges were cut short to prevent what Getty and Naumov called the complete 'suicide of the Party',[11] and the party *nomenklatura* stabilized itself into a 'new class'. And, effectively, it was only during the terrible events of 1928–1933 that the body of

Russian society effectively underwent a radical transformation: in the difficult but enthusiastic years of 1917–1921, the entire society was in a state of emergency; the period of the New Economic Policy (NEP) marked a step backwards, a consolidation of Soviet State power leaving basically intact the texture of the social body (the large majority of peasants, artisans, intellectuals, etc.). It was only the thrust of 1928 that directly and brutally aimed at transforming the very composition of the social body, liquidating peasants as a class of individual owners, replacing the old intelligentsia (teachers, doctors, scientists, engineers, and technicians) with a new one. As Sheila Fitzpatrick suggests in plastic terms: if an emigrant who left Moscow in 1914 were to return in 1924, he would still recognize the same city, with the same array of shops, offices, theatres, and, in most cases, the same people in charge; if, however, he were to return another ten years later, in 1934, he would no longer recognize the city, so different was the entire texture of social life.[12] The difficult thing to grasp about the terrible years after 1929, the years of the great push forward, was that, within all those horrors beyond recognition, one can nonetheless discern a ruthless, but sincere and enthusiastic, will to a total revolutionary upheaval of the social body, to create a new state, intelligentsia, legal system . . . In the domain of historiography, the 'Thermidor' occurred with the forceful reassertion of Russian nationalism, the reinterpretation of the great figures of the Russian past as 'progressive' (including the Tsars Ivan the Terrible and Peter the Great, and conservative composers like Tchaikovsky), the ordered refocusing of historical writing from anonymous mass trends towards great individuals and their heroic acts. In literary ideology and practice, the 'Thermidor' coincides with the imposition of 'socialist Realism' – and here, precisely, one should not miss the mode of this imposition. It was *not* that the doctrine of socialist Realism repressed the thriving plurality of styles and schools; on the contrary, socialist Realism was imposed against the predominance of the 'proletarian-sectarian' RAPP (the acronym for the 'Revolutionary Association of Proletarian Writers'), which, in the epoch of the 'second revolution' (1928–1932), became 'a sort of monster that seemed to be swallowing the small independent writers' organizations one by one'.[13] This is why the elevation of socialist Realism into the 'official' doctrine was greeted by the majority of writers with the sigh of relief: it was perceived (and also intended!) as the defeat of 'proletarian sectarianism', as the assertion of the right of writers to refer to the large corpus of 'progressive' figures of the past, and the primacy of wide 'humanism' over class sectarianism.

It was – again – the unique greatness of Eisenstein that, in his *Ivan the Terrible*, he rendered the libidinal economy of this 'Thermidor'. In the second part of the film, the only colourized reel (the penultimate one) is limited to the hall in which the carnivalesque orgy takes place. It stands for the Bakhtinian fantasmatic space in which 'normal' power relations are inverted, in which the Tsar is the slave of the idiot whom he proclaims a new Tsar; Ivan provides the imbecile Vladimir with all the imperial insignias, then humbly prostrates himself in front of him and kisses his hand. The scene in the hall begins with the obscene chorus and dance of the Oprichniki (Ivan's private army), staged in an entirely 'unrealistic' way: a weird mixture of Hollywood and Japanese theatre, a musical number whose words tell a strange story (they celebrate the axe which cuts off the heads of Ivan's enemies). The song first describes a group of boyars having a rich meal: 'Down the middle . . . the golden goblets pass . . . from hand to hand.' The chorus then asks with pleasurable nervous expectation: 'Come along. Come along. What happens next? Come on, tell us more!' And the solo Oprichnik, bending forward and whistling, shouts the answer: 'Strike with the axes!' We are here at the obscene site where musical enjoyment meets political liquidation. And, taking into account the fact that the film was shot in 1944, does this not confirm the carnivalesque character of the Stalinist purges? We encounter a similar nocturnal orgy in the third part of *Ivan* (which was not shot – see the scenario), where the sacrilegious obscenity is explicit: Ivan and his Oprichniks perform their nightly drinking feast as a black mass, with black monastic robes over their normal clothing. Therein resides the true greatness of Eisenstein: that he detected (and depicted) the fundamental shift in the status of political violence, from the 'Leninist' liberating outburst of destructive energy to the 'Stalinist' obscene underside of the Law.

One must thus learn to look for displaced traces of Stalinist terror in 'official' Soviet culture and art. For instance, the climactic scene of Vsevolod Pudovkin's *Deserter* (1933) presents a weird displacement of the Stalinist show trials: when the film's hero, a German proletarian working in a gigantic Soviet metallurgical plant, is praised in front of the entire collective for his outstanding labour, he replies with a surprising public confession: no, he does not deserve this praise, he merely came to the Soviet Union to work in order to escape his cowardice and betrayal in Germany itself (when the police attacked the striking workers, he stayed at home, because he believed social democratic treacherous propaganda)! The public (simple workers) listen to him with perplexity, laughing and clapping – a properly uncanny scene reminding us of the scene in Kafka's *The Trial* when Josef K. confronts the courts – here also, the public laughs and claps at the most unexpected and inappropriate moments. The worker then returns to Germany to fight the battle at his proper place. This scene is so striking because it stages the secret fantasy of the Stalinist trial: the traitor publicly confesses his crime out of his own free will and feeling of guilt, without any pressure from the secret police.

If there ever was a novel that stands as the absolute classic of literary Stalinism, it is Nikolai Ostrovsky's *How the Steel Was Tempered*. In it, Pavka, a Bolshevik fully engaged first in the Civil War and then, during the 1920s, in the construction of steel-mills, ends up his life in dirty rags and totally crippled, immobilized, deprived of limbs, thus reduced to an almost non-bodily existence. In such a state, he finally marries a young girl named Taya, making it clear that there will be no sex between them, just companionship, with her function being to take care of him. Here we, in a way, encounter the 'truth' of the Stalinist mythology of the Happy New Man: a dirty desexualized cripple, sacrificing everything for the construction of socialism. This fate coincides with that of Ostrovsky himself, who, in the mid 1930s, after finishing the novel, was dying, crippled and blind; and, like Ostrovsky, Pavka – reduced to a living dead, a kind of living mummy – is reborn at the novel's end through writing a novel about his life. (In the last two years of his life, Ostrovsky lived in a Black Sea resort house as a 'living legend', on a street named after himself, his house a site of countless pilgrimages and of great interest to foreign journalists.) This mortification of one's own treacherous body is itself embodied in a piece of shrapnel that has lodged itself in Pavka's eye, gradually blinding him; at this point, Ostrovsky's bland style suddenly explodes into a complex metaphor:

The octopus has a bulging eye the size of a cat's head, a dull-red eye, green in the centre, burning, pulsating with a phosphorescent glow . . . The octopus moves. He can see it almost next to his eyes. The tentacles creep over his body; they are cold and they burn like nettles. The octopus shoots out its sting, and it bites into his head like a leech, and, wriggling convulsively, it sucks at his blood. He feels the blood draining out of his body into the swelling body of the octopus.[14]

To put it in Lacanian–Deleuzian terms, the octopus stands here for an 'organ without body', a partial object that invades our ordinary biological body and mortifies it; it is not a metaphor for the capitalist system squeezing and choking workers within its tentacles (the standard popular use of the metaphor between the two World Wars), but, surprisingly, a 'positive' metaphor for the absolute self-control that a Bolshevik revolutionary must exert over his body (and over his 'pathological', potentially corrupting, bodily desires) – the octopus is a superego organ which controls us from within: when, at the lowest point of despair, Pavka reviews his life, Ostrovsky himself characterizes this moment of reflection as 'a meeting of the Politburo with his "I" about the treacherous behaviour of his body'. Yet another proof of the way that literary ideology can never simply lie: truth articulates itself in it through its very displacements.

If, then, Ostrovsky and Eisenstein stage the obscene underside of the Stalinist universe, what would have been its public face, the Stalinist genre par excellence? My thesis is: not heroic wartime, historic or revolutionary epics, but *musicals*, the unique genre of so-called 'kolkhoz-musicals' that thrived from the mid 1930s to the early 1950s, whose greatest star was Ljubov Orlova, a kind of Soviet counterpart to Ginger Rogers. The representative films of this genre are: *The Merry Children* (a.k.a., *The Shepherd Kostja*), *Volga, Volga* (Stalin's favourite film) and *The Cossacks of the Kuban District*, the swan song of the genre. There are no traitors in these films, and life is fundamentally happy in them: the 'bad' characters are merely opportunists or lazy frivolous seducers, who are, at the film's end, re-educated and gladly assume their place in society. In this harmonious universe, even animals – pigs, cows and chickens – happily dance with humans.

And it is here that the circle of co-dependence with Hollywood closes: not only were these films part of an attempt to build a Soviet version of the Hollywood production system; surprisingly, the influence also went the other way around. Not only is the legendary shot of King Kong on top of the Empire State Building a direct echo of a constructivist project for the Palace of Soviets with a gigantic Lenin statue at its top; in 1942, Hollywood itself produced its own version of the kolkhoz musical, *The North Star*, one of the three directly pro-Stalinist movies which were, of course, part of the wartime propaganda. The image of kolkhoz life that we get here is no poor reflection of its Soviet model: scenario by Lillian Hellmann, words by Ira Gershwin, music by Aaron Copland. Does this strange film not bear witness to an inner complicity between Stalinist cinema and Hollywood?

Pluto's Judgement Day, a Disney classic from 1935, stages a mocking show-trial of Pluto who, after falling asleep near a fire, endures a nightmarish dream about being dragged to a cats' court, where he is designated as a Public Enemy, accused by a series of witnesses of anti-feline behaviour and then condemned to public burning. When Pluto starts to burn, he, of course, awakens: the dream scene of burning incorporated the real-life fact that fire was getting nearer and nearer to his tail. What makes this dream so interesting is not merely the obvious political references (not only was 1935 the first big year of Moscow trials; in the United States itself, the orchestrated campaign against gangster Public Enemies was part of the public relations policy of Hoover's FBI), but, even more, the way the cartoon stages the show-trial as a musical number, with a series of ironic references to popular songs, up to 'Three Little Maids' from Gilbert and Sullivan's *Mikado*. Ten years before Eisenstein, the link between the musical and a political show-trial is established.

Notes

1 Ernst Nolte, *Martin Heidegger – Politik und Geschichte in Leben und Denken*, Berlin, Vittorio Klostermann Verlag, 1992.

2 Nolte, *Martin Heidegger*, p. 296.

3 Nolte, *Martin Heidegger*, p. 277.

4 Bertolt Brecht, *Die Gedichte in einem Band*, Frankfurt, Suhrkamp Verlag, 1999, pp. 1009–10.

5 V. I. Lenin, 'Our revolution (apropos of N. Sukhanov's notes)', in *Selected Works, Volume 3*, Moscow, Progress Publishers, 1975, p. 707:

'Napoleon, I think, wrote, *"On s'engage et puis . . . on voit."* Rendered freely this means, "First engage in a serious battle and then see what happens." Well, we did first engage in a serious battle in October 1917, and then saw such details of development (from the standpoint of world history they were certainly details) as the Brest peace, the New Economic Policy, and so forth. And now there can be no doubt that in the main we have been victorious.' [eds]

6   Quoted in Richard Taylor, *October*, London, British Film Institute, 2002, p. 8.

7   Quoted in Susan Buck-Morss, *Dreamworld and Catastrophe: The Passing of Mass Utopia in East and West*, Cambridge, Harvard University Press, 2001, p. 144.

8   Quoted in Buck-Morss, ibid.

9   See Alain Badiou, 'Qu'est-ce qu'un thermidorien?', in *Abrégé de métapolitique*, Paris, Editions du Seuil, 1998, pp. 139–54. [eds]

10   Sheila Fitzpatrick, *The Cultural Front: Power and Culture in Revolutionary Russia*, Ithaca and London, Cornell University Press, 1992. [eds]

11   J. Arch Getty and Oleg V. Naumov, *The Road to Terror: Stalin and Self-Destruction of the Bolsheviks, 1932–1939*, New Haven, Yale University Press, 1999. [eds]

12   Fitzpatrick, *The Cultural Front*, pp. 9–13. [eds]

13   Katerina Clark, *The Soviet Novel: History as Ritual*, 3rd ed., Bloomington, Indiana University Press, 2000, p. 32.

14   Nikolai Ostrovsky, *How the Steel was Tempered*, Moscow, Progress Publishers, 1979, pp. 195–6.

Chapter 8
Attempts to escape the logic of capitalism

Václav Havel's life would seem to be an unrivalled success story: the Philosopher-King, a man who combines political power with a global moral authority comparable only to that of the Pope, the Dalai Lama or Nelson Mandela. And just as at the end of a fairy tale, when the hero is rewarded for all his suffering by marrying the princess, he is married to a beautiful movie actress. Why, then, did John Keane choose the subtitle of his biography: *Václav Havel: A Political Tragedy in Six Acts* (London, Bloomsbury, 1999)?

In the 1970s, when Havel was still a relatively unknown Czech dissident writer, Keane played a crucial role in making him known in the West: he organized the publication of Havel's political texts and became a close friend. He also did a great deal to resuscitate Havel's notion of 'civil society' as the site of resistance to late socialist régimes. Despite their personal connection, Keane's book is far from hagiography – he gives us the 'real Havel' with all his weaknesses and idiosyncrasies. He divides his life into six stages: the early student years under the Stalinist régime; the playwright and essayist of the 1960s; the defeat of the last great attempt at 'socialism with a human face' in Prague in the Spring of 1968; the years of dissidence and arrest which culminated in Havel's emergence as the leading spokesman for Charter 77; the Velvet Revolution; and, finally, the presidency. Along the way, we get an abundance of 'endearing foibles', which, far from tarnishing Havel's heroic image, seem somehow to make his achievement all the more palpable. His parents were rich 'cultural capitalists', owners of the famous Barrandov cinema studios ('bourgeois origins'). He has always had unreliable habits (a fondness for *eau de toilette* and sleeping late, listening to rock music) and is known for his promiscuity, notwithstanding the celebrated prison letters to his working-class wife Olga. (When he was released from jail in 1977, he spent his first weeks of freedom with a mistress.) In the 1980s, he was ruthless in establishing himself as Czechoslovakia's most important dissident – whenever a potential rival emerged, doubtful rumours would start to circulate about the rival's links with the secret police, etc. As President he used a child's scooter to zoom along the corridors of the huge presidential palace.

The reason for the 'tragedy' of Havel, however, is not the tension between the public figure and the 'real person', nor even his gradual loss of charisma in recent years. Such things characterize every successful political career (with the exception of those touched by the grace of premature demise). Keane writes that Havel's life resembles a 'classical political tragedy', because it has been 'clamped by moments of . . . triumph spoiled by defeat', and notes that 'most of the citizens in President Havel's republic think less of him than they did a year ago'. The crucial issue, in fact, is the tension *between his two public images*: that of the heroic dissident who, in the oppressive and cynical universe of late socialism, practised and wrote about 'living in truth', and that of postmodern President who (not unlike Al Gore) indulges in New Age ruminations that aim at legitimizing NATO military intervention. How do we get from the lone, fragile dissident with a crumpled jacket and uncompromising ethics, who opposed almighty totalitarian power, to the President who babbles about the anthropic principle and the end of the Cartesian paradigm, reminds us that human rights are conferred on us by the Creator, and is applauded in the United States Congress for his defence of Western values? Is this depressing spectacle the necessary outcome, the 'truth', of Havel the heroic dissident? To put it in Hegel's terms: how does the ethically impeccable 'noble consciousness' imperceptibly pass into the servile 'base consciousness'? Of course, for a 'postmodern' Third Way democrat immersed in New Age ideology, there is no tension: Havel is simply following his destiny, and is deserving of praise for not shirking political power. But there is no escape from the conclusion that his life has descended from the sublime to the ridiculous.

Rarely has one individual played so many different parts: the cocky young student in the early 1950s, and member of a closed circle that holds passionate political discussions and somehow survives the worst years of Stalinist terror; the modernist playwright and critical essayist struggling to assert himself in the mild thaw of the late 1950s and 1960s; the first encounter with History – in the Prague Spring – which was also Havel's first big disappointment; the long ordeal of the 1970s and most of the 1980s, when he was transformed from a critical playwright into a key political figure; the miracle of the Velvet Revolution, with Havel emerging as a skilful politician negotiating the transfer of power and ending up as President; finally, the Havel in the 1990s, the man who presided over the disintegration of Czechoslovakia and who is now a proponent of the full integration of the Czech Republic into Western economic and military structures. Havel himself has been shocked by the swiftness of the transformation – a television camera famously caught his look of disbelief as he sat down to his first official dinner as President.

Keane highlights the limitations of Havel's political project, and the Havel he describes is sometimes remarkably naïve, as when, in January 1990, he greeted Chancellor Kohl with the words: 'Why don't we work together to dissolve all political parties? Why don't we set up just one big party, the Party of Europe?' There is a nice symmetry in the two Vaclavs who have dominated Czech politics during the last decade: Havel, the charismatic Philosopher-King, the head of a democratic monarchy, finding an appropriate double in Vaclav Klaus, his Prime Minister – the cold technocratic advocate of full market liberalism who dismisses any talk of solidarity and community.

In 1974, Paul Theroux visited Vietnam after the peace agreement and the withdrawal of the United States Army but before the Communist takeover. He wrote about it in *The Great Railway Bazaar*. A couple of hundred American soldiers were still there – deserters, officially and legally non-existent, living in slum shacks with their Vietnamese wives, earning a living by smuggling or other crimes. In Theroux's hands, these individuals become representative of Vietnam's place in global power politics. From them, he gradually unravels the complex totality of Vietnamese society. When Keane is at his best, he displays the same ability to extract the global context of what was going on in Czechoslovakia from smallest details. The weakest passages in the book are those that attempt to deal more conceptually with the nature of 'totalitarian' régimes or the social implications of modern technology. Instead of an account of the inner antagonisms of Communist régimes, we get the standard liberal clichés about 'totalitarian control', etc.

Towards the end of his book, Keane touches on the old idea of the 'King's Two Bodies', and points to the equivalent importance of the Leader's body in Communist régimes. A 'pre-modern' political order, he writes, relies on having such sacred bodies, while the democratic system, in which the place of power is supposedly empty, is open to competitive struggle. But this contrast fails to grasp the intricacies of 'totalitarianism'. It is not that Keane is too directly anti-Communist, but that his liberal-democratic stance prevents him from seeing the horrifying paradox of the 'Stalinist Leader'.

Lenin's first major stroke, which he suffered in May 1922, left his right side virtually paralysed and for a while deprived him of speech. He realized that his active political life was over and asked Stalin for some poison so that he could kill himself; Stalin took the matter to the Politburo, which voted against Lenin's wish. Lenin assumed that because he was no longer of any use to the revolutionary struggle, death was the only option – 'calmly enjoying old age' was out of the question. Further, the idea of his funeral as a great State event was repulsive to him. This was not modesty: he was simply indifferent to the fate of his body, regarding it as an instrument to be ruthlessly exploited and discarded when no longer useful.

With Stalinism, however, the body of the Leader became 'objectively beautiful'. In 'On the problem of the beautiful in Soviet art', an essay from 1950, the Soviet critic Nedoshivin wrote: 'Amid all the beautiful material of life, the first place should be occupied by images of our great leaders . . . The sublime beauty of the leaders . . . is the basis for the coinciding of the "beautiful" and the "true" in the art of socialist realism.' This has nothing to do with the Leader's physical attributes and everything to do with abstract ideals. The Leader in fact is like the Lady in courtly love poetry – cold, distanced, inhuman. Both the Leninist and the Stalinist Leader are thoroughly alienated, but in opposite ways: the Leninist Leader displays radical self-instrumentalization on behalf of the Revolution, while in the case of the Stalinist Leader, the 'real person' is treated as an appendix to the fetishized and celebrated public image.

It is no wonder the official photos of the Stalinist era were so often retouched, and with a clumsiness so obvious that it almost seemed intentional. It signalled that the 'real person', with all his idiosyncrasies, had been replaced by a wooden effigy. One rumour circulating about Kim Jong Il is that he actually died in a car crash a couple of years ago and a double has taken his place for rare public appearances, so that the crowds can catch a glimpse of the object of their worship. This is the ultimate confirmation that the 'real personality' of the Stalinist leader is thoroughly irrelevant. Havel, of course, is the inverse of this structure: while the Stalinist Leader is reduced to a ritualistically praised effigy, Havel's charisma is that of a 'real person'. The paradox is that a genuine 'cult of personality' can thrive only in a democracy.

Havel's essay on 'The Power of the powerless', written in 1978, was perceptive in explaining how late socialism operated at the domestic, day-to-day level. What was important was not that, deep down, the people believed in the ruling ideology, but that they followed the external rituals and practices by means of which this ideology acquired material existence. Havel's example is the green-grocer, a modest man profoundly indifferent to official ideology. He just mechanically follows the rules: on State holidays, he decorates the window of his shop with official slogans, such as 'Long live socialism!' When there are mass gatherings, he takes part *affectlessly*. Although he privately complains about the corruption and incompetence of 'those in power', he takes comfort in pieces of folk wisdom ('power corrupts', etc.), which enable him to legitimize his stance in his own eyes and to retain a false appearance of dignity. When someone tries to engage him in dissident activity, he protests: 'Why are you getting me mixed up in these things which are bound to be used against my children? Is it really up to me to set the world right?'

Havel saw that if there was a 'psychological' mechanism at work in Communist ideology, it had nothing to do with belief, but rather with shared guilt: in the 'normalization' that followed the Soviet intervention of 1968, the Czech régime made sure that, in one way or another, the majority of people were somehow morally discredited, compelled to violate their own moral standards. When an individual was blackmailed into signing a petition against a dissident (Havel, for example), he knew that he was lying and taking part in a campaign against an honest man, and it was precisely this ethical betrayal that rendered him the ideal Communist subject. The régime relied on and actively condoned the moral bankruptcy of its subjects. Havel's concept of 'living in truth' involved no metaphysics: it simply designated the act of suspending one's participation, of breaking out of the vicious cycle of 'objective guilt'. He blocked off all false escape-routes, including seeking refuge in the 'small pleasures of everyday life'. Such acts of indifference – making fun in private of official rituals, for instance – were, he said, the very means by which the official ideology was reproduced.

A 'sincere' believer in official late socialist ideology was, therefore, potentially much more dangerous to the régime than a cynic. Consider two examples from countries other than Czechoslovakia: first, the emblematic figures of Evald Iljenkov (1924–1979) and Aleksei Losev (1893–1988), the two prototypes of Russian philosophy under late socialism. Losev was the author of the last book published in the USSR (in 1929) which openly rejected Marxism (he called dialectical materialism 'obvious nonsense'). After a short prison term, he was allowed to pursue his academic career and, during World War II, even started lecturing again – his formula for survival was to withdraw into the history of aesthetics. Under the guise of interpreting past thinkers, especially Plotinus and other Neoplatonists, he was able to smuggle in his own spiritualist beliefs, while, in the introductions to his books, paying lip service to the official ideology with a quote or two from Khrushchev or Brezhnev. In this way, he survived all the vicissitudes of Communism and was hailed after 1989 as the representative of an authentic Russian spiritual heritage. Iljenkov, a superb dialectician and expert on Hegel, was, on the other hand, a sincere Marxist–Leninist. He wrote lively, individual prose and endeavoured to engage with Marxism as a serious philosophy rather than as a set of official maxims. This didn't go down well: he was excommunicated and committed suicide.

The second example is Yugoslav 'self-management socialism' and the fundamental paradox contained within it. Tito's official ideology continually exhorted people to take control of their lives outside of the structures of Party and State; the authorized media criticized personal indifference and the escape into privacy. However, it was precisely an authentic, self-managed articulation and organization of common interests that the régime feared most. Between the lines of its propaganda, the government suggested that its official solicitations were not to be taken too literally, that a cynical attitude towards its ideology was what was actually wanted. The greatest catastrophe for the régime would have been for its own ideology to be taken seriously and acted upon by its subjects.

Havel was especially penetrating in his denunciation of the inherent hypocrisy of Western Marxism and of the 'socialist opposition' in Communist countries. Consider the almost total absence of any theoretical confrontation with Stalinism in the works of the Frankfurt School, in contrast to its permanent obsession with fascism. The standard excuse was that Frankfurt School critics did not want to oppose Communism too openly, for fear that they would be playing into the hands of the Cold Warriors in the Western countries where they lived. But this is obviously not sufficient: had they been cornered and made to say where they stood in the Cold War, they would have chosen Western liberal democracy (as Max Horkheimer did explicitly in some of his late writings). 'Stalinism' was a traumatic topic on which the Frankfurt School *had* to remain silent – silence was the only way for its members to retain their underlying solidarity with Western liberal democracy, without losing their mask of radical leftism.

Their ultimate alignment with the Western system is equivalent to the stance of the 'democratic socialist opposition' in the German Democratic Republic. Although members of the opposition criticized Communist Party rule, they endorsed the basic premise of the régime: that the Federal Republic of Germany was a neo-Nazi State, the direct heir of Nazism and, therefore, that the existence of the GDR as an anti-fascist bulwark had to be protected at any cost. When the socialist system was really threatened, the opposition publicly supported it (take Brecht's position on the East Berlin workers' demonstrations in 1953, or Christa Wolf's on the Prague Spring). The opposition retained its belief in the inherent reformability of the system, but argued that true democratic reform would take time. A rapid disintegration of socialism would, it thought, only return Germany to fascism and strangle the utopia of the 'Other Germany', which, in spite of all its horrors and failures, the GDR represented.

This is why opposition intellectuals so deeply distrusted 'the people'. In 1989, they opposed free elections, well aware that, if given the chance, the majority would choose capitalist consumerism. Free elections, Heiner Müller said, had brought Hitler to power. Many Western social democrats played the same game, feeling much closer to 'reform-minded' Communists than to dissidents – the latter somehow embarrassed them as an obstacle to the process of *détente*. It was clear to Havel that Soviet intervention in 1968 had preserved the Western myth of the Prague Spring: the utopian notion that, were the Czechs to be left alone, they would give birth to an authentic alternative to both Real Socialism and Real Capitalism. In fact, had the forces of the Warsaw Pact not intervened in August 1968, either the Czech Communist leadership would have had to impose restraint, and Czechoslovakia would have remained a fully Communist country, or it would have turned into a 'normal' Western capitalist society (though perhaps one with a Scandinavian social-democratic flavour).

Havel also discerned the fraudulence of what I would call the 'interpassive socialism' of the Western academic Left. These leftists aren't interested in activity – merely in 'authentic' experience. They allow themselves to pursue their well-paid academic careers in the West, while using the idealized Other (Cuba, Nicaragua, Tito's Yugoslavia) as the stuff of their ideological dreams: they dream through the Other, but turn their backs on it if it disturbs their complacency by abandoning socialism and opting for liberal capitalism. What is of special interest here is the lack of understanding between the Western Left and dissidents such as Havel. In the eyes of the Western Left, Eastern dissidents were too naïve in their belief in liberal democracy – in rejecting socialism, they threw out the baby with the bath water. In the eyes of the dissidents, the Western Left was playing patronizing games with them, disavowing the true harshness of totalitarianism. The idea that dissidents were somehow guilty for not seizing the unique opportunity provided by the disintegration of socialism to invent an authentic alternative to capitalism was pure hypocrisy.

In dissecting late socialism, Havel was always aware that Western liberal democracy was far from meeting the ideals of authentic community and 'living in truth' on behalf of which he and other dissidents had opposed Communism. He was faced, therefore, with the problem of combining a rejection of 'totalitarianism' with the need to offer critical insights into Western democracy. His solution was to follow Heidegger and to see in the technological hubris of capitalism, its mad dance of self-enhancing productivity, the expression of a more fundamental transcendental-ontological principle – 'will to power', 'instrumental reason' – equally evident in the Communist attempt to overcome capitalism. This was the argument of Adorno and Horkheimer's *Dialectic of Enlightenment*, which first engineered the fateful shift from concrete socio-political analysis to philosophico-anthropological generalization, by means of which 'instrumental reason' is no longer grounded in concrete capitalist social relations, but is instead posited as their quasi-transcendental 'foundation'. The moment that Havel endorsed Heidegger's recourse to quasi-anthropological or philosophical principle, Stalinism lost its specificity, its specific *political* dynamic, and turned into just another example of this principle (as exemplified by Heidegger's remark, in his *Introduction to Metaphysics*, that, in the long run, Russian Communism and Americanism were 'metaphysically one and the same').

Keane tries to save Havel from this predicament by emphasizing the ambiguous nature of his intellectual debt to Heidegger. Like Heidegger, Havel conceived of Communism as a thoroughly modern régime, an inflated caricature of modern life, with many tendencies shared by Western society – for instance, technological hubris and the crushing of human individuality attendant on it. However, in contrast to Heidegger, who excluded any active resistance to the social-technological framework ('only God can save us', as he put it in an interview published after his death), Havel put faith in a challenge 'from below' – in the independent life of 'civil society' outside the frame of State power. The 'power of the powerless', he argued, resides in the self-organization of civil society that defies the 'instrumental reason' embodied in the State and the technological apparatuses of control and domination.

I find this idea of civil society doubly problematic. First, the opposition between State and civil society works *against* as well as *for* liberty and democracy. For example, in the United States, the Moral Majority presents itself (and is effectively organized as) the resistance of local civil society to the regulatory interventions of the liberal State – the recent exclusion of Darwinism from the school curriculum in Kansas is in this sense exemplary. So while in the specific case of late socialism the idea of civil society refers to the opening up of a space of resistance to 'totalitarian' power, there is no essential reason why it cannot provide space for all the politico-ideological antagonisms that plagued Communism, including nationalism and opposition movements of an anti-democratic nature. These are authentic expressions of civil society – 'civil society' designates the terrain of open struggle, the terrain in which antagonisms can articulate themselves, without any guarantee that the 'progressive' side will win.

Second, civil society, as Havel conceived it, is not, in fact, a development of Heidegger's thinking. The essence of modern technology for Heidegger was not a set of institutions, practices and ideological attitudes that can be opposed, but the very ontological horizon that determines how we experience Being today, how reality discloses itself to us. For that reason, Heidegger would have found the concept of 'the *power* of the powerless' suspect, caught in the logic of the 'will to power' that it endeavours to denounce.

Havel's understanding that 'living in truth' could not be achieved by capitalism, combined with his crucial failure to understand the origins of his own critical impulse, has pushed him towards New Ageism. Although the Communist régimes were mostly a dismal failure, generating terror and misery, at the same time they opened up a space for utopian expectations which, among other things, facilitated the failure of Communism itself. What anti-Communist dissidents such as Havel overlook, then, is that the very space from which they criticized and denounced terror and misery was opened and sustained by *Communism's attempt to escape the logic of capitalism*. This explains Havel's continuing insistence that capitalism in its traditional, brutal form cannot meet the high expectations of his anti-Communist struggle – the need for authentic human solidarity, etc. This is, in turn, why Václav Klaus, Havel's pragmatic double, has dismissed Havel as a 'socialist'.

Even the most 'totalitarian' Stalinist ideology is radically ambiguous. While the universe of Stalinist politics was undoubtedly one of hypocrisy and arbitrary terror, in the late 1930s the great Soviet films (say, the Gorky trilogy) epitomized authentic solidarity for audiences across Europe. In one memorable film about the Civil War, a mother with a young son is exposed as a counter-revolutionary spy. A group of Bolsheviks put her on trial and, at the very beginning of the trial, an old Bolshevik demands that the sentence be severe, but just. After she confesses her crime, the court (an informal collective of Bolshevik soldiers) rules that she was seduced into enemy activity by her difficult social circumstances; she is therefore sentenced to be fully integrated into the new socialist collective, to be taught to write and read and to acquire a proper education, while her son, who is unwell, is to be given proper medical care. The surprised woman bursts out crying, unable to understand the court's benevolence, and the old Bolshevik nods: 'Yes, this is a severe but just sentence!' No matter how manipulative such scenes were, no matter how far they were from the reality of 'revolutionary justice', they nonetheless bore witness to a new sense of justice and, as such, gave viewers new ethical standards against which reality could be measured.

Havel seems now to be blind to the fact that his own opposition to Communism was rendered possible by the utopian dimension generated and sustained by Communist régimes. So we get the tragi-comic indignity which is his recent essay in the *New York Review of Books* on 'Kosovo and the end of the nation-state'. In it, he tries to say that the NATO bombing of Yugoslavia placed human rights above the rights of the State, that the NATO alliance's attack on the Federal Republic of Yugoslavia without a direct mandate from the United Nations was not an irresponsible act of aggression, or of disrespect for international Law. It was, on the contrary, according to Havel, prompted by respect for the Law, for a Law that ranks higher than the Law which protects the sovereignty of States. The alliance has acted out of respect for human rights, as both conscience and international treaties dictate.

Havel further invokes this 'higher Law' when he claims that 'human rights, human freedoms . . . and human dignity have their deepest roots somewhere outside the perceptible world . . . while the State is a human creation, human beings are the creation of God.' He seems to be saying that NATO forces were allowed to violate international Law because they acted as direct instruments of the 'higher Law' of God – a clear-cut case of religious fundamentalism. Havel's statement is a good example of what Ulrich Beck, in an article in *Die Süddeutsche Zeitung* in 1999, called 'militaristic humanism' or even 'militaristic pacifism'. The problem with this approach is not that it is inherently contradictory, an Orwellian 'peace is war'. Nor is NATO intervention best met with the pacifist-liberal argument that 'more bombs and killing never bring peace' (it goes without saying that this is wrong). It is not even enough to point out, as a Marxist would, that the targets of bombardment weren't chosen with moral considerations in mind, but were determined by geopolitical and economic interests. The main problem with Havel's argument is that intervention is presented as having been undertaken for the sake of the victims of hatred and violence – that is, justified by a depoliticized appeal to universal human rights.

A report by Steven Erlanger on the suffering of the Kosovo Albanians in the May 1999 edition of the *New York Times* was entitled 'In one Kosovo woman, an emblem of suffering'. This woman is from the outset identified as a powerless victim of circumstance, deprived of political identity, reduced to bare suffering. As such, she is beyond political recrimination – an independent Kosovo is not on her agenda, she just wants the horror over:

> Does she favour an independent Kosovo?
>
> 'You know, I don't care if it's this or that', Meli said. 'I just want all this to end, and to feel good again, to feel good in my place and my house with my friends and family.'
>
> Her support for the NATO intervention is grounded in her wish for the horror to end.
>
> She wants a settlement that brings foreigners here 'with some force behind them'. She is indifferent as to who the foreigners are.
>
> She sympathizes with all sides:
>
> 'There is tragedy enough for everyone,' she says. 'I feel sorry for the Serbs who've been bombed and died, and I feel sorry for my own people. But maybe now there will be a conclusion, a settlement for good. That would be great.'

Meli is the ideal subject-victim to whose aid NATO comes running: not a political subject with a clear agenda, but a subject of helpless suffering, someone who sympathizes with all suffering sides in the conflict, caught in the madness of a local clash that can only be stopped by the intervention of a benevolent foreign power.

The ultimate paradox of the NATO bombing of Serbia is not the one that was regularly rehearsed by Western opponents of the war: that by an attempt to stop ethnic cleansing in Kosovo, NATO triggered cleansing on a larger scale and created the very humanitarian catastrophe it wanted to prevent. A deeper paradox involves the ideology of victimization: when NATO intervened to protect Kosovar victims, it ensured at that same time that they would *remain* victims, inhabitants of a devastated country with a passive population – they were not encouraged to become an active politico-military force capable of defending itself. Here we have the basic paradox of victimization: the Other to be protected is good in so far as it remains a victim (which is why we were bombarded with pictures of helpless Kosovar mothers, children and old people, telling moving stories of their suffering); the moment it no longer behaves as a victim, but wants to strike back on its own, it all of a sudden magically turns into a terrorist, fundamentalist, drug-trafficking Other. This ideology of global victimization, the identification of the human subject as 'something that can be hurt', is the perfect fit for today's global capitalism, though most of the time it remains invisible to the public eye.

Havel praised the NATO bombing of Yugoslavia as the first case of a military intervention in a country with full sovereign power, undertaken not out of any specific economico-strategic interest but because that country was violating the elementary human rights of an ethnic group. To understand the falseness of this, compare this new moralism with the great emancipatory movements inspired by Gandhi and Martin Luther King. These were movements directed not against a specific group of people, but against concrete (racist, colonialist) institutionalized practices; they involved a positive, all-inclusive stance that, far from excluding the 'enemy' (whites, English colonizers), made an appeal to its moral sense and asked it to do something that would restore its own moral dignity. The predominant form of today's 'politically correct' moralism, on the other hand, is that of Nietzschean *ressentiment* and envy: it is the fake gesture of disavowed politics, the assuming of a 'moral', depoliticized position in order to make a stronger political case. This is a perverted version of Havel's 'power of the powerless': powerlessness can be manipulated as a stratagem in order to gain more power, in exactly the same way that today, in order for one's voice to gain authority, one has to legitimize oneself as being some kind of (potential or actual) victim of power.

The ultimate cause of this moralistic depoliticization is the retreat of the Marxist historico-political project. A couple of decades ago, people were still discussing the political future of humanity – will capitalism prevail or will it be supplanted by Communism or another form of 'totalitarianism'? – while silently accepting that, somehow, social life would continue. Today, we can easily imagine the extinction of the human race, but it is impossible to imagine a radical change of the social system – even if life on earth disappears, capitalism will somehow remain intact. In this situation, disappointed leftists, who are convinced that radical change of the existing liberal-democratic capitalist system is no longer possible, but who are unable to renounce their passionate attachment to global change, invest their excess of political energy in an abstract and excessively rigid moralizing stance.

At a recent meeting of the leaders of the Western powers dedicated to the 'Third Way', the Italian Prime Minister Massimo d'Alema said that one should not be afraid of the word 'socialism'. Clinton and, following him, Blair and Schröder, are supposed to have burst out laughing. This says much about the Third Way, which is 'problematic' not least because it exposes the absence of a 'second way'. The idea of a 'third way' emerged at the very moment when, at least in the West, all other alternatives, from old-style conservatism to radical social democracy, crumbled in the face of the triumphant onslaught of global capitalism and its notion of liberal democracy. The true message of the notion of the Third Way is that there is no 'second way', no alternative to global capitalism, so that, in a kind of mocking pseudo-Hegelian 'negation of negation', the Third Way brings us back to the first and only way. Is this not global capitalism with a human face?

This, then, is Havel's tragedy: his authentic ethical stance has become a moralizing idiom cynically appropriated by the knaves of capitalism. His heroic insistence on doing the impossible (opposing the seemingly invincible Communist régime) has ended up serving those who 'realistically' argue that any real change in today's world is impossible. This reversal is not a betrayal of his original ethical stance, but is inherent in it. The ultimate lesson of Havel's tragedy is thus a cruel, but inexorable one: the direct ethical foundation of politics sooner or later turns into its own comic caricature, adopting the very cynicism it originally opposed.

Note

This paper was originally published in the *London Review of Books*, 28 October 1999, pp. 3–7. [eds]

SECTION THREE

Really existing capitalism

Chapter 9
Multiculturalism, or, the cultural logic of multinational capitalism

Those who still remember the good old days of socialist realism are well aware of the key role played by the notion of the 'typical': truly progressive literature should depict 'typical heroes in typical situations'. Writers who presented a bleak picture of Soviet reality were not simply accused of lying; the accusation was rather that they provided a distorted reflection of social reality by depicting the remainders of the decadent past instead of focusing on phenomena that were 'typical', in the sense of expressing the underlying historical tendency of the progress towards Communism. Ridiculous as this notion may sound, its grain of truth resides in the fact that each universal ideological notion is always hegemonized by some particular content that colours its very universality and accounts for its efficiency.

Why is the single mother 'typical'?

In the rejection of the social welfare system by the New Right in the United States, for example, the universal notion of the welfare system as inefficient is sustained by the pseudo-concrete representation of the notorious African-American single mother, as if, in the last resort, social welfare is a programme for black single mothers – the particular case of the 'single black mother' is silently conceived as 'typical' of social welfare and what is wrong with it. In the case of the anti-abortion campaign, the 'typical' case is the exact opposite: a sexually promiscuous professional woman who values her career over her 'natural' assignment of motherhood – although this characterization is a blatant contradiction of the fact that the great majority of abortions occur in lower-class families with a lot of children. This specific twist – a particular content that is promulgated as 'typical' of the universal notion – is the element of fantasy, of the fantasmatic background/support of the universal ideological notion. To put it in Kantian terms, it plays the role of 'transcendental schematism', translating the empty universal concept into a notion that directly relates and applies to our 'actual experience'. As such, this fantasmatic specification is by no means an insignificant illustration or exemplification: it is at this level that ideological battles are won or lost – the moment we perceive as 'typical' the case of abortion in a large lower-class family unable to cope with another child, the perspective changes radically.[1]

This example makes clear in what sense 'the universal results from a constitutive split in which the negation of a particular identity transforms this identity into the symbol of identity and fullness as such':[2] the universal acquires concrete existence when some particular content begins to function as its stand-in. A couple of years ago, the English yellow press focused on single mothers as the source of all of the evils of modern society, from budget crises to juvenile delinquency. In this ideological space, the universality of 'modern social Evil' was operative only through the split of the figure of the 'single mother' into itself in its particularity and itself as the stand-in for 'modern social Evil'. The fact that this link between the Universal and the particular content that acts as its stand-in is *contingent* means precisely that it is the outcome of a *political* struggle for ideological hegemony. However, the dialectic of this struggle is more complex than in its standard Marxist version – that of particular interests assuming the form of universality: 'universal human rights are effectively the rights of white male property owners . . .' In order to be operative, the ruling ideology must incorporate a series of features in which the exploited majority will be able to recognize its authentic longings. In other words, each hegemonic universality must incorporate *at least two* particular contents: the authentic popular content, as well as its distortion by the relations of domination and exploitation. Of course, fascist ideology 'manipulates' authentic popular longings for true community and social solidarity against fierce competition and exploitation; of course, it 'distorts' the expression of this longing in order to legitimize the continuation of the relations of social domination and exploitation. However, in order to be able to achieve this distortion of authentic longing, it has first to incorporate it . . . Étienne Balibar was thus fully justified in reversing Marx's classic formula: the ruling ideas are precisely *not* directly the ideas of those who rule.[3] How did Christianity become the ruling ideology? By incorporating a series of crucial motifs and aspirations of the oppressed – truth is on the side of the suffering and humiliated, power corrupts and so on – and rearticulating them in such a way that they became compatible with the existing relations of domination.

Desire and its articulation

One is tempted to refer here to the Freudian distinction between the latent dream-thought and the unconscious desire expressed in a dream. The two are not the same: the unconscious desire articulates itself, inscribes itself, through the very 'perlaboration' or translation of the latent dream-thought into the explicit text of a dream. In a homologous way, there is nothing 'fascist' (or 'reactionary' and so forth) in the 'latent dream-thought' of fascist ideology (the longing for authentic community and social solidarity); what accounts for the properly fascist character of fascist ideology is the way this 'latent dream-thought' is transformed and elaborated by the ideological 'dream-work' into the explicit ideological text that continues to legitimize social relations of exploitation and domination. And is it not the same with today's right-wing populism? Are liberal critics not too quick in dismissing the very values populism refers to as inherently 'fundamentalist' or 'proto-fascist'?

Non-ideology – what Fredric Jameson calls the utopian moment present even in the most atrocious ideology[4] – is thus absolutely indispensable: ideology is in a way *nothing but the form of appearance, the formal distortion, displacement, of non-ideology*. To take the worst imaginable case, was Nazi anti-Semitism not grounded in the utopian longing for authentic community life, in the fully justified rejection of the irrationality of capitalist exploitation? Our point, again, is that it is theoretically and politically wrong to denounce this longing as a 'totalitarian fantasy', that is, to search within it for the 'roots' of fascism – the standard mistake of the liberal-individualist critique of fascism: what makes it 'ideological' is its articulation, the way this longing is made to function as the legitimization of a very specific notion of what capitalist exploitation is (the result of Jewish influence, of the predominance of financial over 'productive' Capital – only the latter tends towards a harmonious 'partnership' with workers) and of how we are to overcome it (by getting rid of the Jews).

The struggle for ideological and political hegemony is thus always the struggle for the appropriation of the terms that are 'spontaneously' experienced as 'apolitical', as transcending political boundaries. No wonder that the name of the strongest dissident movement in Eastern European Communist countries was Solidarity: a signifier of the impossible fullness of society, if there ever was one. It was as if, in Poland in the 1980s, what Laclau calls the logic of equivalence was brought to an extreme: 'Communists in power' served as *the* embodiment of non-society, of decay and corruption, magically uniting everyone against themselves, including the disappointed 'honest Communists' themselves. Conservative nationalists accused the Communists of betraying Polish interests to the Soviet master; business-orientated individuals saw in them an obstacle to unbridled capitalist activity; for the Catholic Church, Communists were amoral atheists; for the farmers, they represented the force of violent modernization which threw rural life off the rails; for artists and intellectuals, Communism was synonymous with oppressive and stupid censorship; workers saw themselves not only as exploited by the Party bureaucracy, but as even further humiliated by the claims that this was done on their behalf; finally, old disillusioned leftists perceived the régime as the betrayal of 'true socialism'. The impossible *political* alliance between all these divergent and potentially antagonistic positions was possible only under the banner of a signifier which stands, as it were, on the very border that separates the political from the pre-political, and 'Solidarity' was the perfect candidate: it is politically operative as designating the 'simple' and 'fundamental' unity of human beings that should unite them beyond all political differences.[5]

Conservative basic instincts

What does all this tell us about Labour's recent electoral victory in the United Kingdom? It is not only that, in a model hegemonic operation, they reappropriated 'apolitical' notions like 'decency'; what they successfully focused on was the inherent obscenity of Tory ideology. The Tories' explicit ideological statements were always supported by their shadowy double, by an obscene, publicly unacknowledged, between-the-lines message. When, for example, they launched their infamous 'back to basics' campaign, its obscene supplement was clearly indicated by Norman Tebbitt, who is, as Jacqueline Rose puts it, 'never shy about exposing the dirty secrets of the Conservative unconscious': 'Many traditional Labour voters realized that they shared our values – that man is not just a social but also a territorial animal; it must be part of our agenda to satisfy those basic instincts of tribalism and territoriality.'[6] This, then, is what 'back to basics' was really all about: the reassertion of 'basic' egoistic, tribal, barbarian 'instincts' that lurk beneath the semblance of civilized bourgeois society. We all remember the (deservedly) famous scene from Paul Verhoeven's film *Basic Instinct* (1992) in which, in the course of a police investigation, Sharon Stone for a brief moment spreads her legs and reveals to the fascinated policemen what is (or is it?) a glimpse of her pubic hair. A statement like Tebbitt's is undoubtedly the ideological equivalent of this gesture, allowing a brief glance into the obscene intimacy of the Thatcherite ideological edifice. (Lady Thatcher herself was too 'dignified' to perform directly this ideological Sharon-Stone-gesture too often, so poor Tebbitt had to act as her stand-in.) Against this background, the Labour emphasis on 'decency' was not a case of simple moralism – rather, its message was that they are *not* playing the same obscene game, that their statements do not contain, 'between the lines', the same obscene message.

In today's general ideological constellation, this gesture is more important than it may seem, When the Clinton administration resolved the deadlock of gays in the United States army by means of the compromise, 'Don't ask, don't tell!' – by which soldiers are not directly asked if they are gay, so they are also not compelled to lie and deny it, and although they are not formally allowed in the army, they are tolerated as long as they keep their sexual orientation private and do not actively endeavour to engage others in it – this opportunist measure was deservedly criticized for endorsing homophobic attitudes. Although the direct prohibition of homosexuality is not to be enforced, its very existence as a virtual threat compelling gays to remain in the closet affects their actual social status. In other words, what this solution amounted to was an explicit elevation of hypocrisy into a social principle, like the attitude towards prostitution in traditional Catholic countries – if we pretend that gays in the army do not exist, it is as if they effectively do not exist (for the big Other). Gays are to be tolerated, on condition that they accept the basic censorship concerning their identity . . .

While fully justified at its own level, the notion of censorship at work in this criticism, with its Foucauldian background of Power, which, in the very act of censorship and other forms of exclusion, generates the excess it endeavours to contain and dominate, nonetheless seems to fall short at a crucial point: what it misses is the way in which censorship not only affects the status of the marginal or subversive force that the Power discourse endeavours to dominate, but, at an even more radical level, causes a split within the Power discourse itself. One should ask here a naïve, but nonetheless crucial question: why does the army so strongly resist publicly accepting gays into its ranks? There is only one possible consistent answer: not because homosexuality poses a threat to the alleged 'phallic and patriarchal' libidinal economy of the army community, but, on the contrary, because *the army community itself relies on a thwarted/disavowed homosexuality as the key component of the soldiers' male-bonding.*

From my own experience, I remember the way that the old infamous Yugoslav People's Army was homophobic in the extreme – when someone was discovered as having homosexual inclinations, he was instantly turned into a pariah, before being formally dismissed from the army – and yet, at the same time, everyday army life was excessively permeated by an atmosphere of homosexual innuendo. For instance, while soldiers were standing in line for their meal, a common vulgar joke was to stick a finger into the arse of the person ahead of you and then to withdraw it quickly, so that when the surprised victim turned around, he did not know who among the soldiers sharing a stupid obscene smile had done it. A predominant way of greeting a fellow soldier in my unit, instead of simply saying 'Hello!', was to say 'Smoke my prick!' ('Pusi kurac!' in Serbo-Croat); this formula was so standardized that it had completely lost any obscene connotation and was pronounced in a totally neutral way, as a pure act of politeness.

Censorship, power and resistance

This fragile coexistence of extreme and violent homophobia with a thwarted, that is, publicly unacknowledged, 'underground' homosexual libidinal economy, bears witness to the fact that the discourse of the military community can operate only by way of censoring its own libidinal foundation. At a slightly different level, the same goes for the practice of hazing – the ceremonial beating and humiliation of United States marines by their elder peers, who stick medals directly on to their skin and so on. When the public disclosure of these practices (somebody secretly shot them on video) caused such an outrage, what disturbed the public was not the practice of hazing itself (everybody was aware that things like this were going on), but the fact of it being rendered publicly. Outside of the confines of military life, do we not encounter a strictly homologous self-censoring mechanism in conservative populism with its sexist and racist bias? In the election campaigns of Jesse Helms, the racist and sexist message is not publicly acknowledged – at the public level, it is sometimes even violently disavowed – but is instead articulated in a series of double-entendres and coded allusions. This kind of self-censorship is necessary if, in the present ideological conditions, Helms' discourse is to remain effective. If it were to articulate directly, in a public way, its racist bias, this would render it unacceptable in the hegemonic political discourse; if it were effectively to abandon the self-censored coded racist message, it would endanger the support of its targeted electoral body. Conservative populist political discourse thus offers an exemplary case of a Power discourse whose efficiency depends on the mechanism of self-censorship: it relies on a mechanism that is effective only in so far as it remains censored. Against the image, ever-present in cultural criticism, of a radical subversive discourse or practice 'censored' by the Power, one is even tempted to claim that today, more than ever, the mechanism of censorship intervenes predominantly to enhance the efficiency of the Power discourse itself.

The temptation to be avoided here is the old leftist notion that it is 'better for us to deal with an enemy who openly admits his (racist, homophobic . . .) bias, than with the hypocritical attitude of publicly denouncing what one secretly and effectively endorses'. This notion fatefully underestimates the ideological and political significance of *maintaining appearances*: appearance is never 'merely an appearance', but profoundly affects the *actual* socio-symbolic position of those concerned. If racist attitudes were to be rendered acceptable in mainstream ideological and political discourse, this would radically shift the balance of the entire ideological hegemony. This, probably, is what Alain Badiou had in mind when he mockingly designated his work as a search for the 'good terror':[7] today, in the face of the emergence of new racism and sexism, the strategy should be to *make such enunciations unutterable*, so that anyone relying upon them is automatically disqualified – as happens, in our universe, to those who approvingly refer to fascism. While one may be aware of the way in which authentic yearnings for, say, community, are twisted by fascism, one should emphatically *not* discuss 'how many people really died in Auschwitz', 'the good side of slavery', 'the necessity of cutting back on workers' collective rights' and so on; the position should be here quite unabashedly 'dogmatic' and 'terrorist', that these are *not* objects of 'open, rational, democratic discussion'.

This inherent split and self-censorship of the Power mechanism is to be opposed to the Foucauldian motif of the interconnection of Power and resistance. Our point is not only that resistance is immanent to Power, that Power and counter-Power generate each other: it is not only that Power itself generates the excess of resistance that it can no longer dominate; it is also not only that – in the case of sexuality – the disciplinary 'repression' of a libidinal investment eroticizes this gesture of repression itself, as in the case of the obsessional neurotic who gets libidinal satisfaction out of the very compulsive rituals destined to keep the traumatic *jouissance* at bay. This last point must be further radicalized: the Power edifice itself is split from within, that is, to reproduce itself and contain its Other, it has to rely on an inherent excess that grounds it. To put it in the Hegelian terms of speculative identity, Power is always-already its own transgression; if it is to function, it has to rely on a kind of obscene supplement – the gesture of self-censorship is co-substantial with the exercise of Power. It is thus not enough to say that the 'repression' of some libidinal content retroactively eroticizes the very gesture of 'repression' – this 'eroticization' of Power is not a secondary effect of its exertion on its object, but its very disavowed foundation, its 'constitutive crime', its founding gesture that has to remain invisible if Power is to function normally. What we get in the kind of military drill depicted in the first part of Stanley Kubrick's *Full Metal Jacket* (1987), for example, is not a secondary eroticization of the disciplinary procedure that creates military subjects, but the constitutive obscene supplement of this procedure that renders it operative.

The logic of Capital

So, back to the recent Labour victory, one can see how it not only involved a hegemonic reappropriation of a series of motifs that were usually inscribed into the Conservative field – family values, law and order, individual responsibility; the Labour ideological offensive also separated these motifs from the obscene fantasmatic subtext that sustained them in the Conservative field, in which 'toughness on crime' and 'individual responsibility' subtly referred to brutal egotism, to disdain for victims and other 'basic instincts'. The problem, however, is that the New Labour strategy involved its own 'message between the lines': we fully accept the logic of Capital, we will not meddle with it.

Today, financial crisis is a permanent state of things, the reference to which legitimizes the demands to cut social spending, health care, the support of culture and scientific research, in short, the dismantling of the welfare state. Is, however, this permanent crisis really an objective feature of our socio-economic life? Is it not rather one of the effects of the shift of balance from 'class struggle' towards Capital, resulting from the growing role of new technologies as well as the direct internationalization of Capital and the co-dependent diminished role of the Nation-State that was further able to impose certain minimal requirements and limitations to exploitation? In other words, the crisis is an 'objective fact' if and only if one accepts in advance as an unquestionable premise the inherent logic of Capital – as more and more left-wing or liberal parties have done. We are thus witnessing the uncanny spectacle of social-democratic parties that have come to Power with the between-the-lines message to Capital, 'we will do the necessary job for you in an even more efficient and painless way than the Conservatives'. The problem, of course, is that, in today's global sociopolitical circumstances, it is practically impossible effectively to call into question the logic of Capital: even a modest social-democratic attempt to redistribute wealth beyond the limit acceptable to Capital 'effectively' leads to an economic crisis, inflation, a fall in revenues and so on. Nevertheless, one should always bear in mind the way that the connection between 'cause' (rising social expenditure) and 'effect' (economic crisis) is not a direct, objective causal one: it is always-already embedded in a situation of social antagonism and struggle. The fact that, if one does not obey the limits set by Capital, a crisis 'really follows' in no way 'proves' that the necessity of these limits is an objective necessity of economic life. It should rather be conceived of as proof of the privileged position Capital holds in the economic and political *struggle*, as in the situation where a stronger partner threatens that if you do X, you will be punished by Y, and then, upon your doing X, Y effectively ensues.

An irony of history is that, in the Eastern European ex-Communist countries, the 'reformed' Communists were the first to learn this lesson. Why did many of them return to power via free elections? This very return offers the ultimate proof that these states have effectively entered capitalism. That is to say, what do ex-Communists stand for today? Due to their privileged links with the newly emerging capitalists – mostly members of the old *nomenklatura* 'privatizing' the companies they once ran – they are first and foremost the party of big Capital; furthermore, to erase the traces of their brief, but nonetheless rather traumatic experience with politically active civil society, as a rule they ferociously advocate a withdrawal from ideology, a retreat from active engagement in civil society to passive, apolitical consumerism – the very two features that characterize contemporary capitalism. Dissidents are thus astonished to discover that they played the role of 'vanishing mediators' on the path from socialism to capitalism in which the same class as before is in power, but now merely under a new guise. It is therefore wrong to claim that the return of the ex-Communists to power signals the way that people are disappointed with capitalism and long for the old socialist security – rather, in a kind of Hegelian 'negation of negation', it is only with the return to power of ex-Communists that socialism was effectively negated; that is, what the political analysts (mis)perceive as the 'disappointment with capitalism' is effectively disappointment with an ethico-political enthusiasm for which there is no place in 'normal' capitalism.[8]

At a somewhat different level, the same logic underlies the social impact of cyberspace: this impact does not derive directly from technology but relies on the network of social relations, that is, the predominant way that digitalization affects our self-experience is mediated by the frame of the globalized market economy of late capitalism. Bill Gates has commonly celebrated cyberspace as opening up the prospect of what he calls 'frictionless capitalism' – this expression renders perfectly the social fantasy that underlies the ideology of cyberspace capitalism: that of a wholly transparent, ethereal medium of exchange in which the last trace of material inertia vanishes. The crucial point here is that the 'friction' we dispose of in the fantasy of 'frictionless capitalism' does not only refer to the reality of material obstacles that sustain any exchange process, but, above all, to the Real of traumatic social antagonisms, Power relations and so forth that brand the space of social exchange with a pathological twist. In his *Grundrisse* manuscripts, Marx pointed out the way that the very material disposition of a nineteenth-century industrial production site directly materializes the capitalist relationship of domination – the worker as a mere appendix subordinated to the machinery owned by the capitalist;[9] *mutatis mutandis*, the same goes for cyberspace. In the social conditions of late capitalism, the very materiality of cyberspace automatically generates the illusory abstract space of 'frictionless' exchange in which the particularity of the participants' social position is obliterated.

The predominant 'spontaneous ideology of cyberspace' is so-called 'cyber-revolutionism', which relies on the notion of cyberspace – or the world wide web – as a self-evolving 'natural' organism.[10] Crucial here is the blurring of the distinction between 'culture' and 'nature': the obverse of the 'naturalization of culture' (market, society as living organism) is the 'culturalization of nature' (life itself is conceived of as a set of self-reproducing data – 'genes are memes').[11] This new notion of Life is thus neutral with respect to the distinction between natural and cultural or 'artificial' processes. The Earth (as *Gaia*) and the global market both appear as gigantic self-regulated living systems whose basic structure is defined in terms of the process of coding and decoding, of transmitting information. The idea of the world wide web as a living organism is often evoked in contexts that may seem liberating – say, against the State censorship of the Internet. However, this very demonization of the State is thoroughly ambiguous, because it is predominantly appropriated by right-wing populist discourse and/ or market liberalism: its main targets are the State interventions that try to maintain a kind of minimal social balance and security. The title of Michael Rothschild's book – *Bionomics: The Inevitability of Capitalism* – is indicative here.[12] So, while cyberspace ideologists can dream about the next evolutionary step in which we will no longer be mechanically interacting 'Cartesian' individuals, in which each 'person' will cut their substantial link to their body and conceive of themselves as part of the new holistic Mind that lives and acts through them, what is obfuscated in such a direct 'naturalization' of the world wide web or market is the set of power relations – of political decisions, of institutional conditions – that 'organisms' like the Internet (or the market or capitalism . . .) need in order to thrive.

Ideological underground

What one should thus do is to reassert the old Marxist critique of 'reification': today, emphasizing the depoliticized 'objective' economic logic against the allegedly 'outdated' forms of ideological passions is *the* predominant ideological form, because ideology is always self-referential, that is, it always defines itself through some distance towards an Other dismissed and denounced as 'ideological'.[13] Jacques Rancière gave a poignant expression to the 'bad surprise' that awaits today's postmodern ideologues of the 'end of politics': it is as if we are witnessing the ultimate confirmation of Freud's thesis, from *Civilization and its Discontents*, concerning the way that, after every assertion of Eros, Thanatos reasserts itself with a vengeance. At the very moment when, according to the official ideology, we are finally leaving behind 'immature' political passions (the régime of the 'political' – class struggle and other 'out-dated' divisive antagonisms) for the 'mature' post-ideological pragmatic universe of rational administration and negotiated consensus, for a universe, free of utopian impulses, in which the dispassionate administration of social affairs goes hand in hand with aestheticized hedonism (the pluralism of 'ways of life') – at this very moment, the foreclosed political is celebrating a triumphant comeback in its most archaic form: that of pure, distilled racist hatred of the Other that renders the rational tolerant attitude utterly impotent.[14] In this precise sense, contemporary 'postmodern' racism is the *symptom* of multiculturalist late-capitalism, bringing to light the inherent contradiction of the liberal-democratic ideological project. Liberal 'tolerance' condones the folklorist Other deprived of its substance – like the multitude of 'ethnic cuisines' in a contemporary megalopolis; however, any 'real' Other is instantly denounced for its 'fundamentalism', because the kernel of Otherness resides in the regulation of its *jouissance*: the 'real Other' is by definition 'patriarchal', 'violent', never the Other of ethereal wisdom and charming customs. One is tempted to reactualize here the old Marcusean notion of 'repressive tolerance', reconceiving of it as the tolerance of the Other in its aseptic, benign form, which forecloses the dimension of the Real of the Other's *jouissance*.[15]

The same reference to *jouissance* enables us to shed new light on the horrors of the Bosnian war, as they are reflected in Emir Kusturica's film, *Underground* (1995). The political meaning of this film does not reside primarily in its overt tendentiousness, in the way that it takes sides in the post-Yugoslav conflict – heroic Serbs versus the treacherous, pro-Nazi Slovenes and Croats – but, rather, in its very 'depoliticized' aestheticist attitude. That is to say, when, in his conversations with the journalists of *Cahiers du cinéma*, Kusturica insisted that *Underground* is not a political film at all, but a kind of liminal trance-like subjective experience, a 'deferred suicide', he thereby unknowingly placed his true political cards on the table by indicating that *Underground* stages the 'apolitical' fantasmatic background of post-Yugoslav ethnic cleansing and war time cruelties. How? The predominant cliché about the Balkans is that the Balkan people are caught in the fantasmatic whirlpool of historical myth – Kusturica himself endorses this view: 'In this region, war is a natural phenomenon. It is like a natural catastrophe, like an earthquake that explodes from time to time. In my film, I tried to clarify the state of things in this chaotic part of the world. It seems that nobody is able to locate the roots of this terrible conflict.'[16] What we find here, of course, is an exemplary case of 'Balkanism', functioning in a similar way to Edward Said's concept of 'Orientalism': the Balkans as the timeless space on to which the West projects its fantasmatic content. Together with Milche Manchevski's *Before the Rain* (which almost won the Oscar for best foreign film in 1995), *Underground* is thus the ultimate ideological product of Western liberal multiculturalism: what these two films offer to the Western liberal gaze is precisely what this gaze wants to see in the Balkan war – the spectacle of a timeless, incomprehensible, mythical cycle of passions, in contrast to decadent and anaemic Western life.[17]

The weak point of the universal multiculturalist gaze does not reside in its inability to 'throw out the bath water without losing the baby': it is deeply wrong to assert that, when one throws out the nationalist bath water – 'excessive' fanaticism – one should be careful not to lose the baby of 'healthy' national identity, so that one should trace the line of separation between the proper degree of 'healthy' nationalism that guarantees the requisite minimum of national identity and 'excessive' nationalism. Such a common sense distinction *reproduces the very nationalist reasoning that aims to get rid of 'impure' excess*. One is therefore tempted to propose a homology with psychoanalytic treatment, whose aim is also not to get rid of the bath water (symptoms, pathological tics) in order to keep the baby (the kernel of the healthy Ego) safe, but, rather, to throw out the baby (to suspend the patient's Ego) in order to confront the patient with his 'bath water', with the symptoms and fantasies that structure his *jouissance*. In the matter of national identity, one should also endeavour to throw out the baby (the spiritual purity of national identity) in order to render visible the fantasmatic support that structures the *jouissance* in the national Thing. And the merit of *Underground* is that, unknowingly, it renders visible precisely this bath water.

The time machine

Underground brings to the light of day the obscene 'underground' of public, official discourse – represented in the film by the Titoist

Communist régime. One should bear in mind that the 'underground' to which the film's title refers is not only the domain of 'deferred suicide', of the eternal orgy of drinking, singing and copulating, which takes place in the suspension of time and outside public space: it also stands for the 'underground' workshop in which the enslaved workers, isolated from the rest of the world, and misled into thinking that World War II is still going on, work day and night and produce arms sold by Marko, the hero of the film, their 'owner' and the big Manipulator, the only one who mediates between the 'underground' and the public world. Kusturica refers here to the old European fairy-tale motif of diligent dwarfs (usually controlled by an evil magician) who, during the night, while people are asleep, emerge from their hiding-place and accomplish their work (set the house in order, cook the meals), so that when, in the morning, people awaken, they find their work magically done. Kusturica's 'underground' is the last embodiment of this motif that is found from Wagner's *Rheingold* (the Nibelungs who work in their underground caves, driven by their cruel master, the dwarf Alberich) to Fritz Lang's *Metropolis, in* which the enslaved industrial workers live and work deep beneath the earth's surface to produce wealth for the ruling capitalists.

This schema of the 'underground' slaves, dominated by a manipulative evil Master, takes place against the background of the opposition between the two figures of the Master: on the one hand, the 'visible' public symbolic authority; on the other hand, the 'invisible' spectral apparition. When the subject is endowed with symbolic authority, he acts as an appendix to his symbolic title, that is, it is the 'big Other', the symbolic institution, that acts through him: suffice it to recall a judge who may be a miserable and corrupt person, but the moment he puts on his robe and other insignia, his words are those of Law itself. On the other hand, the 'invisible' Master – whose exemplary case is the anti-Semitic figure of the 'Jew' who, invisible to the public eye, pulls the strings of social life – is a kind of uncanny double of public authority: he has to act in shadow, invisible to the public eye, irradiating a phantom-like, spectral omnipotence.[18] Marko from *Underground* is to be located in this lineage of the evil magician who controls an invisible empire of enslaved workers: he is a kind of uncanny double of Tito as the public symbolic Master. The problem with *Underground* is that it falls into the cynical trap of presenting this obscene 'underground' from a benevolent distance. *Underground* is, of course, multi-layered and self-reflective, it plays with a multitude of clichés (the Serbian myth of a true man who, even when bombs fall around him, calmly continues his meal and so on) that are 'not to be taken literally' – however, *it is precisely through such self-distance that 'postmodern' cynical ideology functions*. In a well-known and much-reprinted piece, 'Fourteen theses on fascism' (1995), Umberto Eco enumerated the series of features that define the kernel of the Fascist attitude: dogmatic tenacity, the absence of humour, insensibility to rational argument . . . he couldn't have been more wrong. Today's neofascism is more and more 'postmodern', civilized, playful, involving ironic self-distance, and *yet for all that no less fascist*.

So, in a way, Kusturica was right in his interview with *Cahiers du cinéma*: he does somehow 'clarify the state of things in this chaotic part of the world' by way of bringing to light its 'underground' fantasmatic support. He thereby unknowingly provides the libidinal economy of the ethnic slaughter in Bosnia: the pseudo-Bataillean trance of excessive expenditure, the continuous mad-rhythm of drinking-eating-singing-fornicating. And, *therein consists the 'dream' of the ethnic cleansers, therein resides the answer to the question, 'How were they able to do it?'* If the standard definition of war is that of 'a continuation of politics by other means', then the fact that Radovan Karadžić, the leader of the Bosnian Serbs, is a poet is more than a gratuitous coincidence: ethnic cleansing in Bosnia was the 'continuation of (a kind of) *poetry* by other means'.

'Concrete' versus 'abstract' universality

How, then, is this multiculturalist ideological poetry embedded in today's global capitalism? The problem that lurks beneath it is that of universalism. Étienne Balibar discerned three levels of universality in today's societies: the 'real' universality of the process of globalization and the supplementary process of 'internal exclusions' (the extent to which, now, the fate of each of us hinges on the intricate web of global market relations); the universality of the fiction that regulates ideological hegemony (Church or State as the universal 'imagined communities', which allow the subject to acquire a distance towards his immersion in his immediate social group – class, profession, sex, religion – and posit himself as a free subject); the universality of an Ideal, as exemplified by the revolutionary demand for *égaliberté* (equality freedom), which remains an unconditional excess, setting in motion permanent insurrection against the existing order, and thus can never be 'gentrified', included in the existing order.[19]

The point, of course, is that the boundary between these three universals is never stable and fixed: *égaliberté* can serve as the hegemonic idea that enables us to identify with our particular social role (I am a poor artisan, but precisely as such, I participate in the life of my Nation-State as an equal and free citizen), or as the irreducible excess that destabilizes every fixed social order. In the Jacobin universe, what initially was the destabilizing universality of the Ideal, which, setting in motion the incessant process of social transformation, later became the ideological fiction allowing each individual to identify with his specific place in the social space. In Hegelese, the alternative here is as follows: is the Universal 'abstract' (opposed to concrete content) or 'concrete' (in the sense that I experience my very particular mode of social life as the specific mode of my participation in the universal social order)? Balibar's point, of course, is that the tension between the two is irreducible: the excess of abstract-negative-ideal universality, its unsettling-destabilizing force, can never be fully integrated into the harmonious whole of a 'concrete universality'.[20] However, there is another tension, the tension between the two modes of 'concrete universality' itself, which seems more crucial today. That is to say, the 'real' universality of today's globalization through the global market involves its own fiction (or even ideal) of multiculturalist tolerance, respect and protection of human rights, democracy and so forth; it involves its own pseudo-Hegelian 'concrete universality' of a world order whose universal features of the world market, human rights and democracy allow each specific 'lifestyle' to flourish in its particularity. So a tension inevitably emerges between this postmodern, post-Nation-State, 'concrete universality' and the earlier 'concrete universality' of the Nation-State.

Hegel was the first to elaborate the properly modern paradox of *individualization through secondary identification*.[21] At the beginning, the subject is immersed in the particular life-form into which he was born (family, local community); the only way for him to tear himself away from his primordial 'organic' community, to cut his links with it and to assert himself as an 'autonomous individual', is to shift his fundamental allegiance, to recognize the substance of his being in another, secondary community that is universal and, simultaneously, 'artificial', no longer 'spontaneous' but 'mediated', sustained by the activity of independent free subjects – nation versus local community; a profession in the modern sense (a job in a large anonymous company) versus the 'personalized' relationship between an apprentice and his Master-artisan; the academic community of knowledge versus the traditional wisdom passed from generation to generation. In this shift from primary to secondary identification, primary identifications undergo a kind of transubstantiation: they start to function as the form of appearance of the universal secondary identification – say, precisely by being a good member of my family, I thereby contribute to the proper functioning of my Nation-State. The universal secondary identification remains 'abstract' in so far as it is directly opposed to the particular forms of primary identification, that is, in so far as it compels the subject to renounce his primary identifications; it becomes 'concrete' when it reintegrates primary identifications, transforming them into the modes of appearance of the secondary identification. This tension between 'abstract' and 'concrete' universality is clearly discernible in the precarious social status of the early Christian Church: on the one hand, there was the zealotry of the radical groups that saw no way to combine the true Christian attitude with the existing space of predominant social relations, and thus posed a serious threat to the social order; on the other hand, there were the attempts to reconcile Christianity with the existing structure of domination, so that participation in social life and occupying a place within a hierarchy were compatible with being a good Christian – indeed, accomplishing your determinate social role was not only seen as compatible with being a Christian, it was even perceived as a specific way to fulfil the universal duty of being a Christian.

In the modern era, the predominant social form of the 'concrete universal' is the Nation-State as the medium of our particular social identities: the determinate form of my social life (as, say, worker, professor, politician, farmer, lawyer) is the specific mode of my participation in the universal life of my Nation-State. With regard to this logic of transubstantiation that guarantees the ideological unity of a

Nation-State, the United States plays the unique role of an exception: the key element of standard 'American ideology' consists in the endeavour to transubstantiate the very fidelity to one's particular ethnic roots into an expression of 'being American': in order to be 'a good American', one does not have to renounce one's ethnic roots – Italians, Germans, Africans, Jews, Greeks, Koreans, they are 'all Americans', that is, the very particularity of their ethnic identity, the way they 'stick to it', makes them Americans. This transubstantiation, by means of which the tension between my particular ethnic identity and my universal identity as a member of a Nation-State is surpassed, is threatened today: it is as if the positive charge of pathetic patriotic identification with the universal frame of the American Nation-State has been seriously eroded; 'Americanness', the fact of 'being American', less and less gives rise to the sublime effect of being part of a gigantic ideological project – 'the American dream' – so that the American state is more and more experienced as a simple formal framework for the coexistence of the multiplicity of ethnic, religious or lifestyle communities.

Modernism in reverse

This gradual collapse – or, rather, loss of substance – of the 'American dream' bears witness to the unexpected *reversal* of the passage from primary to secondary identification described by Hegel: in our 'postmodern' societies, the 'abstract' institution of secondary identification is increasingly experienced as an external, purely formal frame that is not really binding, so that one is more and more looking for support in 'primordial', usually smaller (ethnic, religious) forms of identification. Even when these forms of identification are more 'artificial' than national identification – as is the case with gay communities – they are more 'immediate' in the sense of seizing the individual directly and overwhelmingly, in his specific 'way of life', thereby restraining the 'abstract' freedom he possesses in his capacity as the citizen of a Nation-State. What we are dealing with today is thus a reverse process to that of the early modern constitution of a Nation: in contrast to the 'nationalization of the ethnic' – the de-ethnicization, the 'sublation [*Aufhebung*]' of the ethnic into the national – we are now dealing with the 'ethnicization of the national', with a renewed search for (or reconstitution of) 'ethnic roots'. The crucial point here, however, is that this 'regression' from secondary to 'primordial' forms of identification with 'organic' communities is already 'mediated': it is a *reaction* to the universal dimension of the world market – as such, it occurs on its terrain, against its background. For that reason, what we are dealing with in these phenomena is not a 'regression' but rather the form of appearance of its exact opposite: in a kind of 'negation of negation', *this very reassertion of 'primordial' identification signals that the loss of organic-substantial unity is fully consummated.*

To make this point clear, one should bear in mind what is perhaps the fundamental lesson of postmodern politics: far from being a 'natural' unity of social life, a balanced frame, a kind of Aristotelian *entelechia* towards which all previous development advances, the universal form of the Nation-State is rather a precarious, temporary balance between the relationship to a particular ethnic Thing (patriotism, *pro patria mori* and so forth) and the (potentially) universal function of the market. On the one hand, it 'sublates' organic local forms of identification into the universal 'patriotic' identification; on the other hand, it posits itself as a kind of pseudo-natural boundary of the market economy, delimiting 'internal' from 'external' commerce – economic activity is thus 'sublimated', raised to the level of the ethnic Thing, legitimated as a patriotic contribution to the nation's greatness. This balance is constantly threatened from both sides, from the side of previous organic forms of particular identification that do not simply disappear but continue their subterranean life outside the universal public sphere, as well as from the side of the immanent logic of Capital whose 'transnational' nature is inherently indifferent to the boundaries of Nation-State. And today's new 'fundamentalist' ethnic identifications involve a kind of 'desublimation', a process of disintegration of this precarious unity of the 'national economy' into its two constituent parts, the transnational market function and the relationship to the ethnic Thing.[22] It is therefore only today, in contemporary 'fundamentalist' ethnic, religious, lifestyle communities, that the splitting between the abstract form of commerce and the relationship to the particular ethnic Thing, inaugurated by the Enlightenment project, is fully realized: today's postmodern ethnic or religious 'fundamentalism' and xenophobia are not only not 'regressive', but, on the contrary, offer the supreme proof of the final emancipation of the economic logic of the market from the attachment to the ethnic

Thing.[23] Therein resides the highest speculative effort of the dialectic of social life: not in describing the process of mediation of the primordial immediacy – say, the disintegration of organic community in 'alienated' individualist society – but in explaining how this very process of mediation characteristic of modernity can give birth to new forms of 'organic' immediacy. The standard story of the passage from *Gemeinschaft* to *Gesellschaft* should therefore be supplemented by an account of the way that this process of becoming-society of community gives rise to different forms of new, 'mediated' communities – say, 'lifestyle communities'.

Multiculturalism

How, then, does the universe of Capital relate to the form of Nation-State in our era of global capitalism? Perhaps this relationship is best designated as 'auto-colonization': with the direct multinational functioning of Capital, we are no longer dealing with the standard opposition between metropolis and colonized countries; a global company, as it were, cuts its umbilical cord with its mother-nation and treats its country of origin as simply another territory to be colonized. This is what disturbs so much the patriotically oriented right-wing populists, from Le Pen to Buchanan: the fact that the new multinationals have exactly the same attitude towards the French or American local population as they do towards the population of Mexico, Brazil or Taiwan. Is there not a kind of poetic justice in this self-referential turn? Today's global capitalism is thus again a kind of 'negation of negation', after national capitalism and its internationalist/colonialist phase. At the beginning (ideally, of course), there is capitalism within the confines of a Nation-State, with the accompanying international trade (exchange between sovereign Nation-States); what follows is the relationship of colonization in which the colonizing country subordinates and exploits (economically, politically, culturally) the colonized country; the final moment of this process is the paradox of colonization in which there are only colonies, no colonizing countries – the colonizing power is no longer a Nation-State but directly the global company. In the long term, we shall all not only wear Banana Republic shirts, but also live in banana republics.

And, of course, the ideal form of ideology of this global capitalism is multiculturalism, the attitude that, from a kind of empty global position, treats *each* local culture the way the colonizer treats colonized people – as 'natives' whose mores are to be carefully studied and 'respected'. That is to say, the relationship between traditional imperialist colonialism and global capitalist self-colonization is exactly the same as the relationship between Western cultural imperialism and multiculturalism: in the same way that global capitalism involves the paradox of colonization without the colonizing Nation-State metropole, multiculturalism involves patronizing Eurocentrist distance and/or respect for local cultures without roots in one's own particular culture. In other words, multiculturalism is a disavowed, inverted, self-referential form of racism, a 'racism with a distance' – it 'respects' the Other's identity, conceiving of the Other as a self-enclosed 'authentic' community towards which he, the multiculturalist, maintains a distance rendered possible by his privileged universal position. Multiculturalism is a racism which empties its own position of all positive content (the multiculturalist is not a direct racist, he doesn't oppose to the Other the *particular* values of his own culture), but nonetheless retains this position as the privileged *empty point of universality* from which one is able to appreciate (and depreciate) properly other particular cultures – the multiculturalist respect for the Other's specificity is the very form of asserting one's own superiority.

What about the rather obvious counter-argument that the multiculturalist's neutrality is false, since his position silently privileges Eurocentrist content? This line of reasoning is right, but for the wrong reason. The particular cultural background or roots that always support the universal multiculturalist position are not its 'truth', hidden beneath the mask of universality – 'multiculturalist universalism is really Eurocentrist' – but rather the opposite: the stain of particular roots is the fantasmatic screen that conceals the fact that the subject is already thoroughly 'rootless', that his true position is the void of universality. Let me recall here my own paraphrase of de Quincey's witticism about the simple art of murder: how many people have begun with an innocent group sex orgy and ended up sharing meals in a Chinese restaurant![24] The point of this paraphrase is to reverse the standard relationship between the surface-pretext and the unacknowledged wish: sometimes, the most difficult thing is to accept appearance at its surface value – we imagine multiple fantasmatic scenarios in order to cover it up with 'deeper meanings'. It may well be that my 'true desire', discernible behind my refusal to share a Chinese meal, is my fascination with the fantasy of a group orgy, but the key point is that this fantasy which structures my desire is in itself already a defence against my 'oral' drive, which goes its way with absolute coercion . . .

What we find here is the exact equivalent of Darian Leader's example of the man in a restaurant with his date, who, when asking the waiter for the table, says 'Bedroom for two, please!', instead of 'Table for two, please!' One should turn around the standard Freudian explanation ('Of course, his mind was already on the night of sex he planned after the meal!'): this intervention of the subterranean sexual fantasy is rather the screen that serves as the defence against the oral drive that effectively matters more to him than sex.[25] In his analysis of the French Revolution of 1848, Marx provides a similar example of such a double deception:[26] the Party of Order, which took over after the Revolution, publicly supported the Republic, yet secretly, they believed in Restoration – they used every opportunity to mock republican rituals and to signal in any way possible where 'their heart is'. The paradox, however, was that the truth of their activity resided in the external form they privately mocked and despised: this republican form was not a mere semblance beneath which the royalist desire lurked – it was rather the secret clinging to royalism that enabled them to fulfil their actual historical function, to implement the bourgeois republican law and order. Marx himself mentions the way that members of the Party of Order found immense pleasure in their occasional Royalist 'slips of the tongue' against the Republic – referring, for instance, to France as a Kingdom in their parliamentary debates: these slips of the tongue articulated their fantasmatic illusions, which served as the screen enabling them to blind themselves to the social reality of what was taking place *on the surface*.

The machine in the ghost

And, *mutatis mutandis*, the same goes for today's capitalist who still clings to some particular cultural heritage, identifying it as the secret source of his success – Japanese executives participating in tea ceremonies or obeying the bushido code – or for the inverse case of the Western journalist in search of the particular secret of the Japanese success: this very reference to a particular cultural formula is a screen for the universal anonymity of Capital. The true horror does not reside in the particular content hidden beneath the universality of global Capital, but rather in the fact that Capital is effectively an anonymous global machine blindly running its course, that there is effectively no particular secret agent who animates it. The horror is not the (particular living) ghost in the (dead universal) machine, but the (dead universal) machine in the very heart of each (particular living) ghost.

The conclusion to be drawn is thus that the problematic of multiculturalism – the hybrid coexistence of diverse cultural life-worlds – that imposes itself today is the form of appearance of its opposite, of the massive presence of capitalism as *universal* world system: it bears witness to the unprecedented homogenization of the contemporary world. It is effectively as if, since the horizon of social imagination no longer allows us to entertain the idea of an eventual demise of capitalism – since, as we might put it, everybody silently accepts that *capitalism is here to stay* – critical energy has found a substitute outlet in fighting for cultural differences, which leave the basic homogeneity of the capitalist world system intact. So we are fighting our PC battles for the rights of ethnic minorities, of gays and lesbians, of different lifestyles and so on, while capitalism pursues its triumphant march – and today's critical theory, in the guise of 'cultural studies', is doing the ultimate service to the unrestrained development of capitalism by actively participating in the ideological effort to render its massive presence invisible: in a typical postmodern 'cultural criticism', the very mention of capitalism as world system tends to give rise to the accusation of 'essentialism', 'fundamentalism' and other crimes.

The structure here is that of a *symptom*. When one is dealing with a universal structuring principle, one always automatically assumes that – in principle, precisely – it is possible to apply this principle to all of its potential elements, and that the empirical non-realization of the principle is merely a matter of contingent circumstances. A symptom, however, is an element that – although the non-realization of the universal principle in it appears to hinge on contingent circumstances – *must* remain an exception, that is, the point of suspension of the universal principle: if the universal principle were to apply also to this point, the universal system itself would disintegrate. As is well known, in the paragraphs on civil society in his *Philosophy* of Right, Hegel demonstrated how the large class of 'rabble [*Pöbel*]' in modern civil society is not an accidental result of social mismanagement, inadequate government measures or economic bad luck: the inherent structural dynamics of civil society necessarily give rise to a class that is excluded from the benefits of civil society, a class deprived of elementary human rights and therefore also delivered of duties toward society, an element within civil society that negates its universal principle, a kind of 'un-Reason inherent to Reason itself' – in short, its *symptom*.

Are we not witnessing the same phenomenon today, and in an even stronger form, with the growth of an underclass excluded, sometimes for generations, from the benefits of affluent liberal-democratic society? Today's 'exceptions' – the homeless, the ghettoized, the permanently unemployed – are the symptom of the late capitalist universal system, a growing and permanent reminder of how the immanent logic of late capitalism works: the properly capitalist utopia is that, through appropriate measures (for progressive liberals, affirmative action; for conservatives, a return to self-reliance and family values), this 'exception' could be – in the long term and in principle, at least – abolished. And is not a homologous utopia at work in the notion of a 'rainbow coalition': in the idea that, at some utopian future moment, all 'progressive' struggles – for gay and lesbian rights, for the rights of ethnic and religious minorities, the ecological struggle, the feminist struggle and so on – will be united in the common 'chain of equivalences'? Again, this necessity of failure is structural: the point is not simply that, because of the empirical complexity of the situation, all particular 'progressive' fights will never be united, that 'wrong' chains of equivalences will always occur – say, the enchainment of the fight for African-American ethnic identity with patriarchal and homophobic ideology – but rather that emergences of 'wrong' enchainments are grounded in the very structuring principle of today's 'progressive' politics of establishing 'chains of equivalences': the very domain of the multitude of particular struggles with their continuously shifting displacements and condensations is sustained by the 'repression' of the key role of economic struggle – the leftist politics of the 'chains of equivalences' among the plurality of struggles is strictly correlative to the silent abandonment of the analysis of capitalism as a global economic system and to the acceptance of capitalist economic relations as the unquestionable framework.[27]

The falsity of elitist multiculturalist liberalism thus resides in the tension between content and form that already characterized the first great ideological project of tolerant universalism, that of freemasonry: the doctrine of freemasonry (the universal brotherhood of all men based on the light of Reason) clearly clashes with its form of expression and organization (a secret society with its rituals of initiation) – the very form of expression and articulation of freemasonry belies its positive doctrine. In a strictly homologous way, the contemporary 'politically correct' liberal attitude that perceives itself as surpassing the limitations of its ethnic identity (as a 'citizen of the world' without anchors in any particular ethnic community) functions, *within its own society*, as a narrow, elitist, upper-middle-class circle clearly opposing itself to the majority of common people, despised for being caught in their narrow ethnic or community confines.

For a leftist suspension of the law

How, then, do leftists, who are aware of the falsity of this multiculturalist postmodernism, react to it? Their reaction assumes the form of what Hegel called the *infinite judgement*: the judgement which posits the speculative identity of two thoroughly incompatible terms – Hegel's best-known example is from the sub-chapter on phrenology in his *Phenomenology of Spirit*: 'the Spirit is a bone'. The infinite judgement that best encapsulates this reaction is: 'Adorno (the most sophisticated 'elitist' critical theorist) is Buchanan (the lowest of American rightist populism)'. That is to say, those critics of postmodern multiculturalist elitism – from Christopher Lasch to Paul Piccone – risk endorsing neo-conservative populism, with its notions of the reassertion of community, local democracy and active citizenship, as the only politically relevant answer to the all-pervasive predominance of 'instrumental Reason', of the bureaucratization and instrumentalization of our life-world.[28] Of course, it is easy to dismiss today's populism as a nostalgic reactive formation to the process of modernization, and as such inherently paranoiac, in search of an external cause of malignancy, of a secret agent who pulls the strings and is thus responsible for the woes of modernization – Jews, international capital, non-patriotic multiculturalist managers, state bureaucracy and so on; the problem is rather to conceive of this populism as a new form of 'false transparency', which, far from presenting a serious obstacle to capitalist modernization, paves the way for it. In other words, far more interesting than bemoaning the disintegration of community life through the impact of new technologies is to analyse the way that technological progress itself gives rise to new communities that gradually 'naturalize' themselves – like virtual communities.

What these leftist advocates of populism fail to perceive is that today's populism, far from presenting a threat to global capitalism, remains its inherent product. Paradoxically, today's true conservatives are rather the leftist 'critical theorists' who reject liberal multiculturalism as well as fundamentalist populism, those who clearly perceive the complicity between global capitalism and ethnic fundamentalism. They point towards the third domain which belongs neither to global market-society nor to the new forms of ethnic fundamentalism: the domain of the *political*, the public space of civil society, of active, responsible citizenship – the fight for human rights, ecology and so forth. However, the problem is that this very form of political space is more and more threatened by the onslaught of globalization; consequently, one cannot simply return to it or revitalize it. To avoid a misunderstanding: our point is not the old 'economic essentialist' one according to which, in the case of England today, the Labour victory really did not change anything – and as such is even more dangerous than continuing Tory rule, since it gave rise to the misleading impression that there was a change. There are many things the Labour government can achieve; it can contribute a great deal to the passage from traditional English parochial jingoism to a more 'enlightened' liberal democracy with a much stronger element of social solidarity (from health care to education), to the respect for human rights (in its diverse forms, from women's rights to the rights of ethnic groups); one should use the Labour victory as an incentive to revitalize the diverse forms of the struggle for *égaliberté*. (With the socialist electoral victory in France, the situation is even more ambiguous, because Jospin's programme does contain some elements of a direct confrontation with the logic of Capital.) Even when the change is not substantial but the mere semblance of a new beginning, the very fact that a situation is perceived by the majority of the population as a 'new beginning' opens up the space for important ideological and political rearticulations – as we have already seen, the fundamental lesson of the dialectic of ideology is that appearances *do* matter.

Nonetheless, the post-Nation-State logic of Capital remains the Real that lurks in the background, while all three main leftist reactions to the process of globalization – liberal multiculturalism; the attempt to embrace populism by way of discerning, beneath its fundamentalist appearance, the resistance against 'instrumental reason'; the attempt to keep open the space of the political – seem inappropriate. Although the last approach is based on the correct insight about the complicity between multiculturalism and fundamentalism, it avoids the crucial question: *how are we to reinvent political space in today's conditions of globalization?* The politicization of the series of particular struggles that leaves intact the global process of Capital is clearly not sufficient. What this means is that one should reject the opposition that, within the frame of late capitalist liberal democracy, imposes itself as the main axis of ideological struggle: the tension between 'open' post-ideological universalist liberal tolerance and particularist 'new fundamentalisms'. Against the liberal centre that presents itself as neutral and post-ideological, relying on the rule of the Law, one should reassert the old leftist motif of the necessity to suspend the neutral space of Law.

Of course, both the Left and the Right involve their own mode of the suspension of the Law on behalf of some higher or more fundamental interest. The rightist suspension, from anti-Dreyfusards to Oliver North, acknowledges its violation of the letter of the Law, but justifies it via the reference to some higher national interest: it presents its violation as a painful self-sacrifice for the good of the Nation.[29] As to the leftist suspension, suffice it to mention two films, *Under Fire* (Roger Spottiswoode, 1983) and *Watch on the Rhine* (Herman Shumlin, 1943). The first takes place during the Nicaraguan revolution, when an American photo-journalist faces a troublesome dilemma: just prior to the victory of the revolution, Somozistas kill a charismatic Sandinista leader, so the Sandinistas ask the journalist to fake a photograph of their dead leader, presenting him as alive, thus belying the Somozistas' claims about his death – in this way, he would contribute to a swift victory of the revolution and reduce bloodshed. Professional ethics, of course, strictly prohibit such an act, because it violates the unbiased objectivity of reporting and makes the journalist an instrument of the political fight; the journalist nevertheless chooses the 'leftist' option and fakes the picture. In *Watch on the* Rhine, based on a play by Lillian Hellmann, this dilemma is even more aggravated: in the late 1930s, a fugitive family of German political emigrants involved in the anti-Nazi struggle comes to stay with its distant relatives, an idyllic all-American small-town middle-class family; soon, however, the Germans face an unexpected threat in the guise of an acquaintance of the American family, a rightist who blackmails the emigrants and, via his contacts with the German embassy, endangers members of the underground in Germany itself. The father of the emigrant family decides to kill him and thereby puts the American family in a difficult moral dilemma: the empty moralizing solidarity with the victims of Nazism is over; now they have effectively to take sides and dirty their hands by covering up the killing. Here also, the family decides on the 'leftist' option. 'Left' is defined by this readiness to suspend the abstract moral frame, or, to paraphrase Kierkegaard, to accomplish a *political suspension of the Ethical*.

The universality to come

The lesson of all of this, which gained actuality in relation to the Western reaction to the Bosnian war, is that there is no way to avoid being partial, since neutrality involves taking sides – in the case of the Bosnian war, 'balanced' talk about the Balkan ethnic 'tribal warfare' already endorses the Serbian standpoint: the humanitarian liberal equidistance can easily slip into or coincide with its opposite and effectively tolerate the most violent 'ethnic cleansing'. So, in short, the leftist does not simply violate the liberal's impartial neutrality; what he claims is that there is no such neutrality. The cliché of the liberal centre, of course, is that both suspensions, the rightist and the leftist, ultimately amount to the same thing, to a totalitarian threat to the rule of Law. The entire consistency of the Left hinges on proving that, on the contrary, each of the two suspensions follows a different logic. While the Right legitimizes its suspension of the Ethical by its anti-universalist stance, by way of a reference to its particular (religious, patriotic) identity which overrules any universal moral or legal standards, the Left legitimizes its suspension of the Ethical precisely by means of a reference to the true universality to come. Or, to put it in another way, the Left simultaneously accepts the antagonistic character of society (there is no neutral position, struggle is constitutive) *and* remains universalist (speaking on behalf of universal emancipation): in the leftist perspective, accepting the radically antagonistic – that is, *political* – character of social life, accepting the necessity of 'taking sides', is the only way effectively to be *Universal*.

How are we to comprehend this paradox? It can only be conceived of if *the antagonism is inherent to universality itself*, that is, if universality itself is split into the 'false' concrete universality that legitimizes the existing division of the Whole into functional parts and the impossible/ Real demand of 'abstract' universality (Balibar's *égaliberté*). The leftist political gesture par excellence (in contrast to the rightist motif 'to each his or her own place') is thus to question the concrete existing universal order on behalf of its symptom, of the part that, although inherent to the existing universal order, has no 'proper place' within it (say, illegal immigrants or the homeless in our societies). This procedure of *identifying with the symptom* is the exact and necessary obverse of the standard critical and ideological move of recognizing a particular content behind some abstract universal notion ('the "man" of human rights is effectively the white male owner'), of denouncing the neutral universality as false: in it, one pathetically asserts (and identifies with) *the point of inherent exception/exclusion, the 'abject', of the concrete positive order, as the only point of true universality*, as the point which belies the existing concrete universality. It is easy to demonstrate that, say, the subdivision of the people who live in a country into 'full' citizens and temporary immigrant workers privileges 'full' citizens and excludes immigrants from the public space proper – in the same way in which man and woman are not two species of a neutral universal genus of humanity, because the content of the genus as such involves some mode of 'repression' of the feminine; it is far more productive, theoretically as well as politically – because it opens up the way for the 'progressive' subversion of hegemony – to perform the opposite operation of *identifying universality with the point of exclusion*, in our case, of saying 'we are all immigrant workers'. In a hierarchically structured society, the measure of its true universality resides in the way its parts relate to those 'at the bottom', excluded by and from all others – in ex-Yugoslavia, for example, universality was represented by Albanian and Bosnian Muslims, looked down on by all other nations. The recent pathetic statement of solidarity, 'Sarajevo is the capital of Europe', was also an exemplary case of such a notion of exception as embodying universality: the way that enlightened liberal Europe related to Sarajevo bore witness to the way it related to itself, to its universal notion.[30]

This assertion of the universality of antagonism in no way entails that 'in social life, there is no dialogue, only war'. Rightists speak of social (or sexual) *warfare*, while leftists speak of social (or class) *struggle*. There are two variations on Joseph Göbbels' infamous statement, 'When I hear the word "culture", I reach for my pistol': first, 'When I hear the word "culture", I reach for my cheque-book', pronounced by the cynical cinema producer in Godard's *Mépris*, and then the leftist enlightened reversal, 'When I hear the word "gun", I reach for culture'. When today's neo-Nazi street-fighter hears the word 'Western Christian culture', he reaches for his gun in order to defend it from the Turks, Arabs, Jews, thereby destroying what he purports to defend. Liberal capitalism has no need for such direct violence: the market does the job of destroying culture far more smoothly and efficiently. In clear contrast to both these attitudes, the leftist Enlightenment is defined by the wager that culture can serve as an efficient answer to the gun: the outburst of raw violence is a kind of *passage à l'acte* rooted in the subject's ignorance – as such, it can be counteracted by the struggle whose main form is *reflective knowledge*.

Notes

This essay was first published in *New Left Review* 225, 1997, pp. 28–51.

1 Another name for this short-circuit between the Universal and the Particular is, of course, the 'suture': the operation of hegemony 'sutures' the empty Universal to a particular content.

2 Ernesto Laclau, *Emancipation(s)*, London and New York, Verso, 1996, pp. 14–15.

3   Étienne Balibar, 'Ambiguous identities', in *Politics and the Other Scene*, trans. Christine Jones, James Swenson and Chris Turner, London and New York, Verso, 2002, pp. 56–73.

4   Fredric Jameson, 'Reification and utopia in mass culture', in *Signatures of the Visible*, New York and London, Routledge, 1990, p. 30. [eds]

5   Now, when this magic moment of universal solidarity is over, the signifier that, in some post-socialist countries, is emerging as the signifier of the 'absent fullness' of society is *honesty*: it forms the focus of the spontaneous ideology of 'ordinary people' caught in the economic and social turbulence in which the hopes of a new fullness of society that should follow the collapse of socialism were cruelly betrayed, so that, in their eyes, 'old forces' (ex-Communists) and ex-dissidents who entered the ranks of power joined hands in exploiting them even more than before, now under the banner of democracy and freedom. The battle for hegemony, of course, is now focused on the particular content which will give a spin to this signifier: what does 'honesty' mean? And, again, it would be wrong to claim that the conflict is ultimately about the different meanings of the term 'honesty': what gets lost in this 'semantic clarification' is that each position claims that *their honesty is the only 'true' honesty*: the struggle is not simply a struggle among different particular contents, it is a struggle that emerges from the split within the universal itself.

6   Quoted in Jacqueline Rose, *States of Fantasy*, Oxford, Clarendon Press, 1996, p. 149.

7   Alain Badiou, *Ethics: An Essay on the Understanding of Evil*, trans. Peter Hallward, London and New York, Verso, 2001, pp. 72–7. [eds]

8   Retroactively, one thus becomes aware of how deeply the phenomenon of so-called 'dissidence' was embedded in the socialist ideological framework, of the extent to which 'dissidence', in its very utopian 'moralism' (preaching social solidarity, ethical responsibility and so forth) provided the disavowed ethical core of socialism: perhaps, one day, historians will note that – in the same sense in which Hegel claimed that the true spiritual result of the Peloponnesian war, its spiritual End, is Thucydides' book about it – 'dissidence' was the true spiritual result of 'Really Existing Socialism'.

9   Karl Marx, *Grundrisse: Foundations of the Critique of Political Economy*, trans. Martin Nicolaus, London, Penguin/New Left Review, 1973, p. 692. [eds]

10 Tiziana Terranova, 'Digital Darwin: nature, evolution and control in the rhetoric of computer mediated communications', *New Formations* 29, 1996, pp. 69–83.

11 Richard Dawkins, *The Selfish Gene*, Oxford, Oxford University Press, 1989.

12 Michael L. Rothschild, *Bionomics: The Inevitability of Capitalism*, New York, Henry Holt, 1990. [eds]

13 Slavoj Žižek, 'The spectre of ideology', in *Mapping Ideology*, ed. Slavoj Žižek, London and New York, Verso, 1994, pp. 1–33.

14 Jacques Rancière, *On the Shores of Politics*, trans. Liz Heron, London and New York, Verso, 1995, p. 22.

15 For a more detailed account of the role of *jouissance* in the process of ideological identification, see Slavoj Žižek, *The Plague of Fantasies*, London and New York, Verso, 1997, pp. 45–82.

16 'Propos de Emir Kusturica', *Cahiers du cinéma* 492, 1995, p. 69.

17 As to this Western perception of the Balkans as fantasy-screen, see Renata Salecl, *The Spoils of Freedom: Psychoanalysis and Feminism after the Fall of Socialism*, London and New York, Routledge, 1994, pp. 11–19.

18 Slavoj Žižek, '"I hear you with my eyes"; or, The invisible master', in *Gaze and Voice as Love Objects*, ed. Renata Salecl and Slavoj Žižek, Durham, Duke University Press, 1996, pp. 90–126.

19 Étienne Balibar, 'Ambiguous universality', in *Politics and the Other Scene*, pp. 146–75.

20 Here, the parallel is clear with Laclau's opposition between the logic of difference (society as a differential symbolic structure) and the logic of antagonism (society as 'impossible', thwarted by an antagonistic split). Today, the tension between the logic of difference and the logic of antagonism assumes the form of the tension between the liberal-democratic universe of negotiation and the fundamentalist universe of the struggle between Good and Evil.

21 For instance, G. W. F. Hegel, *Elements of the Philosophy of Right*, ed. Allen W. Wood, trans. H.B. Nisbet, Cambridge, Cambridge University Press, 1991, pp. 339–53. [eds]

22 One of the minor, yet tell-tale, events that bear witness to this withering-away of the Nation-State is the slow spreading of the obscene institution of private prisons in the United States and other Western countries: the exercise of what should be the monopoly of the State (physical violence and coercion) becomes the object of a contract between the State and a private company, which exerts coercion on individuals for the sake of profit – what we have here is simply the end of the monopoly on the legitimate use of violence that (according to Max Weber) defines the modern State.

23 These three stages (pre-modern communities, the Nation-State and today's emerging transnational 'universal society') clearly fit the triad of traditionalism, modernism and postmodernism, elaborated by Fredric Jameson: here also, the retro-phenomena that characterize postmodernism should not deceive us – it is only with postmodernism that the break with pre-modernity is fully consummated. The allusion to Jameson's *Postmodernism, or, The Cultural Logic of Late Capitalism* (London and New York, Verso, 1991) in the title of this essay is thus deliberate.

24   Slavoj Žižek, *Enjoy Your Symptom! Jacques Lacan in Hollywood and Out*, New York and London, Routledge, 1992, p. 1.

25   Darian Leader, *Why do women write more letters than they post?*, London, Faber and Faber, 1996, pp. 152–3.

26   Karl Marx, 'The class struggles in France: 1848 to 1850', in *Surveys from Exile: Political Writings, Volume 2*, ed. David Fernbach, trans. Ben Fowkes *et al.*, London, Penguin/New Left Review, 1973, pp. 136–9.

27   Wendy Brown, *States of Injury: Power and Freedom in Late Modernity*, Princeton, Princeton University Press, 1995, pp. 10–18.

28   Paul Piccone, 'Postmodern populism', *Telos* 103, 1995, pp. 45–86. Exemplary here is also the attempt by Elizabeth Fox-Genovese to oppose to upper-middle-class feminism interested in the problems of literary and cinema theory, lesbian rights and so forth, a 'family feminism' that focuses on the actual concerns of ordinary working women and articulates concrete questions of how to survive within the family, with children and work. See Elizabeth Fox-Genovese, *Feminism is Not the Story of My Life*, New York, Anchor, 1996.

29   The most concise formulation of the rightist suspension of public (legal) norms was provided by Eamon de Valera: 'The people has no right to do wrong.'

30   This, perhaps, is how one should read Rancière's notion of *singulier universel*: the assertion of the singular exception as the locus of universality, which simultaneously affirms and subverts the universality in question. When we say, 'We are all citizens of Sarajevo', we are obviously making a 'false' nomination, a nomination that violates a proper geopolitical disposition; however, precisely as such, this violation nominates the injustice of the existing geopolitical order.

Chapter 10
A leftist plea for 'Eurocentrism'

Politics and its disavowals

When one says *Eurocentrism*, every self-respecting postmodern leftist intellectual has as violent a reaction as Joseph Göbbels had to culture – to reach for a gun, hurling accusations of proto-fascist Eurocentrist cultural imperialism. However, is it possible to imagine a leftist appropriation of the European political legacy?

Let us begin with the question: 'What is politics proper?'[1] It is a phenomenon that appeared for the first time in ancient Greece when the members of the *demos* (those with no firmly determined place in the hierarchical social edifice) presented themselves as the representatives, the stand-ins, for the whole of society, for the true universality ('we – the "nothing", not counted in the order – are the people, we are all, against others who stand only for their particular privileged interest'). Political conflict proper thus involves the tension between the structured social body, where each part has its place, and the part of no-part, which unsettles this order on account of the empty principle of universality, of the principled equality of all men *qua* speaking beings, what Étienne Balibar calls *égaliberté*[2] Politics proper thus always involves a kind of short-circuit between the universal and the particular; it involves the paradox of a singular that appears as a stand-in for the universal, destabilizing the 'natural' functional order of relations in the social body. This *singulier universel* is a group that, although without any fixed place in the social edifice (or, at best, occupying a subordinate place), not only demands to be heard on equal footing with the ruling oligarchy or aristocracy (that is, to be recognized as a partner in political dialogue and the exercise of power) but, even more, presents itself as the immediate embodiment of *society as such*, in its universality, against the particular power interests of aristocracy or oligarchy. This identification of the non-part with the whole, of the part of society with no properly defined place (or which resists its allocated subordinate place) with the universal, is the elementary gesture of politicization, discernible in all great democratic events, from the French Revolution (in which the Third Estate proclaimed itself identical to the nation as such against the aristocracy and clergy) to the demise of European socialism, in which such groups as the Czech Civic Forum proclaimed themselves representative of the entire society against the party *nomenklatura*.

The political struggle proper is therefore never simply a rational debate between multiple interests but, simultaneously, the struggle for one's voice to be heard and recognized as that of a legitimate partner. When the excluded, from the Greek *demos* to Polish workers, protested against the ruling elite (the aristocracy or *nomenklatura*), the true stakes were not only their explicit demands (for higher wages, better working conditions, and so forth) but their very right to be heard and recognized as an equal participant in the debate. In Poland, the *nomenklatura* lost the brief moment it had to accept Solidarity as an equal partner. In this precise sense, politics and democracy are synonymous: the basic aim of anti-democratic politics always and by definition is (and was) depoliticization, that is, the unconditional demand that things should return to normal, with each individual doing his or her particular job. Jacques Rancière, of course, emphasizes the way that the line of separation between what he calls policing (in the broad sense of maintaining social order, the smooth running of the social machine) and politics proper is always blurred and contested. In the Marxist tradition, for instance, proletariat can be read as the subjectivization of the part of no-part that elevates its injustice into the ultimate test of universality and, simultaneously, as the operator that will bring about the establishment of a post-political, rational society.[3]

It is thus politicization that re-emerged violently in the disintegration of Eastern European socialism. From my own political past, I remember the way that, after four journalists were arrested and brought to trial by the Yugoslav army in Slovenia in 1988, I participated in the Committee for the Protection of the Human Rights of the Four Accused. Officially, the goal of the Committee was simply to guarantee fair treatment for the journalists; however, the Committee turned into the major oppositional political force, practically the Slovenian version of the Czech Civic Forum or the East German *Neues Forum*, the body that coordinated democratic opposition, a *de facto* representative of civil society. Four items made up the programme of the Committee: while the first three directly concerned the accused, the devil residing in the details, of course, consisted of the fourth item, which said that the Committee wanted to clarify the entire background of the arrest of the four accused and thus to contribute to the creation of the circumstances in which such arrests would no longer be possible – a coded way of saying that we wanted to abolish the existing socialist system. Our demand – 'Justice for the accused four!' – started to function as the metaphoric condensation of the demand for the global overthrow of the socialist régime. For that reason, in almost daily negotiations with the Committee, Communist Party officials were always accusing us of having a hidden agenda, claiming that the liberation of the accused four was not our true goal, that is, that we were exploiting and manipulating the arrest and trial for other, darker political goals. In short, the Communists wanted to play the so-called rational, depoliticized game: they wanted to deprive the slogan 'Justice for the accused four!' of its explosive general connotation and to reduce it to its literal meaning, which concerned merely a minor legal matter; they cynically claimed that it was we, the Committee, who were behaving undemocratically and playing with the fate of the accused, exerting global pressure and using blackmailing strategies instead of focusing on the particular problem of their plight.

Let us take an example from the opposite part of the world, from Japan, where the caste of the untouchables is called the *burakumin*: those who have contact with dead flesh (butchers, leatherworkers, gravediggers), who are sometimes even referred to as *eta*, 'much filth'. Even today, in our supposedly enlightened times, when they are no longer openly despised, they are still silently ignored. Not only do companies still avoid hiring them and parents refuse to allow their children to marry them, but, under the 'politically correct' pretence of not offending them, ignoring the issue altogether is the preferred course of action. The recently deceased author Sue Sumii, in her great series of novels, *The River with No Bridge*, used a reference to the *burakumin* to expose the meaninglessness of the entire Japanese caste hierarchy. Significantly, her primordial traumatic experience was the shock that occurred when, as a child, she witnessed the way that one of her relatives scratched the toilet used by the Emperor to preserve a piece of his shit as a sacred relic. This excremental identification of the *burakumin* is crucial: when Sumii saw her relative cherishing the Emperor's excrement, her conclusion was that, following the tradition of the king's two bodies, in which the king's body stands for the social body as such, the *burakumin* as the excrement of the social body should be cherished in the same way. In other words, Sumii took the structural homology between the Emperor's two bodies more literally and further than usual: even the lowest part, the excrement, of the Emperor's body has to be reduplicated in his other, sublime body, which stands for the body of society. Her predicament was similar to that of Plato who, in *Parmenides*, bravely confronts the embarrassing problem of the exact scope of the relationship between eternal forms/ideas and their material copies: which material objects are ontologically covered by eternal ideas as their models?[4] Is there even an eternal idea of base objects such as mud, filth or excrement? However, the crucial point and the proof of the non-political, corporate functioning of Japanese society is the fact that, although voices like that of Sumii are heard on their behalf, the *burakumin* did not actively *politicize* their destiny or constitute their position as that of *singulier universel*, by claiming that, precisely as the part of no-part, they stand for the true universality of Japanese society.

Although politics proper is thus something specifically 'European', the entire history of European political thought is ultimately nothing but a series of disavowals of the political moment, of the proper logic of political antagonism. There are four main versions of this disavowal:

> *Archipolitics*: the 'communitarian' attempt to define a traditional, close, organically structured, homogeneous social space that allows for no void in which the political moment or event can emerge.

Parapolitics: the attempt to depoliticize politics. One accepts the political conflict but reformulates it into a competition, within the representational space, between acknowledged parties/agents for the (temporary) occupation of the place of executive power. This parapolitics, of course, has a series of different successive versions: the main rupture is that between its classical formulation and its modern Hobbesian version, which focuses on the problematic of social contract, of the alienation of individual rights in the emergence of sovereign power. Habermasian or Rawlsian ethics are perhaps the last philosophical vestiges of this attitude: the attempt to de-antagonize politics by formulating clear rules to be obeyed so that the agonistic procedure of litigation does not explode into politics proper.

Marxist (or utopian socialist) *metapolitics*: political conflict is fully asserted, *but* as a shadow theatre in which events whose proper place is in another scene (that of economic processes) are played out. The ultimate goal of true politics is thus its self-cancellation, the transformation of the administration of people into the administration of things within the fully self-transparent rational order of a collective will. (More precisely, Marxism is here ambiguous since the very term *political economy* also opens up a space for the opposite gesture of introducing politics into the very heart of the economy, that is, of denouncing the apolitical character of the economic processes as the supreme ideological illusion. Class struggle does not express some objective economic contradiction; it is the very form of existence of this contradiction.)

The *ultrapolitics* of Carl Schmitt: the attempt to depoliticize the conflict by way of bringing it to extremes, via the direct militarization of politics. In ultrapolitics, the repressed political returns in the guise of the attempt to resolve the deadlock of political conflict by its false radicalization – that is, by reformulating it as a war between us and them, our enemy, where there is no common ground for symbolic conflict. It is deeply symptomatic, for example, that instead of class *struggle* the radical Right speaks of class (or sexual) *warfare*.

What we have in all four cases is thus an attempt to gentrify the properly traumatic dimension of the political. Something emerged in ancient Greece under the name of the *demos* demanding its rights, and, from the very beginning (that is, from Plato's *Republic* onwards) to the recent revival of liberal political philosophy, political philosophy itself was an attempt to suspend the de-stabilizing potential of the political, to disavow and/or regulate it in one way or another: by bringing about a return to some pre-political social body, by fixing the rules of political competition and so forth. Political philosophy is thus, in all its different shapes, a kind of defence formation, and perhaps its typology could be established by reference to the different modalities of defence against some traumatic experience in psychoanalysis.[5] Archi-, para-, meta- and ultrapolitics form a kind of Greimasian logical square:

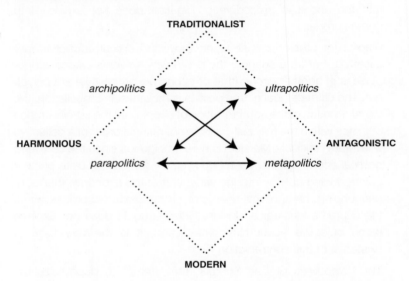

Archi- and ultra- are the two faces of the traditionalist attitude (self-enclosed community versus war of a community against external enemies), and para- and meta- the two versions of modern politics (democratic formal rules versus the notion that this kind of democratic game merely expresses and/or distorts the level of pre-political socioeconomic processes at which things really happen). On the other axis, both meta- and ultrapolitics involve the notions of unsurpassable struggle, conflict and antagonism against the assertion of harmonious collaboration in archi- and parapolitics.

From politics to post-politics

Of importance here is Rancière's critical distance towards Marxist meta-politics. The key feature of metapolitics is that, to put it in the terms of Jacques Lacan's matrix of the four discourses, the place of the agent is occupied by *knowledge*.[6] Marx presented his position as *scientific* materialism, which is to say that metapolitics is a politics that legitimizes itself by means of a direct reference to the scientific status of its knowledge. (It is this knowledge that enables metapolitics to draw a distinction between those immersed in politico-ideological illusions and the Party, which grounds its historical intervention in knowledge of effective socio-economic processes.) This knowledge (about class society and relations of production in Marxism) suspends the classic opposition of *Sein* and *Sollen*, of *Being* and the *Ought*, of that which Is and the ethical Ideal. The ethical Ideal towards which the revolutionary subject strives is directly grounded in (or coincides with) the 'objective', 'disinterested' scientific knowledge of social processes. This coincidence opens up a space for totalitarian violence because, in this way, acts that run against the elementary norms of ethical decency can be legitimized as grounded in (insight into) historical necessity (say, the mass killing of members of the bourgeois class is grounded in the scientific insight that this class is already in itself condemned to disappear, past the moment in which it played a progressive role). Therein resides the difference between the standard, destructive, even murderous dimension of strict adherence to the ethical Ideal and modern totalitarianism. The terrorism of the Jacobins in the French Revolution, grounded in their adherence to the ideal of *égaliberté*, that is, in their attempt to realize directly this Ideal, to impose it directly on to reality, this coincidence of the purest idealism with the most destructive violence, analyzed by Hegel in the famous chapter of his *Phenomenology of Spirit* on absolute terror,[7] is not enough to explain twentieth-century totalitarianism. What the Jacobins lacked was reference to the objective or neutral scientific knowledge of history to legitimize their exercise of unconditional power. It is only the Leninist revolutionary, not yet the Jacobin, who thus occupies the properly perverted position of the pure instrument of historical necessity, made accessible by means of scientific knowledge.

Rancière here follows Claude Lefort's insight into the way that the space for (Communist) totalitarianism was opened by the 'democratic invention' itself: totalitarianism is an inherent perversion of democratic logic.[8] First, we have the traditional master who grounds his authority in some transcendent reason (divine right, for example). What becomes visible with the democratic invention is the gap that separates the positive person of the master from the place he occupies in the symbolic network; with the democratic invention the place of Power is posited as originally *empty*, occupied only temporarily and in a contingent way by different subjects. In other words, it now becomes visible that (to paraphrase Marx) people do not regard somebody as king because he is in himself king; he is king *because* and *as long as* people regard him as king. Totalitarianism takes into account this rupture accomplished by the democratic invention; the totalitarian master fully accepts the logic, 'I am master only insofar as you treat me as one'; that is, his position involves no reference to some transcendent ground. On the contrary, he emphatically tells his followers, 'In myself I am nothing; my whole strength derives from you. I am only the embodiment of your deepest strivings; the moment I lose my roots in you, I am lost.' His entire legitimacy derives from his position as a pure servant of the people. The more he 'modestly' diminishes and instrumentalizes his role, the more he emphasizes that he simply expresses and realizes the strivings of the people itself, which is the true master, the more all-powerful and untouchable he becomes, because, in this case, any attack on him is effectively an attack on the people itself, on its members' innermost longings. The people is thus split into actual individuals (prone to treason and all kinds of human weaknesses) and the People, embodied in the master. So, perhaps these three logics (the traditional master; the democratic, regulated fight for the empty place of power; the totalitarian master) fit the three modes of the disavowal of politics conceptualized by Rancière: the traditional master functions within the space of archipolitics; democracy involves parapolitics, that is, the gentrification of politics proper in regulated agon (the rules of elections and representative democracy, and so forth); and the totalitarian master is only possible within the space of metapolitics.[9]

Rancière is thus right to emphasize the radical ambiguity of the Marxist notion of the gap between formal democracy (the rights of man, political freedom and so forth) and the economic reality of exploitation and domination. One can read this gap between the appearance of *égaliberté* and the social reality of economic and cultural (among other) differences in the standard, meta-political, 'symptomatic' way (the form of universal rights, equality, freedom and democracy is just a necessary but illusory form of expression of its concrete social content, the universe of exploitation and class domination); or, one can read it in the much more subversive sense of a tension in which the appearance of *égaliberté*, precisely, is *not* merely an appearance but evinces an effectivity of its own that allows it to set in motion the process of rearticulating actual socio-economic relations by way of their progressive politicization (why should women not vote? why should conditions at the workplace not be of public political concern? and so forth). One is tempted to use here the old Lévi-Straussian term *symbolic efficiency*: the appearance of *égaliberté* is a symbolic fiction that, as such, possesses an actual efficiency of its own. One should resist the properly cynical temptation of reducing it to a mere illusion that conceals a different actuality.

Crucial here is the distinction between appearance and the postmodern notion of the simulacrum as that which is no longer clearly distinguishable from the Real.[10] The notion of the political as the domain of appearance (opposed to the social reality of class and other distinctions, for example, those of society as the articulated social body) has nothing in common with the postmodern notion that we are entering an era of universalized simulacra, in which reality itself becomes indistinguishable from its simulated double. The nostalgic longing for the authentic experience of being lost in the deluge of simulacra (detectable in Paul Virilio's work) as well as the postmodern assertion that the brave new world of universalized simulacra is the sign that we are finally getting rid of the metaphysical obsession with authentic Being (detectable in the writings of Gianni Vattimo) both miss the distinction between simulacrum and appearance: what gets lost in today's plague of simulations is not the firm, true, non-simulated Real, but *appearance itself*. To put it in Lacanian terms: the simulacrum is Imaginary (illusion), while appearance is Symbolic (fiction); when the specific dimension of Symbolic appearance begins to disintegrate, Imaginary and Real become more and more indistinguishable. The key to today's universe of simulacra, in which the Real is less and less distinguishable from its Imaginary simulation, resides in the retreat of symbolic efficiency. And, in socio-political terms, this domain of appearance (that is, of symbolic fiction) is none other than that of politics, as distinguished from the social body subdivided into parts. There is appearance in so far as we are dealing with a part of no-part, in so far as a part not included in the whole of the social body (or included/excluded in a way it resists) protests against its position, against its allocated place, and symbolizes its position as that of a tort, an injustice, claiming that, against other parts, it stands for the universality of *égaliberté*. We are dealing here with appearance in contrast to the 'reality' of the structured social body. The old conservative motto of 'keeping up appearances' thus today obtains a new twist: it no longer stands for the wisdom according to which it is better not to disturb the rules of social etiquette too much, because social chaos might ensue. Today, rather, keeping up appearances stands for the effort to save the properly political space against the onslaught of the multitude of particular identities of the postmodern, all-embracing social body.[11]

This is also how one has to read Hegel's famous dictum from *Phenomenology of Spirit*, according to which 'the Suprasensible is appearance qua appearance'.[12] In a sentimental answer to a child who asks what God's face looks like, a priest answers that whenever the child encounters a human face radiating benevolence and goodness, no matter to whom this face belongs, he gets a glimpse of His face. The truth of this sentimental platitude is that the suprasensible (God's face) is discernible as a momentary, fleeting appearance, a kind of grimace, of an ordinary face. It is this dimension of appearance that transubstantiates a piece of reality into something that, for a brief moment, illuminates the suprasensible eternity that is missing in the logic of the simulacrum. In the simulacrum, which becomes indistinguishable from the Real, everything is present, so that no other transcendental dimension effectively appears in or through it. Here we return the Kantian problematic of the sublime. In Kant's famous reading of the enthusiasm evoked by the French Revolution in the enlightened public around Europe, the revolutionary events functioned as a sign through which the dimension of trans-phenomenal freedom, of a free society, appeared.[13] Appearance is thus not simply the domain of phenomena but also those magic moments in which the other, noumenal dimension momentarily appears in (or shines through) some empirical or contingent phenomenon. So, back to Hegel, 'the Suprasensible is appearance qua appearance' does not simply mean that the suprasensible is not a positive entity *beyond* the phenomenon, but rather points to the inherent power of negativity, which makes appearance 'merely an appearance', that is, something that is not in itself fully actual but condemned to perish in the process of self-sublation. It also means that the suprasensible comes to exist only in the guise of an appearance of another dimension that interrupts the standard, normal order of phenomena.

Today, however, we are dealing with another form of the denegation of the political, postmodern post-politics, which no longer merely represses the political, trying to contain it and to pacify the returns of the repressed, but much more effectively forecloses it, so that the postmodern forms of ethnic violence, with their irrational, excessive character, are no longer simple returns of the repressed but, rather, present the case of the foreclosed (from the Symbolic), which, as we know from Lacan, returns in the Real. In post-politics, the conflict of global ideological visions embodied in different parties who compete for power is replaced by the collaboration of enlightened technocrats (economists and public opinion specialists, for example) and liberal multiculturalists; via the process of negotiation of interests a compromise is reached in the guise of a more or less universal consensus. The political (the space of litigation in which the excluded can protest the wrong or injustice done to them) foreclosed from the Symbolic then returns in the Real in the guise of new forms of racism. It is crucial to perceive the way that postmodern racism emerges as the ultimate consequence of the post-political suspension of the political, of the reduction of the State to a mere police agent servicing the (consensually established) needs of market forces and multiculturalist, tolerant humanitarianism. The foreigner whose status is never properly 'regulated' is the *indivisible remainder* of the transformation of democratic political struggle into the post-political procedure of negotiation and multiculturalist policing. Instead of the *political subject* 'working class' demanding its universal rights, we get, on the one hand, the multiplicity of particular social strata or groups, each with its problems (the dwindling need for manual workers, and so forth), and, on the other hand, the immigrant increasingly prevented from *politicizing* his predicament of exclusion.[14]

Here one should oppose *globalization* to *universalization*: globalization (not only in the sense of global capitalism, the establishment of a global world market, but also in the sense of the assertion of 'humanity' as the global point of reference of human rights, legitimizing the violation of state sovereignty and policing activities – from trade restrictions to direct military interventions – in parts of the world where global human rights are violated) is precisely the name for the emerging post-political logic that progressively precludes the dimension of universality at work in politicization proper. The paradox is that there is no *universal* proper without the process of political litigation of the part of no-part, of an out-of-joint entity presenting/manifesting itself as the stand-in for the Universal. The otherness excluded from the consensual domain of tolerant/rational post-political negotiation and administration returns in the guise of the inexplicable pure evil whose emblematic image is that of the holocaust. What defines postmodern post-politics is thus the secret solidarity between its Janus faces: on the one hand, the replacement of politics proper by depoliticized, so-called humanitarian operations (the humanitarian protection of human and civil rights and aid to Bosnia, Somalia, Rwanda, North Korea and so forth); on the other hand, the violent emergence of depoliticized pure evil in the guise of excessive ethnic or religious fundamentalist violence. In short, what Rancière proposes here is a new version of the old Hegelian motto, 'Evil resides in the gaze itself which perceives the object as Evil':[15] the contemporary figure of evil too strong to be accessible to political analysis (such as the holocaust) appears as such only to the gaze that constitutes it as such – that is, as depoliticized. Crucial is their speculative identity, that is, the infinite judgement: humanitarian depoliticized compassion *is* the excess of evil over its political forms.

Excessive violence

One should link this problematic to the notion proposed by Balibar of excessive, non-functional cruelty as a feature of contemporary life:[16] a cruelty whose figures range from fundamentalist racist and/or religious slaughter to the supposedly senseless outbursts of violence performed by adolescents and the homeless in our megalopolises, the violence one is tempted to call *id-evil* – violence not grounded in utilitarian or ideological reasons. That is to say, what catches the eye in these cases is the 'primitive' level of their underlying libidinal economy – primitive not in the sense of a regression to some archaic stratum, but in the sense of the utmost *elementary* nature of the relationship between pleasure and *jouissance*, between the circle of the pleasure principle that strives for balance, for the reproduction of its closed circuit, and the extimate foreign body. The libidinal economy that sustains the infamous battle cry, '*Ausländer raus!* [foreigners out!]', can be exemplified by Lacan's schema of the relationship between the *Ich* and *Lust*, where the *Unlust* is defined in the terms of (non)assimilation as 'what remains unassimilable, irreducible to the pleasure principle'.[17] The terms used by Freud and Lacan to describe the relationship of *Ich* and *jouissance* perfectly fit the metaphoric structure of the racist attitude towards foreigners: assimilation and resistance to assimilation, expulsion of a foreign body, disturbed balance. In order to locate this type of evil with regard to the usual types of evil, one is tempted to use as the classificatory principle the Freudian triad of ego, superego and id. The most common kind of evil is *ego-evil*: behaviour motivated by selfish calculation and greed, that is, by disregard for universal ethical principles. The evil attributed to the so-called fundamentalist fanatics, on the contrary, is *superego-evil*: evil accomplished in the name of fanatical devotion to some ideological ideal. In the example of a skinhead beating up foreigners, however, one can discern neither a clear selfish calculation nor a clear ideological identification. All the talk about foreigners stealing work from us, or about the threat they represent to our Western values, should not deceive us: on closer examination, it soon becomes clear that this talk provides a rather superficial secondary rationalization. The answer we ultimately obtain from the skinhead is that it makes him feel good to beat up foreigners, that their presence disturbs him. What we encounter here is *id-evil*, that is, the evil structured and motivated by the most elementary imbalance in the relationship between the *Ich* and *jouissance*, by the tension between pleasure and the foreign body of *jouissance* at the very heart of it. Id-evil thus stages the most elementary short-circuit in the relationship of the subject to the primordially missing object-cause of his desire. What bothers us in the Other (the Jew, the Japanese, the African, the Turk and so forth) is that he appears to entertain a privileged relationship to the object. The Other either possesses the object-treasure, having snatched it away from us (which is why we don't have it), or poses a threat to our possession of the object.[18]

What one should propose here, again, is the Hegelian infinite judgement asserting the speculative identity of this supposedly useless and excessive outburst of violence, which displays nothing but a pure and naked (non-sublimated) hatred of Otherness, with the post-political multiculturalist universe of tolerance for difference in which nobody is excluded. Of course, the term *non-sublimated* is here used in its common meaning, which in this case stands for the exact opposite of its strict psychoanalytic meaning. In short, what takes place in the focusing of our hatred on some representative of the (officially tolerated) Other is the very mechanism of sublimation at its most elementary. The all-encompassing nature of the post-political concrete universality, which accounts for everybody at the level of symbolic inclusion, this multiculturalist vision and practice of unity in difference (all-equal, all different), leaves open, as the only way to mark the difference, the proto-sublimating gesture of elevating a contingent Other (of race, sex, or religion, for example) into the absolute Otherness of the impossible Thing, the ultimate threat to our identity – this Thing which should be annihilated if we are to survive. Therein resides the properly Hegelian paradox: the final arrival of the truly rational concrete universality – the abolition of antagonisms, the mature universe of negotiated coexistence of different groups – coincides with its radical opposite, with thoroughly contingent outbursts of violence.

There are two further Hegelian aspects to this excessive violence. First, Hegel's fundamental rule is that objective excess (the direct reign of abstract universality that imposes its law mechanically, with utter disregard for the concerned subject caught in its web) is always supplemented by subjective excess (the irregular, arbitrary exercise of whims). An exemplary case of this interdependence between objective and subjective excess is provided by Balibar, who distinguishes two opposite, but complementary, modes of excessive violence: the ultra-objective (or structural) violence that is inherent to the social conditions of global capitalism (the automatic creation of excluded and dispensable individuals, from the homeless to the unemployed), and the ultra-subjective violence of newly emerging ethnic and/or religious (in short, racist) fundamentalisms.[19] The second aspect is that this supposedly excessive and groundless violence involves its own mode of knowledge, that of impotent cynical reflection. Back to our example of id-evil, the skinhead who beats up foreigners: when really pressed for the reasons for his violence, and if capable of minimal theoretical reflection, the skinhead will suddenly start to talk like social workers, sociologists and social psychologists, citing diminished social mobility, rising insecurity, the disintegration of paternal authority, the lack of maternal love in his early childhood and so forth. In short, he will provide the more or less precise psycho-sociological account of his acts so dear to enlightened liberals eager to understand the violent youth as the tragic victim of his social and familial conditions.[20] The standard enlightened formula of the efficiency of the critique of ideology from Plato onwards ('they are doing it because they do not know what they are doing', which asserts that knowledge is in itself liberating, as when the erring subject reflects upon what he is doing he will no longer do it) is here turned around: the violent skinhead knows very well what he is doing, but he is nonetheless doing it.[21] This cynically impotent reflective knowledge is the obverse of senseless, excessive violence. We are dealing here with something akin to the well-known unpleasant scene from Terry Gilliam's *Brazil*: in a high-class restaurant, the waiter recommends to his customers the best choices from the daily menu ('Today, our tournedos is really special!'), yet what the customers get is a dazzling colour photo of the meal on a stand above their plates and, on the plates themselves, a loathsome, excremental, paste-like lump. In the same way, the symbolically efficient knowledge embedded in the subject's effective social praxis disintegrates into, on the one hand, excessive, irrational violence with no ideologico-political foundation and, on the other hand, into impotent external reflection that leaves the subject's acts intact. So, in the guise of this cynically impotent, reflecting skinhead who, with an ironic smile, explains to the perplexed journalist the roots of his senselessly violent behaviour, the enlightened, tolerant multi-culturalist bent on understanding forms of excessive violence gets his own message in its inverted, true form. In short, as Lacan would have put it, at this point the communication between him and the object of his study, the intolerant skinhead, is perfectly successful.[22]

Crucial here is the distinction between this excessive, irrational, dysfunctional, cruel violence and the outbursts of obscene violence that serve as the implicit support of the standard ideological universal notion; say, when the rights of man are not really universal but, effectively, the right of white males with property, any attempt to disregard this implicit, underlying set of unwritten rules that effectively constrains the universality of rights is met by outbursts of violence. Nowhere is this contrast stronger than in the case of African Americans in the United States. The old parapolitical, democratic racism excluded blacks from effectively participating in universal political life by way of silently enforcing their exclusion (through verbal and physical threats and so forth). The adequate answer to this standard exclusion from the universal was the great civil rights movement associated with Martin Luther King, Jr., suspending the implicit obscene supplement that enacted the actual exclusion of blacks from formal universal equality. Of course, it was easy for such a gesture to gain the support of a large majority of the white, liberal, upper-class establishment, which dismissed their opponents as dumb, lower-class Southern rednecks. Today, however, the very terrain of the struggle has changed. The post-political liberal establishment not only fully acknowledges the gap between a mere formal equality and its actualization or implementation, it not only recognizes the exclusionary logic of false ideological universality, but it even actively fights this logic by applying to it a vast legal/psychological/sociological network of measures, from identifying the specific problems of each group and subgroup (not only homosexuals but African American lesbians, African American lesbian mothers, African American single unemployed lesbian mothers, and so on) to proposing a set of measures (affirmative action, for example) to amend the wrong. However, what such a tolerant procedure prevents is the gesture of *politicization* proper: although the difficulties of being an African American single unemployed lesbian mother are adequately catalogued, including even the category's most specific features, the concerned subject nonetheless somehow feels that there is something wrong and frustrating in this very effort to render justice for her specific predicament. What she is deprived of is the possibility of the metaphoric elevation of her specific wrong into the stand-in for the universal wrong. The only way openly to articulate this universality – the fact that one, precisely, is *not* merely that specific individual exposed to a set of specific injustices – consists then in its apparent opposite, in the thoroughly irrational, excessive outburst of violence. The old Hegelian rule is here again confirmed: the only way for the universality to come into existence, to posit itself as such, is in the guise of its very opposite, of what cannot but appear as an excessive, irrational whim.

One can see now why the reference to Schmitt is crucial in detecting the deadlocks of post-political liberal tolerance. Schmittean ultrapolitics – the radicalization of politics into the open warfare of us-against-them discernible in different fundamentalisms – *is the form in which the foreclosed political returns in the post-political universe of pluralist negotiation and consensual regulation*. For that reason, the way to counteract this re-emerging ultrapolitics is not more tolerance, more compassion and multicultural understanding, but the *return of the political proper*, that is, the reassertion of the dimension of antagonism that, far from denying universality, is consubstantial with it. Therein resides the key component of the proper *leftist* stance, as opposed to the rightist assertion of particular identity: in the equation of *universalism* with the militant, *divisive* position of engagement in a struggle. True universalists are not those who preach global tolerance of differences and all-encompassing unity but those who engage in a passionate fight for the assertion of the truth that engages them. Theoretical, religious and political examples abound here: from Saint Paul, whose unconditional Christian universalism (everyone can be redeemed, since, in the eyes of Christ, there are no Jews and Greeks, no men and women) made him into a proto-Leninist militant fighting different 'deviations', through Marx, whose notion of class struggle is the necessary obverse of the universalism of his theory, which aims at the 'redemption' of the whole of humanity, up to Freud, and including many great political figures. When de Gaulle, for example, almost alone in England in 1940, launched his call for resistance to German occupation, he was at the same time presuming to speak on behalf of the universality of France and, *for that very reason*, introducing a radical split, a fissure between those who followed him and those who preferred the collaborationist fleshpots of Egypt. To put it in Alain Badiou's terms, it is crucial here not to translate the terms of this struggle, set in motion by the violent and contingent assertion of the new universal truth, into the terms of the order of positive Being with its groups and subgroups, conceiving of it as the struggle between two social entities defined by a series of positive characteristics.[23] Therein resided the 'mistake' of Stalinism, which reduced class struggle to a struggle between classes defined as social groups with a set of positive features (their place in the mode of production, and so forth). From a truly radical Marxist perspective, although there is a link between the working class as a social group and the proletariat as the position of the militant fighting for universal Truth, this link is not a determining causal connection, and the two levels are to be strictly distinguished. To be proletarian involves assuming a certain *subjective stance* (of class struggle destined to achieve redemption through revolution) that, in principle, can occur to any individual; to put it in religious terms, irrespective of his (good) works, any individual can be touched by grace and interpellated as a proletarian subject. The limit that separates the two opposed sides in the class struggle is thus not objective, not the limit separating two positive social groups, but ultimately *radically subjective*; it involves the position individuals assume towards the Event of universal Truth. Again, the crucial point here is that subjectivity and universalism are not only *not* exclusive but are, rather, two sides of the same coin. It is precisely because class struggle interpellates individuals to adopt the subjective stance of a proletarian that its appeal is universal, aiming at everyone with no exceptions. The division it mobilizes is not the division between two well-defined social groups but the division, which runs 'diagonally' to the social division in the Order of Being, between those who recognize themselves in the call of the Truth-Event, becoming its followers, and those who deny or ignore it. In Hegelese, *the existence of the true Universal* (as opposed to the false concrete universality of the all-encompassing global Order of Being) *is that of an endless and incessantly divisive struggle*; it is ultimately the division between the two notions (and material practices) of universality, that which advocates the positivity of the existing global Order of Being as the ultimate horizon of knowledge and action, and that which accepts the efficiency of the dimension of the Truth-Event irreducible to (and unaccountable in terms of) the Order of Being.

From the sublime
to the ridiculous

How do these insights enable us to shed new light on the prospect of today's leftist (re)politicization of our common predicament? Let us return to the disintegration of Eastern European socialism. The passage from Really Existing Socialism to really existing capitalism in Eastern Europe brought about a series of comic reversals, in which sublime democratic enthusiasm was transformed into the ridiculous. The dignified East German crowds gathering around Protestant churches and heroically defying Stasi terror all of a sudden turned into vulgar consumers of bananas and cheap pornography; the civilized Czechs mobilized by the appeal of Václav Havel and other cultural icons all of a sudden turned into cheap swindlers of Western tourists. The disappointment was mutual. The West, which began by idolizing the Eastern dissident movement as the reinvention of its own tired democracy, disappointedly dismissed the present post-socialist régimes as a mixture of the corrupted ex-Communist oligarchy and/ or ethnic and religious fundamentalists (even the dwindling group of liberals is mistrusted as not being politically correct enough: where is their feminist awareness? is but one of many critiques levelled at them). The East, which began by idolizing the West as the example of affluent democracy, finds itself in a whirlpool of ruthless commercialization and economic colonization. Perhaps, however, this double disappointment, this double failed encounter between ex-Communist dissidents and Western liberal democrats is crucial for the identity of Europe; perhaps what transpires in the gap that separates the two perspectives is a glimpse of a Europe worth fighting for.

The hero of Dashiell Hammett's *The Maltese Falcon*, the private detective Sam Spade, tells the story of being hired to find a man who had suddenly left his settled job and family and vanished. Spade is unable to track him down, but a few years later, he encounters the man in another city. Under an assumed name, the man leads a life remarkably similar to the one he fled from (a regular boring job, a new wife and children); however, in spite of this similarity, the man is convinced that beginning again was not in vain, that it was well worth the trouble to cut his ties and start a new life. Perhaps the same goes for the passage from actually existing socialism to actually existing capitalism in ex-Communist Eastern European countries. In spite of the betrayed enthusiastic expectations, something *did* take place in between, in the passage itself, and it is in this event in between, this vanishing mediator, in this moment of democratic enthusiasm, that we should locate the crucial dimension obfuscated by later re-normalization.

It is clear that the protesting crowds in East Germany, Poland and Czechoslovakia wanted something else, a utopian object of impossible fullness designated by a multiplicity of names ('solidarity', 'human rights' and so forth), *not* what they effectively got. Two reactions towards this gap between expectations and reality are possible; the best way to capture them is by reference to the well-known opposition between *fool* and *knave*. The fool is a simpleton, a court jester who is allowed to tell the truth precisely because the performative power (the socio-political efficiency) of his speech is suspended; the knave is the cynic who openly states the truth, a crook who tries to sell the open admission of his crookedness as honesty, a scoundrel who admits the need for illegitimate repression in order to maintain social stability. This opposition has a clear political connotation: today's right-wing intellectual is a knave, a conformist who refers to the mere existence of the given order as an argument for it and mocks the Left for harbouring utopian plans that will necessarily lead to totalitarian or anarchic catastrophe; while the left-wing intellectual is a fool, a court jester who publicly displays the lie of the existing order but in a way that undercuts the socio-political efficiency of his speech. After the fall of socialism, the knave is a neo-conservative advocate of the free market who cruelly rejects all forms of social solidarity as counterproductive sentimentalism, while the fool is a multiculturalist, 'radical' social critic who, by means of ludic procedures designed to subvert the existing order, actually serves as its supplement. With regard to Eastern Europe, a knave dismisses the 'third way' project of the *Neues Forum* in the former East Germany as a hopelessly outdated utopian vision and exhorts us to accept the cruel market reality, while a fool insists that the collapse of socialism effectively opened up a third way, a possibility left unexploited by the Western recolonization of the East.

This cruel reversal of the sublime into the ridiculous was, of course, grounded in the fact that a double misunderstanding was at work in the public (self-)perception of the social protest movements in the last years of Eastern European socialism (from Solidarity to *Neues Forum*). On the one hand, there were attempts by the ruling *nomenklatura* to reinscribe these events in their police/political framework, by way of distinguishing between 'honest critics' with whom one should talk, but in a calm, rational, depoliticized atmosphere, and a bunch of extremist provocateurs who served foreign interests. (This logic was brought to its absurd extreme in the former Yugoslavia, in which the very notion of a workers' strike was incomprehensible because, according to the dominant ideological paradigm, workers already ruled through self-management of their companies – against whom, then, could they strike?) The battle was thus not only for higher wages and better conditions but also, and above all, for the workers to be acknowledged as legitimate partners in negotiations with representatives of the régime. The moment power was forced to accept this, the battle was, in a way, already won. The interesting point here is how, in this struggle within socialism in decay, the very term *political* functioned in an inverted way: it was the Communist Party (standing for the police logic) which 'politicized' the situation (by speaking of counter-revolutionary tendencies and so forth), while the opposition movement insisted on its fundamentally apolitical, civic-ethical character. They merely stood for the so-called simple values of dignity and freedom, for example. No wonder their main signifier was the apolitical notion of solidarity.

When these movements exploded into a broad mass phenomenon, their demands for freedom and democracy (and solidarity and so on) were also misperceived by Western commentators. They saw in them the confirmation that the people of the East wanted what people in the West already had; that is, they automatically translated these demands into the Western liberal-democratic notion of freedom (the multi-party representational political game *cum* global market economy). Emblematic to the point of caricature was the figure of Dan Rather, the American news reader, reporting on Tiananmen Square in 1989, who stood in front of a replica of the Statue of Liberty and claimed that this statue said it all about what the protesting students demanded (in short, if you scratch the skin of a Chinese person, underneath you find an American). What this statue effectively represented was a utopian longing having nothing to do with the actual United States (incidentally, it was the same with many immigrants to America for whom the view of the statue stood for a utopian longing soon crushed down). The perception of the American media thus offered another example of the reinscription of the explosion of Balibar's *égaliberté*, the unconditional demand for freedom and equality that explodes any positive order, within the confines of a given order.

For a leftist appropriation
of the European legacy

Are we then condemned to the debilitating alternative of choosing between a knave or a fool, or is there a *tertium datur*? Perhaps the contours of this *tertium datur* can be discerned by reference to the fundamental European legacy. As we have already seen, politics proper designates the moment at which a particular demand is not simply part of the negotiation of interests but aims at something more, that is, starts to function as the metaphoric condensation of the global restructuring of the entire social space. The contrast is clear between this subjectivization of a part of the social body that rejects its subordinated place in the social-police edifice, and demands to be heard at the level of *égaliberté*, and today's proliferation of postmodern identity politics, whose goal is the exact opposite, that is, precisely the assertion of one's particular identity, of one's proper place within the social structure. The postmodern identity politics of particular (ethnic, sexual and so forth) lifestyles fits perfectly the depoliticized notion of society in which every particular group is accounted for and has its specific status (of victimhood) acknowledged through affirmative action or other measures destined to guarantee social justice. For this kind of justice to be rendered to victimized minorities, an intricate police apparatus is required (for identifying the group in question, for punishing the offenders against its rights, for determining how legally to define sexual harassment or racial injury and so forth, and for providing for the preferential treatment that is intended to outweigh the wrong this group suffered). Postmodern identity politics involves the logic of *ressentiment*, of proclaiming oneself a victim and expecting the dominant social Other to pay for the damage, while *égaliberté* breaks out of the vicious cycle of *ressentiment*. What is usually praised as postmodern politics (the pursuit of particular issues whose resolution is to be negotiated within the 'rational' global order, allocating to a particular component its proper place) is thus effectively the end of politics proper.

Two interconnected traps apropos of the fashionable topic of the end of ideology brought about by the present process of globalization are to be avoided at any cost: first, the commonplace according to which today's main antagonism is between global liberal capitalism and different forms of ethnic/religious fundamentalism; second, the hasty identification of globalization (the contemporary trans-national functioning of Capital) with universalization. As we have already emphasized, the true opposition today is rather between *globalization* (the emerging global market new world order) and *universalism* (the properly political domain of universalizing one's particular fate as representative of global injustice). This difference between globalization and universalism becomes more and more palpable today, when Capital, in the name of penetrating new markets, quickly renounces requests for democracy in order not to lose access to new trade partners. This shameful retreat is then, of course, legitimized as respect for cultural difference, as the right of the (ethnic/religious/cultural) Other to choose the way of life that suits it best – as long as it does not disturb the free circulation of Capital.

This opposition between universalism and globalization is best exemplified by two countries: France and the United States. French republican ideology is the epitome of modernist universalism: of democracy based on a universal notion of citizenship. In clear contrast to it, the United States is a global society, a society in which the global market and legal system serve as the container (rather than the proverbial melting pot) for the endless proliferation of particular group identities. The paradox is that the proper roles seem to be reversed: France, in its republican universalism, is more and more perceived as a *particular* phenomenon threatened by the process of globalization, while the United States, with its multitude of groups demanding recognition of their particular, specific identities, more and more emerges as the universal model. So, perhaps, the parallel between our time and the Roman empire, with the United States rather than Rome as the one global superpower, is not without foundation, especially if one brings into the picture the emergence of Christianity. The first centuries of our era saw the opposition of the *global* 'multicultural' Roman empire and Christianity, which posed such a threat to the empire precisely on account of its *universal* appeal. Furthermore, Christianity opposed itself to two types of discourses: the Greek discourse of philosophical sophistry and the Jewish discourse of obscurantist prophetism, like today's twin brothers of deconstructionist sophistry and New Age obscurantism. Is, then, our task today not exactly homologous to that of Christianity: to undermine the global empire of Capital, not by asserting particular identities, but through the assertion of a new universality?[24]

The re-emerging populist fundamentalism is the inherent product of globalization and, as such, the living proof of the failure of the postmodern abolition of politics, in which the basic economic logic is accepted as the depoliticized Real (a neutral expert knowledge that defines the parameters within which the different strata of population and political subjects are expected to reach a compromise and formulate their common goals). Within this space, the political returns in two guises: on the one hand, rightist populism; on the other hand, the 'wild' demands for social justice, for security of employment and so forth, which are then denounced by supposedly neutral economic specialists as irrational, out of touch with the new reality of the demise of the welfare state, as the remainders of old ideological battles. The (potential) partner is here neutralized, not acknowledged as a partner at all; the position from which he or she speaks is disqualified in advance. Multiculturalist openness versus a new fundamentalism is thus a false dilemma: they are the two faces of today's post-political universe.

The late-capitalist solution is best epitomized by two city-states, Hong Kong and Singapore. In Singapore, we find the paradoxical combination of capitalist economic logic with corporate communitarian ethics aimed at precluding any politicization of social life. Hong Kong under Chinese rule seems to move towards the same solution, albeit in a more Americanized, multiculturalist and pluralist spirit. It is deeply significant that, in the last years of his life, the late Deng Xiaobing himself, the so-called father of Chinese reforms, expressed his admiration for Singapore as the model to be followed in China. The motto of 'wise' Asian rulers like Singapore's Lee Kwan Yew – the combination of the full inclusion of their economies into global capitalism with the traditional Asian values of discipline, respect for tradition and so forth – points precisely toward *globalization without universalism*, that is, with the political dimension suspended. In a different way, the model towards which the United States seems to be moving – the permissive coexistence of a multitude of ways of life within the global capitalist framework – approaches in another way the same result of depoliticization. This rising globalization without universalism demonstrates that the opposition of globalization to particular cultural identity embodied in a specific way of life is deeply misleading. What is effectively threatened by globalization is not the *cosa nostra* (our private secret way of life from which others are excluded, which others want to steal from us) but its exact opposite: universality itself, in its eminently political dimension. One of today's common wisdoms is that we are entering a new medieval society in the guise of the New World Order. The grain of truth in this comparison is that, as in medieval times, the New World Order is global, but not universal, since it strives for a new global order with each part in its allocated place.

A typical advocate of liberalism today throws together workers' protests against the loss of their rights and right-wing insistence on fidelity to the Western cultural heritage; he perceives both as pitiful remainders of the so-called age of ideology that have nothing to do with today's post-ideological universe. However, the two resistances to globalization follow totally incompatible logics: the Right insists on a *particular* communal identity (based on *ethnos* or habitat) threatened by the onslaught of globalization, while for the Left, the threatened dimension is that of politicization, of articulating 'impossible' *universal* demands (impossible from within the existing space of the world order). From the sublime heights of Jürgen Habermas' theory to vulgar market ideologists, we are bombarded by different versions of depoliticization: no longer struggle but dialogic negotiation, regulated competition and so on. No wonder that border control emerges as one of the main points of today's international negotiations – a clear indication that we are dealing with the reduction of politics to social *Polizei*. Against this end-of-ideology politics, one should insist on the potential of democratic politicization as the true European legacy from ancient Greece onwards. *Will we be able to invent a new mode of re-politicization questioning the undisputed reign of global Capital?* Only such a re-politicization of our predicament can break the vicious cycle of liberal globalization destined to engender the most regressive forms of fundamentalist hatred.

Notes

This essay was first published in *Critical Inquiry* 24, 1998, pp. 988–1009. [eds]

1   I rely here on Jacques Rancière, *Disagreement: Politics and Philosophy*, trans. Julie Rose, Minneapolis, University of Minnesota Press, 1999. The present essay develops further the ideas first elaborated in 'Multiculturalism, or, the cultural logic of multinational capitalism' (reprinted as Chapter 9 of this volume).

2   See, for instance, Étienne Balibar, 'Is a European citizenship possible?', in *Politics and the Other Scene*, trans. Christine Jones, James Swenson and Chris Turner, London and New York, Verso, 2002, pp. 104–28.

3   Sometimes the shift from politics proper to policing can simply be a matter of changing the definite to the indefinite article, like when the East German crowds demonstrated against the Communist régime in the last days of the GDR. First they shouted, 'We are *the* people! [*Wir sind das Volk!*], thereby performing the gesture of politicization at its purest. They, the excluded counter-revolutionary 'scum' of the official whole of the people, with no proper place in official space (or, more precisely, with little more than titles such as 'counter-revolutionaries', 'hooligans', or, at best, 'victims of bourgeois propaganda', reserved for their designation), claimed to stand for the people, for 'all'. However, a couple of days later, the slogan changed into, 'We are a/one people! [*Wir sind ein Volk!*]', clearly signalling the closure of the momentary authentic political opening, the reappropriation of the democratic impetus by the thrust towards the re-unification of Germany, which meant rejoining West Germany's liberal-capitalist police/political order.

4   Plato, 'Parmenides', in *Plato IV: Cratylus, Parmenides, Greater Hippias, Lesser Hippias*, trans. Henry N. Fowler, Cambridge, Harvard University Press, 1970, pp. 211–13. [eds]

5   The metaphoric frame that we use in order to account for the political process is thus never innocent and neutral; it schematizes the concrete meaning of politics. Ultra-politics has recourse to the model of war: politics is conceived as a form of social warfare, as the relationship to 'them', to an enemy. Archi-politics today usually has recourse to a medical model: society is a corporate body, an organism, and social divisions are like illnesses of this organism; that is, what we should fight, our enemy, is a cancerous intruder, a pest, a foreign parasite to be exterminated if the health of the social body is to be guaranteed. Para-politics uses a model of agonistic competition, which follows a series of commonly accepted, strictly established rules, much like a sporting event. Post-politics involves the model of business negotiation and strategic compromise.

6   Jacques Lacan, *Le Séminaire de Jacques Lacan XVII: L'envers de la psychanalyse, 1969–70*, ed. Jacques-Alain Miller, Paris, Éditions du Seuil, 1991, pp. 31–59. [eds]

7   G. W. F. Hegel, *Phenomenology of Spirit*, trans. A. V. Miller, Oxford, Oxford University Press, 1977, pp. 355–63. [eds]

8   Claude Lefort, *L'Invention démocratique: Les limites de la domination totalitaire*, Paris, Librarie Arthème Fayard, 1981.

9   Perhaps the distinction between the Communist and the Fascist masters resides in the fact that – in spite of all the talk about racial science and so forth – the innermost logic of fascism is not meta-political, but ultra-political: the Fascist master is a warrior in politics.

10 Rancière, *Disagreement*, pp. 99–104.

11 This crucial distinction between simulacrum (which overlaps with the Real) and appearance is also easily discernible in the domain of sexuality as the distinction between pornography and seduction: pornography 'shows it all', it is 'real sex', and for that very reason produces the mere simulacrum of sexuality, while the process of seduction consists entirely in the play of appearances, hints and promises and thereby evokes the elusive domain of the suprasensible sublime Thing. For a more detailed analysis of the libidinal impact of pornography, see Slavoj Žižek, *The Plague of Fantasies*, London and New York, Verso, 1997, pp. 171–91.

12 Hegel, *Phenomenology of Spirit*, p. 89.

13 Immanuel Kant, 'On the common saying: "This may be true in theory, but it does not apply in practice"', in *Political Writings*, ed. H. S. Reiss, trans. H. B. Nisbet, Cambridge, Cambridge University Press, 1991, pp. 61–92. [eds]

14 Rancière, *Disagreement*, pp. 115–18.

15 Hegel, *Phenomenology of Spirit*, p. 401.

16 Étienne Balibar, 'Violence, ideality and cruelty', in *Politics and the Other Scene*, trans. Christine Jones, James Swenson and Chris Turner, London and New York, Verso, 2002, pp. 136–7, 141–4.

17 Jacques Lacan, *The Seminar of Jacques Lacan XI: The Four Fundamental Concepts of Psychoanalysis, 1964*, ed. Jacques-Alain Miller, trans. Alan Sheridan, New York and London, W. W. Norton, 1977, p. 241; see also p. 240.

18 For a closer examination of these three forms of evil, see Slavoj Žižek, *The Metastases of Enjoyment: Six Essays on Woman and Causality*, London and New York, Verso, 1994, pp. 54–85. My argument here is drawn from material previously published in this work, pp. 70–71.

19 Balibar, 'Violence, ideality and cruelty', pp. 142–4.

20 Slavoj Žižek, *The Indivisible Remainder: An Essay on Schelling and Related Matters*, London and New York, Verso, 1996, p. 199.

21 For a more detailed account of this reflected cynical attitude, see Žižek, *The Indivisible Remainder*, pp. 189–236.

22 See Jacques Lacan, 'Seminar on "The purloined letter"', trans. Jeffrey Mehlman, in *The Purloined Poe: Lacan, Derrida and Psychoanalytic Reading*, ed. John P. Muller and William J. Richardson, Baltimore, Johns Hopkins University Press, 1988, pp. 47–8. [eds]

23 Alain Badiou, *L'être et l'événement*, Paris, Éditions du Seuil, 1988, pp. 121–8.

24 Alain Badiou, *Saint Paul: The Foundation of Universalism*, trans. Ray Brassier, Stanford, Stanford University Press, 2003, pp. 40–54.

Chapter 11
A plea for 'passive aggressivity'

Amish communities practise the institution of *rumspringa* (from the German *herumspringen*, 'to jump around'): at 17 their children (until then subjected to strict family discipline) are set free, allowed, encouraged even, to go out and experience the ways of the 'English' world around them – they drive cars, listen to pop music, watch television, get involved in drinking, drugs, wild sex . . . After a couple of years, they are then expected to decide: will they become members of the Amish community, or leave it and turn into ordinary American citizens? Far from being permissive and allowing the adolescents a truly free choice – i.e., giving them the opportunity to decide based on the full knowledge and experience of both alternatives – such a solution is biased in a most brutal way, a fake choice if ever there was one. When, after long years of discipline and fantasizing about the transgressive illicit pleasures of the outside 'English' world, the adolescent Amish are all of a sudden and unprepared thrown into it, they cannot but indulge in extreme forms of transgressive behaviour. And since, in such a life, they lack any inherent limitation or regulation, such a permissive situation inexorably backlashes and generates unbearable anxiety – it is thus a safe bet that, after a couple of years, they will return to the seclusion of their community. It is no wonder that 90 per cent of the adolescents do exactly that.

And is this not how our academic freedoms function? (This does not *a priori* render them meaningless or 'co-opted' – one should just be aware of it.) There is nothing better for one's proper integration into the hegemonic ideologico-political community than a 'radical' past in which one lived out one's wildest dreams. The latest instalments of this saga are today's American neo-conservatives, a surprising number of whom were in their youth Trotskyites.[1] Is it not possible to ascertain, retroactively, that even the glorious Parisian May '68 was such a collective *rumspringa*, which, in the long term, contributed to the reproductive capacity of the system itself? In his 'The problem of hegemony',[2] Simon Critchley provides a consistent justification of such critical *rumspringa*:

> We inhabit states. . . . Now, it is arguable that the state is a limitation on human existence and we would be better off without it. Such is perhaps the eternal temptation of anarchism, and we will come back to anarchism. However, it seems to me that we cannot hope, at this point in history, to attain a withering away of the state either through anarcho-syndicalism or revolutionary proletarian praxis, or through the agency of the party for example. . . . If class positions are not simplifying, but on the contrary becoming more complex through processes of dislocation, if the revolution is no longer conceivable in Marx's manner, then that means that, for good or ill, let's say for ill, we are stuck with the state, just as we are stuck with capitalism. The question becomes: what should our political strategy be with regard to the state, to the state that we're in? . . . In a period when the revolutionary subject has decidedly broken down, and the political project of a disappearance of the state is not coherent other than as a beautifully seductive fantasy, politics has to be conceived at a distance from the state. Or, better, politics is the praxis of taking up distance with regard to the state, working independently of the state, working in a situation. Politics is praxis in a situation and the work of politics is the construction of new political subjectivities, new political aggregations in specific localities, new political sequences.
>
> Perhaps it is at this intensely situational, indeed local level that the atomising force of capitalist globalization is to be met, contested and resisted. That is, it is not to be resisted by constructing a global

anti-globalisation movement that, at its worst, is little more than a highly-colourful critical echo of the globalisation it contests. It is rather to be resisted by occupying and controlling the terrain upon which one stands, where one lives, works, acts and thinks. This needn't involve millions of people. It needn't even involve thousands. It could involve just a few at first. It could be what Julia Kristeva has recently called the domain of 'intimate revolt'. That is, politics begins right here, locally, practically and specifically, around a concrete issue and not by running off to protest at some meeting of the G8. You shouldn't meet your enemy on their ground, but on your own, on the ground that you have made your own. Also, think of the money and time you save on travel! . . .

[True democracy is thus] enacted or even simply acted – practically, locally, situationally – at a distance from the state. . . . It calls the state into question, it calls the established order to account, not in order to do away with the state, desirable though that might well be in some utopian sense, but in order to better it or attenuate its malicious effects.[3]

The main ambiguity of this position resides in a strange *non sequitur* that it contains: if the State is here to stay, if it is impossible to abolish the State (and capitalism), why act with a *distance* towards the State? Why not *with(in) the State?* Why not accept the basic premise of the Third Way? Perhaps it is time to take seriously Stalin's obsessive critique of 'bureaucracy', and appreciate in a new (Hegelian) way the necessary work done by State bureaucracy itself. In other words, does Critchley's position not rely on the fact that someone else will assume the task of running the State machinery, enabling us critically to distance ourselves from the State? Furthermore, if the space of democracy is defined by this 'distance', is Critchley not abandoning the field (of the State) all too easily to the enemy? Is it not crucial *what* form the State power has? Does not Critchley's position lead to the reduction of this crucial question to a secondary place: whatever State we have, it is inherently non-democratic?

This brings us to the second ambiguity: is the sentiment that the State 'is here to stay' a temporary withdrawal, a specific claim about today's historico-political situation, or a transcendental limitation conditioned by human finitude? That is to say, when Critchley defines today's political constellation as one in which the State is permanent and in which we are caught within multiple displacements, etc., this thesis is radically (and necessarily) ambiguous: (1) is it – as some of his formulations appear (for instance, 'In a period when the revolutionary subject has decidedly broken down, and the political project of a disappearance of the State is not coherent other than as a beautifully seductive fantasy . . .') – that this is merely today's historical constellation, in which progressive political forces are in retreat; or (2) is it that this is a general 'truth' to which we were blind when we believed in essentialist utopian political ideologies (for instance, 'The revolution is not going to be generated out of systemic or structural laws. We are on our own and what we do we have to do for ourselves. Politics requires subjective invention. No ontology or eschatological philosophy of history is going to do it for us . . .')? Again, the ambiguity is here necessary:

> The revolution is not going to be generated out of systemic or structural laws. We are on our own and what we do we have to do for ourselves. Politics requires subjective invention. No ontology or eschatological philosophy of history is going to do it for us. Working at a distance from the state, a distance that I have tried to describe as democratic, we need to construct political subjectivities in specific situations, subjectivities that are not arbitrary or relativistic, but which are articulations of an ethical demand whose scope is universal and whose evidence is faced in a situation. This is dirty, detailed, local, practical and largely unthrilling work. It is time we made a start.[4]

Is this dilemma not *all too coarse?* Is it not effectively a case of 'binary opposition'? That is to say, even if emancipatory progress cannot be directly grounded in some 'objective' social necessity, even if it is true that 'what we do we have to do for ourselves' (incidentally, this is a thesis with which the Lukács of *History and Class Consciousness*, the ultimate straw-man of the critics of 'teleological' Hegelian-Marxism, would fully agree – he provided the most convincing version of it), it presupposes a certain specific historical site, what Alain Badiou called 'an evental site [*un site événementiel*]'.[5] Is then Critchley not paradigmatic of the position of an ideal supplement to the Third Way

Left: the 'revolt' against it which poses no effective threat since it endorses in advance the logic of hysterical provocation, bombarding the Power with 'impossible' demands, demands which are not meant to be met? Critchley is therefore consequent in his assertion of the primacy of the ethical over the political: the ultimate motivating force of political interventions is the experience of *injustice*, of the ethical unacceptability of the state of things.[6]

Against Critchley's call for the modest local 'practical' action, one is thus tempted to evoke Badiou's provocative thesis: 'It is better to do nothing than to contribute to the invention of formal ways of rendering visible that which Empire already recognizes as existent.'[7] Better to do nothing than to engage in localized acts whose ultimate function is to make the system run more smoothly (acts like providing the space for the multitude of new subjectivities, etc.). The threat today is thus not passivity, but *pseudo-activity*, the urge to 'be active', to 'participate', to mask the Nothingness of what goes on. People intervene all the time, academics participate in meaningless 'debates', etc., but the truly difficult thing is to step back from activity, to withdraw from it. Those in power often even prefer 'critical' participation, a dialogue, to silence – they would prefer to engage us in a 'dialogue', just to make sure that our ominous passivity is broken.

However, the ultimate argument against 'big' political interventions which aim at global transformation is, of course, the terrifying experience of the catastrophes of the twentieth century, catastrophes that unleashed previously unheard of modes of violence. There are three main ways of theorizing these catastrophes: (1) the way epitomized by Habermas: while Enlightenment is in itself a positive emancipatory process with no inherent 'totalitarian' potential, these catastrophes are merely an indicator that it remains an unfinished project, so our task should be to bring 'Enlightenment' itself to completion; (2) the way associated with Adorno and Horkheimer's 'dialectic of Enlightenment', as well as, today, with Agamben:[8] the 'totalitarian' potential of the Enlightenment is inherent and crucial, the 'administered world' is the truth of Enlightenment, the concentration camps and genocide of the twentieth century are a kind of negative-teleological endpoint of the entire history of the West; (3) the 'third way', developed by Étienne Balibar, among others: modernity opens up a field of new freedoms, but at the same time of new dangers, and there is no ultimate teleological guarantee of the outcome – the battle is an open one, as yet undecided.

The starting point of Balibar's remarkable intervention is the insufficiency of the standard Hegelian-Marxist notion of 'converting' violence into an instrument of historical Reason, a force which begets new social formations: the 'irrational' brutality of violence is thus *aufgehoben*, 'sublated' in the strict Hegelian sense, reduced to a particular stain that contributes to the overall harmony of historical progress.[9] The twentieth century confronted us with catastrophes, some of them directed against Marxist political forces and some of them generated by the Marxist political engagement itself, which cannot be 'rationalized' in this way: their instrumentalization into the tools of the 'cunning of reason' is not only ethically unacceptable but also theoretically wrong, *ideological* in the strongest sense of the term. In his close reading of Marx, Balibar nonetheless discerns an oscillation between this teleological 'conversion'-theory of violence and a much more interesting notion of history as an open, undecided process of antagonistic struggles whose final 'positive' outcome is not guaranteed by any all-encompassing historical Necessity.

According to Balibar, for necessarily structural reasons, Marxism is unable to conceive of an excess of violence that cannot be integrated into the narrative of historical progress – more specifically, it cannot provide an adequate theory of fascism and Stalinism and their 'extreme' expressions, the Shoah and gulag. The task then becomes double: to deploy a theory of historical violence as something that cannot be mastered, instrumentalized by any political agent, which threatens to engulf this very agent in a self-destructive cycle, and – the other side of the same task – to pose the question of how to 'civilize' revolution, of how to make the revolutionary process itself a 'civilizing' force. Recall the infamous St Bartholomew's Day Massacre – what went wrong? Catherine de Medici's goal was limited and precise: hers was a Machiavellian plot to have Admiral de Coligny, a powerful Protestant pushing for war with Spain in the Netherlands, assassinated and let the blame fall on the all-powerful Catholic Guise family. In this way, Catherine hoped that the final outcome would be the fall of both houses that posed a menace to the unity of the French State. But this ingenious plan to play her enemies against each other degenerated into an uncontrolled frenzy of blood: in her ruthless pragmatism,

Catherine was blind to the passion with which people cling to their beliefs.

Balibar further proposes the notion of excessive, non-functional cruelty as a feature of contemporary life:[10] a cruelty whose figures range from 'fundamentalist' racist and/or religious slaughter to the 'senseless' outbursts of violence performed by adolescents and the homeless in our megalopolises, a violence one is tempted to call *Id-Evil*, a violence grounded in no utilitarian or ideological reason. All the talk about foreigners stealing work from us or the threat they represent to our Western values should not deceive us: under closer examination, it soon becomes clear that this talk provides a rather superficial secondary rationalization. The answer we ultimately obtain from skinheads is that it makes them feel good to beat foreigners, that their very presence is what is disturbing . . . Such Id-Evil is structured around and motivated by the most elementary imbalance in the relationship between the Ego and *jouissance*, by the tension between pleasure and the foreign body of *jouissance* at its very heart. Id-Evil thus stages the most elementary 'short-circuit' in the relationship of the subject to the primordially missing object-cause of his desire: what bothers us in the 'other' (Jew, Japanese, African, Turk, etc.) is that he appears to entertain a privileged relationship to the object – the other either possesses the *agalma*, having snatched it away from us (which is why we don't have it), or he poses a threat to our possession of the object. What one should propose here, again, is the Hegelian 'infinite judgement', which asserts the speculative identity of these 'useless' and 'excessive' outbursts of violence that display nothing but a naked ('non-sublimated') hatred of Otherness, with the post-political multiculturalist universe of tolerance for difference in which no one is excluded.

(Of course, we are using the term *non-sublimated* in its common, vulgar meaning, which, in this case, stands for the exact opposite of its strict psychoanalytic meaning. In short, what takes place when we focus our hatred on some representative of the [officially tolerated] Other is the very mechanism of sublimation at its most elementary: the all-encompassing nature of post-political 'concrete universality', which accounts for everybody at the level of symbolic inclusion, this multi-culturalist vision and practice of 'unity in difference' [e.g., 'everyone is equal, everyone is different'], leaves open, as the only way to mark difference, the proto-sublimatory gesture of elevating a contingent Other [race, sex, religion, etc.] into the 'absolute Otherness' of the impossible Thing, the ultimate threat to our identity – this Thing that must be annihilated if we are to survive. Therein resides the properly Hegelian paradox: the final arrival of a truly rational 'concrete universality' – the abolition of antagonisms, the 'mature' universe of a negotiated co-existence of different groups – coincides with its radical opposite, with thoroughly contingent outbursts of violence.)

Hegel's fundamental rule is that 'objective' excess (the direct reign of abstract universality which imposes its law 'mechanically', with utter disregard for the concerned subject caught in its web) is always supplemented by a 'subjective' excess (the irregular, arbitrary exercise of the whims of the individual).[11] An exemplary case of this interdependence is provided by Balibar, who distinguishes two opposite but complementary modes of excessive violence: the *ultra-objective* ('structural') violence that is inherent to the social conditions of global capitalism (the 'automatic' creation of excluded and dispensable individuals, from the homeless to the unemployed), and the *ultra-subjective* violence of newly emerging ethnic and/or religious (in short, racist) 'fundamentalisms'. This excessive, groundless violence involves its own mode of knowledge, that of impotent cynical reflection – back to our example of Id-Evil, of a skinhead beating up foreigners: when really pressed for reasons for his violence, and if capable of minimal theoretical reflection, he would suddenly begin to speak like a social worker, sociologist or social psychologist, quoting diminished social mobility, rising insecurity, the disintegration of paternal authority, the lack of maternal love in his early childhood, etc.; in short, he would provide a more-or-less precise psycho-sociological account of his acts, so as to endear him to enlightened liberals eager to 'understand' the violent youth as a tragic victim of social and familial conditions. The standard enlightened formula for the efficiency of the 'critique of ideology' from Plato onwards ('they are doing it because they do not know what they are doing', i.e., knowledge is in itself liberating: when the erring subject reflects upon what he is doing, he will no longer be doing it) is here inverted: the violent skinhead 'knows very well what he is doing, but he is nonetheless doing it'.[12] The symbolic efficiency of knowledge embedded in the subject's effective social praxis disintegrates into, on the one hand, excessive 'irrational' violence with no ideological-political foundation and, on the other hand, impotent external reflection that leaves the subject's behaviour intact. While the skinhead, in the guise of this cynically-impotent reflection, explains to the perplexed journalist the roots of his senseless violent behaviour, the enlightened tolerant multiculturalist bent on 'understanding' these forms of excessive violence receives his own message in its inverted, true form – in short, as Lacan would have put it, at this point, the communication between him and the 'object' of his study, the intolerant skinhead, is thoroughly successful.

But the complementarity of these modes of excessive violence is nowhere more apparent than in the dynamics of capitalism itself. On one level, capitalism entails the radical secularization of social life – it mercilessly tears apart any aura of authentic nobility, sacredness and honour. However, the fundamental lesson of the 'critique of political economy' elaborated by the mature Marx in the years following the *Manifesto* is that this reduction of all heavenly chimeras to brutal economic reality generates a quasi-theological spectrality of its own.[13] When Marx describes the mad self-enhancing circulation of Capital, whose solipsistic process of self-fecundation[14] reaches its apogee in today's meta-reflexive speculations on futures, it is far too simplistic to claim that the spectre of this self-engendering monster that pursues its path disregarding any human or environmental concern is an ideological abstraction, and that one should never forget that, behind this abstraction, there are real people and natural objects on whose productive capacities and resources Capital's circulation is based and on which it feeds itself like a gigantic parasite. The problem is that this 'abstraction' is not merely in the misperception of social reality, but that it is 'Real' in the precise sense of determining the structure of the material social processes themselves: the fate of an entire strata of the population and sometimes of whole countries can be decided by the 'solipsistic' speculative dance of Capital, which pursues its goal of profitability in a blessed indifference towards the way its movement will affect social reality. Therein resides the fundamental character of the systemic violence of capitalism, which is much more uncanny than direct pre-capitalist socio-ideological violence: this violence can no longer be attributed to concrete individuals and their 'evil' intentions, but is purely 'objective', structural, anonymous.

Here we encounter the Lacanian difference between reality and the Real: 'reality' is the lived social experience of actual people involved in the productive process, while the Real is the inexorable 'abstract' spectral logic of Capital that determines what goes on in social reality. And, again, today is this not more accurate than ever? Do phenomena usually designated as 'virtual capitalism' (futures trading and other abstract financial speculations) not point towards the immanent reign of 'real abstraction' at its purest? The ideological rationalizations of this process are those different theories of 'postmodernism' or 'second modernization' that emphasize the notion of global reflexivity: today, the process of the dissolution of all traditional authorities described by Marx, the process through which 'all that is solid melts into air', has reached an unprecedented peak far beyond what Marx and Engels were able to imagine, penetrating even the intimate domain of sexuality.[15]

Hannah Arendt's insights at this point are particularly fitting. She emphasized the distinction between political power and the mere exercise of (social) violence: organizations run by direct non-political authority – for instance, by an order of command that is not politically grounded (as in the army, church, family or school) – represent examples of violence [Gewalt], not of political power in the strict sense of the term. Here, however, it would be productive to introduce the distinction between public symbolic Law and its obscene supplement: the notion of an obscene superegoic 'double' of Power implies that there is no power without violence. Power must always rely on an obscene stain of violence; political space is thus never 'pure', but always involves some kind of reliance on 'pre-political' violence. Of course, the relationship between political Power and pre-political violence is one of mutual implication: not only is violence the necessary supplement to Power, but (political) Power is itself always-already present at the core of every apparently 'non-political' social bond. The accepted violence and direct relationship of subordination in the army, church, family and other 'non-political' social forms are themselves simply the 'reified' expressions of certain ethico-political struggles – the task of critical analysis is to discern the hidden political processes that sustain all these 'non-' or 'pre-political' forms. In human society, the political is the encompassing structuring principle, so that every neutralization of some partial social content as 'non-political' is itself a political gesture par excellence.

This acceptance of violence, this 'political suspension of the ethical', is the limit that even the most 'tolerant' liberal stance is unable to cross – witness the uneasiness of 'radical' post-colonialist Afro-American studies apropos of Frantz Fanon's fundamental insight into the unavoidability of violence in the process of effective decolonization. Consider Fredric Jameson's suggestion that, in a revolutionary process, violence plays the same role as worldly wealth in the Calvinist logic of predestination: although it has no intrinsic value, it is a sign of the authenticity of the revolution, of the fact that this process is effectively disturbing the existing Power relations.[16] In other words, the dream of a revolution without violence is precisely the dream of a 'revolution without revolution' (Robespierre). On the other hand, the role of the fascist spectacle of violence is exactly the opposite: it is a violence whose aim is to *prevent* true change – something spectacular happens constantly so that, precisely, nothing really happens.

But, again, the ultimate argument against this perspective is the simple encounter with excessive suffering generated by political violence. Sometimes, one cannot but be shocked by the excessive indifference towards suffering, even and especially when this suffering is widely reported in the media and condemned – it is as if the very outrage at suffering is what turns us into immobilized fascinated spectators. Recall, in the early 1990s, the three-years-long siege of Sarajevo, whose population was starving and constantly exposed to shelling and sniper fire. The real enigma is this: although the media were full of pictures and reports, why didn't the UN forces, NATO or the United States accomplish the seemingly insignificant act of *breaking the siege of Sarajevo*, of imposing a corridor through which people and provisions could pass freely? It would have cost nothing: with a little bit of serious pressure on the Serb forces, the prolonged spectacle of an encircled Sarajevo exposed to such ridiculous terror would have been over. There is only one answer to this enigma, the one proposed by Rony Brauman himself who, on behalf of the Red Cross, coordinated the aid to Sarajevo: the very presentation of the crisis in Sarajevo as 'humanitarian', the very recasting of the political-military conflict into humanitarian terms, was sustained by an eminently *political* choice, that of, basically, taking the side of Serbia in the conflict. Especially ominous and manipulative here was the role of Mitterand:

> The celebration of 'humanitarian intervention' in Yugoslavia took the place of a political discourse, disqualifying in advance all conflicting debate . . . It was apparently not possible, for François Mitterand, to express his analysis of the war in Yugoslavia. With the strictly humanitarian response, he disovered an unexpected source of communication or, more precisely, of cosmetics, which is a little bit the same thing. . . . Mitterand remained in favour of the maintenance of Yugoslavia within its borders and was persuaded that only a strong Serbian power was in the position to guarantee a certain stability in this explosive region. This position rapidly became unacceptable in the eyes of the French people. All the bustling activity and the humanitarian discourse permitted him to reaffirm the unfailing commitment of France to the Rights of Man in the end, and to mimic an opposition to greater Serbian fascism, all in giving it free rein.[17]

From this specific insight, one should then move to the more general level of rendering problematic the very 'depoliticized' humanitarian politics of 'human rights' as the ideology of military interventionism serving specific economic-political purposes. As Wendy Brown insists apropos of Michael Ignatieff, such humanitarianism 'presents itself as something of an antipolitics – a pure defence of the innocent and the powerless against power, a pure defence of the individual against immense and potentially cruel or despotic machineries of culture, state, war, ethnic conflict, tribalism, patriarchy, and other mobilizations or instantiations of collective power against individuals'.[18] However, the real question is, 'what kind of politicization [do those who intervene on behalf of human rights] set in motion against the powers they oppose? Do they stand for a different formulation of justice or do they stand in opposition to collective justice projects?'[19] It is clear, for instance, that the American gesture of overthrowing Saddam Hussein, legitimized in terms of ending the suffering of the Iraqi people, was not only motivated by other politico-economic interests (i.e., oil), but also relied on a determinate idea of the political and economic conditions (Western liberal democracy, guarantee of private property, inclusion in the global market economy, etc.) that should open up the prospect of freedom to the Iraqi people. The purely humanitarian anti-political politics of simply preventing suffering thus effectively amounts to the implicit prohibition of elaborating a positive collective project of socio-political transformation.

And, at an even more general level, one should problematize the very opposition between the universal (pre-political) human rights that belong to every human being 'as such' and the specific political rights of citizens, members of a particular political community; along these lines, Balibar argues for the '*reversal* of the historical and theoretical relationship between "man" and "citizen"' which proceeds by 'explaining how *man is made by citizenship* and not citizenship by man'.[20] He is referring here to Hannah Arendt's insight apropos of the twentieth-century phenomenon of refugees: 'The conception of human rights based upon the assumed existence of a human being as such broke down at the very moment when those who professed to believe in it were for the first time confronted with people who had indeed lost all other qualities and specific relationships – except that they were still human.'[21] This line, of course, leads straight to Agamben's notion of *homo sacer* as a human being reduced to 'bare life': in a properly Hegelian paradoxical dialectics of the universal and the particular, it is precisely when a human being is deprived of his particular socio-political identity, which accounts for his determinate citizenship, that he, in the very same gesture, is no longer recognized and/or treated as human. In short, the paradox is that one is deprived of human rights precisely when one is effectively, in one's social reality, reduced to a human being 'in general', without citizenship, profession, etc. – that is to say, *precisely when one effectively becomes the ideal bearer of 'universal human rights'* (which belong to me independently of my profession, sex, citizenship, religion, ethnic identity . . .).

We thus arrive at the standard 'postmodern', 'anti-essentialist' position, a kind of political version of Foucault's notion of sex as generated by a multitude of sexual practices: 'man', the bearer of human rights, is generated by a set of political practices which materialize citizenship – but is this sufficient? Jacques Rancière has proposed a very elegant and precise solution to the antinomy between human rights (belonging to 'man as such') and the politicization of citizens:[22] while human rights cannot be posited as an unhistorical essentialist 'Beyond' with regard to the contingent sphere of political struggles, as universal 'natural rights of man' exempted from history, they also should not be dismissed as a reified fetish, a product of concrete historical processes of the politicization of citizens. The gap between the universality of human rights and the political rights of citizens is thus not a gap between the universality of man and a specific political sphere; rather, it 'separates the whole of the community from itself',[23] as Rancière put it in a precise Hegelian way. Far from being pre-political, 'universal human rights' designate the very space of politicization proper: what they amount to is *the right to universality as such*, the right of a political agent to assert its radical non-coincidence with itself (in its particular identity), i.e., to posit itself – precisely in so far as it is the 'surnumerary' one, the 'part with no part', the one without a proper place in the social edifice – as an agent of the universality of the Social as such. This paradox is thus a very precise one, and symmetrical to the paradox of universal human rights as the rights of those reduced to inhumanity: *at the very moment when we try to conceive political rights of citizens without the reference to universal 'meta-political' human rights, we lose politics itself*, i.e., we reduce politics to a 'post-political' play of negotiated particular interests. What, then, happens to human rights when they are reduced to the rights of *homo sacer*, of those excluded from the political community, those reduced to 'bare life'? Rancière proposes here an extremely salient dialectical reversal:

> When they are of no use, you do the same as charitable persons do with their old clothes. You give them to the poor. Those rights that appear to be useless in their place are sent abroad, along with medicine and clothes, to people deprived of medicine, clothes, and rights. It is in this way, as the result of this process, that the Rights of Man become the rights of those who have no rights, the rights of bare human beings subjected to inhuman repression and inhuman conditions of existence. They become humanitarian rights, the rights of those who cannot enact them, the victims of the absolute denial of right. For all this, they are not void. Political names and political places never become merely void. The void is filled by somebody or something else . . . If those who suffer

inhuman repression are unable to enact Human Rights that are their last recourse, then somebody else has to inherit their rights in order to enact them in their place. This is what is called the 'right to humanitarian interference' – a right that some nations assume to the supposed benefit of victimized populations, and very often against the advice of the humanitarian organizations themselves. The 'right to humanitarian interference' might be described as a sort of 'return to sender': the disused rights that had been sent to the rightless are sent back to the senders.[24]

The reference to Lacan's formula of communication (in which the sender gets back from the receiver-addressee his own message in its inverted, i.e., true, form) is here especially pertinent: in the reigning discourse of humanitarian interventionism, the developed West is getting back from the victimized Third World its own message in its true form.[25] And the moment human rights are in this way depoliticized, the discourse dealing with them has to change its register to that of ethics, mobilizing some reference to the pre-political opposition of Good and Evil. Today's 'new reign of Ethics',[26] clearly discernible in, say, Michael Ignatieff's work, thus relies on a violent gesture of depoliticization, of denying political subjectivization to the victimized other. And, as Rancière has pointed out, liberal humanitarianism à la Ignatieff unexpectedly meets the 'radical' position of Foucault or Agamben with regard to this depoliticization: the Foucauldian–Agambenian notion of 'biopolitics' as the culmination of the whole of Western thought ends up getting caught in a kind of 'ontological trap' in which concentration camps appear as an 'ontological destiny: each of us would be in the situation of the refugee in a camp. Any difference grows faint between democracy and totalitarianism and any political practice proves to be already ensnared in the biopolitical trap'.[27] When, in a shift from Foucault, Agamben identifies sovereign power and biopolitics (in today's generalized state of exception, the two overlap), he thus precludes the very possibility of the emergence of political subjectivity.

However, the rise of political subjectivity takes place against the background of a certain limit of the 'inhuman', so that one should continue to endorse the paradox of the inhumanity of the human being deprived of citizenship, and posit the 'inhuman' pure man as a necessary excess of humanity over itself, its 'indivisible remainder', a Kantian limit-concept of the phenomenal notion of humanity. Just as, in Kant's philosophy, the sublime noumenal appears as pure horror when we come too close to it, man 'as such', deprived of all phenomenal qualifications, appears as an inhuman monster, something like Kafka's *odradek*. The problem with human rights humanism is that it covers up the monstrosity of this 'human as such', presenting it as a sublime human essence.

What then is the way out of this deadlock? Balibar concludes his paper on 'human civic rights' with an ambiguous reference to Mahatma Gandhi. It is true that Gandhi's formula, 'Be yourself the change you would like to see in the world', encapsulates perfectly the basic attitude of emancipatory change: do not wait for the 'objective process' to generate the expected/desired change – if you merely wait for it, it will never come. Instead, throw *yourself* into it, *be* this change, take upon yourself the risk of enacting it directly. However, is not the ultimate limitation of Gandhi's strategy the fact that it only works against a liberal-democratic régime which adheres to certain minimal ethico-political standards – i.e., in which, to put it in pathetic terms, those in Power still 'have a conscience'? Recall Gandhi's reply, in the late 1930s, to the question of what the Jews in Germany should do against Hitler: they should commit collective suicide and thus arouse the conscience of the world . . . One can easily imagine the Nazi reaction: OK, we will help you, where do you want the poison delivered?

There is, however, another way in which Balibar's plea for a renunciation of violence can be given a specific twist. Recall the two symmetrically opposed modes of the 'living dead', when one finds oneself in the uncanny place 'between two deaths [*l'êntre deux morts*]': one is either biologically dead while symbolically alive (surviving one's biological death as a spectral apparition or the symbolic authority of the Name), or symbolically dead while biologically alive (those excluded from the socio-symbolic order, from Antigone to today's *homo sacer*). And what if we apply the same logic to the opposition of violence and non-violence, identifying the two ways in which they intersect?[28] We all know the pop-psychological notion of 'passive-aggressive behaviour', usually applied to a housewife who, instead of actively opposing her husband, passively sabotages him (and this brings us back to our beginning): perhaps this attitude of *passive aggressivity* is a proper radical political gesture, in contrast to aggressive passivity, the standard 'interpassive' mode of our participation in socio-ideological life in which we are active all the time in order to make sure that nothing will happen, that nothing will really change. In such a constellation, the first truly critical ('aggressive', violent) step is to *withdraw* into passivity, to refuse to participate – this is the necessary first step that, as it were, clears the ground for a true activity, for an act that will effectively change the coordinates of today's constellation.

Notes

1 One should, of course, resist the stupid temptation to use this fact as grounds for the retroactive legitimization of Stalin's brutal suppression of Trotskyism ('So Stalin was nonetheless right when he pointed out how Trotskyism ends up directly serving imperialism – he was half a century ahead of his time!'); such a line of reasoning can only end up in a cheap paraphrase of de Quincey: 'How many an honest man started with a modest leftist critique of Stalinism and ended up as servants of imperialism . . .'

2 Simon Critchley, 'The problem of hegemony', lecture from the 2004 *Albert Schweitzer Series on Ethics and Politics* at New York University. It appears on the *Political Theory* website [www.politicaltheory.info/essays/critchley.htm]. Page references are taken from this site. [eds]

3 Critchley, 'Problem of hegemony', pp. 3–4. [eds]

4 Critchley, 'Problem of hegemony', p. 5. [eds]

5 Alain Badiou, *L'être et l'événement*, Paris, Éditions du Seuil, 1988, pp. 195–6. [eds]

6 Critchley, 'Problem of hegemony', p. 5. [eds]

7 Alain Badiou, 'Fifteen theses on contemporary art', lecture presented at the launch of *lacanian ink* 22, The Drawing Center, New York, 4 December 2003. See also Badiou's commentary on his theses in *lacanian ink* 23, 2004, pp. 103–19. [eds]

8 See Max Horkheimer and Theodor Adorno, *Dialectic of Enlightenment: Philosophical Fragments*, ed. Gunzelin Schmid Nörr, trans. Edmund Jephcott, Stanford, Stanford University Press, 2002; Giorgio Agamben, *Homo Sacer: Sovereign Power and Bare Life*, trans. Daniel Heller-Roazen, Stanford, Stanford University Press, 1998; and *Remnants of Auschwitz: The Witness and the Archive*, trans. Daniel Heller-Roazen, New York, Zone, 1999. [eds]

9 Étienne Balibar, 'Three concepts of politics: emancipation, transformation, civility', in *Politics and the Other Scene*, trans. Christine Jones, James Swenson and Chris Turner, London and New York, Verso, 2002, pp. 23–35. [eds]

10 Étienne Balibar, 'Violence, ideality and cruelty', in *Politics and the Other Scene*, pp. 136–7, 141–4.

11 G. W. F. Hegel, *Phenomenology of Spirit*, trans. A. V. Miller, Oxford, Oxford University Press, 1977, pp. 151–7; and *Elements of the Philosophy of Right*, trans. H. B. Nisbet, Cambridge, Cambridge University Press, 1991, pp. 54–7. [eds]

12 Žižek is here referring to the 'fetishist disavowal' famously elaborated by Octave Mannoni in his, 'I know well, but all the same . . .', in *Perversion and the Social Relation*, ed. Molly Anne Rothenberg, Dennis A. Foster and Slavoj Žižek, Durham, Duke University Press, 2003, 68–92. [eds]

13 See, for instance, Karl Marx, *Capital: A Critique of Political Economy, Volume 1*, trans. Ben Fowkes, London, Penguin/New Left Review, 1976, p. 256. Marx's formulation here is crucial: '[I]nstead of simply representing the relations of commodities, [value] now enters into a private relationship with itself, as it were. It differentiates itself as original value from itself as surplus-value, just as God the Father differentiates himself from himself as God the Son, although both are of the same age and form, in fact one single person. Value therefore now becomes value in process, money in process, and, as such, capital.' [eds]

14 See, for instance, Karl Marx, *Capital: A Critique of Political Economy, Volume 3*, trans. David Fernbach, London, Penguin/New Left Review, 1981, p. 966: 'Capital thereby already becomes a very mystical being, since all the productive forces of social labour appear attributable to it, and not to labour as such, as a power springing forth from its own womb.' [eds]

15 See Balibar, 'Violence, ideality and cruelty', pp. 143–4. [eds]

16 Slavoj Žižek, *The Puppet and the Dwarf: The Perverse Core of Christianity*, Cambridge, MIT Press, 2003, p. 175 n. 26. [eds]

17 Rony Brauman, 'From philanthropy to humanitarianism', *South Atlantic Quarterly* 103, 2004, pp. 398–9, 416.

18 Wendy Brown, 'Human rights as the politics of fatalism', *South Atlantic Quarterly* 103, 2004, p. 453.

19 Brown, 'Human rights as the politics of fatalism', p. 454.

20 Étienne Balibar, 'Is a philosophy of human civic rights possible?', *South Atlantic Quarterly* 103, 2004, pp. 320–1.

21 Hannah Arendt, *The Origins of Totalitarianism*, New York, Meridian, 1958, p. 297.

22   See Jacques Rancière, 'Who is the subject of the rights of man?', *South Atlantic Quarterly* 103, 2004, pp. 297–310.

23   Rancière, 'Who is the subject of the rights of man?', p. 305.

24   Rancière, 'Who is the subject of the rights of man?', pp. 307–9.

25   And this is also where we should look for candidates for the position of 'universal singular', a particular group whose fate stands for the injustice of today's world. Palestine is today the site of a potential event precisely because all of the standard 'pragmatic' solutions to the 'Middle East crisis' repeatedly fail, so that the utopian invention of a new space is the only 'realistic' choice. Furthermore, Palestinians are particularly good candidates on account of their paradoxical status of being *the victims of the ultimate Victims themselves* (i.e., Jews), which, of course, puts them in an extremely difficult position: when they resist, their resistance can immediately be denounced as a prolongation of anti-Semitism, as a secret solidarity with the Nazi 'final solution'. Indeed, if – as Lacanian Zionists like to claim – Jews are the *objet petit a* among nations, the troubling excess of Western history, how can one resist them with impunity? Is it possible to be the *objet a* of *objet a* itself? It is precisely this ethical blackmail that one should reject.

There is, however, a privileged site among these other candidates: the slums of the new megalopolises and their inhabitants. The explosive growth of slums in the last few decades – particularly in Third World megalopolises from Mexico City and other Latin American capitals through Africa (e.g., Lagos, Chad) to India, China, the Philippines and Indonesia – is perhaps the crucial geopolitical event of our times. While one should certainly resist the easy temptation to elevate and idealize slum-dwellers into a new revolutionary class, one should nonetheless, in Badiou's terms, perceive slums as one of the few authentic 'evental sites' in today's society – slum-dwellers are literally a collection of those who are the 'part of no-part', the 'surnumerary' element of society, excluded from the benefits of citizenship, the uprooted and dispossessed, those who effectively 'have nothing to lose but their chains'.

26   Rancière, 'Who is the subject of the rights of man?', p. 309.

27   Rancière, 'Who is the subject of the rights of man?', p. 301.

28   In what follows, I rely on certain ideas developed by Rob Rushing (University of Illinois, Champaign-Urbana).

Chapter 12
The three faces of Bill Gates

There is more than one story to be told about Bill Gates.

First, there is the American success story: a young boy starting a company in his garage a mere quarter of a century ago, borrowing ridiculously small amounts of money from his neighbours and relatives, who is now the richest man in the world – the latest proof of the infinite opportunities of America, the American dream at its purest.

Then, there is the story of Bill Gates the evil monopolist, the ominous master with his weird smile, whom we all love to hate – the obverse of the American dream, one of the ideal figures of American paranoia. In spite of its apparent anti-capitalist stance, this story is no less ideological than the first one: it is sustained by another myth, that of American freedom, of a freedom fighter destroying the bad Institution (from the Watergate journalists to Noam Chomsky). In short, what these two stories share is the fetishized personification of social struggles: the belief in the key role of the heroic individual.

Finally, there is the Bill Gates of 'frictionless capitalism', the emblem of post-industrial society in which we witness the 'end of labour', in which software is winning over hardware and the young nerd over the old top manager in black suit – in the new company headquarters, there is little external discipline, (ex-)hackers who dominate the scene work long hours, enjoying free drinks in green surroundings, etc. How, then, do these three stories relate? Let us begin, in the good old

Marxist way, with the last narrative, that of the historical vicissitudes of capitalism.

Perhaps it is only today, within global capitalism in its 'post-industrial' form, that, to put it in Hegelian terms, 'really existing capitalism' is achieving the level of its notion: perhaps, one should once again follow Marx's infamous anti-evolutionist motto (incidentally, taken verbatim from Hegel) that 'human anatomy contains a key to the anatomy of the ape', i.e., that, in order to deploy the inherent notional structure of a social formation, one must start with its most developed form.[1] As is well known, Marx located capitalism's elementary antagonism in the opposition between use- and exchange-value: in capitalism, the potentials of this opposition are fully realized, the domain of exchange-values acquires autonomy, and is transformed into the spectre of self-propelling speculative Capital which uses the productive capacities and needs of actual people only as its dispensable temporal embodiment. Marx derived the very notion of economic crisis from this gap: a crisis occurs when reality catches up with the illusory self-generating mirage of money begetting more money – this speculative madness cannot go on indefinitely, it has to explode in ever stronger crises. The ultimate root of the crisis is for him the gap between use- and exchange-value: the logic of exchange-value follows its own path, its own mad dance, irrespective of the real needs of real people. It may appear that this analysis is more actual today than ever, when the tension between the virtual universe and the Real is reaching almost palpably unbearable proportions: on the one hand, we have crazy solipsistic speculations about futures, mergers, etc., following their own inherent logic; on the other hand, reality is catching up in the guise of ecological catastrophes, poverty, the Third World collapse of social life, Mad Cow Disease, etc. This is why cyber-capitalists can appear as the paradigmatic capitalists today, and why Bill Gates can dream of cyberspace as providing the frame for what he calls 'frictionless capitalism'. What we have here is an ideological short-circuit between the two versions of the gap between reality and virtuality: the gap between real production and the virtual/spectral domain of Capital, and the gap between experiential reality and the virtual reality of cyberspace. The actual horror of the motto 'frictionless capitalism' is that, since actual 'frictions' continue to insist, they become invisible, repressed into the netherworld outside our 'postmodern' post-industrial universe; this is why the 'frictionless' universe of digitalized communication, technological gadgets, etc., is always haunted by the notion that there is a global catastrophe waiting around the corner, threatening to explode at any moment.

Jeremy Rifkin designated this new stage of commodification as 'cultural capitalism'.[2] In 'cultural capitalism', the relationship between an object and its symbol-image is inverted: the image does not represent the product, but, rather, the product represents the image.[3] We buy a product – say, an organic apple – because it represents the image of a healthy lifestyle. This reversal is brought to its extreme when a secondary association becomes the ultimate point of reference, as in the case of Mozart's Piano Concerto No. 20: when, decades ago, its second movement was used for the soundtrack of the popular Swedish sentimental love story, *Elvira Madigan*, even its 'serious' recordings as a rule added the film's title to it – e.g., Mozart, Piano Concerto No. 20 ('Elvira Madigan') – so that, when we buy and listen to the CD, we are in fact buying the experience of that insipid Romantic melodrama. Along the same lines, the main reason why so many people still continue to visit 'real' stores (as opposed to on-line shopping) is not so much that you can 'see and feel' the products there, but that you can 'enjoy browsing itself as a recreational activity'.[4]

As the example of buying an organic apple indicates, the very ecological protest against capitalist ruthless exploitation of natural resources is already caught in the commodification of experiences: although ecology perceives itself as a protest against the digitalization/ virtualization of our daily lives and advocates a return to the direct experience of sensual material reality in all its unpredictable fragility and inertia, ecology itself is branded as a new lifestyle – what we are effectively buying when we buy 'organic food', for instance, is already a certain cultural experience, the experience of a 'healthy, ecologically-friendly lifestyle'. And the same goes for every return to 'reality': in a recent publicity spot widely broadcast on all the main American television stations, a group of ordinary people is depicted as engaged in a barbecue picnic with country music and dancing, with the accompanying message: 'Beef. Real food for real people.' The irony is that the beef offered here as the symbol of a certain lifestyle ('real' grass-roots working-class Americans) is much more chemically and genetically manipulated than the 'organic' food consumed by 'artificial' yuppies.

What we are witnessing today, the defining feature of 'postmodern' capitalism, is the direct commodification of our experience: what we are buying on the market less and less are products (material objects) that we want to own, and more and more life-experiences – experiences of sex, eating, communication, cultural consumption, participation in a lifestyle. Material objects serve merely as props for such experiences, increasingly offered for free in order to seduce us into buying the true 'experiential commodity'[5] (like free cellular phones if we sign a one-year contract):

> As cultural production comes to dominate the economy, goods increasingly take on the qualities of props. They become mere platforms or settings around which elaborate cultural meanings are acted out. They lose their material importance and take on symbolic importance. They become less objects and more tools to help facilitate the performance of lived experiences.[6]

The logic of market exchange is here brought to a kind of Hegelian self-relating identity: we no longer buy objects, we ultimately buy (the time of) our lives. Michel Foucault's notion of turning one's self itself into a work of art thus gets an unexpected confirmation: I buy my 'body' by visiting fitness clubs; I buy my spiritual enlightenment by enrolling in courses on transcendental meditation; I buy my public persona by going to the restaurants visited by people with whom I want to be associated, etc.

Although this shift may appear as a break with capitalist market economy, one can argue that it brings its logic to its consequent climax. Industrial market economy involves a temporal gap between the purchase of a commodity and its consumption: from the standpoint of the seller, the affair is over the moment he sells the commodity – what happens afterwards (what the purchaser does with it, the direct consumption of the commodity) does not concern him. But in the commodification of experience, this gap is closed, and *consumption itself is the commodity purchased*. However, the possibility of closing this gap is inscribed into the very nominalist logic of the modern society and its community. That is to say, since the purchaser buys a commodity for its use-value, and because this use-value can be decomposed into its components (when I buy a Land Rover, I do this in order to drive myself and other people around, *plus* to signal my participation in a certain life-style associated with it), there is a logical next step towards the commodification and direct sale of these components (leasing a car instead of buying, etc.). At the end of the road is thus the solipsistic fact of subjective experience: because the subjective experience of individual consumption is the ultimate goal of production as a whole, is it not logical to bypass the object and sell directly this experience? And, perhaps, instead of interpreting this commodification of experience as the result of a shift in the predominant mode of subjectivity (from the classical bourgeois subject focused on the possession of objects to the 'postmodern' Protean subject focused on the wealth of his experiences), one should rather conceive of this Protean subject itself as the effect of the commodification of experience.[7]

This, of course, compels us thoroughly to reformulate the standard Marxist topic of 'reification' and 'commodity fetishism', insofar as this topic still relies on the notion of fetish as a solid object whose stable presence obfuscates its social mediation. Paradoxically, fetishism reaches its acme precisely when the fetish itself is 'dematerialized', turned into a fluid 'immaterial' virtual entity; money fetishism will culminate in its passage to electronic form, when the last traces of its materiality disappear – electronic money is the third form, after 'real' money, which directly embodies its value (gold, silver), and paper money, which, although a 'mere sign' with no intrinsic value, still clings to its material existence. And it is only at this stage, when money becomes a purely virtual point of reference, that it finally assumes the form of an indestructible spectral presence: I owe you $1,000, and no matter how many material notes I burn, I will still owe you $1,000 – the debt is inscribed somewhere in virtual digital space. It is only through this 'dematerialization', when Marx's famous old thesis from the *Manifesto*, according to which 'all that is solid melts into air', acquires a much more literal meaning than the one Marx had in mind, when not only our material social reality is dominated by the spectral/speculative movement of Capital, but when reality itself is progressively 'spectralized' (the 'Protean Self' instead of the old self-identical subject, the elusive fluidity of its experiences instead of the stability of owned objects), in short, when the usual relationship between firm material objects and fluid ideas is reversed (objects are progressively dissolved in fluid experiences, while the only stable things are virtual symbolic obligations) – it is at this point that what Derrida called the spectral aspect of capitalism is fully actualized.[8]

The inherent analysis of 'cultural capitalism' thus brings us to a new type of subjectivity that emerges out of the disintegration of paternal authority. This disintegration has two facets: on the one hand, symbolic prohibitive norms are increasingly replaced by imaginary ideals (of social success, of bodily fitness, etc.); on the other hand, the lack of symbolic prohibition is supplemented by the re-emergence of ferocious superego figures. So, we have a subject who is extremely narcissistic, i.e., who perceives everything as a potential threat to his precarious imaginary balance (this is the universalization of the logic of the victim: every contact with another human being is experienced as a potential threat – if the other smokes, if he casts a covetous glance at me, he is already hurting me); however, far from allowing him to float freely in an undisturbed balance, this narcissistic self-enclosure leaves the subject to the (not so) tender mercies of the superego injunction to enjoy. This so-called 'postmodern' subjectivity thus involves a kind of direct 'superegoization' of the imaginary Ideal, caused by the lack of proper symbolic Prohibition; exemplary are here the 'postmodern' hackers– programmers, those extravagant eccentrics hired by large corporations to pursue their programming hobbies in an informal environment. They are under the injunction to be what they are, to follow their innermost idiosyncrasies, they are allowed to ignore social norms of dress and behaviour (what they obey are just some elementary rules of polite tolerance of each other's idiosyncrasies); they thus seem to realize a kind of proto-socialist utopia of overcoming the opposition between alienated business (where you actually earn money) and private hobby-activity (that you pursue for pleasure). In a way, their job is their hobby, which is why they spend long hours at weekends in their workplace behind the computer screen: when one is paid for indulging in one's hobby, the result is that one is exposed to a superego pressure incomparably stronger than that of the good old 'Protestant work ethic'. Therein resides the unbearable paradox of postmodern 'disalienation': the tension is no longer between my innermost idiosyncratic creative impulses and the Institution that either doesn't appreciate them or wants to crush them in order to 'normalize' me: what the superego-injunction of the postmodern Corporation (like Microsoft) targets is precisely this core of my idiosyncratic creativity – I become useless for them the moment

I start losing this 'imp of perversity', the moment I lose my 'counter-cultural' subversive edge and start to behave like a 'normal' mature subject. There thus emerges a strange alliance between the rebellious subversive core of my personality and the external Corporation.

And it is interesting to note how the public image of Bill Gates reproduces this tension between narcissistic satisfaction and superego anxiety. What matters is not the factual accuracy ('Is Gates really like that?'), but the very fact that a certain figure started to function as an icon, to fill in some fantasmatic slot – if the features do not correspond to the 'true' Gates, they are all the more indicative of an underlying fantasmatic structure. Gates is not only no longer the patriarchal Father-Master, he is also no longer the corporate Big Brother running a stiff bureaucratic empire, dwelling in the inaccessible top floor, guarded by a host of secretaries and deputies. He is rather a kind of 'Little Brother': his very ordinariness functions as an indication of its opposite, of some monstrous dimension so uncanny that it can no longer publicly be rendered in the guise of some symbolic title. What we encounter here in a most violent way is the deadlock of the 'double', the *doppelgänger* who is simultaneously like us and the harbinger of an uncanny, properly monstrous dimension – indicative of this is the way title-pages, drawings or photo-montages present Gates as an ordinary guy, whose devious smile nonetheless points towards a wholly different underlying dimension of monstrosity beyond representation that threatens to shatter his 'ordinary guy' image. In this respect, it is also a crucial feature of Gates as icon that he is (perceived as) the ex-hacker who made it – one should confer on the term 'hacker' all of the subversive, marginal, anti-establishment connotations of those who wanted to disturb the smooth functioning of large bureaucratic corporations. At the fantasmatic level, the underlying notion here is that Gates is a subversive marginal hooligan who has taken over and dresses himself up as a respectable chairman.

In Bill Gates, the Little Brother, the average ugly guy, thus coincides with and contains the figure of the Evil Genius who aims at total control of our lives. In the 1960s and 1970s, it was possible to buy soft-porn postcards with a girl clad in bikini or wearing a proper gown; however, when one moved the postcard a little bit or looked at it from a slightly different angle, the dress magically disappeared and one was able to see the naked body of the girl – is something similar not happening with the image of Bill Gates, whose benevolent features, when viewed from a slightly different perspective, magically acquire a sinister and threatening dimension? In the early James Bond movies, the Evil Genius was still an eccentric figure, dressed up extravagantly or in a proto-Communist Maoist grey uniform – in the case of Gates, this ridiculous charade is no longer needed: the Evil Genius turns out to be the obverse of the common 'guy next door'. In other words, what we encounter in the icon of Bill Gates is a kind of reversal of the motif of the hero endowed with supernatural powers, but who is in daily life a common, confused, clumsy guy (like Superman, who is in his ordinary existence a clumsy, bespectacled journalist): here it is the bad guy who is characterized by this kind of a split. The ordinariness of Bill Gates is thus not of the same order as the emphasis on the so-called ordinary human features of the traditional patriarchal Master. The fact that this Master never lived up to his mandate, that he was always imperfect, marked by some failure or weakness, not only did not impede his symbolic authority, but even served as its support, rendering palpable the constitutive gap between the purely formal function of symbolic authority and the empirical individual who occupies its position. In contrast to this gap, Bill Gates' ordinariness points to a different notion of authority, that of the obscene superego that operates in the Real.

There is an old European fairy-tale motif of diligent dwarfs (usually controlled by an evil magician) who, during the night, while people are asleep, emerge from their hiding-place and accomplish their work (set the house in order, cook the meals, etc.), so that when, in the morning, people awaken, they find their work magically done. This motif appears in places such as Richard Wagner's *Rheingold* (the Nibelungs who work in their underground caves, driven by their cruel master, the dwarf Alberich) and Fritz Lang's *Metropolis* (in which enslaved industrial workers live and work deep beneath the earth's surface to produce wealth for the ruling capitalists). This dispositif of the 'underground' slaves dominated by a manipulative evil Master brings us back to the old duality of the two modes of the Master, the public symbolic Master and the secret evil magician who effectively pulls the strings and does his work at night. Are the two 'Bills' who ran the United States during the 1990s, Bill Clinton and Bill Gates, not the ultimate exemplification of this duality? And, perhaps, this link between the two 'Bills' is more telling than it may first appear: the Gates figure is no longer the ultimate emblem of capitalism – after 11 September 2001, it turned into a nostalgic symbol of what now appears as *la belle époque* of the Clintonian 'roaring 90s', irretrievably lost under the impact of this new violence.

When the subject is endowed with symbolic authority, he acts as an appendix to his symbolic title, i.e., it is the big Other, the symbolic institution, who acts through him: suffice it to recall a judge, who may be a miserable and corrupt person, but the moment he puts on his robe and other insignia, his words are the words of Law itself. On the other hand, the 'invisible' Master (whose exemplary case is the anti-Semitic figure of the 'Jew' who, invisible to the public eye, pulls the strings of social life) is a kind of uncanny double of public authority: he has to act in shadow, irradiating a phantom-like, spectral omnipotence. This, then, is the conclusion to be drawn from the Bill Gates icon: how the disintegration of patriarchal symbolic authority, of the Name-of-the-Father, gives rise to the new figure of Master who is simultaneously our common peer, our 'neighbour', our imaginary double, and for this very reason, fantasmatically endowed with another dimension of Evil Genius. In Lacanian terms: the suspension of the Ego Ideal, of the feature of Symbolic identification (i.e., the reduction of the Master to an Imaginary ideal) necessarily gives rise to its monstrous obverse, to the superego figure of an omnipotent Evil Genius who controls our lives. In this figure, the Imaginary (semblance) and the Real (of paranoia) overlap, due to the suspension of proper Symbolic efficiency.

The point of our insistence that we are dealing with Bill Gates as an *icon* is that it would be mystifying to elevate the 'real' Gates into some kind of Evil Genius who masterminds a plot to achieve global control over our lives. Here, more than ever, it is crucial to remember the lesson of the Marxist dialectic of fetishization: the 'reification' of relations between people (the fact that they assume the form of fantasmagorical 'relations between things') is always redoubled by the apparently opposite process, by the false 'personalization' of what are effectively objective social processes. It was already in the 1930s that the first generation of Frankfurt School theoreticians drew attention to the way – at the very moment when global market relations began to exert their full domination, making the individual producer's success or failure dependent on capricious market cycles – that the notion of a charismatic 'business genius' reasserted itself in the 'spontaneous ideology of capitalism', attributing the success or failure of a businessman to some mysterious *je ne sais quoi* which he possesses. And does the same not hold even more today, when the abstraction of market relations that run our lives is brought to its extreme? The book market is overflowing with psychology manuals advising us how to succeed, how to outdo our partner or competitor – in short, making our success dependent on our proper 'attitude'. So, in a way, one is tempted to invert Marx's famous formula: in contemporary capitalism, objective market 'relations between things' tend to assume the fantasmagorical form of pseudo-personalized 'relations between people'. No, Bill Gates is no genius, good or bad; he is just an opportunist who knew how to seize the moment, and as such the result of the capitalist system runs amok. The question to ask is not, 'How did Gates do it?', but rather, 'How is the capitalist system structured? What is wrong with it, so that an individual can achieve such disproportionate power?'

Phenomena like that of Bill Gates thus seem to point towards their own solution: once we are dealing with a gigantic global network formally owned by a single individual or corporation, is it not that ownership becomes in a way irrelevant to its functioning (there is no longer any worthwhile competition, profit is guaranteed), so that it becomes possible simply to cut off this head and socialize the entire network without greatly perturbing its operation? Does such an act not amount to a purely formal conversion that simply brings together what *de facto* already belongs together: the collective of individuals and the global communications network they are all using, and which thus forms the substance of their social lives?

We can see, now, that the three stories of Bill Gates belong together: in order to get the complete picture, one should add a *fourth* story, one that would supplement the third (the ideology of 'frictionless capitalism') in the same way the ominous figure of Gates the evil monopolist supplements the figure of the next-door boy who made it and became the richest man in the world – namely, the (Marxist) narrative of the inherent antagonisms and destructive potentials of capitalism.

Notes

1 Karl Marx, *Grundrisse: Foundations of the Critique of Political Economy*, trans. Martin Nicolaus, London, Penguin/New Left Review, 1973, p. 105.

As Marx puts it: 'Bourgeois society is the most developed and the most complex historic organization of production. The categories which express its relations, the comprehension of its structure, thereby also allow insights into the structure and the relations of production of all the vanished social formations . . . The bourgeois economy thus supplies the key to the ancient, etc.' [eds]

2   See Jeremy Rifkin, *The Age of Access: The New Culture of Hypercapitalism, Where All of the Life Is a Paid-for Experience*, New York, Putnam, 2000.

3   Fuat Firat and Alladi Venkatesh, quoted from Rifkin, *The Age of Access*, p. 173.

4   Quoted from Rifkin, *The Age of Access*, p. 35.

5   Rifkin, *The Age of Access*, p. 35.

6   Rifkin, *The Age of Access*, p. 173.

7   For an attempt to assert the potentially liberating aspects of the rise of the 'Protean subject', see Robert Lifton, *The Protean Self: Human Resilience in an Age of Fragmentation*, Chicago, University of Chicago Press, 1999.

8   Jacques Derrida, *Spectres of Marx: The State of Debt, the Work of Mourning and the New International*, trans. Peggy Kamuf, London and New York, Routledge, 1994.

Chapter 13
The prospects of radical politics today

Today, in a time of continuous swift changes, from the 'digital revolution' to the retreat of old social forms, thought is more than ever exposed to the temptation of 'losing its nerve', of precociously renouncing the old conceptual coordinates. The media is bombarding us constantly with the need to abandon 'old paradigms': if we are to survive, we have to change our most fundamental notions of personal identity, society, environment, etc. New Age wisdom claims that we are entering a new 'post-human' era; psychoanalysts hasten to concede that the Oedipal matrix of socialization is no longer operative, that we live in times of universalized perversion, that the concept of 'repression' is of no use in our permissive times; postmodern political thought tells us that we are entering a post-industrial society, in which the old categories of labour, collectivity, class, etc., are theoretical zombies, no longer applicable to the dynamics of modernization . . . Third Way ideology and political practice are effectively the model of this defeat, of this inability to recognize how the New is here to enable the Old to survive. Against this temptation, one should rather follow the unsurpassed example of Pascal and ask the difficult question: How are we to remain faithful to the Old in the new conditions? It is *only* in this way that we can generate something effectively New.

Habermas designated the present era as that of the *neue Unübersichtlichkeit* – the new opacity.[1] More than ever, our daily experience is mystifying: modernization generates new obscurantisms, the reduction of freedom is presented to us as the arrival of new freedoms.

Today, in the era of 'risk society', the ruling ideology endeavours to sell us the insecurity caused by the dismantling of the Welfare State as an opportunity for new freedoms. Do you have to change jobs every year, relying on short-term contracts instead of a long-term stable appointment? Why not see it as liberation from the constraints of a fixed job, as a chance to reinvent yourself again and again, to become aware of and realize the hidden potentials of your personality? Can you no longer rely on standard health insurance and retirement plans, so that you have to pay for additional coverage? Why not perceive it as an additional opportunity to choose: either better life now or long-term security? And if this predicament causes you anxiety, the postmodern or 'second modernity' ideologists will immediately accuse you of being unable to assume full freedom, of an 'escape from freedom', of an immature grasping of old stable forms . . . Even better, when this is inscribed into the ideology of the subject as the psychological individual pregnant with innate abilities and tendencies, then I, as it were, automatically interpret all these changes as the result of my personality, not of being tossed around by market forces.

In these circumstances, one should be especially careful not to confuse the ruling ideology with the ideology which *seems* to dominate. More than ever, one should bear in mind Walter Benjamin's reminder that it is not enough to ask how a certain theory (or art) declares itself with regard to social struggles – one should also ask how it effectively functions in these very struggles.[2] In sex, the hegemonic attitude is not patriarchal repression, but promiscuity; in art, provocations in the style of the notorious *Sensation* exhibitions are the norm, an example of art fully integrated into the establishment. I am therefore tempted to reverse Marx's thesis 11: the first task today is precisely *not* to succumb to the temptation to act, to intervene directly and change things (which then inevitably ends in a cul-de-sac of debilitating impossibility: 'What can one do against global Capital?'), but to question the hegemonic ideological coordinates. If, today, one follows a direct call to act, this act will not be performed in an empty space – it will be an act *within* the hegemonic ideological coordinates: those who 'really want to do something to help people' get involved in (undoubtedly honourable) exploits like Médecins sans Frontières, Greenpeace, feminist and anti-racist campaigns, which are all not only tolerated, but even supported by the media, even if they seemingly enter economic territory (say, denouncing and boycotting companies that do not respect ecological conditions or that use child labour) – they are tolerated and supported as long as they do not get too close to a certain limit.

Let us take two predominant topics of today's American radical academia: postcolonial and queer (gay) studies. The problem of post-colonialism is undoubtedly crucial; however, 'postcolonial studies' tends to translate it into the multiculturalist problematic of colonized minorities' 'right to narrate' their experience of victimization, of the power mechanisms that repress 'otherness', so that, at the end of the day, we learn that the root of postcolonial exploitation is our intolerance towards the Other, and, furthermore, that this intolerance itself is rooted in our intolerance towards the 'Stranger in Ourselves', in our inability to confront what we repressed in and of ourselves. The politico-economic struggle is thus imperceptibly transformed into a pseudo-psychoanalytic drama of the subject unable to confront its inner traumas . . . The true corruption of American academia is not primarily financial, it is not only that they are able to buy many European critical intellectuals (myself included – up to a point), but conceptual: notions of 'European' critical theory are imperceptibly translated into the benign universe of Cultural Studies chic.

My personal experience is that practically all of the 'radical' academics silently count on the long-term stability of the American capitalist model, with a secure tenured position as their ultimate professional goal (a surprising number of them even play on the stock market). If there is one thing they are genuinely horrified of, it is a radical shattering of the (relatively) safe living environment of the 'symbolic classes' in developed Western societies. Their excessive Politically Correct zeal when dealing with sexism, racism, Third World sweatshops, etc., is thus ultimately a defence against their own innermost identification, a kind of compulsive ritual whose hidden logic is: 'Let's talk as much as possible about the necessity of radical change in order to make sure that nothing will really change!' Symptomatic here is the journal *October*: when you ask one of the editors to what the title refers, they will half-confidentially signal that it is, of course, *that* October – in this way, one can indulge in jargonistic analyses of modern art, with the hidden assurance that one is somehow retaining a link with the radical revolutionary past . . . With regard to this radical chic, the first gesture towards Third Way ideologues and practitioners should be that of praise: they, at least, play their game straight and are honest in their acceptance of global capitalist coordinates, in contrast to the pseudo-radical academic leftists who adopt an attitude of utter disdain towards the Third Way, while their own radicality ultimately amounts to an empty gesture which obliges no one to anything determinate.

From human to animal rights

We live in a 'postmodern' era in which truth-claims as such are dismissed as expressions of hidden power mechanisms – as the reborn pseudo-Nietzscheans like to emphasize, truth is the lie that is most efficient in asserting our will to power. The very question, 'Is it true?', apropos of some statement is supplanted by another question: 'Under what power conditions can this statement be uttered?' What we get, instead of universal truth, is a multitude of perspectives, or, as it is fashionable to put it today, 'narratives' – not only literature, but also politics, religion, science, they are all different narratives, stories we tell ourselves about ourselves, and the ultimate goal of ethics is to guarantee the neutral space in which this multitude of narratives can peacefully coexist, in which everyone, from ethnic to sexual minorities, will have the right and ability to tell his/her story. *The* two philosophers of today's global capitalism are the two great Left-liberal 'progressives', Richard Rorty and Peter Singer – both honest in their respective stances. Rorty defines the basic coordinates: the fundamental dimension of a human being is the ability to suffer, to experience pain and humiliation – consequently, because humans are symbolic animals, the fundamental right is to narrate one's experience of suffering and humiliation.[3] Singer then provides the Darwinian background.[4]

Singer – usually designated as a 'social Darwinist with a collectivist socialist face' – begins innocently enough, trying to argue that people would be happier if they led lives committed to ethics: a life spent trying to help others and reduce suffering is truly the most moral and fulfilling one.[5] He thus radicalizes and actualizes Jeremy Bentham, the father of utilitarianism: the ultimate ethical criterion is not the dignity (rationality, soul) of man, but the ability to *suffer*, to experience pain, which man shares with animals.[6] With inexorable radicality, Singer levels the animal/human divide: better to kill an old suffering woman than a healthy animal . . . Look an orang-utan straight in the eye and what do you see? A none-too-distant cousin – a creature worthy of all the legal rights and privileges that humans enjoy. One should thus extend aspects of equality – the right to life, the protection of individual liberties, the prohibition of torture – at least to the non-human great apes (chimpanzees, orang-utans, gorillas).[7]

Singer argues that 'speciesism' (privileging the human species) is no different from racism: our perception of a difference between humans and (other) animals is no less illogical and unethical than our one-time perception of an ethical difference between, say, men and women, or blacks and whites. Intelligence is no basis for determining ethical stature: the lives of humans are not worth more than the lives of animals simply because they display more intelligence (if intelligence were a standard of judgement, Singer points out, we could perform medical experiments on the mentally retarded with moral impunity).[8] Ultimately, all things being equal, an animal has as much interest in living as a human. Therefore, all things being equal, medical experimentation on animals is immoral: those who advocate such experiments claim that sacrificing the lives of 20 animals will save millions of human lives – however, what about sacrificing 20 humans to save millions of animals? As Singer's critics like to point out, the horrifying extension of this principle is that the interests of 20 people outweigh the interests of one, which gives the green light to all sorts of human rights abuses.

Consequently, Singer argues that we can no longer rely on traditional ethics for answers to the dilemmas that our universe imposes on us; he proposes a new ethics meant to protect the quality, not the sanctity, of human life.[9] As sharp boundaries disappear between life and death, between humans and animals, this new ethics casts doubt on the morality of animal research, while offering a sympathetic assessment of infanticide. When a baby is born with severe defects of the sort that once killed babies, are doctors and parents now morally obliged to use the latest technologies, regardless of cost? *No.* When a pregnant woman loses all brain function, should doctors use new procedures to keep her body living until the baby can be born? *No*. Can a doctor ethically help terminally ill patients to kill themselves? *Yes*.

The first thing to discern here is the hidden utopian dimension of such a survivalist stance. The easiest way to detect ideological surplus-enjoyment in an ideological formation is to read it as a dream and analyse the displacement at work in it. Freud reports a dream of one of his patients which consists of a simple scene: the patient is at the funeral of a relative.[10] The key to the dream (which repeats a real-life event from the previous day) is that, at this funeral, the patient unexpectedly encounters a man, her old love for whom she still feels very deeply – far from being a masochistic dream, this dream thus simply articulates the patient's joy at meeting again her old love. Is the mechanism of displacement at work in this dream not strictly homologous to the one elaborated by Fredric Jameson apropos of science-fiction films which take place, typically, in California in the near future, after a mysterious virus or some other catastrophe has quickly killed a great majority of the population?[11] When the films' heroes, for instance, wander empty shopping malls, with all the merchandize intact and at their disposal, is this libidinal gain of having access to material goods without the alienating market machinery not the true point of the film occluded by the displacement of the official focus of the narrative on to the catastrophe caused by the virus? At an even more elementary level, is not one of the commonplaces of sci-fi theory that the true point of novels or movies about a global catastrophe resides in the sudden reassertion of social solidarity and the spirit of collaboration among the survivors? It is as if, in our society, global catastrophe is the price one has to pay for gaining access to solidary collaboration . . .

When my son was a small boy, his most cherished personal possession was a special 'survival knife', whose handle contained a compass, a sack of powder to disinfect water, a fishing-hook and line, and other similar items – totally useless in our social reality, but perfectly fitting the survivalist fantasy of finding oneself alone in wild nature. It is this same fantasy that, perhaps, provides the clue to the success of Joshua Piven and David Borgenicht's surprise best-seller, *The Worst-Case Scenario Survival Handbook*.[12] Suffice it to mention two of the finest examples from it: What do you do if an alligator has closed its jaws on one of your limbs? (Answer: you should tap or punch it on the snout, because alligators automatically react to it by opening their mouths.) What do you do when confronted by a lion that is threatening to attack you? (Answer: try to make yourself appear bigger than you are by opening your coat.) The joke of the book thus consists in the discord between its enunciated content and its position of enunciation: the situations it describes are effectively serious and the solutions correct – the only problem is, *Why is the author telling us all this? Who needs this advice?*

The underlying irony is that, in our individualistic competitive society, the most useless advice concerns survival in extreme physical situations – what one effectively needs is the very opposite, the Dale Carnegie type of book that tells us how to win over (manipulate) other people: the situations rendered in *The Worst-Case Scenario* lack any symbolic dimension, they reduce us to pure survival machines. In short, *The Worst-Case Scenario* became successful for the very same reason as Sebastian Junger's *The Perfect Storm*, a story (and movie) about the struggle for survival of a fishing vessel caught in the 'storm of the century' east of the Canadian coast in 1991: they both stage the fantasy of a pure encounter with a natural threat in which the socio-symbolic dimension is suspended. In a way, *The Perfect Storm* even provides the secret utopian background of *The Worst-Case Scenario*: it is only in such extreme situations that an authentic intersubjective community, held together by solidarity, can emerge. Let us not forget that *The Perfect Storm* is ultimately a book about the solidarity of a small working-class collective! The humorous appeal of *The Worst-Case Scenario* can thus be read as bearing witness to our utter alienation from nature, exemplified by the shortage of contact with 'real life' dangers.

On account of its utter 'realism', *The Worst-Case Scenario* is a Western book par excellence; its Oriental counterpart is *chindogu*, arguably the finest spiritual achievement of Japan in the last few decades, the art of inventing objects which are sublime in the strictest Kantian sense of the term – practically useless on account of their very excessive usefulness (for instance, glasses with electric miniature windscreen wipers, so that your view will remain clear even if you have to walk through the rain without an umbrella; or butter contained in a lipstick tube, so that you can carry it with you and spread it on bread without a knife). That is to say, in order to be recognized, *chindogu* objects must meet two basic criteria: it must be possible actually to construct them and they should work; simultaneously, they must not be 'practical', that is, it should not be feasible to market them.

This comparison between *The Worst-Case Scenario Survival Handbook* and *chindogu* offers us a unique insight into the difference between the Eastern and Western Sublime, an insight far superior to New Age pseudo-philosophical treatises. In both cases, the effect of the Sublime resides in the way that the uselessness of the product is the outcome of an extremely 'realistic' and pragmatic approach. However, in the case of the West, we get simple realistic advice for problems (or situations) that most of us will never encounter (who of us will really have to face a hungry lion?); in the case of the East, we get impractically complicated solutions for problems that all of us encounter (who of us has not been caught in the rain?). The Western Sublime offers a practical solution for a problem that does not arise; the Eastern Sublime offers a useless solution for a common problem.

So, back to Singer, one cannot simply dismiss him as a monstrous exaggeration – what Adorno said about psychoanalysis (that its truth resides in its very exaggerations)[13] fully applies to Singer: he is so traumatic and intolerable because his scandalous 'exaggerations' directly render visible the truth of so-called postmodern ethics. Is not the ultimate horizon of postmodern 'identity politics' effectively Darwinian – defending the right of some particular species of humankind within the panoply of their proliferating multitude (gays with AIDS, single black mothers, etc.)? The very opposition between 'conservative' and 'progressive' politics can thus be conceived of in Darwinian terms: ultimately, conservatives defend the right of those with might (their very success proves that they won the struggle for survival), while progressives advocate the protection of endangered human species (i.e., those losing the struggle for survival).

In an incident in American academia a couple of years ago, a lesbian feminist claimed that today gays are the privileged victims, so that an analysis of the way that gays are underprivileged provides the key to understanding all other exclusions, repressions, acts of violence (religious, ethnic, class), etc. What is problematic about this thesis is precisely its implicit (or, in this case, even explicit) *universal* claim: it makes exemplary victims of those that are not, of those who can be fully integrated into public space much more easily than religious or ethnic Others, and who thus can enjoy full rights. There is a long tradition of leftist gay bashing, whose traces are discernible up to Adorno – suffice it to mention Maxim Gorky's infamous remark from his essay 'Proletarian Humanism' (1934): 'Exterminate [*sic!*] homosexuals, and fascism will disappear.'[14] This cannot be reduced to a merely opportunistic flirtation with the traditional patriarchal sexual morality of the working classes, or with the Stalinist reaction against the liberation of the first years following the October Revolution; one should remember that Gorky's above-quoted statement, as well as Adorno's reservations about homosexuality (his conviction about the libidinal link between homosexuality and the spirit of military male-bonding), are both based on the same historical experience: that of the SA, the 'revolutionary' paramilitary Nazi organization of street-fighting thugs, in which homosexuality abounded (including its head, Ernst Röhm). The first thing to note here is that it was Hitler himself who purged the SA in order to make the Nazi régime publicly acceptable by cleansing it of its obscene-violent excess/excesses, and that he justified slaughtering the SA leadership precisely by evoking their 'sexual depravity'. In order to function as the support of a 'totalitarian' community, homosexuality has to remain a publicly disavowed 'dirty secret', shared by those who are 'in'. Does this mean that, when gays are persecuted, they deserve only qualified support, a kind of, 'Yes, we know we should support you, but nonetheless . . . (you are partly responsible for Nazi violence)'? No, but one *should* insist that the political overdetermination of homosexuality is far from simple, that the homosexual libidinal economy can be co-opted by different political orientations, and that it is *here* that one should avoid the 'essentialist' mistake of dismissing rightist 'militaristic' homosexuality as a secondary distortion of 'authentic' subversive homosexuality.

In the chapter on Reason in *Phenomenology of Spirit*, Hegel speaks about *das geistige Tierreich* (the spiritual animal kingdom): the social world that lacks any spiritual substance, so that, in it, individuals effectively interact as 'intelligent animals'. They use reason, but only in order to assert their individual interests, to manipulate others into serving their own pleasures.[15] Is not a world in which the highest rights are human rights precisely such a 'spiritual animal kingdom'? There is, however, a price to be paid for such liberation – in this kind of universe, human rights ultimately function as *animal* rights. This, then, is the ultimate truth of Singer: our universe of human rights is the universe of animal rights.

This, then, is what gets lost in Singer's *geistige Tierreich*: the Thing, something to which we are unconditionally attached irrespective of its positive qualities. In Singer's universe, there is a place for mad cows, but no place for an Indian sacred cow. In other words, what gets lost here is simply the dimension of truth – *not* 'objective truth' as the notion of reality from a point of view which somehow floats above the multitude of particular narratives, but truth as the Singular Universal. When Lenin says, 'The Marxist doctrine is omnipotent because it is true',[16] everything depends on how we understand 'truth' here: is it neutral 'objective knowledge', or the truth of an engaged subject? Lenin's wager – today, in our era of postmodern relativism, more actual than ever – is that universal truth and partisanship, the gesture of taking sides, are not only not mutually exclusive, but condition each other: in a concrete situation, its *universal* truth can only be articulated from a thoroughly *partisan* position – truth is by definition one-sided. This, of course, goes against the predominant ethic of compromise, of finding a middle path among the multitude of conflicting interests. If one does not specify the *criteria* of the different, alternate narrativizations, then this endeavour courts the danger of endorsing, in the Politically Correct mood, ridiculous 'narratives' like the ones about the supremacy of some aboriginal holistic wisdom, or that dismiss science as just another narrative on a par with pre-modern superstitions.

On closer analysis, one could expose the way that the cultural relativism of the 'right-to-narrate' contains its own apparent opposite, the fixation on the Real of some trauma that resists narrativization. This properly dialectical tension sustains today's academic 'holocaust-industry'. My own experience of the holocaust-industry police occurred in 1997 at a round-table at the Centre Georges Pompidou in Paris: I was viciously attacked for an intervention in which (among other things) I claimed, against the neoconservatives deploring the decline of faith today, that the basic need of a normal human being is not to be a believer himself, but to have another subject who will believe for him, in his place.[17] The reaction of one of the distinguished participants was that, by claiming this, I am ultimately endorsing holocaust revisionism, justifying the claim that, since everything is a discursive construct, this includes the holocaust as well, so it is meaningless to search for what really happened . . . Apart from displaying hypocritical paranoia, my critic was doubly wrong. First, holocaust revisionists (to my knowledge) *never* argue in the terms of postmodern discursive constructivism, but in the terms of empirical factual analysis: their claims range from the 'fact' that there is no written documentation in which Hitler ordered the holocaust, to the weird mathematics of 'taking into account the number of gas ovens in Auschwitz, it was not possible to burn so many corpses'. Furthermore, not only is the postmodern logic of 'everything is a discursive construct, there are no direct firm facts', never used to deflate the holocaust; in a paradox worth noting, it is precisely the postmodern discursive constructivists (like Lyotard) who tend to elevate the holocaust into the supreme ineffable metaphysical Evil – the holocaust functions as an untouchable-sacred Real, as the negative of contingent language games.

The Möbius strip of politics and economy

What all of the new French (or French-orientated) theories of the Political – from Étienne Balibar through Jacques Rancière to Alain Badiou – aim at is, to put it in traditional philosophical terms, the reduction of the sphere of economy (of material production) to an 'ontic' sphere deprived of 'ontological' dignity. Within this horizon, there is simply no place for the Marxian 'critique of political economy': the structure of the universe of commodities and Capital in Marx's *Capital* is *not* just that of a limited empirical sphere, but a kind of socio-transcendental *a priori*, the matrix that generates the totality of social and political relations. The relationship between economy and politics is ultimately that of the well-known visual paradox of the 'two faces or a vase': one sees either two faces or a vase, never both of them – in other words, one has to make a choice.[18] In the same way, one either focuses on the political, and the domain of economy is reduced to the empirical 'servicing of goods', or one focuses on economy, and politics is reduced to a theatre of appearances, to a passing phenomenon which will disappear with the arrival of a developed communist (or technocratic) society, in which, as Engels put it, the 'administration of people' will vanish in the 'administration of things'. (Does not the same 'vase/faces' paradox occur in the case of the holocaust and gulag? We either elevate the holocaust into the ultimate crime, and Stalinist terror is thereby half-redeemed, reduced to a minor role as an 'ordinary' crime; or we focus on the gulag as the ultimate result of the logic of modern revolutionary terror, and the holocaust is thereby at best reduced to another example of the same logic. Somehow, it does not seem possible to deploy a truly 'neutral' theory of totalitarianism, without giving a hidden preference to either the holocaust or gulag.)

What we are dealing with here is another version of the Lacanian *il n'y a pas de rapport* . . .: if, for Lacan, there is no sexual relationship, then, for Marxism proper, there is no relationship between economy and politics, no 'metalanguage' enabling us to grasp both two levels from the same neutral standpoint, although – or, rather, *because* – these two levels are inextricably intertwined. 'Political' class struggle takes place in the very midst of economy (recall that the very last paragraph of *Capital* 3, where the text abruptly stops, tackles class struggle), while, at the same time, the domain of economy serves as the key enabling us to decode political struggles. It is no wonder that the structure of this impossible relationship is that of the Möbius strip: first, we have to progress from the political spectacle to its economic infrastructure; then, in the second step, we have to confront the irreducible dimension of the political struggle at the very heart of economy.

In this context, the first myth to be debunked is that of the diminishing role of the State. What we are witnessing today is a shift in its functions: while partially withdrawing from its welfare obligations, the State is strengthening its apparatuses in other domains of social regulation. In order to start a business now, one has to rely on the State to guarantee not only law and order, but the entire infrastructure (access to water and energy, means of transportation, ecological criteria, international regulations, etc.), to an incomparably larger extent than a hundred years ago. The recent electricity debacle in California makes this point palpable: for a couple of weeks in January and February 2001, the privatization ('deregulation') of the electricity supply changed southern California, one of the most highly developed 'post-industrial' landscapes in the entire world, into a Third World country with regular blackouts. Of course, its defenders claimed that the deregulation was not thorough enough, thereby engaging in the old false syllogism of 'my fiancée is never late for an appointment, because the moment she is late, she is no longer my fiancée': deregulation by definition works, so if it does not work, it was not truly a deregulation . . . Does the recent panic over Mad Cow Disease (which probably presages dozens of similar phenomena that await us in the near future) also not point towards the need for strict State and global institutionalized control of agriculture?

The key antagonism of the so-called new (digital) industries is thus: how to maintain the form of (private) property – the only context in which the logic of profit can be maintained (see also the 'Napster' problem, the free circulation of music). And do the legal complications in biogenetics not point in the same direction? The key element of the new international trade agreements is the 'protection of intellectual property': whenever, in a merger, a large First World company takes over a Third World company, the first thing they do is close down the research department. What we have here is the emergence of phenomena which bring the notion of property to extraordinary dialectical paradoxes: in India, local communities suddenly discover that medical practices and materials they have been using for centuries are now owned by American companies, so that the rights to them now have to be bought; with the patenting of genes of biogenetic companies, we are discovering that parts of ourselves, our genetic components, are already copyrighted, owned by others . . .

However, the outcome of this crisis of private property, of the means of production, is in no way guaranteed – it is *here* that one should take into account the ultimate paradox of Stalinist society: against capitalism, which is class-based society, though in principle egalitarian, without direct hierarchical divisions, 'mature' Stalinism was a classless society articulated in precisely defined hierarchical groups (top *nomenklatura*, technical intelligence, the army, etc.). What this means is that, already for Stalinism, the classical Marxist notion of class struggle is no longer adequate to describe its hierarchy and domination: in the Soviet Union from the late 1920s onwards, the key social division was not defined by property but by the direct access to power mechanisms and to the privileged material and cultural conditions of life (food, housing, health care, freedom of travel and education). And, perhaps, the ultimate irony of history will be that, in the same way that Lenin's vision of 'central bank socialism' can be properly read only retroactively, from today's world wide web, the Soviet Union provided the first model of a developed 'post-property' society, of true 'late capitalism' in which the ruling class will be defined by direct access to the (informational, administrative) means of social power and control and attendant material and social privileges: the point will no longer be to own companies, but to run them directly, to have the right to use a private jet, to have access to top health care, etc. – privileges which will be acquired not by property but by other (educational, managerial, etc.) mechanisms. The ultimate answer to the reproach that radical Left proposals are utopian should thus be that, today, the true utopia is the belief that the present liberal-democratic capitalist consensus could go on indefinitely, without radical changes. We are thus back to the old '68 motto, 'Soyons realistes, demandons l'impossible!': in order to be truly a 'realist', one must consider breaking from the constraints of what appears 'possible' (or, as we usually put it, 'feasible').

Today, we can already discern the signs of a kind of general unease – recall the series of events usually grouped under the nomination 'Seattle'. The ten-year honeymoon of triumphant global capitalism is over, the long-overdue 'seven-year itch' is here; witness the panicky reactions of the big media, which – from *Time* magazine to CNN – all of a sudden began to warn about Marxists manipulating the crowd of 'honest' protesters. The problem is now a strictly Leninist one: how to *actualize* the media's accusations, how to invent the organizational structure which will confer upon this unrest the *form* of a universal political demand? Otherwise, the momentum will be lost, and what will remain is a marginal disturbance, perhaps organized as a new Greenpeace, with a certain efficiency, but also strictly limited goals, a marketing strategy, etc. In other words, the key 'Leninist' lesson today is: *politics without the organizational form of the party is politics without politics*, so the answer to those who want just the (quite adequately named) 'new *social* movements' is the same as the answer of the Jacobins to the Girondin compromisers: 'You want revolution without a revolution!' Today's blockade is that there are two ways open for socio-political engagement: either play the game of the system, engage in the 'long march through the institutions', or get active in new social movements, from feminism through ecology to anti-racism. And, again, the limit of these movements is that they are not *political* in the sense of the Universal Singular: they are 'single-issue movements' which lack the dimension of the Universal, that is, they do not relate to the social *totality*.

Here, Lenin's reproach to liberals is crucial: they only *exploit* the discontent of the working class to strengthen their position vis-à-vis the conservatives, instead of identifying with it to the end.[19] Is this also not the case with today's leftist liberals? They like to evoke racism, ecology, workers' grievances, etc., to score points over the conservatives *without endangering the system*. Recall how, in Seattle, Bill Clinton himself deftly referred to the protesters on the streets outside, reminding the gathered leaders inside the guarded palaces that they should listen to the message of the demonstrators (a message that, of course, Clinton interpreted, depriving it of its subversive sting, which was attributed to dangerous extremists introducing chaos and violence into the majority of peaceful protesters). It is the same with all 'New Social Movements', up to the Zapatistas in Chiapas: systemic politics is always ready to 'listen to their demands'. The system is by definition ecumenical, open, tolerant, ready to 'listen' to all – even if one insists on one's demands, they are deprived of their universal political sting by the very form of negotiation. The true Third Way we have to look for is this third way between institutionalized parliamentary politics and new social movements.

Gilles Deleuze's and Felix Guattari's *Anti-Oedipus* was the last great attempt to combine in a subversive synthesis the Marxist and psychoanalytic traditions. They fully recognized the revolutionary, deterritorializing impact of capitalism, which, in its inexorable dynamics, undermines all stable traditional forms of human interaction; what they reproached capitalism with is that its deterritorialization is not thorough enough, that it generates new re-territorializations – a verbatim repetition of Marx's claim that the ultimate obstacle to capitalism is capitalism itself, that capitalism unleashes a dynamic that it will not be able to contain.[20] Far from being outdated, this claim seems to gain actuality with today's growing deadlock in/of globalization in which the inherently antagonistic nature of capitalism belies its worldwide triumph. However, the real problem is this: is it still possible to imagine communism (or another form of post-capitalist society) as a formation that sets free the deterritorializing dynamics of capitalism, liberating it from its inherent constraints? Marx's fundamental vision was that a new, higher social order (communism) is possible, an order that would not only maintain, but even raise to a higher degree and effectively fully release the potential of the self-increasing spiral of productivity which, in capitalism, on account of its inherent obstacle/contradiction, is again and again thwarted by socially destructive economic crises. What Marx overlooked is that, to put it in standard Derridean terms, this inherent obstacle/antagonism as the 'condition of impossibility' of the full deployment of the productive forces of capitalism is simultaneously its 'condition of possibility': if we abolish the obstacle, the inherent contradiction of capitalism, we do not get the fully unleashed drive towards productivity finally delivered of its impediment, but we lose precisely this productivity that seemed to be generated and simultaneously thwarted by capitalism – if we take away the obstacle, the very potential thwarted by this obstacle dissipates . . . Therein would reside a possible Lacanian critique of Marx, focusing on the ambiguous overlapping between 'surplus-value [*la plus-value*]' and 'surplus-enjoyment [*le plus-de-jouir*]'.[21] (It is often said that the ultimate products of capitalism are piles of trash – useless computers, cars, televisions and VCRs: places like the famous 'graveyard' of hundreds of abandoned planes in the Mojave desert confront us with the obverse truth of capitalist dynamics, its inert objectal remainder. And it is against this background that one should read the ecological dream-notion of total recycling – in which every remainder is used again – as the ultimate capitalist dream, even if it is couched in terms of the retention of the natural balance on Planet Earth; the dream of the self-propelling circulation of Capital which would succeed in leaving behind no material residue – proof of the way that capitalism can appropriate ideologies which seem to oppose it.)

While this constant self-propelling revolution still holds for high Stalinism, with its total productive mobilization, 'stagnant' late Real Socialism legitimizes itself (between the lines, at least) as a society in which one can live peacefully, avoiding capitalist competitive stress. This was the last line of defence when, from the late 1960s onwards, after the fall of Khrushchev (the last enthusiast who, during his visit to the United States, prophesied that 'your grandchildren will be Communists'), it became clear that Real socialism was losing the competitive edge in its war with capitalism. So stagnant late Real Socialism was, in a way, already 'socialism with a human face': silently abandoning great historical tasks, it provided the security of everyday life enduring in a benevolent boredom. Today's *Ostalgie* for defunct socialism mostly consists in such conservative nostalgia for the self-satisfied constrained way of life; even nostalgic anti-capitalist artists from Peter Handke to Joseph Beuys celebrate this aspect of socialism: the absence of stressful mobilization and frantic commodification. Of course, this unexpected shift tells us something about the deficiency of the original Marxist project itself: it points towards the limitation of its goal of unleashed productive mobilization.

Fetishism today

The ultimate postmodern irony is the strange exchange currently taking place between Europe and Asia: at the very moment when, at the level of 'economic infrastructure', 'European' technology and capitalism are triumphing worldwide, at the level of 'ideological superstructure', the Judaeo-Christian legacy is threatened in the European space itself by the onslaught of New Age 'Asiatic' thought, which, in its different guises, from 'Western Buddhism' (today's counterpoint to Western Marxism, as opposed to 'Asiatic' Marxism–Leninism) to different 'Taos', is establishing itself as the hegemonic ideology of global capitalism. Therein resides the highest speculative identity of opposites in today's global civilization: although 'Western Buddhism' presents itself as the remedy to the stressful tension of capitalist dynamics, allowing us to uncouple and retain inner peace and *Gelassenheit* [placidity], it actually functions as its perfect ideological supplement. One should mention here the well-known topic of 'future shock', that is, of how, today, people are no longer psychologically able to cope with the dazzling rhythm of technological development and the social changes that accompany it – things simply move too fast; before one can accustom oneself to an invention, this invention is already supplanted by a new one, so that one more and more lacks the most elementary 'cognitive mapping'.[22] The recourse to Taoism or Buddhism offers a way out of this predicament, which definitely works better than the desperate escape into old traditions: instead of trying to cope with the accelerating rhythm of technological progress and social change, one should rather renounce the very endeavour to retain control over what goes on, rejecting such control as an expression of the modern logic of domination – one should, instead, 'let oneself go', drift along, while retaining an inner distance and indifference towards the mad dance of accelerated process, a distance based on the insight that all of this social and technological upheaval is ultimately just an insubstantial proliferation of semblances which do not really concern the innermost kernel of one's being . . . One is almost tempted to resuscitate here the old infamous Marxist cliché of religion as the 'opiate of the people', as the imaginary supplement of terrestrial misery: the 'Western Buddhist' meditative stance is arguably the most efficient way, for us, fully to participate in capitalist dynamics, while retaining the appearance of sanity. If Max Weber were to live today, he would definitely have written a second, supplementary, volume to his *Protestant Ethic*, entitled *The Taoist Ethic and the Spirit of Global Capitalism*.

'Western Buddhism' thus perfectly fits the fetishist mode of ideology in our allegedly 'post-ideological' era, as opposed to its traditional symptomal mode, in which the ideological lie that structures our perception of reality is threatened by symptoms *qua* 'returns of the repressed', cracks in the fabric of the ideological lie. The fetish is effectively a kind of symptom *à l'envers*. That is to say, a symptom is the exception which disturbs the surface of false appearance, the point at which the repressed truth erupts, while a fetish is the embodiment of the lie which enables us to sustain the unbearable truth. Let us take the case of the death of a loved one: when I 'repress' this death, I try not to think about it, but the repressed trauma persists and returns in symptoms. For instance, after my beloved wife dies of breast cancer, I try to repress this fact by throwing myself into hard work or a vivacious social life, but then there is always something that reminds me of her, I cannot escape her ghost. In the case of a fetish, on the contrary, I 'rationally' accept this death entirely, I am able to talk about her most painful moments in a cold and clear way, because I cling to the fetish, to some feature that embodies for me the disavowal of this death. In this sense, a fetish can play a very constructive role of allowing us to cope with harsh reality: fetishists are not dreamers lost in their private worlds, they are thorough 'realists', able to accept the way things are – *because* they have their fetish to which they can cling in order to defuse the full impact of reality.[23]

So, when we are bombarded by claims that, in our post-ideological cynical era, nobody believes in the proclaimed ideals, when we encounter a person who claims he is cured of any beliefs, accepting social reality the way it really is, one should always counter such claims with the question: 'OK, but where is the fetish that enables you to (pretend to) accept reality "the way it really is"?' 'Western Buddhism' is such a fetish: it enables you fully to participate in the frantic pace of the capitalist game, while sustaining the perception that you are not really in it, that you are well aware how worthless this spectacle really is – what really matters to you is the peace of the inner self to which you know you can always withdraw . . .

Perhaps the most succinct definition of ideology was produced by Christopher Hitchens, when he tackled the difficult question of what the North Koreans effectively think about their 'Beloved Leader' Kim Jong Il: 'mass delusion is the only thing that keeps a people sane.'[24] This paradox points towards the fetishist split at the very heart of an effectively functioning ideology: individuals transpose their beliefs on to the big Other (embodied in the collective), which thus believes in their place – individuals thus remain sane *qua* individuals, maintaining the distance towards the 'big Other' of the official discourse. It is not only the direct identification with the ideological 'delusion' that would render individuals insane, but also the suspension of their (disavowed, displaced) belief. In other words, if individuals were to be deprived of this belief (projected on to the 'big Other'), they would have to jump in and themselves directly assume the belief. (Perhaps this explains the paradox that many a cynic becomes a sincere believer at the very point of the disintegration of 'official' belief.) This is what Lacan aimed at in his claim that the true formula of atheism is not 'God doesn't exist' but 'God is unconscious'[25] – suffice it to recall what, in a letter to Max Brod, Milena Jesenska wrote about Kafka: 'Above all, things like money, the stock exchange, foreign currency administration, the typewriter, are for him thoroughly mystical (what they effectively are, only not for us, but for the others).'[26] One should read this statement against the background of Marx's analysis of commodity fetishism: the fetishist illusion resides in our real social life, not in our perception of it – a bourgeois subject knows very well that there is nothing magic about money, that money is just an object which stands for a set of social relations, but he nevertheless *acts* in real life as if he believed that money is a magical thing. This, then, gives us a precise insight into Kafka's universe: Kafka was able to experience directly these fantasmatic beliefs that we 'normal' people disavow – Kafka's 'magic' is what Marx liked to refer to as the 'theological freakishness' of commodities.

This definition of ideology indicates the best way to answer the tedious standard reproach against the application of psychoanalysis to social-ideological processes: is it 'legitimate' to expand the use of the notions that were originally deployed for the treatment of individuals to collective entities and to speak, say, of religion as a 'collective compulsive neurosis'? The focus of psychoanalysis is entirely different: the 'social', the field of social practices and socially held beliefs, is not simply at a different level than individual experience, but something to which the individual him/herself must relate, which the individual him/herself must experience as an order that is minimally 'reified', externalized. The problem is, therefore, not 'how to jump from the individual to the social level'; the problem is: how should the decentred socio-symbolic order of institutionalized practices and beliefs be structured, if the subject is to retain his/her 'sanity', his/her 'normal' functioning? Which delusions should be deposited there so that individuals can remain sane? Recall the proverbial egotist, cynically dismissing the public system of moral norms: as a rule, such a subject can only function if this system is 'out there', publicly recognized – i.e., in order to be a private cynic, he has to presuppose the existence of naïve other(s) who 'really believe'. This is how a true 'cultural revolution' should be conducted: not by directly targeting individuals, endeavouring to 're-educate' them, to 'change their reactionary attitudes', but by depriving individuals of support in the 'big Other', in the institutional symbolic order.

It is easy to be 'radical' apropos of gay marriage, incest, etc. – however, what about child sex and torture? On what grounds are we justified in opposing them without having recourse to the 'legal fiction' of the adult autonomous subject responsible for his/her acts? (And, incidentally, *why* should marriage be constrained to *two* persons, gay or not? Why not three or more? Is this not the last remainder of 'binary logic'?) More generally, if we adopt the standard postmodern mantra of the autonomous responsible subject as a legal fiction, what are the consequences of this denial when dealing with, say, child rapists? Is it not deeply symptomatic how the very same theorists who denounce the liberal autonomous subject as a Western legal fiction *at the same time* fully endorse the discourse of victimization, treating the perpetrators of sexual harassment as guilty (i.e., responsible) for their acts? Furthermore, the attitude towards sex between adults and children is the best indicator of the changes in sexual mores: three or four decades ago, in the heyday of the Sexual Revolution, child sex was *celebrated* as overcoming the last barrier, the ideologically enforced desexualization of children, while the Politically Correct ideology of victimization offers the sexually abused child as the ultimate image of horror.

In a recent pamphlet against the 'excesses' of May '68 and, more generally, the 'sexual liberation' of the 1960s, *The Independent* brought back to memory what the radicals of '68 thought about child sex. A quarter of a century ago, Daniel Cohn-Bendit wrote about his experience as an educator in a kindergarten: 'My constant flirt with all the children soon took on erotic characteristics. I could really feel how from the age of five the small girls had already learned to make passes at me . . . Several times a few children opened the flies of my trousers and started to stroke me . . . When they insisted, I then stroked them.' Shulamith Firestone went even further, expressing her hopes that, in a world 'without the incest taboo . . . relations with children would include as much genital sex as they were capable of – probably considerably more than we now believe'.[27] Decades later, when confronted with these statements, Cohn-Bendit played them down, claiming that 'this did not really happen, I only wanted to provoke people. When one reads it today, it is unacceptable.'[28] However, the question still hovers: how, at that time, was it possible to provoke people, presenting sexual games among preschool children as something appealing, when today the same 'provocation' would immediately give rise to an outburst of moral disgust? After all, child sexual harassment is one of *the* notions of Evil today.

Without directly taking sides in this debate, one should read it as a sign of the change in our mores from the utopian energies of the 1960s and early 1970s to the contemporary stale Political Correctness, in which every authentic encounter with another human being is denounced as a victimizing experience. What we are unable even to conjecture today is the idea of *revolution*, be it sexual or social. Perhaps, in today's stale times of proliferating pleas for tolerance, one should take the risk of recalling the liberating dimension of such 'excesses'.

Notes

This paper was first published in *Democracy Unrealized: Documenta 11 – Platform 1*, ed. Okwui Enwezor *et al.*, Kassel, Documenta, 2002, pp. 67–85. [eds]

1   Jürgen Habermas, *Die neue Unübersichtlichkeit*, Frankfurt am Main, Suhrkamp Verlag, 1985.

2   Walter Benjamin, 'The work of art in the age of technological reproducibility (second version)', in *Selected Writings: Volume 3, 1935–1938*, ed. Howard Eiland and Michael W. Jennings, trans. Edmund Jephcott, Howard Eiland *et al.*, Cambridge, Belknap, 2002, pp. 101–22. [eds]

3   Richard Rorty, 'The contingency of liberal community', in *Contingency, Irony, Solidarity*, Cambridge, Cambridge University Press, 1989, pp. 44–69.

4   See Peter Singer, *Practical Ethics*, 2nd edn, Cambridge, Cambridge University Press, 1993, pp. 72–8; and *A Darwinian Left: Politics, Evolution and Cooperation*, New Haven and London, Yale University Press, 1999. [eds]

5   Singer, *Practical Ethics*, pp. 314–35. [eds]

6   Singer, *Practical Ethics*, pp. 72–8; and *Animal Liberation*, 2nd edn, London, Jonathan Cape, 1990, pp. 5–23. [eds]

7   Singer, *Practical Ethics*, pp. 117–19. [eds]

8   Singer, *Practical Ethics*, pp. 59–60. [eds]

9   Peter Singer, *Rethinking Life and Death: The Collapse of Our Traditional Ethics*, Melbourne, Text Publishing, 1994, pp. 187–222. [eds]

10   Sigmund Freud, *The Penguin Freud Library, 4: The Interpretation of Dreams*, ed. and trans. James Strachey, Harmondsworth, Penguin, 1976, pp. 235–7, 348. [eds]

11   The examples of such analyses in Jameson's work are legion. See, for instance, Fredric Jameson, 'After Armageddon: character systems in *Dr Bloodmoney*', *Science-Fiction Studies* 2, 1975, pp.31–42; *The Geopolitical Aesthetic: Cinema and Space in the World System*, London, British Film Institute, 1992, pp. 87–113. [eds]

12   Joshua Piven and David Borgenicht, *The Worst-Case Scenario Handbook*, New York, Chronicle Books, 1999.

13   Theodor Adorno, *Minima Moralia: Reflections from Damaged Life*, trans. Edmund Jephcott, London and New York, Verso, 1974, p. 49.

14   Quoted in Siegfried Tornow, 'Männliche homosexualität und politik in Sowjet-Russland', in *Homosexualität und Wissenschaft II*, Berlin, Rosa Winkel, 1992, p. 281.

15 G. W. F. Hegel, *Phenomenology of Spirit*, trans. A. V. Miller, Oxford, Oxford University Press, 1977, p. 178.

16 V. I. Lenin, 'The three sources and three component parts of Marxism', in *Selected Works, Volume 1*, Moscow, Progress Publishers, 1968, p. 20. [eds]

17 For the text of his intervention, see Slavoj Žižek, 'Le sujet interpassif', *traverses* 3 [www2.centrepompidou.fr/traverses/numero3/f2a-zizek.html], especially pp. 1–4. [eds]

18 Fredric Jameson, 'The concept of revisionism', paper presented at *Towards a Politics of Truth: The Retrieval of Lenin*, 2–4 February 2001, Kulturwissenschaftlichen Institut, Essen, Germany.

19 See V. I. Lenin, *What Is To Be Done?*, trans. Joe Fineberg and George Hanna, London, Penguin, 1962, pp. 120–30. [eds]

20 Gilles Deleuze and Félix Guattari, *Anti-Oedipus: Capitalism and Schizophrenia*, trans. Robert Hurley, Mark Seem and Helen P. Lane, Minneapolis, University of Minnesota Press, 1983, pp. 302–3. [eds]

21 Jacques Lacan, *Le Séminaire de Jacques Lacan XVII: L'envers de la psychanalyse, 1969–70*, ed. Jacques-Alain Miller, Paris, Éditions du Seuil, 1991, pp. 18–19. [eds]

22 Žižek derives the notion of 'cognitive mapping' from Fredric Jameson, who in turn first developed it in 'Postmodernism, or the cultural logic of late capitalism', *New Left Review* 146, 1984, pp. 89–92. [eds]

23 See Louis Althusser's crucial differentiation of the fetish from the symptom in *Reading Capital*, trans. Ben Brewster, London and New York, Verso, 1970, pp. 14–30. [eds]

24 Christopher Hitchens, 'Visit to a small planet', in *Love, Poverty, and War: Journeys and Essays*, New York, Nation Books, 2004, pp. 373–86. [*Editorial note*: There is no passage in Hitchens' article that corresponds to this citation. The nearest equivalent is, on p. 379, the following: 'The scenes of hysterical grief when Fat Man [Kim Il Sung] died were not all feigned; there might be a collective nervous breakdown if it was suddenly announced that the Great Leader had been a verbose and arrogant fraud.']

25 Jacques Lacan, *The Seminar of Jacques Lacan XI: The Four Fundamental Concepts of Psychoanalysis, 1964*, ed. Jacques-Alain Miller, trans. Alan Sheridan, New York and London, W. W. Norton, 1977, p. 59. [eds]

26 Quoted in Jana Cerna, *Kafka's Milena*, Evanston, Northwestern University Press, 1993, p. 174.

27 Both quotes from Maureen Freely, 'Polymorphous sexuality in the Sixties', *The Independent*, 29 January 2001, p. 4.

28 Quoted in *Konkret* 3, March 2001, p. 9.

SECTION FOUR

What is (not) to be done

Chapter 14
Against the double blackmail

The prize winner in the contest for the greatest blunder of 1998 was a Latin-American patriotic terrorist who sent a letter bomb to a United States consulate in order to protest against America's interference in local politics. As a conscientious citizen, he wrote his return address on the envelope, but he did not put enough stamps on it, and so the letter was returned to him. Forgetting what he put in it, he opened it and blew himself up – a perfect example of how, ultimately, a letter always arrives at its destination. And is something similar not happening to the Slobodan Milošević régime with the recent NATO bombing? (Over the last few days, incidentally, it has been interesting to watch Serbian satellite state television, which is aimed at the foreign public: no reports on atrocities in Kosovo; refugees are mentioned only as people fleeing NATO bombing; the overall image is that Serbia – an island of peace, the only place in ex-Yugoslavia not to be touched by the war raging all around – is being attacked irrationally by NATO madmen, who destroy bridges, hospitals . . .) For years, Milošević has been sending letter bombs to his neighbours, from the Albanians to Croatia and Bosnia, keeping himself out of the conflict while igniting fire all around Serbia – finally, his last letter returned to him. Let us hope that the result of the NATO intervention will be that Milošević will be proclaimed the political blunderer of the year.

And there is a kind of poetic justice in the fact that the West has finally intervened apropos of Kosovo – let us not forget that it was there that it all began with the ascension to power of Milošević: this ascension was legitimized by the promise to amend the underprivileged situation of Serbia within the Yugoslav federation, especially with regard to Albanian 'separatism'. Albanians were Milošević's first target; afterwards, he turned his wrath on to other Yugoslav republics (Slovenia, Croatia, Bosnia), until, finally, the focus of the conflict returned to Kosovo – as in a closed loop of Destiny, the arrow returned to the one who fired it by way of setting free the spectre of ethnic passions. This is the key point worth remembering: Yugoslavia did not start to disintegrate when the Slovene 'secession' triggered the domino effect (first Croatia, then Bosnia, Macedonia); it was already at the moment of Milošević's constitutional reforms in 1987, depriving Kosovo and Vojvodina of their limited autonomy, that the fragile balance on which Yugoslavia rested was irretrievably disturbed. From that moment onwards, Yugoslavia continued to live only because it didn't yet notice it was already dead – it was like the proverbial cat in the cartoon walking over the precipice, floating in mid-air, and falling only when it becomes aware that it has no ground under its feet. From Milošević's seizure of power in Serbia onwards, the only actual chance for Yugoslavia to survive was to reinvent its formula: either a Yugoslavia under Serb domination or some form of radical decentralization, from a loose confederacy to the full sovereignty of its units.

It is thus easy to praise the NATO bombing of Yugoslavia as the first case of an intervention – not into the confused situation of a civil war, but – into a country with full sovereign power. Is it not comforting to see the NATO forces intervene not for any specific economico-strategic interests, but simply because a country is cruelly violating the elementary human rights of an ethnic group? Is this not the only hope in our global era – to see some internationally acknowledged force as a guarantee that all countries will respect a certain minimum of ethical (and, hopefully, also health, social, ecological) standards? However, the situation is more complex, and this complexity is indicated already in the way that NATO has justified its intervention: the violation of human rights is always accompanied by the vague, but ominous reference to 'strategic interests'. The story of NATO as the enforcer of respect for human rights is thus only one of two coherent stories that can be told about the recent bombings of Yugoslavia, and the problem is that each story has its own rationale. The second story concerns the other side of the much-praised new global ethical politics in which one is allowed to violate the sovereignty of a state due to the violation of human rights. The first glimpse into this other side is provided by the way the Western media selectively elevate some local 'warlord' or dictator into the embodiment of Evil: Saddam Hussein, Milošević, up to the unfortunate (now forgotten) Aidid in Somalia – at every point, it is or was 'the community of civilized nations against . . .'. And on what criteria does this selection rely? Why Albanians in Serbia and not also Palestinians in Israel, Kurds in Turkey, and so on? Here, of course, we enter the shady world of international Capital and its strategic interests.

According to *Project CENSORED*, the top censored story of 1998 was that of a half-secret international working agreement, called the Multilateral Agreement on Investment (MAI). The primary goal of MAI is to protect the foreign interests of multinational companies. The agreement will basically undermine the sovereignty of nations by assigning power to corporations almost equal to those of the countries in which these corporations are located. Governments will no longer be able to treat their domestic firms more favourably than foreign firms. Furthermore, countries that do not relax their environmental, land-use, health and labour standards to meet the demands of foreign firms may be accused of acting illegally. Corporations will be able to sue sovereign states if they impose too severe ecological or other standards – under NAFTA (which is the main model for MAI), Ethyl Corporation is already suing Canada for banning the use of its gasoline additive MMT. The greatest threat, of course, is to the developing nations that will be pressured into depleting their natural resources for commercial exploitation. Renato Ruggerio, director of the World Trade Organization, the sponsor of MAI, is already hailing this project, elaborated and discussed in a clandestine manner, with almost no public debate or media attention, as the 'constitution for a new global economy'. And, in the same way in which, already for Marx, market relations provided the true foundation for the notion of individual freedoms and rights, *this* is also the obverse of the much-praised new global morality celebrated even by some neo-liberal philosophers as signalling the beginning of the new era in which the international community will establish and enforce some minimal code preventing sovereign states from engaging in crimes against humanity even within its own territory. And the recent catastrophic economic situation in Russia, far from being the heritage of old socialist mismanagement, is a direct result of this global capitalist logic embodied in MAI.

This other story also has its own ominous military side. The ultimate lesson of the last American military interventions, from Operation Desert Fox against Iraq at the end of 1998 to the present bombing of Yugoslavia, is that they signal a new era in military history – battles in which the attacking forces operate under the constraint that it can sustain no casualties (as elaborated by General Colin Powell). When the first stealth-fighter crashed in Serbia, the emphasis of the American media was that there were no casualties – the pilot was saved! And was not the counterpoint to this coverage the almost surreal way that CNN reported on the war: not only was it presented as a television event, but the Iraqis themselves seemed to treat it this way – during the day, Baghdad was a 'normal' city, with people milling around and conducting their business, as if the bombing was an unreal nightmarish spectre that occurred only at night and effectively did not take place in reality?

Let us recall what went on during the final American assault on the Iraqi lines during the Gulf War: no photos, no reports, just rumours that tanks with bulldozer-like shields in front of them rolled over Iraqi trenches, simply burying thousands of troops in earth and sand – what went on was allegedly considered too cruel in its sheer mechanical efficiency, too different from the standard notion of heroic face-to-face combat, so that images would perturb too much public opinion and a total media blackout was strictly imposed. Here we have the two aspects joined together: the new notion of war as a purely technological event, taking place behind radar and computer screens, without casualties, *and* extreme physical cruelty too unbearable for the gaze of the media – not the crippled children and raped women, victims of caricaturized local ethnic 'fundamentalist warlords', but thousands of nameless soldiers, victims of anonymous, efficient, technological warfare. When Jean Baudrillard made the claim that the Gulf War did not take place, this statement could also be read in the sense that such traumatic pictures that stand for the Real of this war were totally censored . . .

How, then, are we to think these two stories together, without sacrificing the truth of each of them? What we have here is a political example of the famous Gestalt drawing in which we recognize the contours either of a rabbit's head or of a goose's head, depending on our mental focus. If we look at the situation in a certain way, we see the international community enforcing minimal standards of human rights on a nationalist neo-Communist leader engaged in ethnic cleansing, ready to ruin his own nation just to retain power. If we shift focus, we see NATO, the armed hand of the new capitalist global order, defending the strategic interests of Capital in the guise of a disgusting travesty, posing as a disinterested enforcer of human rights, attacking a sovereign country which, in spite of the problematic nature of its régime, nonetheless acts as an obstacle to the unbridled assertion of the New World Order.

However, what if one should reject this double blackmail (if you are against the NATO bombings, you are for Milošević's proto-fascist régime of ethnic cleansing; if you are against Milošević, you support the global capitalist New World Order)? What if this very opposition between enlightened international intervention against ethnic fundamentalism and the heroic last pockets of resistance against the New World Order is a false one? What if phenomena like Milošević's régime are not the opposite of the New World Order, but rather its *symptom*, the place from which the hidden *truth* of the New World Order emerges? Recently, one of the American negotiators said that Milošević is not only part of the problem, he is *the* problem itself. However, was this not clear *from the very beginning*?

Why, then, the interminable procrastination of the Western powers, playing for years into Milošević's hands, acknowledging him as a key factor of stability in the region, misreading clear cases of Serb aggression as civil or even tribal warfare, initially putting the blame on those who immediately saw what Milošević stood for and, for that reason, desperately wanted to escape his grasp (see James Baker's public endorsement of a 'limited military intervention' against Slovene secession), supporting the last Yugoslav prime minister Ante Marković, whose programme was, in an incredible case of political blindness, seriously considered as the last chance for a democratic, market-orientated, unified Yugoslavia, etc.? When the West fights Milošević, it is *not* fighting its enemy, one of the last points of resistance against the liberal-democratic New World Order; it is rather fighting its own creature, a monster that grew as the result of the compromises and inconsistencies of Western politics itself. (And, incidentally, it is the same as with Iraq: its strong position in the region is also the result of the American strategy to contain Iran.)

So, precisely as a leftist, my answer to the dilemma, 'Bomb or not?', is: *not yet enough* bombs, and they are already *too late*. During the last decade, the West followed a Hamlet-like procrastination towards the Balkans, and the present bombings have all the signs of Hamlet's final murderous outburst in which many people unnecessarily die (not only the King, his true target, but also his mother, Laertes, Hamlet himself . . .), because Hamlet acted too late, when the proper moment was already missed. So the West, in the present intervention, which displays all the signs of a violent outburst of impotent aggressivity without a clear political goal, is now paying the price for years of entertaining illusions that one can make a deal with Milošević: with the recent hesitations about the ground intervention in Kosovo, the Serbian régime is, under the pretext of war, launching the final assault on Kosovo to purge it of most of the Albanians, cynically accepting the bombings as the price to be paid. When the Western forces repeat constantly that they are not fighting the Serbian people but only their corrupted régime, they rely on the typically liberal false premise that the Serbian people are just victims of their evil leadership personified in Milošević, and are manipulated by him. The painful fact is that Serb aggressive nationalism enjoys the support of the vast majority of the population – no, Serbs are not passive victims of nationalist manipulation, they are not Americans in disguise, just waiting to be delivered from the bad nationalist spell.

More precisely, the misperception of the West is double: this notion of the bad leadership manipulating the good people is accompanied by the apparently contradictory notion according to which the Balkan people are living in the past, fighting once again old battles, perceiving the current situation through old myths . . . One is tempted to say that these two notions should be precisely *turned around*: not only are the people not 'good', because they let themselves be manipulated with obscene pleasure, there are also no 'old myths' that we need to study if we are really to understand the situation; there is just the *present* outburst of racist nationalism which, according to its needs, opportunistically resuscitates old myths.

So, on the one hand, we have the obscenities of Serb state propaganda: they regularly refer to Clinton not as 'the American president', but as 'the American Führer'; two of the placards on their state-organized anti-NATO demonstrations were 'Clinton, come here and be our Monica!' (i.e., suck our . . .), and 'Monica, did you also suck out his brain?' The atmosphere in Belgrade is, at least for the time being, carnivalesque in a faked way – when they are not in shelters, people dance to rock or ethnic music on the streets, under the motto 'With poetry and music against bombs!', playing the role of defiant victims (since they know that NATO does not really bomb civilian targets and that, consequently, they are safe!). This is where the NATO strategists got it wrong, caught in their schemes of tactical reasoning, unable to predict that the Serb reaction to the bombings would be recourse to a collective Bakhtinian carnivalization of social life. This pseudo-authentic spectacle, although it may fascinate some confused leftists, is effectively the other, public, face of ethnic cleansing: in Belgrade people are defiantly dancing on the streets while, 300 kilometres to the South, a genocide of African proportions is taking place . . . And the Western counterpoint to this obscenity is the more and more openly racist tone of its reporting: when the three American soldiers were taken prisoners, CNN dedicated the first ten minutes of the news to their predicament (although everyone knew that *nothing* would happen to them!), and only then reported on the tens of thousands of refugees, burned villages and Pristina turning into a ghost town. Where is the much-praised Serb 'democratic opposition' to protest *this* horror taking place in their own backyard, not only the bombings, which, until now at least, have involved relatively few casualties?

In the recent struggle of the so-called 'democratic opposition' in Serbia against Milošević's régime, the truly touchy topic is the stance towards Kosovo: as to this topic, the large majority of the 'democratic opposition' unconditionally endorses Milošević's anti-Albanian nationalist agenda, even accusing him of making compromises with the West and thus 'betraying' Serb national interests in Kosovo. In the course of the student demonstrations against the Milošević socialist party's falsification of the election results in the winter of 1996, the Western media, which closely followed events and praised the revived democratic spirit in Serbia, rarely mentioned the fact that one of the regular slogans of the demonstrators against the special police forces was, 'Instead of kicking us, go to Kosovo and kick out the Albanians!' In today's Serbia, the absolute *sine qua non* of an authentic political act would thus be to reject unconditionally the ideological topos of the 'Albanian threat to Serbia'.

One thing is for sure: the NATO bombing of Yugoslavia will change the global geopolitical coordinates. The unwritten pact of peaceful co-existence (respect for each state's full sovereignty, i.e., non-interference in internal affairs, even in the face of grave violations of human rights) is over. However, the very first act of the new global police usurping the right to punish sovereign states for their wrongdoings already signals its end, its own undermining, since it immediately becomes clear that this 'universality of human rights' as its legitimization is false, i.e., that the attacks on selective targets protect particular interests. The NATO bombing of Yugoslavia also signals the end of any serious role of the United Nations and its Security Council: it is NATO under American guidance that effectively pulls the strings. Furthermore, the silent pact with Russia that held until now is broken: in the terms of this pact, Russia was publicly treated as a superpower, allowed to maintain the appearance of being one, on the condition that it did not act as one. Now, Russia's humiliation is public, and any pretence of dignity is unmasked: Russia can only openly resist or openly comply with Western pressure. The further logical result of this new situation will be, of course, the renewed rise of anti-Western resistance from Eastern Europe to the Third World, with the sad consequence that criminal figures like Milošević will be elevated into model fighters against the New World Order.

So the lesson is that the alternative between the New World Order and the neo-racist nationalism opposing it is a false one: these are the two sides of the same coin – the New World Order itself breeds the monstrosities that it fights. This is why protests against the bombing from the reformed Communist parties all around Europe, including the PDS, are totally misdirected: these false protesters against the NATO bombing of Serbia are like the caricaturized pseudo-leftists who oppose the trial of a drug dealer, claiming that his crime is the result of the social pathology of the capitalist system. The way to fight the capitalist New World Order is not by supporting local proto-fascist resistances to it, but to focus on the only serious question today: how to build *transnational* political movements and institutions strong enough seriously to constrain the unlimited rule of Capital, and to render visible and politically relevant the fact that local fundamentalist resistances against the New World Order, from Milošević to Le Pen and the extreme Right in Europe, are part of it?

Note

Various versions of this paper were circulating until it was finally published in *New Left Review* 234, 1999, pp. 76–82. This text dates from 7 April 1999, and contains several passages that, interestingly, were omitted from the official *NLR* version. [eds]

Chapter 15
Welcome to the desert of the Real (reflections on 11 September 2001)

Seizing the Real

Alain Badiou identified the 'passion for the Real [*la passion du réel*]'[1] as the key feature of the twentieth century: in contrast to the utopian or 'scientific' projects and ideals, and plans about the future, of the nineteenth century, this century aimed at delivering the thing itself, at directly realizing the longed-for New Order. The ultimate and defining experience of the twentieth century was the direct experience of the Real as opposed to everyday social reality – the Real in its extreme violence as the price to be paid for peeling off deceptive layers of reality. Already in the trenches of World War I, Carl Jünger was celebrating face-to-face combat as the authentic intersubjective encounter: authenticity resides in the act of violent transgression, from the Lacanian Real – the Thing confronted by Antigone when she violates the order of the city – to Bataillean excess.

As Badiou demonstrated apropos of the Stalinist show trials, this violent effort to distil the pure Real from elusive reality necessarily ends up in its opposite, in the obsession with pure appearance: in the Stalinist universe, the passion for the Real (the ruthless enforcement of socialist development) thus culminates in ritualistic stagings of a theatrical spectacle in the truth of which no one believes. The key to this reversal resides in the impossibility ultimately to draw a clear distinction between deceptive reality and some firm positive kernel of the Real: every positive bit of reality is *a priori* suspicious, because (as we know from Lacan) the Real Thing is ultimately another name for the Void. The pursuit of the Real thus equals total annihilation, a (self-)destructive fury within which the only way to trace the distinction between the semblance and the Real is, precisely, to *stage* it as a fake spectacle. The fundamental illusion here is that, once the violent work of purification is done, the New Man will emerge *ex nihilo*, freed from the filth of past corruption. Within this horizon, 'really-existing men' are reduced to the stock of raw material which can be ruthlessly exploited for the construction of the New – the Stalinist revolutionary definition of man is thus a circular one: 'man is what is to be crushed, stamped on, mercilessly worked over, in order to produce a new man.' We have here the tension between the series of 'ordinary' elements ('ordinary' men as the 'material' of history) and the exceptional 'empty' element (the socialist 'New Man', which at first is nothing but an empty place to be filled up with positive content through revolutionary turmoil). In a revolution, there is no *a priori* positive determination of this New Man: a revolution is not legitimized by the positive notion of what constitutes Man's essence, 'alienated' in present conditions and to be realized through the revolutionary process – the only legitimization of a revolution is negative, a will to break with the past. One should formulate things here in a very precise way: the reason why the Stalinist fury of purification was so destructive resides in the very fact that it was sustained by the belief that, after the destructive work of purification was accomplished, *something will remain*, the sublime 'indivisible remainder', the paragon of the New. It is in order to conceal the fact that there is nothing beyond this purification, in a strictly perverse way, that the revolutionary has to cling to violence as the only index of his authenticity, and it is at this level that critics of Stalinism as a rule misperceive the cause of the Communist's attachment to the Party. When, say, in 1939–41, pro-Soviet Communists twice had to change their Party line overnight (after the Soviet–German pact, it was imperialism, not fascism, that was elevated to the role of the primary enemy; from 22 June 1941, when Germany attacked the Soviet Union, it was again the popular front against the fascist beast), the brutality of the imposed changes of position was what attracted them. Along the same lines, the purges themselves exerted an uncanny fascination, especially on intellectuals: their 'irrational' cruelty served as a kind of ontological proof, bearing witness to the fact that we are dealing with the Real, not just with empty plans – the Party is ruthlessly brutal, so it must mean business . . .

So, if the passion for the Real ends up with the pure semblance of political theatre, then, in an exact inversion, the 'postmodern' passion of the semblance of the Last Men ends up with a kind of Real. Recall the phenomena, strictly correlative to the virtualization of our environment, of 'cutters' (mostly women who experience an irresistible urge to cut themselves with razors or otherwise hurt themselves): they stand for a desperate strategy to return to the Real of the body. As such, cutting is to be contrasted with standard tattooing, which guarantees the subject's inclusion in the (virtual) symbolic order – with cutters, the problem is the opposite one, namely, the assertion of reality itself. Far from being suicidal, far from signalling a desire for self-annihilation, cutting is a radical attempt to (re)gain a stronghold in reality, or (another aspect of the same phenomenon) firmly to ground our ego in bodily reality, against the unbearable anxiety of perceiving oneself as non-existent. The standard report of cutters is that, after seeing the warm red blood flowing out of their self-inflicted wound, they feel alive again, firmly rooted in reality. So although, of course, cutting is a pathological phenomenon, it is nonetheless a pathological attempt to regain some kind of normalcy, to avoid a total psychotic breakdown. On today's market, we find a whole series of products deprived of their malignant property: coffee without caffeine, cream without fat, beer without alcohol, etc. Virtual Reality simply *generalizes* this procedure of offering a product deprived of its substance: it provides *reality itself* deprived of the resisting hard kernel of the Real – in the same way that decaffeinated coffee smells and tastes like the real coffee without being the real thing, Virtual Reality is experienced as reality without being so. However, at the end of this process of virtualization, the inevitable Benthamian conclusion awaits us: reality is its own best semblance.

And was the collapse of the World Trade Center, apropos of Hollywood's catastrophe movies, not like snuff pornography versus ordinary sadomasochistic porn films? Herein resides the element of truth in Karl-Heinz Stockhausen's provocative statement that the planes hitting the WTC towers was the ultimate work of art: one can effectively perceive the collapse of the WTC towers as the climactic conclusion of twentieth century art's 'passion for the real' – the terrorists themselves did not do it primarily to provoke real material damage, but *for the spectacular effect of it*. The authentic twentieth-century passion to penetrate the Real Thing (ultimately, the destructive Void) through the cobweb of semblances that constitute our reality thus culminates in the thrill of the Real as the ultimate 'effect', sought after from digitalized special effects through reality television and amateur pornography up to snuff films (which, in their very attempt to deliver the 'real thing', are perhaps the ultimate truth of Virtual Reality). There is an intimate connection between the virtualization of reality and the emergence of an infinite and infinitized bodily pain, much stronger than the usual one: do the combination of biogenetics and Virtual Reality not open up new 'enhanced' possibilities of *torture*, unheard-of horizons for extending our ability to endure pain (through widening our sensory capacity to sustain pain, through the invention of new ways to inflict it)? Perhaps, the ultimate Sadean image of an 'undead' victim of torture who can sustain endless pain without having at his/her disposal the escape into death also waits to become reality.

The ultimate American paranoiac fantasy is that of an individual living in an idyllic Californian town, a consumerist paradise, who suddenly starts to suspect that the world he lives in is a fake, a spectacle staged to convince him that he lives in a real world, while everyone around him is effectively an actor or extra in a gigantic show. The most recent example of this is Peter Weir's *The Truman Show* (1998), with Jim Carrey playing a small-town clerk who gradually discovers the truth that he is the hero of a television show which airs 24 hours a day: his hometown is constructed inside a gigantic studio, with cameras following him permanently. Among its predecessors, it is worth mentioning Philip K. Dick's *Time Out of Joint* (1959), in which a hero living a modest daily life in a small Californian town of the late 1950s gradually discovers that the whole town is a fake staged to keep him satisfied. The underlying experience of *Time Out of Joint* and *The Truman Show* is that late capitalist consumerist Californian paradise is, in its very hyper-reality, in a way *unreal*, substanceless, deprived of material inertia. And the same 'derealization' of the horror went on after the WTC attacks: while the number of 6,000 victims is repeated constantly, it is surprising how little of the actual carnage we see – no dismembered bodies, no blood, no desperate faces of dying people . . . in clear contrast to the reporting of Third World catastrophes, in which the whole point is to produce a scoop of some gruesome detail: Somalis dying of hunger, raped Bosnian women, men with their throats slit. These shots are always accompanied with the advance warning that 'you may find some of the images disturbing . . .' – a warning that we *never* heard in the reports of the WTC collapse. Is this not yet another proof of how, even in these tragic moments, the distance which separates Us from Them, our reality from their reality, is maintained? The real horror always happens *there*, not *here*.[2]

So, it is not only that Hollywood stages a semblance of real life deprived of the weight and inertia of materiality – in late capitalist consumerist society, *'real social life' itself somehow acquires the features of a staged fake*, with our neighbours behaving in 'real' life as stage actors and extras. Again, the ultimate truth of the capitalist (utilitarian) de-spiritualized universe is the de-materialization of 'real life' itself, its reversal into a spectral show. Among others, Christopher Isherwood gave expression to this unreality of American daily life, exemplified in the motel room: 'American motels are unreal! . . . They are deliberately designed to be unreal . . . The Europeans hate us because we've retired to live inside our advertisements, like hermits going into caves to contemplate.' Peter Sloterdijk's notion of the 'sphere' – a gigantic metal sphere that envelops and isolates the entire city – is here literally realized. Years ago, a series of science-fiction films like *Zardoz* or *Logan's Run* forecast today's postmodern predicament by extending this fantasy to the community itself: an isolated group living an aseptic life in a secluded area longs for the experience of the real world of material decay. Is the endlessly repeated shot of the plane approaching and hitting the second WTC tower not the real-life version of the famous scene from Hitchcock's *Birds*, superbly analysed by Raymond Bellour, in which Melanie approaches the Bodega Bay pier after crossing the bay on the small boat? When, while approaching the wharf, she waves to her (future) lover, a single bird (first perceived as an undistinguished dark blot) unexpectedly enters the frame from the upper right and hits her head.[3] Was the plane that hit the WTC tower not the ultimate Hitchcockian blot, the anamorphic stain which denaturalized the idyllic, well-known New York landscape?

The Wachowski brothers' hit, *The Matrix* (1999), brought this logic to its climax: the material reality we all experience and see around us is a virtual one, generated and coordinated by a gigantic mega-computer to which we are all attached; when the hero (played by Keanu Reeves) awakens into 'real reality', he sees a desolate landscape littered with burnt-out ruins – what remained of Chicago after a global war. The resistance leader, Morpheus (Laurence Fishburne), utters the ironic greeting: 'Welcome to the desert of the real.' Was it not something of a similar order that took place in New York on 11 September? Its citizens were introduced to the 'desert of the real' – to us, corrupted by Hollywood, the landscape and the shots we saw of the collapsing towers could not but remind us of the most breathtaking scenes from those great catastrophe films.

When we hear how the attacks were totally unexpected, how the unimaginable 'Impossible' happened, one should recall the other defining catastrophe from the beginning of the twentieth century, the *Titanic*: it was also a shock, but the space for it had already been prepared by ideological fantasizing, since the *Titanic* was the symbol of the might of nineteenth-century industrial civilization. Does the same not also hold for these attacks? Not only were the media bombarding us all the time with talk about the terrorist threat; this threat was also obviously libidinally invested – just recall the series of movies from *Escape from New York* to *Independence Day*. Therein resides the rationale for the often-mentioned association of the attacks with Hollywood disaster movies: the unthinkable that happened was the object of fantasy, so that, in a way, *America got what it fantasized about* – and this was the greatest surprise.

One should therefore invert the standard reading, according to which the events of 11 September were the intrusion of the Real that shattered our illusory sphere: quite the contrary, it is prior to the WTC collapse that we lived in our reality, perceiving Third World horrors as something that are not effectively part of our social reality, as something that exists (for us) as a spectral apparition on the (television) screen – and what happened on 11 September is that *this fantasmatic screen apparition entered our reality*. It is not that reality entered our imaginary domain: the image entered and shattered our reality (i.e., the symbolic coordinates that determine what we experience as reality). The fact that, after 11 September, the premières of a number of 'blockbusters' containing scenes that bore resemblances to the attacks (large buildings on fire or under siege, terrorist activities, etc.) were postponed (in some cases, the films were even shelved), is thus to be read as *the 'repression' of the fantasmatic background* responsible for the impact of the WTC collapse. The point, of course, is not to play a pseudo-postmodern game of reducing 11 September to just another media spectacle, reading it as a catastrophic version of snuff films; the question we should have asked ourselves when we stared at the television screens on 11 September is simply: *haven't we already seen this same thing over and over again?*

The symbolism of a catastrophe

It is precisely now, when we are dealing with the raw Real of a catastrophe, that we should bear in mind the ideological and fantasmatic coordinates which determine its perception. If there is any symbolism in the collapse of the WTC towers, it is not so much the old-fashioned notion of the 'centre of financial capitalism', but rather the notion that the two WTC towers stood for the centre of *virtual* capitalism, of financial speculations disconnected from the sphere of material production. The shattering impact of the attacks can be accounted for only against the background of the borderline that today separates the digitalized First World from the Third World 'desert of the Real'. It is the awareness that we live in an insulated artificial universe which generates the notion that some ominous agent is threatening us all the time with total destruction.

Consequently, is Osama bin Laden, the suspected mastermind behind the attacks, not the real-life counterpart of Ernst Stavro Blofeld, the master-criminal in most of the James Bond films, involved in the acts of global destruction? What one should recall here is that the only place in Hollywood films where we see the production process in all its material intensity is when Bond penetrates the master-criminal's secret domain and locates there a site of intense labour (distilling and packaging drugs, constructing a rocket that will destroy New York, etc.). When the master-criminal, after capturing Bond, takes him on a tour of his illegal factory, is this not the closest Hollywood comes to the socialist-realist proud presentation of factory production? And the function of Bond's intervention, of course, is spectacularly to destroy this site of production (usually punctuated by an enormous explosion), allowing us to return to the daily semblance of our existence in a world with a 'disappearing working class'. Is it not that, in the destruction of the WTC towers, this violence directed at the threatening Outside turned back on us?

A distilled version of our own essence

The safe sphere in which Americans live is experienced as under threat from the Outside of terrorist attackers who are ruthlessly self-sacrificing *and* cowards, cunningly intelligent *and* primitive barbarians. The letters of deceased attackers are quoted as 'chilling documents' – why? Are they not exactly what one would expect from dedicated fighters on a suicide mission? If one takes away references to the Koran, how do they differ from, say, CIA special manuals? Were the CIA manuals for the Nicaraguan contras, with their detailed descriptions of how to perturb daily life, up to how to clog toilet water, not of the same order – if anything, were they not *more* cowardly? When, on 25 September 2001, the Taliban leader Mullah Mohammad Omar appealed to Americans to exercise their own judgement when responding to the devastating attacks on the World Trade Center and Pentagon rather than blindly following their government's policy to attack his country ('You accept everything your government says, whether it is true or false. . . . Don't you have your own thinking? . . . So it will be better for you to use your sense and understanding . . .'), were these statements, taken in a literal-abstract, decontextualized sense, not quite appropriate? Today, more than ever, one should bear in mind that the large majority of Arabs are not fanaticized dark crowds, but scared, uncertain, aware of their fragile status – witness the anxiety the attacks caused in Egypt.

Whenever we encounter such a purely evil Outside, we should gather the courage to endorse the Hegelian lesson: in this pure Outside, we should recognize the distilled version of our own essence. For the last five centuries, the (relative) prosperity and peace of the 'civilized' West was bought by exporting ruthless violence and destruction to this 'barbarian' Outside: this narrative stretches from the conquest of the Americas to the slaughter in the Congo. Cruel and indifferent as it may sound, we should also, now more than ever, bear in mind that the actual effect of these terrorist attacks is much more symbolic than real: in Africa, *every single day* more people die of AIDS than all the victims of the WTC collapse, and the death toll there can be easily reduced at a relatively low cost. The United States simply got a taste of what goes on around the world on a daily basis, from Sarajevo to Grozny, from Rwanda and the Congo to Sierra Leone. If one adds to the situation in New York gangs of rapists and a dozen or so snipers blindly targeting people walking along the streets, one gets an idea of what Sarajevo was like a decade ago.

The falsity of 'reality television'

When, days after 11 September 2001, our gaze was transfixed by images of the plane hitting one of the WTC towers, we were all forced to experience precisely what the 'compulsion to repeat' and *jouissance* beyond the pleasure principle are: we wanted to see it again and again, the same shots were repeated *ad nauseam*, and the uncanny satisfaction we got from them was *jouissance* at its purest. It is when we watched the two towers collapsing on the television screen that it became possible to experience the falsity of 'reality television shows': even if these shows are 'for real', people still *act* in them – they simply *play themselves*. The standard disclaimer in a novel ('the characters in this text are fictional; any resemblance to actual individuals is purely accidental') holds for participants in reality soaps as well: what we see there are fictional characters, even if they play themselves 'in reality'. Of course, the 'return to the Real' can be given different twists: one already hears some conservatives claim that what made us so vulnerable is our very openness – with the inevitable conclusion lurking in the background that, if we are to protect our 'way of life', we will have to sacrifice some of our freedoms which were exploited by the enemies of freedom. This logic should be rejected *tout court*: is it not a fact that our First World 'open' countries are the most controlled countries in the entire history of humanity? In the United Kingdom, all public spaces, from buses to shopping malls, are constantly videotaped, not to mention the almost total control of all forms of digital communication.

An impotent *passage à l'acte*

Following 11 September, rightist commentators like George Will immediately proclaimed the end of America's 'holiday from history' – the impact of reality shattering the isolated tower of liberal tolerance and the cultural studies focus on textuality. Now, we are forced to strike back, to deal with real enemies in the real world . . . But *whom* to strike? Whatever the response, it will never hit the *correct* target, bringing us full satisfaction. The ridiculousness of America retaliating against Afghanistan cannot but strike the eye: if the so-called 'only remaining superpower' destroys one of the world's poorest countries, in which peasants barely survive on barren hills, will this not be the ultimate case of an impotent *passage à l'acte?* Afghanistan is otherwise an ideal target: a country *already* reduced to rubble, with no infrastructure, repeatedly destroyed by war over the last two decades . . . one cannot avoid the conclusion that the choice of Afghanistan was also determined by economic considerations: is it not the best procedure to act out one's anger at a country for whom no one cares and where there is nothing to destroy? Unfortunately, the choice of Afghanistan recalls the anecdote about the madman who searches for a lost key beneath a street light; when asked why he is searching there when he lost the key in a dark corner, he answers: 'But it is easier to search under a strong light!' Is not the ultimate irony that the whole of Kabul already looks like downtown Manhattan after 11 September?

To succumb to the urge to act now means precisely to *avoid* confronting the true dimension of what occurred on 11 September – it represents an act whose true aim is to lull us into the secure conviction that nothing has *really* changed. The real long-term threat is the prospect of further acts of mass terror in comparison to which the memory of the WTC collapse will pale, acts less spectacular, but much more horrifying. What about bacteriological warfare, the use of lethal gas, the prospect of DNA terrorism (the development of poisons that will only affect people who share a determinate gene)? In contrast to Marx who relied on the notion of fetish as a solid object whose stable presence obfuscates its social mediation, one should assert that fetishism reaches its acme precisely when the fetish itself is 'dematerialized', turned into a fluid, 'immaterial', virtual entity; money fetishism will culminate with its passage to electronic form, when the last traces of its materiality disappear – it is only at this stage that it will assume the form of an indestructible spectral presence: I owe you $1,000, and no matter how many material notes I burn, I will still owe you $1,000; the debt is inscribed somewhere in virtual digital space. Does the same not hold for warfare? Far from pointing towards the nature of warfare in the twenty-first century, the collapse of the WTC towers was rather the last spectacular cry of twentieth-century warfare. What awaits us is something far more uncanny: the spectre of an 'immaterial' war in which the attack is invisible – viruses, poisons that can be both everywhere and nowhere. At the level of visible material reality, nothing happens, no big explosions, and yet the known universe begins to collapse, life itself disintegrates. We are entering a new era of paranoiac warfare in which the greatest task will be to identify the enemy and its weapons. Instead of a hasty *passage à l'acte*, one should confront these difficult questions: What will 'war' mean in the twenty-first century? Who will 'they' be, if they are, clearly, neither states nor criminal gangs? One cannot resist the temptation to recall here the Freudian opposition of public Law and its obscene superego double: along the same lines, are 'international terrorist organizations' not the obscene double of large multinational corporations – the ultimate rhizomatic machine, all-present, and yet with no clear territorial base? Are they not the form in which nationalist and/or religious 'fundamentalism' accommodated itself to global capitalism? Do they not embody the ultimate contradiction, with their particular/exclusive content and their global dynamic functioning?

The 'clash of civilizations'

There is a partial truth to the notion of a 'clash of civilizations' attested here – witness the surprise of the average American: 'How is it possible that these people display such disregard for their own lives?' Is the obverse of this surprise not the rather sad fact that we, in First World countries, find it more and more difficult even to imagine a public or universal Cause for which one would be prepared to sacrifice one's own life? When, after the attacks, even the Taliban foreign minister said that he could 'feel the pain' of the American children, did he not thereby confirm the hegemonic, ideological role of this trademark phrase of Bill Clinton? It effectively appears as if the split between First and Third World runs more and more along the lines of the opposition between leading a long satisfying life full of material and cultural wealth, and dedicating one's life to some transcendent Cause. Two philosophical references immediately impose themselves apropos of this ideological antagonism between Western consumerism and Muslim radicalism: Hegel and Nietzsche. Is this antagonism not the one between what Nietzsche called 'passive' and 'active' nihilism? We in the West are the Nietzschean Last Men, immersed in stupid daily pleasures, while the Muslim radicals are ready to risk everything, engaged in the struggle up to the point of their own self-destruction. (One cannot but note the significant role played by the stock exchange in the attacks: the ultimate proof of their traumatic impact was that the New York Stock Exchange was closed for four days, and its opening the following Monday was presented as a sign that things are beginning to return to normal.) Furthermore, if one perceives this opposition through the lens of the Hegelian struggle between Master and Servant, one cannot avoid noting the paradox: although we in the West are perceived as exploiting masters, we are the ones who occupy the position of the Servant who, because he clings to life and its pleasures, is unable to risk his life (recall Colin Powell's notion of a high-tech war with no human casualties), while the poor Muslim radicals are the Master, prepared to risk everything . . .

However, this notion of the 'clash of civilizations' must be thoroughly rejected: what we are witnessing today is rather clashes *within* each civilization. A brief look at the comparative history of Islam and Christianity tells us that the 'human rights record' of Islam (to use this anachronistic term) is much better than that of Christianity: in past centuries, Islam was significantly more tolerant towards other religions than Christianity. *Now* is the time to remember that it was also through the Arabs that, in the Middle Ages, Western Europe regained access to its ancient Greek legacy. While I am in no way excusing today's acts of terrorism, these facts nonetheless clearly demonstrate that we are not dealing with a feature inscribed into Islam 'as such', but with the outcome of modern socio-political conditions.

On closer inspection, what *is* this 'clash of civilizations' effectively about? Are all real-life 'clashes' not clearly related to global capitalism? The target of Muslim 'fundamentalism' is not just global capitalism's corrosive effect on social life, but *also* the corrupted 'traditionalist' régimes in Saudi Arabia, Kuwait, etc. The most horrifying slaughters (those in Rwanda, the Congo and Sierra Leone) not only took place – and are taking place – within the *same* 'civilization', but they are also clearly related to the interplay of global economic interests. Even in the few cases that would vaguely fit the definition of a 'clash of civilizations' (Bosnia and Kosovo, southern Sudan, etc.), the shadow of other interests is easily discernible.

L'Amérique profonde

The very feature attributed to the Other is already present in the very heart of the United States. Take, for instance, murderous fanaticism. There are today in America itself more than two million Right-populist 'fundamentalists' who practise a terrorism of their own, legitimized by (their understanding of) Christianity. Since America is in a way 'harbouring' them, shouldn't the United States Army have punished the Americans themselves after the Oklahoma City bombing? And what about the way Jerry Falwell and Pat Robertson reacted to the attacks, perceiving them as a sign that God has removed his protection from the United States because of the sinful lives of Americans, placing the blame squarely on hedonist materialism, liberalism and rampant sexuality, claiming that America got what it deserved? The fact that the very same condemnation of 'liberal' America issued from the heart of *l'Amérique profonde* as that from the Muslim Other should make one pause to consider. And what about America as a safe haven? When a New Yorker commented on how, after 11 September, one can no longer walk the city streets safely, the irony was that, well before the attacks, the streets of New York were well known for the dangers of being attacked or, at least, mugged – if anything, the attacks gave rise to a new sense of solidarity; recall the scenes of young African-Americans helping an old Jewish gentleman to cross the street, scenes unimaginable a couple of days previously.

Bad omens

Now, in the days immediately following the attacks, it is as if we dwell in a unique time between a traumatic event and its symbolic impact, like in that brief moment after we are deeply cut, before the full extent of the pain strikes us – it remains uncertain how events will be symbolized, what their symbolic efficiency will be, what acts they will be evoked to justify. If nothing else, one can clearly sense yet again the limitation of our democracy: decisions are being made that will affect the fate of us all, and we just wait, aware of being utterly powerless. But even here, in these moments of heightened tension, this association is not automatic. We are already seeing the first bad omens: the irruption, like a sudden resurrection, in public discourse of the old Cold War term 'free world' – the struggle is now between the 'free world' and the forces of darkness and terror. The question to be asked here, of course, is: who then belongs to the *unfree world*? Are, say, China or Egypt part of this free world? The actual message is, in fact, that the old division between Western liberal-democratic countries and all the others is once again enforced.

A new Berufsverbot

On 12 September 2001, I received a message from a journal that was just about to publish a long text of mine on Lenin, informing me that they decided to postpone its publication – they considered it inopportune to publish a text on Lenin immediately after the attacks. Does this not point towards the ominous ideological rearticulations that will follow, with a new *Berufsverbot* (prohibition to employ radicals) much stronger and more widespread than the one in Germany in the 1970s? These days, one often hears the sentiment that the struggle today is for democracy – true, but not quite in the way this phrase is usually intended. Already, some leftist friends of mine have told me that, in these difficult times, it is better to keep one's head down and not push ahead with our agenda. Against this temptation to weather the crisis, one should insist that *now* is the time for the Left to provide a better analysis – otherwise, it concedes in advance its political *and* ethical defeat in the face of acts of quite genuine, ordinary, popular heroism (like the passengers who, as a model of a rational ethical act, overtook the kidnappers and provoked the premature crash of one of the planes: if one is condemned to die soon, one should gather the strength and die in such a way as to prevent the deaths of others).

This very innocence is not innocent

When, in the aftermath of 11 September, Americans *en masse* rediscovered their American pride, displaying flags and singing together in public, one should emphasize more than ever that there is nothing 'innocent' about this rediscovery of American innocence, this getting rid of the sense of historical guilt or irony which prevented many of them from fully assuming being American. What this gesture amounted to was 'objectively' to assume the burden of all that being 'American' represented in the past – an exemplary case of ideological interpellation, of fully assuming one's symbolic mandate, which comes about after the perplexity caused by some historical trauma. In the traumatic aftermath of 11 September, when the old security seemed momentarily shattered, what could be a more 'natural' gesture than to take refuge in the innocence of a firm ideological identification?[4] However, it is precisely such moments of transparent innocence, of a 'return to basics', when the gesture of identification seems 'natural', that are, from the standpoint of the critique of ideology, most obscure – they are even, in a certain way, *obscurity itself*. Let us recall another such transparent moment, the endlessly repeated footage from Beijing's Avenue of Eternal Peace at the height of the 'struggles' in 1989: a young man standing on his own in front of an advancing tank, courageously trying to prevent its forward movement:

> The representation is so powerful that it demolishes all other understandings. This street scene, this time and this event, have come to constitute the compass point for virtually all Western journeys into the interior of the contemporary political and cultural life of China.[5]

Again, this very moment of supposed transparent clarity (things are rendered at their most naked: a single man against the brute force of the State) is, for our Western gaze, sustained by a cobweb of ideological assumptions, embodying a series of oppositions: individual versus State, peaceful resistance versus State violence, man versus machine, the inner force of a tiny individual versus the impotence of the powerful machine . . . These assumptions, against the background of which the scene exerted its full impact, these 'mediations' that sustain the scene's immediate effect, are *not* present for a Chinese observer, since the above-mentioned oppositions are inherent to the European ideological legacy. And the same ideological background overdetermines, say, our perception of the horrifying images of tiny individuals jumping from the burning WTC tower to their certain death.

What happened on 11 September?

So what about the phrase which now reverberates everywhere: 'Nothing will be the same after 11 September'? Significantly, this phrase is never further elaborated – it is merely a hollow attempt to say something 'deep' without really knowing what to say. So, should our first reaction not be: *Really?* Rather, is it not that the only thing that effectively changed was that America was forced to realize the kind of world to which it belongs? On the other hand, such changes in perception are never without consequences, because the way we perceive our situation determines the way we act in it. Recall the process of collapse of a political régime – for instance, the collapse of the Communist régimes in Eastern Europe in 1990: at a certain moment, people all of a sudden became aware that the game is over, that Communism is lost. The break was purely symbolic, nothing changed 'in reality' – and, nonetheless, from this moment on, the final collapse of the régime was just a question of days. What if something of the same order *did in fact* occur on 11 September?

We don't yet know what consequences this event will have in the economy, ideology, politics, war, etc., but one thing is certain: the United States, which, until now, perceived itself as an island exempted from this kind of violence, witnessing such violence only through the safe medium of the television screen, is now directly involved. So the alternative is: will Americans decide further to fortify their 'sphere', or will they risk stepping out of it? Either: America will persist in, strengthen even, the deeply *immoral* attitude of, 'Why should this happen to us? Things like this don't happen *here*!', leading to more aggressiveness toward the threatening Outside – in short, to a paranoiac acting out; or, America will finally risk stepping through the fantasmatic screen separating it from the Outside, accepting its arrival into the 'real world', making the long-overdue move from, 'A thing like this should not happen *here*!', to 'A thing like this should not happen *anywhere*!' Therein resides the true lesson of the attacks: the only way to ensure that it will not happen *here* again is to prevent it from going on *anywhere else*. In short, America should learn humbly to accept its own vulnerability as part of this world, enacting the punishment of those responsible as a sad duty, not an exhilarating retaliation.

Resisting the double blackmail

The WTC attacks confront us again with the necessity of resisting the temptation of a double blackmail. If one simply, only and unconditionally condemns the attacks, one cannot but appear to endorse the blatantly ideological position of American innocence under threat from Third World Evil; if one draws attention to the deeper socio-political causes of Arab extremism, one cannot but appear to blame the victims who ultimately got what they deserved . . . Consequently, the only solution is to reject this very opposition and to adopt both positions simultaneously, which can only be done if one resorts to the dialectical category of *totality*: there is no choice between these two positions, each is one-sided and false. Far from offering a case apropos of which one can adopt a clear ethical stance, we encounter here *the limit of moral reasoning*: from the moral standpoint, the victims are innocent, the act was an abominable crime; however, *this very innocence is not innocent* – to adopt such an 'innocent' position in today's global capitalist universe is itself a false abstraction. The same goes for the more overtly ideological clash of interpretations: one can claim that 11 September was an attack on what is worth fighting for in democratic freedom – the decadent Western way of life condemned by Muslim and other fundamentalists is the universe of women's rights and multiculturalist tolerance; however, one can also claim that it was an attack on the very centre and symbol of global financial capitalism. This, of course, in no way entails the compromise of shared guilt (terrorists are to blame, but, partially, Americans are also responsible . . .) – the point is, rather, that the two sides are not really opposed, that they belong to the same field. The fact that global capitalism is a totality means that it is the dialectical unity of itself and its other, of the forces which resist it on 'fundamentalist' ideological grounds.

Consequently, of the two possible interpretations that emerged from 11 September, *both are worse*, as Stalin would have put it. The American patriotic narrative – innocence under siege, the surge of patriotic pride – is, of course, vain; however, is the leftist narrative (with its *Schadenfreude*: the United States got what they deserved, what they had been for decades doing to others) really any better? The predominant reaction of European, but also American, leftists was nothing less than scandalous: all imaginable stupidities were said and written, up to the 'feminist' point that the WTC towers were two phallic symbols, waiting to be destroyed ('castrated'). Was there not something petty and miserable in the purely mathematical version, analogous to the contentions of holocaust revisionism (what are the 6,000 dead when compared to the millions in Rwanda, Congo, etc.)? And what about the fact that the CIA (co-)created the Taliban and bin Laden, financing and helping them to fight the Soviet forces in Afghanistan? Why was this fact cited as an argument *against* attacking them? Would it not be much more logical to claim that it is precisely their duty to destroy the monster they created? The moment one thinks in terms of the qualification, 'Yes, 11 September was a tragedy, but one should not be in full solidarity with the victims because this would mean supporting American imperialism', the ethical catastrophe has already occurred: the only appropriate stance is *unconditional solidarity with all victims*. The ethical stance proper is here replaced with the moralizing mathematics of guilt and horror which misses the key point: the terrifying death of each individual is absolute and incomparable. In short, let us attempt a simple mental experiment: if you detect in yourself any restraint towards fully empathizing with the victims of the WTC collapse, if you feel the urge to qualify your empathy with, 'Yes, but what about the millions who suffer in Africa . . .', you are not demonstrating your Third World sympathy, but merely the *mauvaise foi* which bears witness to your implicitly patronizing racist attitude towards Third World victims. (More precisely, the problem with such comparative statements is that they are necessary and inadmissible: one *has* to make them, one *has* to make the point that much worse horrors are taking place around the world on a daily basis – but one has to do so without getting entangled in the obscene mathematics of guilt.)

'Collateral damage'

It must be said that, within the scope of these two extremes (the violent retaliatory act versus the new reflection about the global situation and America's role within it), the reaction of the Western powers until now has been surprisingly considerate. (No wonder it caused the violent anti-American outburst of Ariel Sharon!) Perhaps the greatest irony of the situation is that the primary 'collateral damage' of the Western reaction is the focus on the plight of Afghani refugees, and, more generally, on the catastrophic food and health situation in Afghanistan, so that, sometimes, military action against the Taliban is almost presented as a means to guarantee safe delivery of humanitarian aid – as Tony Blair said, perhaps we will have to bomb the Taliban in order to secure the food transportation and distribution. Although, of course, such large-scale publicized humanitarian actions are in themselves ideologically charged, involving the debilitating degradation of the Afghani people to helpless victims, and reducing the Taliban to a parasite terrorizing them, it is significant to acknowledge that the humanitarian crisis in Afghanistan presents a much larger catastrophe than the WTC attacks.

The stupidity of the Left

Another way in which the Left miserably failed is that, in the weeks following the attacks, it reverted to the old mantra, 'Give peace a chance! War does not stop violence!' – a true case of hysterical precipitation, reacting to something that would not even occur in the expected form. Instead of a concrete analysis of the new complex situation after 11 September, of the chances provided to the Left to propose its own interpretation of the events, we got the stupid ritualistic chant, 'No war!', which fails to address even the elementary fact, *de facto* acknowledged by the United States government itself (through its postponing of retaliatory action), that this is not a war like others, that the bombing of Afghanistan is not a solution. A sad situation, in which George W. Bush showed more power of reflection than the majority of the Left!

'Small nationalism'

It is no wonder that anti-Americanism was most discernible in 'big' European nations, especially France and Germany: it functions as part of their resistance to globalization. One often hears the complaint that the recent trends of globalization threaten the sovereignty of Nation-States; here, however, one should qualify this statement: *which* states are most exposed to this threat? It is not the small states, but the second-rung (former) world powers, countries like the United Kingdom, Germany and France: what they fear is that, once fully immersed in the newly emerging global Empire, they will be reduced to the same level as, say, Austria, Belgium or even Luxemburg. The refusal of 'americanization' in France, shared by many leftists and rightist nationalists, is thus ultimately the refusal to accept the fact that France itself is losing its hegemonic role in Europe. The results of this refusal are often comical – at a recent philosophical colloquium, a French leftist philosopher complained how, apart from him, there are now practically no French philosophers in France: Derrida has sold out to American deconstructionism, academia is overwhelmed by Anglo-Saxon cognitivism . . . A simple mental experiment is indicative here: let us imagine someone from Serbia claiming that he is the only remaining truly Serb philosopher – he would have been immediately denounced and ridiculed as a nationalist. The levelling of importance between larger and smaller Nation-States should thus be counted among the beneficial effects of globalization: beneath the contemptuous derision of new Eastern European post-Communist states, it is easy to discern the contours of the wounded narcissism of those 'great nations' of old Europe. Here, a good dose of Lenin's sensitivity for the small nations (recall his insistence that, in the relationship between large and small nations, one should always allow for a greater degree of 'small' nationalism) would be helpful.[6] Interestingly, the same matrix was reproduced within ex-Yugoslavia: not only for the Serbs, but even for the majority of Western powers, Serbia was self-evidently perceived as the only ethnic group with enough substance to form its own state. Throughout the 1990s, even the radical democratic critics of Milošević who rejected Serb nationalism acted on the presupposition that, among ex-Yugoslav republics, it was only Serbia that had democratic potential: after overthrowing Milošević, Serbia alone could turn into a thriving democratic state, while other ex-Yugoslav nations were too 'provincial' to sustain democratic autonomy . . . does this not echo Friedrich Engels' well-known scathing remarks about how small Balkan nations are politically reactionary because their very existence is a reaction, a survival of the past?

Evil resides in the innocent gaze

America's 'holiday from history' was a fake: its peace was paid for by the catastrophes occurring elsewhere. These days, the predominant point of view is that of an innocent gaze confronting an unspeakable Evil which struck from the Outside – and, again, apropos of this gaze, one should gather the strength to bring Hegel's well-known dictum to bear on the situation: that the Evil resides (also) in the innocent gaze which perceives Evil all around itself.[7] There is thus an element of truth even in the most restrictive Moral Majority vision of a depraved America dedicated to mindless pleasures, in the conservative horror at this netherworld of sexploitation and pathological violence: what they don't get is simply the Hegelian speculative identity between this netherworld and their own position of fake purity – the fact that so many fundamentalist preachers turned out to be secret sexual perverts is more than a contingent empirical fact. When Jimmy Swaggart infamously claimed that his frequent visits to prostitutes supplied additional strength to his preaching (he knew through intimate struggle what he was preaching against), although undoubtedly hypocritical at the immediate subjective level, his claim was nonetheless *objectively true*.

'Infinite justice'

Can one imagine a greater irony than the fact that the initial codename for the first of the United States Army's operations against terrorism was 'Infinite Justice' (later changed in response to the reproach from American Islamic clerics that only God can exert infinite justice)? Taken seriously, this name is profoundly ambiguous: either it means that the Americans have the right ruthlessly to destroy not only all terrorists but also all who provided them with material, moral and ideological support (and this process will be by definition endless in the precise sense of Hegelian 'bad infinity' – the work will never really be accomplished because there will always remain some other terrorist threat . . .); or it means that the justice exerted must be truly infinite in the strict Hegelian sense, i.e., that, in relating to others, it has to relate to itself – in short, that it has to ask the question of how we ourselves, who enforce justice, are involved in what we are fighting against. When, on 22 September 2001, Jacques Derrida received the Theodor Adorno award, he made reference in his speech to the WTC attacks: 'My unconditional compassion, addressed to the victims of September 11, does not prevent me from saying it loudly: with regard to this crime, I do not believe that anyone is politically guiltless.' This self-relating, this inclusion of oneself in the picture, is the only true 'infinite justice'.

'Love thy neighbour'

In his 2000 electoral campaign, President Bush named the most important person in his life as being Jesus Christ. Now he has a unique chance to prove that he was serious: for him, as for all Americans today, 'Love thy neighbour!' means 'Love the Muslims!', *or it means nothing at all*.

Notes

Like Chapter 14, 'Against the double blackmail', and Chapter 16, 'The Iraq War – where is the true danger?', this text passed through multiple versions – from its hurried initial electronic circulations in September 2001, to the more polished version published in the spring of 2002 *(South Atlantic Quarterly* 101, 2002, pp. 385–9), before reaching its final, book-length version, *Welcome to the Desert of the Real*, London and New York, Verso, 2002. This chapter dates from 7 October 2001, and constitutes a kind of 'prolegomena towards a response to 11 September'. We have supplied all sub-headings to impose some order on the otherwise random sequence of the text. [eds]

1 Alain Badiou, *Le siècle*, Paris, Éditions du Seuil, 2005, p. 54. [eds]

2 In another case of ideological censorship: when the firemen's widows were interviewed by CNN, most of them gave the expected performance: tears, prayers . . . all except one of them who, without a tear, said that she does not pray for her deceased husband, because she knows that prayer will not get him back. When asked if she dreams of revenge, she calmly said that that would be the true betrayal of her husband: if he were to survive, he would insist that the worst thing to do is to succumb to the urge to retaliate . . . Needless to say that this fragment was only shown once and then disappeared from further repetitions of the same block.

3 Raymond Bellour, 'The obvious and the code', in *The Analysis of Film*, Bloomington, Indiana University Press, 2000, pp. 69–76.

4 See my critical elaboration of Althusser's notion of interpellation in *The Metastases of Enjoyment: Six Essays on Woman and Causality*, London and New York, Verso, 1994, pp. 57–62.

5 Michael Dutton, *Streetlife China*, Cambridge, Cambridge University Press, 1998, p. 17.

6 See, for instance, V. I. Lenin, 'The Socialist Revolution and the right of nations to self-determination', in *Selected Works, Volume 1*, Moscow, Progress Publishers, 1968, pp. 158, 163–5. [eds]

7 G. W. F. Hegel, *Phenomenology of Spirit*, trans. A. V. Miller, Oxford, Oxford University Press, 1977, pp. 401–2. [eds]

Chapter 16
The Iraq War – where is the true danger?

The borrowed kettle

We all remember the old joke about the borrowed kettle that Freud tells in order to render the strange logic of dreams:

> A. borrowed a copper kettle from B. and after he had returned it was sued by B. because the kettle now had a big hole in it which made it unusable. His defence was: 'First, I never borrowed a kettle from B. at all; secondly, the kettle had a hole in it already when I got it from him; and thirdly, I gave him back the kettle undamaged.'[1]

For Freud, such an enumeration of inconsistent arguments confirms *per negationem* what it endeavours to deny – that I returned a broken kettle to you . . . Do we not encounter the same inconsistency when high United States officials try to justify the attack on Iraq? (1) There is a link between Saddam's régime and al-Quaida, so Saddam should be punished as part of the retaliation for 11 September; (2) even if there is no link between the Iraqi régime and al-Quaida, they are united in their hatred of the United States – Saddam's régime is thus extremely dangerous, a threat not only to the United States, but also to its neighbours and the Iraqi people; (3) the change of régime in Iraq will create the conditions for the resolution of the Israeli–Palestinian conflict. The problem is that there are *too many* reasons for the attack. Furthermore, one is almost tempted to claim that, within the space of this reference to the Freudian logic of dreams, Iraqi oil acts as the famous 'umbilical cord' of the series of justification(s) – almost tempted, because it would perhaps be more reasonable to claim that there are also three *real* reasons for the attack: (1) control of the Iraqi oil reserves; (2) the urge brutally to assert and signal unconditional American hegemony; and (3) the 'sincere' ideological belief that the United States is bringing democracy and prosperity to other nations. And it seems as if these three 'real' reasons provide the 'truth' of the three official reasons: (1) the liberation of the Iraqi people is motivated by the desire to control the oil reserves; (2) the instability in the Middle East will only be resolved by the unconditional assertion of American hegemony; and (3) the connection between Iraq and al-Quaida is, in fact, *brought about* by the very attempt to bring democracy to Iraq. And, incidentally, opponents of the war seemed merely to repeat the same inconsistent logic: (1) Saddam is a tyrant, and we also want to see him toppled, but we should give the United Nations weapons inspectors more time; (2) the whole thing is a pretext for the control of oil and American hegemony – the true rogue state that terrorizes others is America itself; and (3) even if successful, the attack on Iraq will provide new impetus for a new wave of anti-American terrorism.

The only good argument for war is the one recently evoked by Christopher Hitchens: one should not forget that the majority of Iraqis effectively are Saddam's victims, and they would be genuinely glad to be rid of him.[2] He was such a catastrophe for his country that an American occupation in *whatever* form may represent a much brighter future for them in terms of day-to-day survival and general levels of fear. We are not speaking here of 'bringing Western democracy to Iraq', but simply of getting rid of the nightmare called Saddam. In the face of this majority, the caution expressed by Western liberals cannot but appear deeply hypocritical – do they really care about how the Iraqi people feel? However, it is all too easy to slip from this fact to the notion that, at bottom, 'Iraqis are just like us, and really want the same things that we do'. The old story then repeats itself: America brings new hope and democracy to a people, but, instead of hailing the American forces, the ungrateful people are suspicious of an unwanted gift within the gift; America then feels hurt because of the ingratitude of those it selflessly helped.

The underlying presupposition is an old one: beneath our skin, if we scratch the surface, we are all Americans, that is our true desire – so all that is needed is just to give people a chance, liberate them from their imposed external constraints and they will join us in our ideological dream. It is no wonder that, in February 2003, an American representative used the term 'capitalist revolution' to describe what the United States was now doing – exporting their revolution all around the world; no wonder they moved from merely 'containing' the enemy to a far more aggressive stance. It is the United States which is now, as the defunct USSR was decades ago, the subversive agent of an international revolution. So when Bush recently said, 'Freedom is not America's gift to other nations; it is God's gift to humanity', this apparent modesty nonetheless, in the best totalitarian fashion, conceals its opposite: yes, *but* it is nonetheless the United States that perceives itself as the chosen instrument of its distribution!

The idea of 'repeating Japan in 1945', of bringing democracy to Iraq, which will then serve as model for the entire Arab world, enabling people to get rid of their corrupt régimes, immediately faces an insurmountable obstacle: what about Saudi Arabia, where it is vital for the American interests in that country that it does *not* turn into a democracy? The result of democracy in Saudi Arabia would be a repetition of either Iran in 1953 (a populist régime with an anti-imperialist twist) or Algeria a couple of years ago, where 'fundamentalists' *won* the free election.

Europe and globalization I

There is a grain of truth in Rumsfeld's ironic quip against the 'old Europe'. The French–German united opposition to the United States policy apropos of Iraq should be read against the background of the recent French–German summit in which Chirac and Schröder basically proposed a kind of dual Franco–German hegemony over the European Community. So it is no wonder that anti-Americanism is at its strongest among the 'big' European nations, especially France and Germany: it is part of their resistance to globalization. One often hears the complaint that the current trends of globalization threaten the sovereignty of Nation-States; here, however, one should qualify this statement: *which* states are most exposed to this threat? It is not the small states, but the second-rung (former) world powers, countries like the United Kingdom, Germany and France: what they fear is that, once fully immersed in the newly emerging global Empire, they will be reduced to the same level as, say, Austria, Belgium, or even Luxembourg. The refusal of 'americanization' in France, shared by many leftists and rightist nationalists, is thus ultimately the refusal to accept the fact that France itself is losing its hegemonic role in Europe. The levelling of importance between larger and smaller Nation-States should thus be counted among the beneficial effects of globalization: beneath the contemptuous derision of new Eastern European post-Communist states, it is easy to discern the contours of the wounded narcissism of those 'great nations' of old Europe. And this 'great-state-nationalism' is not just a feature external to the (failure of the) present opposition; it affects the very way that France and Germany have articulated their opposition. Instead of doing, with greater urgency, precisely what the United States is doing – *mobilizing* the 'new European' states, *organizing* a new common front – France and Germany arrogantly acted alone.

Is there not a clear echo of the 'old decadent' Europe in France's resistance to the war on Iraq? One escapes the problem by inactivity, by new resolutions upon resolutions – all this reminiscent of the impotence of the League of Nations against Germany in the 1930s. But the pacifist mantra to 'let the inspectors do their work' *is*, in fact, hypocritical: they are only able to do their work because of the credible threat of military intervention. Then there is the dark role of French neo-colonialism in Africa (from Congo-Brazzaville to the Rwanda massacres) or in the Bosnian War. And is it not significant how, immediately after the commencement of the Iraq War, the same 'Europe' that opposed the war (i.e., France and Germany) adopted the attitude of, 'OK, now that war is here, let us move on to the next topic: the post-war reconstruction of Iraq' – as if to present the message, 'We performed our formal duty and opposed the war; now let us get back to business as usual!' (Not to mention Chirac's properly *racist* outbursts against post-Communist Eastern European states that supported the United States . . .) However, while everyone is complaining that the European opposition to the United States was weak and inconsequential, that

Europe failed in asserting itself as an autonomous political agent, is this very overwhelming awareness of failure not in itself a positive sign? Does it not, in a negative way, bear witness to the fact that Europe clearly perceives its lack of assertiveness as a failure?

Europe and globalization II

Is the war on Iraq not the moment of truth when 'official' political distinctions are blurred? Generally, we live in a topsy-turvy world in which Republicans freely spend money, creating record budget deficits, while Democrats practise fiscal responsibility; in which Republicans, who rage against big government and preach the devolution of power to states and local communities, are in the process of creating the strongest state mechanism of control in the entire history of humanity. And the same applies to post-Communist countries. Symptomatic here is the case of Poland: the most ardent supporter of the United States' international policy in Poland is the ex-Communist president Kwasniewski (who has even been mentioned as the future secretary of NATO, after George Robertson), while the main opposition to Poland's participation in the 'coalition of the willing' comes from the right-wing parties. Towards the end of January 2003, Polish bishops also demanded that the government add a specific paragraph to the contract which regulates Poland's membership in the European Union guaranteeing that Poland will 'retain the right to keep its fundamental values as they are formulated in its constitution' – by which they mean, of course, the prohibition of abortion, euthanasia and same-sex marriages.

The very ex-Communist countries which are the most ardent supporters of the 'war on terror' are deeply worried that their cultural identities, their very survival as nations, are threatened by the onslaught of cultural 'americanization', the price for their immersion in global capitalism – we thus witness the paradox of pro-Bush anti-Americanism. In Slovenia, my own country, there is a similar inconsistency: the rightist nationalists criticized the ruling Centre-Left coalition for publicly supporting NATO and the American campaign against terrorism, but for doing so opportunistically, not out of conviction. At the same time, however, they also reproached the ruling coalition for wanting to undermine Slovene national identity by advocating Slovenia's full integration into Western global capitalism, and thus drowning Slovenes in contemporary American pop-culture. The idea is that the ruling coalition sustains pop culture, stupid television amusement, mindless consumption, etc., in order to turn Slovenes into an easily manipulated crowd incapable of serious reflection and firm ethical positions. In other words, the underlying motif is that the activities of the ruling coalition represent a 'liberal-Communist plot': ruthless, unrestrained immersion in global capitalism is perceived as the latest strategy of ex-Communists, enabling them to retain their secret hold on power.

The almost tragic misunderstanding is that the nationalists, on the one hand, unconditionally support NATO (under the United States' command), accusing the ruling coalition of secretly supporting anti-globalization and anti-American pacifists, while, on the other hand, worrying about the fate of Slovene identity in the process of globalization, claiming that the ruling coalition wants to throw Slovenia into a global whirlpool. Ironically, the new emerging socio-ideological order these nationalist conservatives are bemoaning reads like the old 'New Left' description of 'repressive tolerance' and capitalist freedom as the mode of appearance of un-freedom. Here, the example of Italy is crucial: Berlusconi, the Italian prime minister, is *both* the staunchest supporter of the United States *and* the agent of the idiotizing (through television) of public opinion, turning politics into an on-screen spectacle and running a large advertisement and media company.

Pro et contra

Where, then, do we stand with reasons *pro et contra* the war? Abstract pacifism is intellectually stupid and morally wrong – one must oppose a threat. Of course the fall of Saddam's régime would have been a relief to a large majority of the Iraqi people. Of course militant Islam is a horrifying ideology. Of course there is something hypocritical about objections to the war (the revolt should come from the Iraqi people themselves; we should not impose our values on them; war is never a solution; etc.). *But*, although this is true, the war is wrong – and it is *who does it* that makes it wrong. The reproach should thus be: *who are you to do this*? It is not war versus peace, it is rather the correct 'gut feeling' that there is something terribly wrong with *this* war, that something will irreversibly change because of it.

One of Jacques Lacan's most outrageous statements is that, even if what a jealous husband claims about his wife (that she is sleeping around with other men) is true, his jealousy is still pathological.[3] Along the same lines, one could say that, even if most of the Nazi claims about Jews were true (that they exploit Germans, seduce German girls, etc.), their anti-Semitism would still be (and was) pathological – because the very 'truthfulness' of the claims represses the true reason *why* the Nazis *needed* anti-Semitism in order to sustain their ideological position. And the same should be said today apropos of the United States' claim that 'Saddam has weapons of mass destruction!' – even if this claim is true (and it probably is, at least to some extent), it is still false with regard to the position from which it is enunciated.

The true danger . . .

Everyone fears a catastrophic outcome to the American invasion of Iraq: an ecological catastrophe of gigantic proportions, high American casualties, further terrorist attacks in the West . . . In doing so, we have already accepted the United States' terms of reference – and it is easy to imagine how, if the war is over quickly, if Saddam's régime disintegrates, in a kind of repetition of the 1991 Gulf War, there would be a universal sigh of relief, even among the many critics of the current American policy of unilateral action. One is even tempted to propose the hypothesis that the United States is purposefully fomenting the fear of an impending catastrophe, counting on the universal relief when the catastrophe does *not* occur. This, however, is arguably the true danger of the Iraq War. That is to say, one should gather the courage to proclaim the opposite: perhaps, the American forces taking a bad military turn would be the best thing that could happen, a sobering piece of bad news which would compel all participants to rethink their positions.

The end of the 'roaring 90s'

On 11 September 2001, the Twin Towers collapsed; 12 years earlier, on 9 November 1989, the Berlin Wall fell. The latter date announced the commencement of the 'roaring 90s', Francis Fukuyama's dream of the 'end of history', the belief that liberal democracy had in principle won, that the search is over, that the advent of a global liberal world community is just around the corner, that the obstacles to this Hollywood-style happy ending are merely empirical and contingent, local pockets of resistance in which their leaders have not yet grasped that their time is over. By contrast, 11 September 2001 is the primary symbol of the end of the Clintonite 'roaring 90s', of the forthcoming era in which new walls are emerging everywhere, between Israel and the West Bank, around the European Union, on the United States–Mexican border. The prospect of a new global crisis is looming: economic collapses, military and other catastrophes, emergency states.

'The decisive moment . . .'

During the first days of the Iraq War, there was an obscene overlapping of its military and humanitarian aspects: there were complaints that Iraqi resistance in Basra was preventing the distribution of aid to Iraqis; listening to Blair and some other politicians, one would have thought that the purpose of the bombing and occupation of Iraq was to be able to dispense humanitarian aid there. And when politicians begin directly to justify their actions in such ethical terms, one can be sure that ethics is being mobilized in order to conceal the dark and threatening horizons of their activity. It is thus the very inflation of abstract ethical rhetoric in George W. Bush's recent public statements (of the 'Does the world have the courage to act against the Evil or not?' type) which manifests the utter *ethical misery* of the United States' stance – the function of an ethical reference is here purely mystifying; it merely serves to mask the true political stakes, which are not difficult to discern. In their recent *The War Over Iraq*, William Kristol and Lawrence F. Kaplan wrote:

> If America does not shape this new epoch, we can be sure that others will shape it for us . . . For the United States, then, this is the decisive moment . . . The decision about what course to take in dealing with Iraq is particularly significant because it is so clearly about more than Iraq. It is about more even than the future of the

Middle East and the war on terror. It is about what sort of role the United States intends to play in the world in the twenty-first century.[4]

One cannot but agree: it is effectively the future of the international community which is now at stake – the new rules that will regulate it, what the New World Order will be. What is going on now is thus the next logical step of the United States' dismissal of the Hague Court.

The first permanent global war crimes tribunal (the ICC) commenced on 1 July 2002 in The Hague, empowered to tackle genocide, crimes against humanity and war crimes. Anyone, from a head of state to an ordinary citizen, will be liable to ICC prosecution for human rights violations, including systematic murder, torture, rape and sexual slavery; or, as Kofi Annan put it: 'There must be a recognition that we are all members of one human family. We have to create new institutions. This is one of them. This is another step forward in humanity's slow march toward civilization.' However, while human rights groups have hailed the Court's establishment as the most important milestone for international justice since leading Nazis were tried by an international military tribunal in Nuremberg after World War II, the Court faces stiff opposition from the United States, Russia and China. The United States says the ICC infringes national sovereignty and could lead to politically motivated prosecutions of its officials or soldiers working outside American borders; the United States Congress is even considering legislation authorizing American forces to invade The Hague, in the event that prosecutors grab an American national. The noteworthy paradox here is that the United States has thus rejected the jurisdiction of a Court which was constituted with the full support (and vote) of the United States itself![5] Why, then, should Milošević, who now sits before the ICC, not be given the right to claim that, in the same way that the United States has rejected the legality of the international jurisdiction of the Court, the same argumentation should hold also for him? And the same goes for Croatia: the United States is now exerting tremendous pressure on the Croat government to deliver to the ICC a couple of its generals accused of war crimes during the struggles in Bosnia – their reaction, of course, is how can they demand this of *us* when *they* themselves refuse to recognize the legitimacy of the ICC? Or, are American citizens effectively 'more equal than others'? If one simply universalizes the underlying principles of the Bush-doctrine, does India not have full right to attack Pakistan? After all, Pakistan does directly support and harbour anti-Indian terrorists in Kashmir, and it possesses (nuclear) weapons of mass destruction. Not to mention the right of China to attack Taiwan, and so on, with unthinkable consequences . . .

The same logic of exception applies also to economic reflations. The BBC reported, on 21 December 2002, that the 'United States blocks cheap drugs agreement':

> The United States has blocked an international agreement to allow poor countries to buy cheap drugs. This means millions of poor people will still not have access to medicines for diseases such as HIV/AIDS, malaria and tuberculosis. 'One-hundred and forty-three countries stood on the same ground, we were hoping to make that unanimous.' The principle of allowing developing countries access to cheap versions of drugs still protected by copyright had been agreed at WTO talks a year ago.

The ultimate irony here is that, in the anthrax scare after 11 September, the United States exerted considerable pressure on the German company Bayer when it failed immediately to lower its prices for anti-anthrax pills.

The 'soft revolution'

Are we aware that we are in the midst of a 'soft revolution', in the course of which the unwritten rules that determine the most elementary international logic are changing? The United States scolded Gerhard Schröder, a democratically elected leader, for maintaining a stance supported by the vast majority of the German population (plus, according to the polls in mid-February 2003, by around 59 per cent of the American population itself – who opposed any strike against Iraq without UN support). In Turkey, according to opinion polls, 94 per cent of the population are opposed to the presence of United States troops in Iraq – where is democracy here? Every old leftist remembers Marx's reply in The Communist Manifesto to critics who reproached the Communists that they aim at undermining family, property, etc.: it is the capitalist order itself whose economic dynamics are destroying the traditional family order (incidentally, a fact more true today than in Marx's time), as well as expropriating a large majority of the population. In the same vein, is it not precisely that those who pose today as global defenders of democracy are effectively undermining it? In a perverse rhetorical twist, when the pro-war leaders are confronted with the brutal fact that their politics is out of tune with the majority of their population, they revert to the commonplace wisdom that, 'a true leader leads, he does not follow' – this sentiment from leaders otherwise obsessed with opinion polls!

The present crisis thus compels us to rethink democracy itself as today's master signifier. 'Democracy' is not merely the 'power of, by and for the people'; it is not enough simply to claim that, in democracy, the will and interests (the two in no way automatically coincide) of the majority determine decisions of State. Democracy – in the way the term is used today – concerns, above all, *formal legality*: its minimal definition is the unconditional adherence to a certain set of formal rules which guarantee that antagonisms are fully absorbed into the agonistic game. 'Democracy' means that, whatever electoral manipulation takes place, every political agent will unconditionally respect the results. In this sense, the American presidential elections of 2000 were effectively 'democratic': despite obvious electoral manoeuvrings, and the patent meaninglessness of the fact that a few hundred Floridian voices will decide who will be the President, the Democratic candidate accepted his defeat. In the weeks of uncertainty following the elections, Bill Clinton made an appropriately acerbic comment: 'The American people have spoken; we just don't know what they said.' This comment should be taken more seriously than it was intended: even now, we don't know what the American people said – and, maybe, it is because there was no substantial 'message' behind the result at all. This is the sense in which one should render democracy problematic: why should the Left always and unconditionally respect the formal, democratic 'rules of the game'? Why should it not, in some circumstances, at least, call into question the legitimacy of the outcome of a formal democratic procedure? Interestingly enough, there is at least one scenario in which formal democrats themselves (or, at least, a substantial portion of them) would tolerate the suspension of democracy: what if a 'free election' was won by an antidemocratic party whose platform promised the abolition of formal democracy? (This did happen, among other places, in Algeria a couple of years ago.) In such a case, many a democrat would concede that the people were not yet 'mature enough' to be entrusted with democracy, and that some kind of enlightened despotism, whose aim would be to educate the majority into proper democrats, is preferable. A crucial component of any populism is also the dismissal of the formal democratic procedure: even if its rules are still respected, it is always emphasized that they do not provide the necessary legitimacy to political agents – populism rather evokes the direct pathetic link between charismatic leadership and the crowd, verified through plebiscites and mass gatherings.

The true dangers of the Iraq War are thus the long-term ones. In what resides perhaps the greatest danger of the prospect of the American occupation of Iraq? The present régime in Iraq is ultimately a secular nationalist one, out of touch with Muslim fundamentalist populism – it is obvious that Saddam only superficially flirts with pan-Arab Islamic sentiment. As his past clearly demonstrates, he is a pragmatic ruler who strives for power, shifting alliances whenever it suits his purposes – first with the United States against Iran in order to seize their oil fields, then against Kuwait for the same reason, pitting himself against a pan-Arab coalition allied to the United States. What Saddam is *not* is a fundamentalist obsessed with the 'great Satan', ready to destroy the world just to strike at him. However, what now *can* emerge as the result of the American occupation is precisely a truly fundamentalist Muslim anti-American movement, directly linked to such movements in other Arab countries or countries with a strong Muslim presence. The ultimate politico-ideological outcome of the Iraq War may well turn out to be the elevation of Saddam, this despicable tyrant who brought ruin to his country, to the status of a Third World and Muslim legend, the hero of resistance against the superior United States Army . . .

One can surmise that the United States is well aware that Saddam's era in Iraq and his non-fundamentalist régime is coming to an end, and that the attack on Iraq probably represents a far more radical pre-emptive strike – not against Saddam, but against the main contender for his political successor, a truly fundamentalist Islamic régime. In this way, the vicious cycle of American intervention gets even more complex: the danger is that this very American intervention will contribute to the emergence of what America most fears, namely, a united anti-American

Muslim front. Iraq is the first case of a direct American occupation of a large and significant Arab state – how could this not generate an almost universal hatred in response? One can already imagine thousands of young people dreaming of becoming suicide bombers, and the way that will force the United States government to impose a permanent 'high alert' emergency state. However, at this point, one cannot resist a slightly paranoid temptation: what if the people around Bush *know* this, what if this 'collateral damage' is the true aim of the entire operation? What if the *true* target of the 'war on terror' is American society itself, i.e., the disciplining of its emancipatory excesses?

On 5 March 2003, on the 'Buchanan & Press' news programme on NBC, there appeared a photo of the recently captured Khalid Shakh Mohammed, the 'third man of al-Quaida' – a mean, moustached-face, dressed in an indeterminate nightgown-like prison uniform, half opened and with something like half-discernible bruises (hints that he had already been tortured?) – while Pat Buchanan's rapid voice was asking, 'Should this man, who knows all the names, all the detailed plans for future terrorist attacks on the United States, be tortured, so that we get all this out of him?' The horror of it was that the photo, with its details, already suggested its own answer – no wonder the response of other commentators and the calls of viewers was an overwhelming 'Yes!' – this makes one nostalgic for the good old days of the colonial war in Algeria, when the torture practised by the French army was a dirty secret. In effect, was this not a close realization of what Orwell imagined in *Nineteen Eighty-Four*, in his vision of 'hate sessions', in which citizens are shown photos of traitors, and are supposed to boo and yell at them? But the story goes on: a day later, on Fox TV, a commentator claimed that one should be allowed to do with this prisoner whatever is necessary – not only to deprive him of sleep, but to break his fingers, etc. – because he is 'a piece of human garbage with no rights whatsoever'. *This* is the true catastrophe: that such public statements are possible today.

We should therefore be very careful not to fight false battles: the debates on how bad Saddam is, even on how much the war will cost, are false debates. The focus should be on what effectively is occurring in our societies, on what kind of society is emerging *here* as a result of the 'war on terror'. Instead of talking about hidden conspiratorial agendas, one should shift the focus on to what is happening, what kinds of changes are taking place here and now. The ultimate result of this war will be a change in *our* political order.

Right-populism with a human face

The danger represented by the Iraq War can best be exemplified by the actual role of the populist Right in Europe – namely, to introduce certain topics (like the foreign threat, the necessity of limiting immigration, etc.) that could then be silently taken over not only by conservative parties, but even by the *de facto* politics of 'socialist' governments. Today, the need to 'regulate' the status of immigrants, etc., is part of the mainstream consensus: as the story goes, Le Pen *did*, in fact, address and exploit actual problems that concern people. One is almost tempted to say that, if there were no Le Pen in France, he would have been invented: he is the perfect example of a person one loves to hate, the hatred of whom guarantees the wide liberal 'democratic pact', the pathetic identification with democratic values of tolerance and respect for diversity. However, after shouting, 'Le Pen is horrible! How dark and uncivilized! This is wholly unacceptable! It is a threat to our basic democratic values!', the outraged liberals then proceed to act like 'Le Pen with a human face', to do the same thing in a more 'civilized' way, along the lines of, 'Nevertheless, the racist populists are manipulating the legitimate worries of ordinary people, so we do have to take some measures . . .'

What we have here is a kind of perverted Hegelian 'negation of negation': in a first negation, the populist Right disturbs the aseptic liberal consensus by giving voice to passionate dissent, clearly arguing against the 'foreign threat'; in a second negation, the 'decent' democratic centre, in the very gesture of pathetically rejecting this populist Right, integrates its message in a 'civilized' way – between these two moments, the *entire field* of 'unwritten rules' has already changed to the extent that no one even notices and everyone is simply relieved that the anti-democratic threat is over. And the true danger is that something similar will happen apropos of the 'war on terror': so-called 'extremists' like John Ashcroft will be discarded, but their legacy will remain, imperceptibly interwoven into the invisible ethical fabric of our societies. Their defeat will be their ultimate triumph: they will no longer be needed, since their message will have been incorporated into the mainstream.

Notes

Unlike the previous chapter, whose initial associative qualities were eventually translated into more precise, book-length form, this text (dated 23 April 2003) never lost its original character: it began as a related series of impressions on the Iraq War, and its inevitable book version (*Iraq: The Borrowed Kettle*, London and New York, Verso, 2004) retains the same formal quality. In the introduction to the book, Žižek attempts to thematize this very fact: 'The hidden literary model for this book is what I consider E. L. Doctorow's masterpiece, the supreme exercise in literary post modernism, far superior to his bestselling *Ragtime*, or *Billy Bathgate*: his *Lives of the Poets: Six Stories and a Novella* – six totally heterogeneous short stories . . . accompanied by a novella which conveys the confused impressions of the day-to-day life of a writer in contemporary New York who, as we soon guess, is the author of the six stories. The charm of the book is that we can reconstruct the process of the artistic working-through of the raw material of this day-to-day life. In the same way, the main chapter of *Iraq: The Borrowed Kettle* is a *bric-à-brac* of the author's immediate impressions and reactions to the unfolding story of the US attack on Iraq, followed by two appendices which provide more consistent theoretical analyses distilled from the immediate reactions to the Iraqi war.' (p. 7) . . . Once again, we have supplied all sub-headings to suggest some sequence to the text. [eds]

1　Sigmund Freud, *The Penguin Freud Library, 6: Jokes and their Relation to the Unconscious*, ed. and trans. James Strachey, Harmondsworth, Penguin, 1976, p. 100. [eds]

2　Christopher Hitchens, *Régime Change*, London, Penguin, 2003, pp. 49–56. [eds]

3　See Jacques Lacan, *The Seminar of Jacques Lacan III: The Psychoses, 1955–56*, ed. Jacques-Alain Miller, trans. Russell Grigg, New York and London, W. W. Norton, 1993, pp. 76–7. [eds]

4　William Kristol and Lawrence F. Kaplan, *The War Over Iraq: Saddam's Tyranny and America's Mission*, San Francisco, Encounter, 2003, pp. vii–viii. [eds]

5　At this point, one should even not be afraid to ask the naïve question: the United States as a global policeman – why not? The post-Cold War situation effectively calls for some global power to fill the void. The real problem resides elsewhere: recall the common perception of the United

States as a new Roman Empire. *The problem with the United States today is not that it represents a new global Empire, but that it does not, i.e., that, while pretending to be Imperial, it continues to act as a Nation-State, ruthlessly pursuing its own interests.* It is as if the guidelines for America's recent international politics were a kind of weird reversal of the well-known 'Green' motto: *act globally, think locally.*

Chapter 17

Some politically incorrect reflections on violence in France and related matters

Two parallels are often evoked in relation to the recent outbursts of violence in France: the looting that took place in New Orleans in the aftermath of Hurricane Katrina, and the student riots that shook Paris in May 1968. Despite their considerable differences, lessons can nonetheless be drawn from both. With respect to the first, the Paris fires had a sobering effect on those European intellectuals who used New Orleans to emphasize the advantage of the European welfare state model over the rampant capitalism of the USA. They had to acknowledge that such a thing can happen *here* as well. And those who attributed the violence in New Orleans to the lack of European-style solidarity are no less mistaken than the American free-market liberals who now gleefully demonstrate that it was the rigidity of state interventionism – which limits competition and regulates the market dynamics – that stymied the economic prosperity of marginalized immigrants in France (in contrast to the USA, where many immigrant groups are among the most successful).

On the other hand, what is particularly striking in the comparison between the most recent Parisian riots and those in May '68 is the current absence of any positive utopian prospect among the protesters: if May '68 was a revolt fuelled by a utopian vision, these riots are merely outbursts without any pretence of some positive content. There were not even any particular demands made by in the rioters in Paris, just an insistence on *recognition* based on a vague, unarticulated, *ressentiment*: most of those interviewed referred to how unacceptable were the comments of the interior minister, Nicolas Sarkozy, who called them 'scum' (i.e., in a weird self-referential short-circuit, they protested against the very reaction to their protests). It is here that 'populist reason' encounters its irrational limit: it is a 'zero-level' protest, a violent act that demands nothing.[1] It is therefore not without irony to observe the way that various sociologists – 'bleeding heart' intellectuals eager to understand their plight – desperately tried to confer 'meaning' on to the protests ('we have to do something about the integration of immigrants, about welfare, job opportunities . . .'), thereby obfuscating the central enigma: these protesters, although effectively underprivileged, *de facto* excluded and so on, were in no way living on the edge of survival. People living in far worse material conditions and under severe physical or ideological oppression have been able to organize themselves as political agents with a clear – or not so clear – programme. The fact that there was *no programme*, no organization to the Paris riots is thus itself a fact to be interpreted: it says a great deal about our own ideologico-political predicament. What does it say about the socio-political universe in which we now live, which hails itself as a society of choice, but in which the only alternative to the enforced democratic consensus is a blind *passage à l'acte*? Is this sad fact – that opposition to the system cannot articulate itself in the form of a realistic alternative, or at least some meaningful utopian project, but only as a meaningless outburst of violence – not the strongest indictment of our predicament? Where is our celebrated freedom of choice, when the only choice is between playing by the rules and (self-)destructive violence, a violence that is almost exclusively directed against one's own interests (the cars and schools that were torched were not from rich neighbourhoods but the hard-won acquisitions of the very strata from which the protesters originated)?

The true aim of these riots was thus not to protest against an actual socio-economic condition; even less did they represent some kind of assertion of Islamic fundamentalism (one of the first objects burned, apart from a social welfare office, was a mosque, which is why the Muslim religious bodies immediately condemned the violence). Rather, they were a desperate effort simply to gain *visibility*. A social group that, though part of France and composed of French citizens, experienced itself as excluded from the political and social space proper, and wanted to render its presence palpable to the general public: *whether or not you want to admit it, no matter how much you pretend not to see us, we are here* . . . That is to say, commentators failed to note the crucial fact that the protesters did not claim for themselves the special status of a particular (religious or ethnic) community that is striving for its own self-enclosed way of life; on the contrary, their main premise was that they want to be, and in fact *are*, French citizens, but are not fully recognized as such. Alain Finkelkraut created a scandal in France when, in an interview for *Ha'aretz*, he described the current unrest as an 'anti-republican pogrom' and 'an ethnic-religious revolt', thereby totally missing the point: the message of the riots was not that the protesters found their ethnic-religious identity threatened by French republican universalism, but, on the contrary, that they were not included within it, that they found themselves on the wrong side of the frontier that separates the visible from the invisible part of the republican social space. They were neither offering a solution nor constituting a movement that demanded a solution; on the contrary, it was their sole aim to create a problem, to signal that they are an issue that can no longer be ignored. This is what made the violence necessary: had they simply organized a non-violent march, the most they would have received would have been a small note on the bottom of the page in a newspaper.

Recall the old joke about a man suspected of smuggling: every day for twenty years a man pushed a wheelbarrow full of sand across the border-crossing. The customs inspector would dig through the sand but never discovered any illegal goods. He nevertheless remained convinced that he was dealing with a smuggler. On the last day before his retirement, the inspector asked the smuggler what he had been smuggling all these years and how he did it. The man replied, of course, that he had been smuggling wheelbarrows. Does the same not hold for the Paris riots? These well-meaning sociologists were searching for the meaning behind the violence, all the while missing the obvious point – i.e., that, as Marshall McLuhan would have put it, the medium itself is the message: we are dealing with a case of what

Roman Jakobson called 'phatic communication', in which the meaning of the act *is* the act of communication as such, the establishment of a link, the rendering visible of the speaker. At this point, one is even tempted to speculate on the appeal that fascism might have had for these protesters: one should not forget that the first pacifying gesture made by Hitler (indeed, by fascism generally) was to guarantee each social group that their specific place within the social edifice, and thus their dignity, would be recognized, that they should be proud of their contribution to the smooth functioning of the social whole, and in this way would counteract the threat of those who experience themselves as 'part of no-part'. This, perhaps, was the hidden meaning of Chirac's assertion that the crisis was effectively a 'crisis of meaning [*une crise du sens*]'. (I am not, of course, implying that the riots were 'proto-fascist': the point is just that fascism is ultimately always a reaction to a potential emancipatory event, a 'failed revolution'.)

This brings us back to Alain Badiou's suggestion that our social space is increasingly experienced as 'worldless' – in such a space, the only form protest can take is that of 'meaningless' violence. Even Nazi anti-Semitism opened up a 'world': by describing the present critical situation, by naming the enemy (the 'Jewish conspiracy'), the goal and the means of overcoming it (the 'final solution'), Nazism constructed reality in such a way that it allowed its subjects to achieve a global 'cognitive mapping', inclusive of the space for their meaningful engagement. Perhaps it is here that one should locate the true danger of capitalism: although it is global, encompassing the entire world, it sustains a *stricto sensu* 'worldless' ideological constellation, depriving the large majority of people of any meaningful 'cognitive mapping'. Capitalism is the first socio-economic order that *de-totalizes meaning*: it is not global at the level of meaning (there is no global 'capitalist worldview', no 'capitalist civilization' proper – the fundamental lesson of globalization is precisely that capitalism can accommodate itself to all civilizations, from Christian to Hindu and Buddhist); its global dimension can only be formulated at the level of a truth-without-meaning, as the 'Real' of the global market economy. Consequently, insofar as capitalism already enacts the rupture between meaning and truth, it can be opposed at two levels: either at the level of meaning (those conservative attempts to re-frame capitalism within some social field of meaning, to contain its self-propelling movement within the confines of a system of shared 'values' that bind a community in its 'organic unity'), or to question the Real of capitalism with regard to its truth-outside-meaning (this was, essentially, Marx's aim).[2] It thus becomes clear that the injunction, the 'ideological interpellation', proper to global capitalism is no longer that of sacrificial devotion to a Cause, but, in contrast to previous modes of ideological interpellation, the reference to an obscure unnameable – '*Enjoy!*' (in all its modes, from the most perverse sexual gratification to the most ethereal mystical self-realization).

The first conclusion to be drawn from this is that both the conservative and liberal reactions to the Paris riots clearly failed. The conservatives emphasized the 'clash of civilizations' and, predictably, the need for law and order: immigrants should not abuse our hospitality, they are our guests, so they should respect our customs; our society has the right to safeguard its unique culture and way of life (plus, there is no excuse for crimes and violent behaviour; what young immigrants need is not more welfare but discipline and hard work . . .) Leftist liberals, no less predictably, maintained their old mantra about neglected social programmes and failed integration efforts which are depriving the younger generation of immigrants of any clear economic prospects, thus leaving violent outbursts as the only way for them to articulate their dissatisfaction. As Stalin would have put it, it is meaningless to debate which of these responses is worse: they are *both* worse, inclusive of the warning, formulated by both sides, that the real danger of these outbursts was the predictably racist or populist reaction of the French crowd.

The Fundamentalist Impasse

So what can a philosopher do at this point? One should bear in mind that the philosopher's task is not to propose solutions, but to reformulate the problem itself, to shift the ideological framework within which we have hitherto perceived the problem. Perhaps a good starting point would be to place the recent outbursts into the series they constitute with two other types of violence that the liberal majority today perceives as threats to our way of life: (1) direct 'terrorist' attacks; (2) Rightist populist violence; and (3) suburban juvenile 'irrational' outbursts.

The first step of our analysis is to confront each of these modes of violence with its opposite or supposedly preventative measure: the counter-pole to 'terrorism' is the USA's neo-colonial doctrine of global policing; the counter-pole to Rightist populist violence is welfare state control and regulation; the counter-pole to juvenile outbursts is the anonymous violence of the capitalist system. In all three instances, violence and counter-violence are caught in a deadly vicious cycle, each generating the very opposite it tries to overcome. Furthermore, what all three modes share, in spite of their fundamental differences, is the logic of a blind *passage à l'acte*: in each case, violence is an implicit admission of impotence.

So, let us begin with the problem of fundamentalism – who, in fact, *are* fundamentalists? To put it simply, a fundamentalist does not *believe* in something, but rather *knows* it directly. In other words, both liberal-sceptical cynicism and fundamentalism share a basic underlying feature: the loss of the ability to believe in the proper sense of the term. For both of them, religious statements are quasi-empirical statements of direct knowledge: fundamentalists accept these statements as such, while sceptics mock them. What is unthinkable for both is the 'absurd' act of a *decision* which installs every authentic belief, a decision that cannot be grounded in the chain of 'reason', in positive knowledge: take the 'sincere hypocrisy' of somebody like Anne Frank who, in the face of the terrifying depravity of the Nazis, in a true act of *credo qua absurdum*, asserted her belief in the fundamental goodness of all humans. It is no wonder that religious fundamentalists are among the most passionate computer hackers, and are always prone to combine their religious stance with the latest scientific findings: for them, religious and scientific statements belong to the same order of positive knowledge. (In this sense, the status of 'universal human rights' is also that of pure belief: they cannot be grounded in one's knowledge of human nature, and are thus an axiom posited by our decision.) One would thus risk the following paradoxical conclusion: in the opposition between traditional secular humanists and religious fundamentalists, it is the humanists who stand for belief, while fundamentalists stand for knowledge – in short, the true danger of fundamentalism does not reside in the fact that it poses a threat to secular scientific knowledge, but in the fact that it poses a threat to authentic belief itself.

We should bear in mind here the way that the opposition between knowledge and faith echoes the one between the 'constative' and the 'performative': faith (or, rather, trust) is the basic ingredient of speech as the medium of the social link, of the subject's engaged participation in this link, while science – exemplarily in its formalization – reduces language to neutral register. Let us not forget that science has, for Lacan, the status of a 'knowledge in the Real [*savoir dans le réel*]':[3] the language of science is not the language of subjective engagement, but language deprived of its performative dimension, de-subjectivized language. The predominance of scientific discourse entails the retreat, the suspension, of the very symbolic function as the metaphor constitutive of human subjectivity. The hegemony of scientific discourse thus potentially suspends the entire network of symbolic traditions that sustain the subject's identifications.

The 'worldless' character of capitalism is linked to the hegemonic role of scientific discourse in modernity (a feature already identified by Hegel who wrote that, for us, art and religion no longer command absolute respect: we admire them, but we no longer kneel down before them – today, only science [conceptual knowledge] is deserving of this respect[4]): the growing suspension of the 'performative' aspect of the symbolic order curtails the subject's full engagement in a symbolic universe ('world'), which provides the horizon of meaning for its experience – instead of symbolic identification, the subject is increasingly reliant on the obscure superego demand for an unnameable *jouissance*.

'Postmodernity', as the 'end of grand narratives', is but one of the names for this predicament, in which an imaginary multitude of local fictions thrives against the background of scientific discourse as the only remaining universality, though deprived of meaning. This is why the politics advocated by many on the Left today – that of countering the devastating world-dissolving effect of capitalist modernization by inventing new fictions, imagining 'new worlds' (like the Porto Allegre slogan, 'A new world is possible!') – is not only insufficient but at best profoundly ambiguous: it all depends on how these fictions relate to the underlying Real of capitalism: do they just supplement it with imaginary multitude, as in the case of postmodern 'local narratives', or do they *disturb* its functioning? In other words, the true task today is to produce *a symbolic fiction (a truth) that intervenes in the Real*.

We can also see how wrong the Left is in its reproach that Lacan fetishized the Symbolic into a quasi-transcendental Order: as was already clear to Lacan back in 1938, when he wrote his *Les complexes familiaux dans le formation de l'individu*, the very birth of psychoanalysis is linked to the crisis and disintegration of what he then called the 'paternal image' – or, as he was to put it decades later, the subject of psychoanalysis is none other than the Cartesian subject of modern science.[5] And to those who misread this diagnosis as implying a call – or, at least, nostalgia – for the good old days when paternal authority remained uncontested and fully functional, let us recall that, for Lacan, the crisis of paternal authority that gave birth to psychoanalysis is *stricto sensu* symptomal: it represents the unique point of exception that allows us to formulate the underlying universal Law.

It is thus only psychoanalysis that can fully disclose the contours of the shattering impact of modernity (in both of its aspects – the hegemony of scientific discourse and capitalism) on the way our identity is performatively grounded in symbolic identifications, on the way we rely on the symbolic order to constitute the horizon that allows us to locate every experience within a meaningful totality. The necessary obverse of modernity is the 'crisis of meaning' (to evoke Chirac), the disintegration of the link – identity even – between Truth and Meaning. Because, in Europe, modernization was spread over centuries, we had the time to accommodate to this rupture, to soften its shattering impact through *Kulturarbeit*, through the formation of new social narratives and myths; by contrast, other societies – particularly Muslim – were exposed to this impact directly, without a protective screen or temporal delay, so that their symbolic universe was arrested even more brutally, such that they lost their (symbolic) ground with no chance to establish a new (symbolic) balance. It is no wonder, then, that the only way for some of these societies to avoid total disintegration was to erect the panic shield of 'fundamentalism', the psychotic-delirious-incestuous reassertion of religion as direct insight into the divine Real, with all the terrifying consequences that such a reassertion entails, up to the vengeful return of the obscene superego divinity who demands sacrifice.

The Terrorist *Ressentiment*

As to the 'terrorist' attacks of fundamentalists, the first thing to observe is the inadequacy of the idea, developed most systematically by Donald Davidson, that human acts are rational-intentional, accountable in terms of the beliefs and desires of the agent.[6] This approach is typical of the racist bias of theories of 'rationality': while their aim is to understand the motives and intentions of the Other (to walk in their shoes, as it were), these theories end up attributing to the Other the most ridiculous beliefs (up to the infamous 72 virgins awaiting the martyr in Paradise as the 'rational' explanation for his willingness to blow himself up) – i.e., they make the Other preposterously weird in the very effort to try to make them 'comprehensible'. Take, for instance, the following passage from one of the propaganda texts distributed by North Korea during the Korean War:

> Hero Kang Ho-yung was seriously wounded in both arms and both legs in the Kamak Hill Battle, so he rolled into the midst of the enemy with a hand grenade in his mouth and wiped them out, shouting: 'My arms and legs were broken. But on the contrary my retaliatory spirit against you scoundrels became a thousand times stronger. I will show the unbending fighting will of a member of the Workers' Party of Korea and unflinching will firmly pledged to the Party and the Leader!'[7]

Although it is easy to laugh at the ridiculously non-realistic character of this description (how could poor Kang talk if he was holding a grenade in his mouth? and how is it that, in the midst of a fierce battle, there was time for such a long oration?), the true mistake is to read this passage as a realistic description, thus imputing ridiculous beliefs to the Koreans. If directly asked, it is clear how a North Korean would respond: of course this story is not literally true, but is meant simply to render the unconditional spirit of sacrifice and readiness of the Korean people to do the impossible in order to defeat the imperialist aggressors on their land. Why not regard this passage – which sounds operatic in its pathos – in the same way that we would Act III of Wagner's *Tristan*, in which the mortally wounded Tristan sings his (extremely demanding) dying chant for almost an hour? Who among us is prepared to impute to Wagner the belief that such a scenario is possible? Can we not effectively imagine Kang singing an aria before rolling under the tank – in that properly operatic moment in which the flow of real time is suspended, and when, in song, the hero reflects on what he is about to do?

The perplexing fact about 'terrorist' acts of violence is that they do not fit our standard opposition of Evil as egotism, as disregard for the common Good, and Good as the spirit of sacrifice for some higher Cause. Terrorists cannot but appear as somehow akin to Milton's Satan, with his 'Evil, be thou my Good': while they pursue (what appears to us to be) evil goals through evil means, the very *form* of their activity meets the highest ethical standard of the Good. The resolution of this enigma is simple, one that was already familiar to Rousseau: egotism (the concern for one's well-being) is not opposed to common Good, because altruistic norms can easily be deduced from egotistic concerns.[8] Individualism versus communitarianism, utilitarianism versus universal normativism are thus *false* oppositions, because the two opposed poles are identical in terms of their result. Critics who complain that authentic values are absent from today's hedonistic-egotistic society totally miss the point: the true opposite of egotistic self-love is not altruism, concern for common Good, but envy, *ressentiment*, which makes me act *against* my own interests. Freud, of course, was already aware of this: death drive is opposed to the pleasure principle as well as to the reality principle – i.e., true 'Evil' (death drive) involves self-sabotage. Dupuy is thus wrong in his characterization of Lacanian psychoanalysis as part of the ongoing 'mechanization of the mind'.[9] Psychoanalysis, on the contrary, *reintroduces* notions of Evil and responsibility into our ethical vocabulary: 'death drive' is the name for what *disturbs* the homeostatic mechanism of rational pleasure-seeking, the weird reversal in which I sabotage my own interests. If *this* is the true Evil, then even this 'mechanization of the mind' in cognitive sciences should be conceived as not itself 'evil', but as a *defence* against Evil.

The problem with human desire is that, as Lacan put it, it is always a 'desire of the Other', in the senses both of *genitivus subjectivus* and *genitivus objectivus*: desire for the Other, desire to be desired by the Other, and, especially, desire for what the Other desires. Envy and *ressentiment* are thus constitutive components of human desire, as Augustine knew so well – recall the passage from his *Confessions*, often quoted by Lacan, in which he describes a baby jealous of his brother sucking at the mother's breast: 'I have personally watched and studied a jealous baby. He could not speak and, pale with jealousy and bitterness, glared at his brother sharing his mother's milk.'[10]

Based on this insight, Dupuy proposes a convincing critique of John Rawls' theory of justice: in the Rawlsian model of a just society, social inequalities are tolerated only insofar as they also assist those at the bottom of the social ladder, and insofar as they are based not on inherited hierarchies but on natural inequalities which are considered contingent, not meritorious.[11] What Rawls fails to observe is the way that such a society would create the conditions for an uncontrolled explosion of *ressentiment*: in such a society, I would know that my lower social status is fully 'justified', and would thus be deprived of the ability to excuse my failures as the result of social injustice. Rawls proposes the terrifying model of a society in which hierarchy is *directly* legitimized by natural properties, thereby missing the simple lesson of an anecdote about a Slovene peasant who is given a choice by a benevolent witch: she will either give him one cow and his neighbour two cows, or take from him one cow and from his neighbour two cows – the peasant immediately chooses the second option. (In a more morbid version, the witch tells him: 'I will do to you whatever you wish, but I warn you, I will do it to your neighbour twice!' The peasant, with a cunning smile, tells her, 'Take one of my eyes!'.) It is no wonder that even today's conservatives are ready to endorse Rawls' notion of justice: on 8 November 2005, David Cameron, the newly elected leader of the British Tories, signalled his intention to turn the Conservative Party into a defender of the underprivileged, declaring that, 'I think the test of all our policies should be: what does it do for the people who have the least, the people on the bottom rung of the ladder?'

As Friedrich Hayek observed, it is much easier to accept inequalities if one can claim that they result from a blind, impersonal force.[12] The good thing about the 'irrationality' of market success or failure within capitalism (recall Marx's comparison between the inscrutable market dynamics and the ancient conception of Fate[13]) is that it allows me to perceive my failure (or success) as undeserved, and thus contingent. The fact that capitalism is not 'just' is thus a key feature that makes it palatable to the majority of people – I can accept my failure much more easily if I know that it is not due to my inferior qualities but to chance.

What Nietzsche and Freud share is the idea that justice *qua* equality is founded on envy – envy of the Other who has what we do not have, and who is enjoying it. The demand for justice is thus ultimately the demand that the excessive enjoyment of the Other should be curtailed, so that everyone's access to *jouissance* should be equal. The necessary outcome of this demand, of course, is asceticism: because it is not possible to impose an equal measure of *jouissance*, what one *can* impose is an equal deprivation through a shared *prohibition*. However, one should not forget that today, in our allegedly permissive society, this asceticism assumes precisely the form of its opposite, that of the generalized superego injunction to 'Enjoy!' We are all under the rule of this injunction, with the result that our enjoyment is more hindered than ever – just think of the yuppie who combines narcissistic 'self-fulfilment' with the utterly ascetic disciplines of jogging, eating health food and so on. This, perhaps, is what Nietzsche had in mind with his notion of the Last Man: it is only today that we can truly discern the contours of the Last Man in the guise of yuppie hedonistic asceticism. Nietzsche thus did not simply urge life-assertion against asceticism: he was well aware that a certain asceticism is the obverse of decadent excessive sensuality, and therein resides his criticism of Wagner's *Parsifal* and, more generally, of late Romantic decadence, which oscillated between damp sensuality and obscure spiritualism.

So what exactly is envy? Recall once again the Augustinian scene of a sibling envying his brother who is suckling the mother's breast: the subject does not envy the Other's possession of the prized object as such, but rather the way the Other is able to *enjoy* this object. This is why it is not enough for him simply to steal, and thus gain possession of, the object: his true aim is to destroy the Other's ability to enjoy the object. As such, envy is to be located within the triad of envy, thrift and melancholy – the three forms of *not* being able to enjoy the object (and, reflexively, of enjoying this very impossibility). In contrast to the subject of envy, who envies the Other's possession and/or enjoyment of the object, the miser possesses the object but cannot enjoy it – his satisfaction derives merely from possessing it, elevating it into a sacred, untouchable entity, which should under no conditions be consumed. This very hindrance that prevents the consumption of the object guarantees its status as the object of desire. The melancholic subject, like the miser, possesses the object but has lost the cause that made him desire it in the first place: this figure, the most tragic of them all, has free access to everything he wants, but finds no satisfaction in anything.

This excess of envy is the basis of Rousseau's well-known distinction, from his first dialogue, between egotism, *amour de soi*, and *amour-propre*, the perverted preference of oneself to others in which I focus not on achieving the goal, but on destroying the obstacle to it:

The primitive passions, which all directly tend toward our happiness, make us deal only with objects which relate to them, and whose principle is only *amour de soi*, are all in their essence lovable and tender; however, when, diverted from their objects by obstacles, they are more occupied with the obstacle they try to get rid of than with the object they try to reach, they change their nature and become irascible and hateful. This is how *amour de soi*, which is a noble and absolute feeling, becomes *amour-propre*, that is to say, a relative feeling by means of which one compares oneself, a feeling which demands preferences, whose enjoyment is purely negative and which does not strive to find satisfaction in our own well-being, but only in the misfortune of others.[14]

For Rousseau, an evil person is *not* an egotist, 'thinking only about his own interests': a true egotist is too busy with taking care of his own good to have time to cause misfortune to others, while the primary vice of an evil person is precisely that he is more occupied with others than with himself. Rousseau describes here a precise libidinal mechanism: the inversion that generates the shift of the libidinal investment *from* the object *to* the obstacle itself. Far from being opposed to the spirit of sacrifice, Evil is thus the very spirit of sacrifice, the readiness to ignore one's own well-being ('if, through my sacrifice, I can deprive the Other of his *jouissance* . . .').

This is why the notion of *evaluation* is crucial for the functioning of a democratic society: if, at the level of their symbolic identity, all subjects are equal, if, at this point, *un sujet vaut l'autre*, if they can indefinitely be substituted one for another, since each of them is reduced to an empty punctual place, to a 'man without qualities-properties' (to recall the title of Robert Musil's *magnum opus*) – if, consequently, every reference to their properly symbolic mandate is prohibited – how then, are they to be distributed within the social edifice, how can their occupations be legitimized? The answer, of course, is *evaluation*:

one must evaluate – as objectively as possible, and through all possible means, from the quantified testing of their abilities to more 'personalized' in-depth interviews – their relative potential. The ideal behind this notion is to produce characterizations that exclude all traces of their symbolic identities.[15] Here the standard Leftist criticism of the hidden cultural bias of evaluations completely misses the point: the problem with evaluation, with its total objectification of criteria, is not that it is unjust, but precisely that it *is* just.

What this means is that the 'deconstructionist' or 'risk society' commonplace – according to which the contemporary individual experiences himself as thoroughly de-naturalized, with even their most 'natural' features (from his ethnic identity to their sexual preferences) experienced as things that are chosen, historically contingent, and thus to be learned – is profoundly deceptive: what we are effectively witnessing today is the opposite process of an unheard of *re-naturalization*: all of the major 'public issues' are (re)translated into questions about the regulation of intimate, natural or even 'personal' idiosyncrasies. This is also why, at a more general level, pseudo-naturalized ethnic-religious conflicts are the form of struggle most appropriate to global capitalism: in our age of 'post-politics', when politics proper is progressively being replaced by expert social administration, the only remaining legitimate source of conflict is cultural (religious) or natural (ethnic) tensions. So, perhaps, the time has come to reassert, as the truth of 'evaluation', the perverted logic to which Marx ironically refers in his description of commodity fetishism when he quotes Dogberry's advice to Seacoal from Shakespeare's *Much Ado About Nothing* (Act 3, Scene 3) at the conclusion of the first chapter of *Capital*: 'To be a well-favoured man is the gift of fortune; but reading and writing comes by nature.' Today, in our time of evaluation, to be a computer expert or a successful manager is a gift of nature, while to have beautiful lips or eyes is a fact of culture.

Escape from New Orleans

This same deadlock is clearly perceptible behind the social unrest in New Orleans. One of the popular heroes of the Iraq war, enjoying fame for a while and now entirely forgotten, was Muhammed Saeed al-Sahaf, the unfortunate Iraqi information minister who, in his daily press conferences, heroically denied even the most evident facts and stuck to the Iraqi line: while American tanks were only a few hundred yards from his office, he persisted in his claim that the television images of the tanks on Baghdad streets were just Hollywood special effects. Sometimes, however, he struck a strange truth – when, for instance, confronted with the claim that American soldiers were in control of parts of Baghdad, he snapped back: 'They are not in control of anything – they can't even control themselves!' It is as if, with New Orleans' descent into chaos, Marx's old saying that tragedy repeats itself as farce was inverted: Saeed's comic repartee turned into tragedy. The USA's government, this global policeman who endeavours to contain every threat to peace, freedom and democracy around the world, lost control of New Orleans itself: for a few days, the city regressed to a kind of game preserve of free looting, killing and rape, becoming a city of the dead and dying, a post-apocalyptic zone in which those whom Giorgio Agamben calls *homini sacer* – those excluded from the civil order – wandered around like zombies. A great deal can be said about this fear that permeates our lives – the fear that, because of some technological or natural catastrophe (electricity failure, earthquake, etc.), our entire social fabric will disintegrate. (Simply recall the paranoia over the 'Millennium Bug'.) This feeling of the fragility of our social bonds is itself a social symptom: at the precise point that one would expect a surge of social solidarity in the face of a disaster, the most ruthless egotism explodes.

But this is not the time for any kind of *Schadenfreude* (the USA got what it deserved) – the tragedy is immense. What we saw was no ordinary flooding: because New Orleans is below sea level, the water will not simply subside by itself. But it *is* the time for analysis. All these television images recall something that we've witnessed before – but where? The first association, of course, is that of reports from Third World cities descending into chaos during a civil war (Kabul, Baghdad, Somalia, Liberia, etc.) – and this accounts for our genuine surprise over the New Orleans catastrophe: what we are used to see happening *there* is now taking place *here*. (The irony is that Louisiana is often designated as America's own 'banana republic', the Third World portion of the USA.) This is probably one of the reasons why the authorities responded so late: although one rationally knew what could have happened, no one really believed that it would happen, as with the threat of ecological disaster – although we know all about it, we somehow do not really believe that it will happen.

However, it has *already* happened in the USA: just recall the series of *Escape from . . .* films (*Escape from New York* and *Escape from Los Angeles*), in which an American megalopolis is cut off from the domain of public order and taken over by criminal gangs. More interesting in this respect is David Koepp's *The Trigger Effect* (1996), in which society begins to disintegrate when there is a massive power failure in a major city. The film plays imaginatively with race relations and our prejudicial attitudes toward strangers – as the publicity for the film put it, 'When nothing works, anything goes.' Lurking even further behind the social veneer is the mythology of New Orleans as the city of vampires, voodoo and the living dead, where a dark spiritual force always threatens to disrupt the fabric of society. So again, as with the events of 11 September 2001, our surprise was no ordinary surprise: what happened was not that the self-enclosed ivory tower of American life was shattered by the intrusion of the Third World reality of social chaos, violence and hunger, but, on the contrary, that (what was hitherto perceived as) something that is not part of our reality, something that we were only vaguely aware of as a fictional presence on television and movie screens, brutally entered our reality.

So what was the catastrophe that took place in New Orleans? Upon closer inspection, the first thing one can note is its strange temporality. Immediately after the hurricane passed, there was a moment of relief: its eye had missed New Orleans by about 25 miles, only ten people were reported dead, and thus the worst-case scenario had seemingly been avoided. Then, in the aftermath, things started to go terribly wrong: a portion of the levee walls collapsed, the city became submerged in water, and the already flimsy social order began to disintegrate. The supposedly 'natural' disaster thus revealed itself as being 'socially mediated' in a number of ways. First, there are good reasons to believe that the USA is getting more hurricanes than usual due to global warming. Second, the immediate catastrophic aftermath of the hurricane – the city submerged and the shortage of drinking water – was to a large extent due to human failure: the levees were not strong enough and the authorities were not prepared for the (predictable) humanitarian needs that would follow. But then came the delayed reaction: it was as if the natural disaster had repeated itself as a social disaster. How are we to understand this social breakdown?

The first reaction is the standard conservative one: the events in New Orleans confirm yet again how fragile the social order is, how we need strong law enforcement and ethical pressure to prevent an explosion of violent passions. Humanity is by nature evil, and so the descent into social chaos is a constant threat. This argument can, of course, be given an additional racial twist: those who lashed out violently were almost exclusively black, so here we have further proof that blacks are not really civilized. Natural disasters simply bring to light the decay that is barely kept in check under normal conditions.

The obvious counter-argument is that the chaos in New Orleans merely rendered visible the persistent racial divide in the USA: New Orleans was predominantly populated by blacks who are largely poor and underprivileged; they had no means to leave the city in time and were left behind, starving and without care – it is no wonder they erupted in violence. (Their violent reactions should thus be seen in a series with the Rodney King riots in Los Angeles, or even the outbursts in Detroit and Newark in the late 1960s.)

But what if, more fundamentally, the tension that led to the chaos in New Orleans was not between 'human nature' and the forces of civilization that keep it in check, but the tension between two aspects of our very civilization? What if, in their attempt to control situations like New Orleans, the forces of law and order were confronted with the 'nature' of capitalism at its purest – the logic of individualist competition, of ruthless self-assertion, generated by the capitalist dynamic – a 'nature' much more threatening and violent than any hurricane or earthquake? In his theory of the sublime (*das Erhabene*), Immanuel Kant interpreted our fascination with the unleashed power of nature as a negative proof of the superiority of spirit over nature: no matter how ferocious the display of nature's aggression, it cannot touch the moral law in ourselves.[16] Does the catastrophe of New Orleans not provide a similar example of the sublime? No matter how brutal the vortex of the hurricane, it cannot compare to the vortex of the capitalist dynamic.

The Subject Supposed
to Loot and Rape

There is, however, another aspect of the New Orleans catastrophe that is no less crucial with regard to the ideological mechanisms that regulate our lives. According to a well-known anthropological anecdote, the 'primitives' to whom were attributed certain superstitious beliefs, when directly asked about these beliefs, answered: 'Of course not – we're not that stupid! But I was told that some of our ancestors did in fact believe that . . .' In short, they had transferred their beliefs on to another. In an uncanny way, some beliefs always seem to function 'at a distance': in order for the belief to function, there *must be* some ultimate guarantor of it, and yet this guarantor is always deferred, displaced, never present *in persona*. (Is this need to find another who 'really believes' also not that which propels us to stigmatize the Other as a – religious or ethnic – 'fundamentalist'?) The point, of course, is that this 'subject who is supposed to believe' need not exist for the belief to be operative: it is enough for their existence to be presupposed.

The events in post-Katrina New Orleans provide a new entry to this series of 'subjects supposed to . . .': *the subject supposed to loot and rape*. We all heard reports of the disintegration of public order, the explosion of black violence, instances of rape and looting – however, later inquiries demonstrated that, in the vast majority of cases, these alleged orgies of violence simply *did not occur*: unverified rumours were reported as facts by the media. For example, on 4 September 2005, the Super-intendent of the New Orleans Police Department was quoted in *The New York Times* concerning conditions at the convention centre: 'The tourists are walking around there, and as soon as these individuals see them, they're being preyed upon. They are beating, they are raping them in the streets.' In an interview two weeks later, he conceded that some of his most shocking statements turned out to be untrue: 'We have no official reports to document any murder. Not one official report of rape or sexual assault.'[17] The reality of poor blacks, abandoned, left without the means to survive, was thus transformed into the spectre of the irruption of black violence, of tourists being robbed and killed on streets that had descended into anarchy and of a

Super Dome ravaged by gangs that were raping women and children. These reports were not merely words; they were words that had precise *material effects*: they generated fears that led the authorities to change troop deployments, delayed medical evacuations, drove police officers to quit, grounded helicopters and so on. For example, the Acadian Ambulance Company's vehicles were locked down after word came that a firehouse in Covington had all its water stolen by armed robbers – a report that proved totally untrue.

Of course, this sense of menace had been ignited by genuine disorder and violence: looting *did* begin the moment the storm passed over New Orleans, ranging from vulgar thievery to foraging for the necessities of life. However, the (isolated) instances of crime in no way justified those 'reports' of the total breakdown of law and order – not because these reports were 'exaggerated', but on account of something much more radical. Lacan once claimed that, even if the analysand's wife is 'really' sleeping with other men, his jealousy is still to be treated as a pathological condition; in a homologous way, even if wealthy Jews in Germany in the early 1930s 'really' exploited German workers, seduced their daughters, dominated the popular press, Nazi anti-Semitism was still emphatically 'untrue', a pathological ideological condition – why? What made anti-Semitism pathological was its disavowed libidinal investment in the figure of the Jew: the cause of all social antagonisms was projected on to the figure of the 'Jew', the object of a perverse love-hatred, the spectral figure of mixed fascination and disgust. The same goes for the looting in New Orleans: *even if every report of violence and rape was proven to be factually true, the stories circulating about them would still be 'pathological' and racist*, because what motivated these stories were not facts but racist prejudices, the satisfaction felt by those who wanted to be able to say, 'You see, blacks are really like that, violent barbarians under the thin veneer of seeming civilized!' In other words, we are here dealing with another instance of *lying in the guise of truth*: even if what I am saying is factually true, my motivations for saying it are false.

Of course, we do not openly admit such motivations – from time to time, however, they surface in our public space in censored form, in the guise of denegation, evoked as an option and then immediately disavowed. Recall the comments William Bennett, the neo-conservative author of *The Book of Virtues*, made on his talk-back programme

'Morning in America' on 28 September 2005: 'But I do know that it's true that if you wanted to reduce crime, you could, if that were your sole purpose, you could abort every black baby in this country, and your crime rate would go down. That would be an impossibly ridiculous and morally reprehensible thing to do, but your crime rate would go down.'[18] A White House spokesperson immediately responded, 'The president believes the comments were not appropriate.' Then, two days later, Bennett qualified his statement: 'I was putting a hypothetical proposition . . . and then said about it, it was morally reprehensible to recommend abortion of an entire group of people. But this is what happens when you argue that ends can justify the means.'[19] This is precisely what Freud meant when he wrote that the unconscious knows no negation: the official (Christian, democratic, or whatever) discourse is accompanied and sustained by a whole nest of obscene racist or sexist fantasies, which can only be admitted in censored form.

But we are not dealing here simply with old-fashioned racism; something greater is at stake – namely, a fundamental feature of the emerging 'global' society. On 11 September 2001 (11/9), the Twin Towers collapsed. Twelve years earlier, on 9 November 1989 (9/11), the Berlin Wall fell. This latter date announced the beginning of the 'roaring 90s', Francis Fukuyama's dream of the 'end of history', the belief that liberal democracy had, in principle, won, that the search is over, that the advent of a global, liberal world community lies just around the corner, and that the obstacles to this 'happy ending' are merely empirical and contingent (local pockets of resistance that have not yet realized that their time is over). By way of contrast, 11 September was the symbol of the end of the Clintonite 'roaring 90s', marking an era in which new walls are emerging everywhere – between Israel and the West Bank, around the European Union, on the American-Mexican border and so on. (The rise of the populist New Right is just the most conspicuous example of the compulsion to erect these new walls.)

A couple of years ago, an ominous decision of the European Union passed almost unnoticed: the plan to establish an all-European border police force to secure the Union's territory and thus stem the influx of immigrants. *This* is the truth of globalization: the construction of new walls safeguarding prosperous Europe from the immigrant flood. I am tempted here to resuscitate the old Marxist 'humanist' opposition of 'relations between things' and 'relations between persons': within the much celebrated free-market opened up by global capitalism, it is 'things' (commodities) that freely circulate, while the circulation of 'persons' is increasingly regulated. We are thus not dealing with 'globalization as an unfinished project', but with a true 'dialectics of globalization': the segregation of people *is* the reality of economic globalization. This new racism of the developed is in a way much more brutal than the old vulgar racism: its implicit legitimization is neither naturalist (we in the West are 'by nature' superior) nor cultural (we in the West also want to preserve our cultural identity), but rather based on unashamed economic egotism – the fundamental divide lies between those included in the sphere of (relative) economic prosperity and those excluded from it.

In October 2005, the Spanish police announced a strategy to deal with the problem of how to stop the influx of desperate African immigrants trying to penetrate the small Spanish territory across from Gibraltar: they proposed to build a wall on the Spanish-Moroccan border. The plans uncannily resembled those of the Berlin Wall, only with the opposite intention: it was designed to prevent people from coming in, not getting out. The cruel irony of the situation is that it was the Zapatero government, at this moment arguably the most anti-racist and tolerant in Europe, that was forced to adopt these measures of segregation – a clear sign of the limits of multicultural 'tolerance', which preaches open borders and the acceptance of Others. If one were to open the borders, the first to rebel would be local working classes. It is thus becoming clear that the solution is not to 'tear down the walls and let them all in' – this is the empty demand of bleeding-heart liberal 'radicals'. The only true solution is to tear down the *true* wall, the socio-economic wall: to change society in such a way that people will no longer try desperately to escape their own world.

This brings us back to the rumours and 'reports' of 'subjects supposed to loot and rape': New Orleans is an American city that is among the most heavily marked by the internal wall that separates the affluent from ghettoized blacks. And it is about those on the other side of the wall that we fantasize: they increasingly live in another world, in a blank zone that offers itself as a screen for the projection of our fears, anxieties and secret desires. *The 'subject supposed to loot and rape' is on the other side of the wall* – it is about *this* subject that Bennett can afford to make his slip of the tongue and confess his murderous dreams in a censored form. More than anything else, the rumours and false reports in the aftermath of Katrina bear witness to the deep class divisions within American society.

Class Struggle in France, Again

Do the recent riots in Paris not bear witness to the existence of the same wall in Europe itself? When we are confronted with shocking reports and images of cars burning in Paris suburbs, the important thing is to avoid the 'hermeneutic temptation': to search for some deeper meaning or hidden message behind these outbursts. It is most difficult to accept that these acts are entirely meaningless: rather than a form of protest, such violence is a *passage à l'acte*, which bears witness not only to the impotence of the perpetrators, to their inability to locate the experience of their situation within a meaningful Whole. The true question is thus: what are the roots of this disorientation?

As I stated before, social theorists like to repeat that today's society is thoroughly 'reflexive': there is no nature or tradition that would provide a firm foundation on which one can rely, and even our most basic inner orientations are more and more experienced as something chosen. However, the ultimate deadlock of the risk society resides in the gap between knowledge and decision: there is no one who 'really knows' what to do, the situation is radically 'undecidable', but we nonetheless *must decide*. The problem is not that of a forced choice (I am free to choose, on condition that I make the right choice), but the opposite: the choice is effectively free and, for this very reason, is experienced as even more frustrating.

We increasingly find ourselves having to decide about matters that will dramatically affect our lives, but without the requisite knowledge needed to make the decisions; far from being liberating, this compulsion 'freely' to decide provokes an acute anxiety. Is this not a kind of ironic reversal of predestination? I am held accountable for decisions that I was forced to make without proper knowledge of the situation or awareness of their consequences. There is no guarantee that the democratization of crucial decisions, the active involvement of thousands of interested individuals, will necessarily improve the quality or accuracy of their decisions and thus effectively lessen the risks. (I am tempted here to evoke the answer of a devoted Catholic to the reproach of a liberal atheist that Catholics are stupid for believing in the infallibility of the Pope: 'At least we Catholics believe in the infallibility of only *one* person. Does democracy not rely on the much more risky notion that the majority of the people are infallible?') The subject thus finds himself in a Kafkaesque situation of being guilty of not knowing of what (if anything) they are guilty: I am forever haunted by the prospect that I have already made decisions that will endanger me and everyone around me, but, if I ever learn the truth, it will only be once it is too late.

What do these violent outbursts in Paris have to do with the fact that we live in a 'risk society' of perpetual choice? In short – everything. These 'meaningless' and 'excessive' outbursts of violence are the obverse of the 'reflexivization' of our daily lives. Nowhere is this clearer than in the fate of psychoanalytic interpretation. Today, the formations of the unconscious (from dreams to hysterical symptoms) have finally lost their innocence and are thoroughly reflexivized: the 'free associations' of an educated analysand consist of attempts to provide a psychoanalytic explanation of their disturbances, so that one is quite justified in saying that we not only have Jungian, Kleinian and Lacanian interpretations of these symptoms, but symptoms themselves that are Jungian, Kleinian and Lacanian – i.e., whose reality involves implicit reference to some psychoanalytic theory. The unfortunate result of this global reflexivization of interpretation (everything becomes interpretation, the unconscious interprets itself) is that the analyst's interpretation itself is deprived of its performative 'symbolic efficiency', and leaves the symptom intact in the immediacy of its idiotic *jouissance*.

What happens in psychoanalytic treatment is strictly homologous to the response of a neo-Nazi skinhead who, when pressed for the reasons for his violence, suddenly begins to speak like a social worker, sociologist or social psychologist: he quotes diminished social mobility, rising insecurity, the disintegration of paternal authority, the lack of maternal love in his early childhood and so on. Here the unity of practice and its inherent ideological legitimization disintegrates into raw violence and its impotent, inefficient interpretation. The re-emergence of the brutal Real of 'irrational' violence, impermeable by and insensitive to any reflexive interpretation, is the necessary obverse of the universalized reflexivity hailed by risk-society theorists. So the more that social theory proclaims the end of nature and/or tradition and the emergence of a 'risk society', the more the implicit reference to 'nature' pervades our daily discourse: even when not speaking directly of the 'end of history', are we not putting forward the same message when we claim that we are entering a 'post-ideological', pragmatic era, which is just another way of claiming that we are entering a post-political order in which the only legitimate conflicts are ethnic-cultural?

Typically, in today's political discourse, the term 'worker' has disappeared from the vocabulary and has been substituted for 'immigrants' (i.e., immigrant workers: Algerians in France, Turks in Germany, Mexicans in the USA, etc.) – in this way, the class problematic of workers' exploitation is translated into the multiculturalist problematic of the 'intolerance of Otherness'. Do not the disproportionate concerns of liberals to protect immigrants' ethnic rights draw their energy from this very 'repressed' class dimension? Although Francis Fukuyama's thesis on the 'end of history' quickly fell into disrepute, we still silently presume that the liberal-democratic capitalist global order is somehow the 'natural' social régime. We thus implicitly conceive of conflicts in the Third World as a subspecies of natural catastrophes, as outbursts of quasi-natural violent passions, or as conflicts based on a fanatical identification with one's ethnic roots – and what does 'ethnic' represent here if not a code word for nature?

There is a well-known anecdote about Picasso: during World War II, a German officer visited his studio and, upon seeing *Guernica*, was shocked by the modernist confusion of the painting. He then asked: 'Did you do this?' Picasso calmly replied: 'No, *you* did this!' Today, many liberals, when faced with violent outbursts like the riots in Paris, ask us, the few remaining Leftists who still count on a radical social transformation: 'Didn't you do this? Isn't *this* what you want?' And we should reply, like Picasso: 'No, *you* did this! This is the result of *your* politics!'

Notes

This paper was completed on 24 November 2005, and then revised for publication on 15 July 2006. [eds]

1 On Žižek's further critique of 'populism', see his 'Against the Populist Temptation', *Critical Inquiry* 32 (2006), pp. 551–74. [eds]

2 I rely here, of course, on conversations with Alain Badiou.

3 Jacques Lacan, *Le Séminaire de Jacques Lacan XXI: Les non-dupes errent, 1973–74* (unpublished), session of 21 May 1974. See also Jacques Lacan, *Le triomphe de la religion, précédé de Discours aux catholiques*, Paris, Éditions du Seuil, 2005, pp. 73–81. [eds]

4 G.W.F. Hegel, *The Encyclopedia Logic: Part 1 of the Encyclopedia of Philosophical Sciences (with the Zusätze)*, trans. T.F. Geraets, W.A. Suchting and H.S. Harris, Indianapolis, Hackett, 1991, pp. 11–17. [eds]

5 Jacques Lacan, 'Science and Truth', in *Écrits: The First Complete Edition in English*, trans. Bruce Fink, New York, W.W. Norton, 2006, pp. 726–7. [eds]

6 See Donald Davidson, *Essays on Actions and Events*, Oxford, Oxford University Press, 1980.

7 Quoted in Bradley K. Martin, *Under the Loving Care of the Fatherly Leader*, New York, Thomas Dunne, 2004, p. 85.

8 See, for example, Robert Axelrod, *The Evolution of Cooperation*, New York, Basic Books, 1984.

9 See Jean-Pierre Dupuy, *Avions-nous oublié le mal? Penser la politique après le 11 septembre*, Paris, Bayard, 2002.

10 Augustine, *Confessions*, trans. Henry Chadwick, Oxford, Oxford University Press, 1991, p. 9. [eds]

11 See John Rawls, *A Theory of Justice*, Cambridge, Harvard University Press, 1971.

12 See Friedrich Hayek, *The Road to Serfdom*, Chicago, University of Chicago Press, 1994.

13 Karl Marx and Friedrich Engels, 'Manifesto of the Communist Party', in *The Revolutions of 1848: Political Writings, Volume 1*, ed. David Fernbach, London, Penguin/New Left Review, 1973, pp. 70–1. [eds]

14 Jean-Jacques Rousseau, *Rousseau Judge of Jean-Jacques: Dialogues, Collected Writings of Rousseau, Volume 1*, ed. Roger D. Masters and Christopher Kelly, trans. Judith R. Bush, Christopher Kelly and Roger D. Masters, Hanover and London, University Press of New England, 1990, p. 9. [eds]

15 See Jacques-Alain Miller and Jean-Claude Milner, *Voulez-vous être évalué?*, Paris, Grasset, 2004.

16 Immanuel Kant, *Critique of the Power of Judgment*, ed. Paul Guyer, trans. Paul Guyer and Eric Matthews, Cambridge, Cambridge University Press, 2000, p. 264. [eds]

17 Jim Dwyer and Christopher Drew, 'Fear Exceeded Crime's Reality in New Orleans', *The New York Times*, 29 September 2005.

18 See also Steven D. Levitt and Stephen J. Dubner, *Freakonomics: A Rogue Economist Explores the Hidden Side of Everything*, London, Allen Lane, 2005, pp. 117–44. [eds]

19 For a newspaper article outlining these events, see Dan Glaister, 'Abort all black babies and cut crime, says Republican', *The Guardian International*, 1 October 2005, p. 14. [eds]

Author's afterword
Where do we stand today?

The arch-conservative William Butler Yeats was correct in his diagnosis of the twentieth century:

> The blood-dimmed tide is loosed, and everywhere
> the ceremony of innocence is drowned;
> the best lack all conviction, while the worst
> are full of passionate intensity.
>
> ('The Second Coming', 1920)

The key to his diagnosis is contained in the phrase 'the ceremony of innocence', which is to be taken in the precise sense of Edith Wharton's 'age of innocence': Newton's wife, the 'innocent' referred to in the title, was not a naïve believer in her husband's fidelity – she knew well of his passionate love for Count Olenska, but just politely ignored it and staged the belief in his fidelity. Or, take the angry response of Groucho Marx when caught in a lie: 'Whom do you believe, your eyes or my words?' This apparently absurd logic renders perfectly the functioning of the symbolic order, in which the symbolic mask-mandate matters more than the direct reality of the individual who wears this mask and/or assumes this mandate. This functioning involves the structure of fetishist disavowal: 'I know very well that things are the way I see them – i.e., that this person is a corrupt weakling – but I nonetheless treat him respectfully, because he wears the insignia of a judge, so that when he speaks, it is the Law itself which speaks through him.' So, in a way, I effectively believe his words, not my eyes, i.e., I believe in another domain (that of pure symbolic authority), which matters more than the reality of its spokesmen. The cynical reduction to reality thus falls short: when a judge speaks, there is in a way more truth in his words (the words of the institution of Law) than in the direct reality of the person of judge – if one limits oneself to what one sees, one simply misses the point. This paradox is what Lacan aims at with his phrase, 'les non-dupes errent': those who do not let themselves be caught in the symbolic deception/fiction and continue to believe their eyes are the ones who err most. What is missed by a cynic who 'only believes his eyes' is the efficiency of the symbolic fiction, the way this fiction structures our experience of reality. The same gap is at work in our most intimate relationship with our neighbours: we behave *as if* we do not know that they also smell badly, secrete excrement, etc. – a minimum of idealization, of fetishistic disavowal, is the basis of our co-existence. And doesn't the same disavowal account for the sublime beauty of the idealizing gesture discernible from Anne Frank to American Communists who continued to believe in the Soviet Union? Although we know that Stalinist Communism was an appalling thing, we nonetheless admire the victims of McCarthyism who heroically persisted in their belief in Communism and support for the Soviet Union. The logic here is the same as that of Anne Frank who, in her diaries, expresses belief in the ultimate goodness of man in spite of the horrors accomplished by men against Jews in World War II: what renders such an assertion of belief (in the essential goodness of man, in the truly human character of the Soviet régime) sublime is the very gap between it and the overwhelming factual evidence to the contrary, i.e., the active will to disavow the actual state of things. Perhaps therein resides the most elementary metaphysical gesture: in this refusal to accept the Real in its idiocy, to disavow it and to search for another domain behind it. The big Other is thus *the order of the Lie*, the domain of lying sincerely. And it is in this sense that 'the best lack all conviction, while the worst are full of passionate intensity': even the best are no longer able to sustain their symbolic innocence, their full engagement in symbolic ritual, while 'the worst', the mob, engage in (racist, religious, sexist . . .) fanaticism. Is this opposition not a good description of today's split between tolerant but anaemic liberals and fundamentalists full of 'passionate intensity'?

What is thus gradually suspended is *symbolic efficiency*, the performative power of signifying systems best encapsulated by the Pascalean formula used by Alcoholics Anonymous: 'Fake it until you make it'. This causality of the habit is more complex than it may appear: far from offering an explanation of the way that beliefs emerge, it itself calls for an explanation. The first thing to specify is that Pascal's formula, 'Kneel and you will believe!', must be understood as involving a kind of self-referential causality: 'Kneel and you will believe *that you knelt down because you believed!*' The second thing is that, in the 'normal' cynical functioning of ideology, belief is displaced on to another, on to a 'subject supposed to believe', so that the true logic is: 'Kneel and you will thereby *make someone else believe!*' One has to take this literally and even risk a kind of inversion of Pascal: 'Do you believe too much, too directly? Do you find your belief too oppressing in its raw immediacy? Then kneel, act as if you believe, and *you will get rid of your belief* – you will no longer have to believe yourself, your belief will already exist objectified in your act of praying!' That is to say, what if one kneels down and prays not so much to regain one's own belief but, to the contrary, to *rid oneself* of belief, of its over-proximity, to acquire the breathing space of a minimal distance towards it? To believe – to believe 'directly,' without the externalizing mediation of a ritual – is a heavy, oppressive, traumatic burden, which, by engaging in a ritual, one has a chance to transfer on to an Other . . .

Today, theists are no longer opposed to atheists – on the contrary, one of their standard rhetorical strategies is to emphasize the way that, when abandoning the abstract 'God of philosophers', atheists are much closer to the 'true' God than metaphysical theologians: 'The god-less thinking which must abandon the god of philosophy, god as *causa sui*, is thus perhaps closer to the divine God. Here this means only: god-less thinking is more open to Him than onto-theo-logic would like to admit.'[1] Even in the late Derrida, one finds a variation on this ploy: in his reflections on prayer, he proposes not only that atheists also pray but, today, it is perhaps *only atheists that truly pray*.[2] Against this rhetoric, one should assert the *literal* truth of Lacan's statement that theologians are the only true materialists.

Niels Bohr, who gave the right response to Einstein's claim 'God doesn't play dice' ('Don't tell God what to do!'), also provided the perfect example of the way that such a fetishist disavowal of belief works in ideology: seeing a horseshoe on his door, the surprised visitor said that he isn't superstitious and doesn't believe that such things bring luck, to which Bohr snapped: 'I don't believe in it either; I keep it there because I was told that it works even if one doesn't believe in it!' What this paradox renders clearly is the way belief is a reflexive attitude: it is never a case of just believing, one has to believe in belief itself. Kierkegaard was thus right to claim that we do not really believe (in Christ), we just believe in order to believe; Bohr simply confronts us with the logical negative of this reflexivity (one can also *not* believe in one's beliefs . . .).

The obverse of this gradual suspension of symbolic efficiency is the fact that, today, politics is increasingly the politics of *jouissance*, concerned with ways of soliciting or controlling and regulating *jouissance*. Is the entire opposition between liberal Western tolerance and Islamic fundamentalism not condensed in the opposition between, on the one hand, a woman's right to free sexuality – inclusive of the freedom to display/expose oneself and provoke/disturb a man – and, on the other hand, the desperate male attempt to eradicate or, at least, keep this threat under control? (Recall the ridiculous Taliban prohibition of metal heels for women; it is as if, even if women were completely covered, the metallic sound of their heels would still drive men crazy!) And, of course, both sides ideologically/morally mystify their position: for the liberal West, the right provocatively to expose oneself to male desire is legitimized as the right freely to offer one's body and to enjoy it as one wants; for Islam, the control of feminine sexuality is, of course, legitimized as the defence of woman's dignity against the threat of being reduced to an object of male sexual exploitation. So while, when the French government prohibited women from wearing veils in schools, one can claim that they were enabled to dispose of their bodies, one can also point out that the truly disturbing point for critics of Muslim 'fundamentalism' was that there *were* women who did not participate in the game of offering their bodies for seduction, for the social circulation/exchange involved in it. What the two opposing attitudes – liberal tolerance and fundamentalism – share is the extreme *disciplinary* approach, which is in each case differently directed: 'fundamentalists' regulate the feminine self-presentation in great detail in order to prevent sexual provocation; politically-correct feminist liberals impose a no-less-severe regulation of behaviour aimed at containing different forms of harassment.

One should nonetheless add a qualification here. What we have today is not so much the *politics* of *jouissance* but, more precisely, the *regulation* (or administration) of *jouissance*, which is *stricto sensu* post-political. *Jouissance* is in itself limitless, the obscure excess of the unnameable, and the fundamental task is to regulate this excess. The superego imperative to 'Enjoy!' thus functions as the reversal of Kant's 'Du kannst, denn du sollst! [You can, because you must!]' – it relies on, 'You must, because you can!' That is to say, the superego dimension of today's 'non-repressive' hedonism (the constant provocation we are exposed to, enjoining us to explore all modes of *jouissance* to their end) resides in the way that permitted *jouissance* necessarily turns into obligatory *jouissance*.

However, the question here is: does the capitalist injunction to enjoy effectively aim at soliciting *jouissance* in its excessive character, or rather are we ultimately dealing with a kind of universalized pleasure-principle, with a life dedicated to pleasures? In other words, are not the injunctions to have a good time, to acquire self-realization and self-fulfilment, etc., precisely injunctions to *avoid* excessive *jouissance*, to find a kind of homeostatic balance? Is the Dalai Lama's advice not advice as to how to maintain a balanced 'proper measure' and avoid disturbing extremes? The situation here is more complex: the problem is that, although the immediate and explicit injunctions call for the rule of the pleasure-principle that would maintain homeostasis, the effective functioning of the injunction explodes these constraints into a striving towards excessive enjoyment.

I am tempted here to oppose the post-'68 leftist push towards *jouissance* (to reach the extreme of forms of sexual pleasures that would dissolve all social links and allow one to find a climax in the solipsism of absolute *jouissance*) to the consumption of commodities promising *jouissance*: the first still stands for a radical, 'authentic' even, subjective position, while the second signals defeat, a surrender to market forces. Is, however, this opposition quite so clear? Is it not all too easy to denounce the *jouissance* offered on the market as 'false', as providing only the empty package-promise with no substance? Rather, is the hole, the void, at the very heart of our pleasures not the structure of every *jouissance*? Furthermore, is it not precisely that the commodified provocations to enjoy that bombard us constantly push us towards an autistic-masturbatory, 'asocial' *jouissance*, whose supreme case is addiction? Are drugs not, at the same time, the means for the most radical autistic experience of *jouissance* and the commodity par excellence?

The drive to pure autistic *jouissance* (through drugs or other trance-inducing means) arose at a precise political moment: when the emancipatory 'sequence' of '68 exhausted its potential. At this critical point (in the mid 1970s), the only remaining option was a kind of direct, brutal *passage à l'acte*, a push-towards-the-Real, which assumed three main forms: the search for extreme forms of sexual *jouissance*; leftist political terrorism (the Red Army Faction in Germany, the Red Brigade in Italy, etc.), whose wager was that, in an epoch in which the masses are totally immersed in a capitalist ideological sleep, the standard critique of ideology is no longer operative, so that only a resort to the raw Real of direct violence – *l'action directe* – can awaken the masses; and, finally, the turn towards the Real of an inner experience (Oriental mysticism). What all three share is their withdrawal from concrete socio-political engagement to a direct contact with the Real.

Freud's 'naïve' reflections on the way that the artist renders embarrassing, disgusting even, intimate fantasies socially palpable by way of wrapping them up in a socially acceptable form – i.e., by way of 'sublimating' it, of offering the pleasure of the beautiful artistic form as a lure which seduces us into accepting the otherwise repulsive excessive pleasure of intimate fantasizing[3] – obtain new actuality in today's era of permissiveness, when performance and other artists are under pressure directly to stage the innermost private fantasies in their desublimated nakedness. Such 'transgressive' art confronts us immediately with *jouissance* in its most solipsistic form, with pure masturbatory phallic *jouissance*. And, far from being individualist, such *jouissance* precisely characterizes individuals in so far as they are caught in a 'crowd': what Freud called 'crowd [*Masse*]' is *not* an articulated communal network, but a direct conglomerate of solipsistic individuals – as the saying goes, one is by definition lonely in a crowd. The paradox is thus that a crowd is a fundamentally *anti-social* phenomenon.

The problem with today's superego injunction to enjoy is that, in contrast to previous modes of ideological interpellation, it opens up no 'world' proper – it just refers to an obscure Unnameable. Even Nazism opened up a world: by describing the present critical situation, naming the enemy ('Jewish conspiracy'), the goal and the means to achieve it,

Nazism disclosed reality in a way that allowed its subjects to acquire a global 'cognitive mapping', inclusive of the space for their meaningful engagement. Perhaps, it is here that one should locate the 'danger' of capitalism: although it is global, encompassing the entire world, it sustains a *stricto sensu* 'worldless' ideological constellation, depriving the large majority of people of any meaningful 'cognitive mapping'.[4]

In what, more precisely, does this 'worldlessness' consist? As Lacan points out in his *Seminar XX, jouissance* involves a logic strictly homologous to that of the ontological proof of the existence of God.[5] In the classic version of this proof, my awareness of myself as a finite, limited being immediately gives birth to the notion of an infinite, perfect being, and because this being is perfect, its very notion contains its existence; in the same way, our experience of *jouissance* accessible to us as finite, located, partial, 'castrated', immediately gives birth to the notion of a full, achieved, unlimited *jouissance* whose existence is necessarily presupposed by the subject who imputes it to another subject, his/her 'subject supposed to enjoy'.

Our first reaction here is, of course, that this absolute *jouissance* is a myth, that it never effectively existed, that its status is purely differential, i.e., that it exists only as a negative point of reference with regard to which every actually experienced *jouissance* falls short ('pleasurable as this is, it's not *that!*'). However, the recent advances in cognitive studies have opened up another approach: one can (no longer only) imagine the situation in which pain (or pleasure) is not generated through sensory perceptions, but through a direct excitation of the appropriate neuronal centres (by means of drugs or electrical impulses) – what the subject experiences in this case would be 'pure' pain, pain 'as such', the *Real* of pain, or, to put it in precise Kantian terms, non-schematized pain, pain that is not yet grounded in the experience of reality constituted by transcendental categories.

In order properly to grasp what is taking place here, one has to take a detour through what Lacan called *la jouissance de l'Autre* – what is this mysterious *jouissance*? Imagine (a real clinical case, though) two lovers who arouse each other by verbalizing, telling each other, their innermost sexual fantasies to such a degree that they reach full orgasm without touching, just as the effect of 'mere talking'. The result of such an excess of intimacy is not difficult to guess: after such a radical mutual exposure, they will no longer be able to maintain their amorous link – too much had been said, or, rather, the spoken word, the big Other, was too directly flooded by *jouissance*, so the two are embarrassed by each other's presence and slowly drift apart, start to avoid one another. *This*, not a full perverse orgy, is the true excess: not 'practising your innermost fantasies instead of just talking about them', but, precisely, *talking* about them, allowing them to invade the medium of the big Other to such an extent that one can literally 'fuck with words', so that the elementary, constitutive barrier between language and *jouissance* breaks down. Measured by this standard, the most extreme 'real orgy' is but a poor substitute.

The presentation of the sexual act in Adrian Lyne's *Unfaithful* renders perfectly the logic of the feminine *jouissance de l'Autre*: after the couple (the married Diane Lane and the young Frenchman) embrace in his apartment, there is a direct cut to Diane Lane returning home on the suburban train, sitting alone and reminiscing. Her remembering (rendered through a wonderful display of embarrassed smiles, tears, gestures of incredulity at what happened, etc.) is intercepted with short, fragmented flashbacks of the couple making love – we thus only see the love act as it were in *futur antérieur*, as it is recollected. The direct sexual *jouissance* is immediately 'sublated' in the *jouissance* of the Other; the two magically overlap. The lesson is that the 'true' *jouissance* is neither in the act itself nor in the expectant thrill of the pleasures to come, but in the melancholic remembrance of it. And here is the enigma: is it possible to imagine a sexual act in which the participants, while 'really doing it', already adopt the imagined position of the remembering it, from which they *now* enjoy it? Furthermore, can one say that this melancholic position of *futur antérieur* is feminine, while the *jouissance* engendered by the thrill of pleasures to come is masculine? Recall the famous scene in Bergman's *Persona* of Bibi Andersson telling about a beach orgy and passionate love-making in which she participated: we see no flashback pictures, and nonetheless the scene is one of the most erotic in the entire history of cinema – the excitement is in the way she tells it, and this excitement that resides in speech itself is *jouissance féminine* . . .

And it is this dimension of the *jouissance* of the Other that is threatened by the prospect of 'pure' *jouissance*. Is such a short-circuit not the basic and most disturbing feature of consuming drugs to generate the experience of enjoyment? What drugs promise is a purely autistic *jouissance*, a *jouissance* accessible without the detour through the Other (of the symbolic order) – *jouissance* generated not by fantasmatic representations, but by directly attacking our neuronal pleasure-centres. It is in this precise sense that drugs involve the suspension of symbolic castration, whose most elementary meaning is precisely that *jouissance* is accessible only through the medium of (as mediated by) symbolic representation. This brutal Real of *jouissance* is the obverse of the infinite plasticity of imagining, no longer constrained by the rules of reality. Significantly, the experience of drugs encompasses both these extremes: on the one hand, the Real of noumenal (non-schematized) *jouissance* that bypasses representations; on the other hand, the wild proliferation of fantasizing (recall the proverbial reports on how, after taking a drug, you imagine scenes you never thought you were able to access – new dimensions of shapes, colours, smells . . .).

One should thus learn to discern the lesson of recent bio-technological advances. In 2003, Japanese telecom carriers came up with the world's first mobile phone that enables users to listen to calls inside their heads by conducting sound through bone. The phone is equipped with a 'Sonic Speaker', which transmits sounds through vibrations that move from the skull to the cochlea in the inner ear, instead of relying on the usual method of sound hitting the outer eardrum. With the new handset, the key to better hearing in a noisy situation is thus to plug your ears to prevent outside noise from drowning out bone-conducted sounds. Here we encounter the Lacanian distinction between reality and the Real: this spectral voice that we hear in our interior, although it has no place in external reality, is the Real at its purest.

In a step further, in 2003, at the Center for Neuro-Engineering at Duke University, monkeys with brain implants were trained to move a robot arm with their thoughts: a series of electrodes containing tiny wires were implanted in the brains of two monkeys; a computer then recorded signals produced by the monkeys' brains as they manipulated a joystick controlling the robotic arm in exchange for a reward (sips of juice). The joystick was later unplugged and the arm, which was in a separate room, was controlled directly by the brain signals coming from the implants. The monkeys eventually stopped using the joystick, as if they knew their brains were controlling the robot arm. The Duke researchers have now moved on to researching similar implants in humans: in the summer of 2004, it was reported that they succeeded at temporarily implanting electrodes in the brains of volunteers; the volunteers then played videogames while the electrodes recorded the brain signals – the scientists trained a computer to recognize the brain activity corresponding to the different movements of the joystick. This procedure of 'eavesdropping' on the brain's digital crackle with electrodes (where computers use zeros and ones, neurons encode our thoughts in all-or-nothing electrical impulses), and transmitting the signals to a computer that can read the brain's code and then use the signals to control a machine, already has an official name: brain–machine interface. Further prospects include not only more complex tasks (say, implanting the electrodes in the language centres of the brain and thus wirelessly transmitting a person's inner voice to a machine, so that one can speak 'directly', bypassing voice or writing), but also sending the brain signals to a machine thousands of miles away and thus directing it from a great distance. And what about sending the signals to somebody standing nearby with electrodes implanted in his hearing centres, so that he can 'telepathically' listen to my inner voice?[6] The Orwellian notion of 'thought control' will thus acquire a much more literal meaning.

Even Stephen Hawking's proverbial little finger – the minimal link between his mind and the outside reality, the only part of his paralysed body that he can move – will thus no longer be necessary: with my mind, I can *directly* cause objects to move, i.e., it is the brain itself that will directly serve as the remote control machine. In the terms of German Idealism, this means that what Kant called 'intellectual intuition [*intelektuelle Anschauung*]' – the closing of the gap between mind and reality, a mind-process that, in a causal way, directly influences reality, this capacity that Kant attributed only to the infinite mind of God – is now potentially available to all of us, i.e., we are potentially deprived of one of the basic features of our finitude. And because, as we learned from Kant as well as from Freud, this gap of finitude is at the same time the resource of our creativity (the distance between 'mere thought' and causal intervention into external reality enables us to test the hypotheses in our mind and, as Karl Popper put it, let them die instead of ourselves), the direct short-circuit between mind and reality implies the prospect of a radical closure.

It may seem that this scientific-technological breakthrough brings to the extreme Freud's story of three successive humiliations of man, three 'narcissistic illnesses' ('Copernicus-Darwin-Freud'), which is much more complex than it may appear. The first thing to add is that the latest scientific breakthroughs seem to add to it a whole series of further 'humiliations' which radicalize the first three, so that, as Peter Sloterdijk perspicuously noted, with regard to today's 'cognitive sciences', psychoanalysis rather seems to belong to the traditional 'humanist' field threatened by the latest humiliations. Is the proof of it not the predominant reaction of psychoanalysts to the latest advances in cognitive sciences? Their defence of psychoanalysis often reads as just another variation of the standard philosophico-transcendental gesture of pointing out the way that a positive science can never encompass and account for the very horizon of meaning within which it is operative. There are, however, some complications to this image. First: from the very beginning of modernity, humiliation, the 'narcissistic illness', seems to generate a sense of superiority paradoxically grounded in the very awareness of the miserable character of our existence. As Pascal has already put it in an unsurpassable way, man is a mere insignificant speck of dust in the infinite universe, but he *knows* about his nullity, and that makes all the difference. Paradigmatically modern is this notion of greatness not as simply opposed to misery, but as a misery aware of itself . . . The second complication concerns the precise status of this knowledge: it is not only knowledge about our own vanity, but also its inherent obverse, technological *savoir-faire*, knowledge as power. Strictly correlative to the 'humiliation' of man is the exponential growth of humankind's technological domination over nature in modernity.

These two features combined give us the basic paradox of the modern philosophy of subjectivity: the couplet of the humiliation of empirical man and the elevation of the transcendental subject. It was Descartes, already, who asserted the *cogito* as the starting point of philosophy, simultaneously reducing all of reality, life included, to mere *res extensa*, the field of matter obeying mechanical laws. In this precise sense, the thought of modern subjectivity is *not* 'humanism', but, from the very outset, 'anti-humanist': humanism characterizes Renaissance thought which celebrated man as the crown of creation, the highest term in the chain of created beings, while modernity proper occurs only when man loses his privileged place and is reduced to just another element of reality – and correlative to this loss of privilege is the emergence of subject as the pure immaterial void, not as a substantial part of reality. The Kantian sublime itself is grounded in this gap: it is the very experience of the impotence and nullity of man (as a part of nature) when he is exposed to a powerful display of natural forces that evokes in a negative way his greatness as a noumenal ethical subject.

These two complications, however, are part of the standard narrative of modernity; it is only the third one which effectively disturbs the received image: the fact that the twentieth-century 'humiliations' are much more ambiguous than it may appear – and, retroactively, render visible the ambiguity of these classical humiliations. That is to say, in a first approach, Marx, Nietzsche and Freud all share the same 'desublimating' hermeneutics of suspicion: a 'higher' capacity (ideology and politics, morality, consciousness) is unmasked as a shadow-theatre that is effectively governed by the conflict of forces that takes place on another 'lower' scene (economic processes, conflict of unconscious desires). And, today, things go much further: in cognitivism, human thinking itself is conceived as modelled after the functioning of a computer, so that the very gap between understanding (the experience of meaning, of the openness of a world) and the 'mute' functioning of a machine potentially disappears; in neo-Darwinism (not only) human individuals are conceived of as mere instruments or, rather, vehicles, of the reproduction of 'their' genes, and, in a homologous way, human culture, the cultural activity of the mankind, as a vehicle for the proliferation of 'memes'. However, one is tempted to say that, in so far as nineteenth-century 'demystification' is a reduction of the noble appearance to some 'lower' reality (Marx-Nietzsche-Freud), then the twentieth century adds to it another turn of the screw by rehabilitating (a weird, previously unheard-of) appearance itself. Indicative is here Husserlian *phenomenology*, the first true event of twentieth-century philosophy, with its stance of 'reduction', which aims at observing the phenomena 'as such', in their autonomy, not as mere attributes/expressions/effects of some underlying 'real entities' – a line is opened up here that leads to figures as different as Bergson, Deleuze, Wittgenstein and quantum physics, each of them focusing on the autonomy of the pure flux-event of becoming with regard to real entities ('things').

What is even more crucial is that this insight into the autonomy of phenomena enables us to approach the classic 'demystifiers' themselves in a new way. What we find in Marx is not only the 'reduction' of ideology to an economic base and, within this base, of exchange to production, but a much more ambiguous and mysterious phenomenon of 'commodity fetishism', which designates a kind of proto-'ideology' inherent to the reality of the 'economic base' itself. Freud accomplishes a strictly homologous breakthrough with regard to the paradoxical status of fantasy: the ontological paradox, scandal even, of the notion of fantasy resides in the fact that it subverts the standard opposition of 'subjective' and 'objective': of course, fantasy is by definition not 'objective' (in the naïve sense of 'existing independently of the subject's perceptions'); however, it is also not 'subjective' (in the sense of being reducible to the subject's consciously experienced intuitions). Fantasy rather belongs to the 'bizarre category of the objectively subjective – the way things actually, objectively seem to you even if they don't seem that way to you' (as Dennett put it in his acerbic critical remark against the notion of qualia).[7] When, for example, we claim that someone who is consciously well disposed towards Jews nonetheless harbours profound anti-Semitic prejudices he is not consciously aware of, do we not claim that (in so far as these prejudices do not render the way Jews really are, but the way they appear to him) he is not aware of the way Jews really seem to him?

Apropos of commodity fetishism, Marx himself uses the term 'objectively-necessary appearance'. So, when a critical Marxist encounters a bourgeois subject immersed in commodity fetishism, the Marxist's reproach should not be, 'The commodity may seem to you a magical object endowed with special powers, but it really is just a reified expression of relations between people'; but rather, 'You may think that the commodity appears to you as a simple embodiment of social relations (that, for example, money is just a kind of voucher entitling you to a part of the social product), but this is not how things really seem to you – in your social reality, by means of your participation in social exchange, you bear witness to the uncanny fact that a commodity really appears to you as a magical object endowed with special powers . . .' This difference between the two appearances (the way things *really* appear to us versus the way they *appear* to appear to us) is linked to the structure of the well-known Freudian joke about a Jew who complains to his friend, 'Why are you telling me you are going to Lemberg when you are really going to Lemberg?': say, in the case of commodity fetishism, when I immediately perceive money as just a knot of social relations, not any kind of magic object, and I only treat it like a fetish in my practice, so that the site of fetishism is my actual social practice, I could effectively be reproached with: 'Why are you saying that money is just a knot of social relations, when money really *is* just a knot of social relations?' Jean Laplanche wrote about the hysteric's 'primordial lie' which articulates the original fantasy: 'The term *proton pseudos* aims at something different from a subjective lie; it renders a kind of passage from the subjective to the founding, even, one could say, to the transcendental; in any case, a kind of objective lie, inscribed into the facts.'[8] Is this not also the status of Marxian commodity fetishism – not simply a subjective illusion, but an 'objective' illusion, an illusion inscribed into facts (social reality) themselves? Let us read carefully the famous first sentence of the section on 'Commodity Fetishism' in *Capital*:

> A commodity appears at first sight an extremely obvious, trivial thing. But its analysis brings out that it is a very strange thing, abounding in metaphysical subtleties and theological niceties.[9]

Kojin Karatani is right to link this passage to the starting point of the Marxian critique, the famous lines from 1843, that 'the criticism of religion is the presupposition of all criticism':[10] with it, the circle is in a way closed upon itself, i.e., at the very bottom of the critique of actual life (of the economic process), we again encounter the theological dimension inscribed into social *reality* itself. Karatani refers here to the Freudian notion of drive [*Trieb*] as opposed to the multitude of human desires: capitalism is grounded in the Real of a certain quasi-theological impersonal 'drive', the drive to reproduce and grow, to expand and accumulate profit.

This is also one of the ways of clarifying the meaning of Lacan's assertion of the subject's constitutive 'decentrement': its point is not that my subjective experience is regulated by objective unconscious mechanisms that are 'decentred' with regard to my self-experience and, as such, beyond my control (a point asserted by every materialist), but rather something much more unsettling – I am deprived of even my most intimate 'subjective' experience, the way things 'really seem to me', that of the fundamental fantasy that constitutes and guarantees the core of my being, because I can never consciously experience it and assume it. According to the standard view, the dimension that is constitutive of subjectivity is that of the phenomenal (self-)experience – I am a subject the moment I can say to myself: 'No matter what unknown mechanism governs my acts, perceptions and thoughts, nobody can take from me what I see and feel now.' Say, when I am passionately in love, and a biochemist informs me that all my intense sentiments are just the result of biochemical processes in my body, I can respond by clinging to the appearance: 'All that you're saying may be true, but, nonetheless, no one can take from me the intensity of the passion that I am experiencing now . . .' Lacan's point, however, is that the psychoanalyst is the one who, precisely, *can* take this from the subject, i.e., his ultimate aim is to deprive the subject of the very fundamental fantasy that regulates the universe of his (self-)experience. The Freudian 'subject of the unconscious' emerges only when a key aspect of the subject's phenomenal (self-)experience (his 'fundamental fantasy'), becomes inaccessible to him, i.e., is 'primordially repressed'. At its most radical, the unconscious is the *inaccessible phenomenon*, not the objective mechanism that regulates my phenomenal experience. So, in contrast to the commonplace that we are dealing with a subject the moment an entity displays signs of 'inner life', i.e., of a fantasmatic self-experience that cannot be reduced to external behaviour, one should claim that what characterizes human subjectivity proper is rather the gap that separates the two, i.e., the fact that fantasy, at its most elementary, becomes inaccessible to the subject; it is this inaccessibility that makes the subject 'empty'. We thus obtain a relationship that totally subverts the standard notion of the subject who directly experiences himself, his 'inner states': an 'impossible' relationship between the empty, non-phenomenal subject and the phenomena that remain inaccessible to the subject. When David Chalmers opposes phenomenal and psychological concepts of mind (conscious awareness/experience and what mind does), he quotes the Freudian unconscious as the exemplary case of the psychological mind external to the phenomenal mind:[11] what Freud describes as the work of the unconscious is a complex network of mental causality and behavioural control that takes place 'on the other scene', without being experienced. However, is it really like that? Is not the status of the unconscious fantasy nonetheless, in an unheard-of sense, *phenomenal*? Is *this* not the ultimate paradox of the Freudian unconscious – that it designates the way things 'really appear' to us, beyond their conscious appearance?

Another version of this shift in the logic of 'demystification' is discernible in two opposite readings of Lacan's famous thesis on 'Kant avec Sade' (Sade as the truth of Kantian ethics) – what does Lacan's 'Kant with Sade' effectively mean? The first association here is, of course: what's all the fuss about? Today, in our post-idealist Freudian era, doesn't everybody know what the point of the 'with' is – the truth of Kant's ethical rigourism is the sadism of the Law, i.e., the Kantian Law is a superego agency that sadistically enjoys the subject's deadlock, his inability to meet its inexorable demands, like the proverbial teacher who tortures pupils with impossible tasks and secretly savours their failings? Lacan's point, however, is the exact opposite of this first association: it is not Kant who was a closet sadist, it is Sade who is a closet Kantian. That is to say, what one should bear in mind is that the focus of Lacan is always Kant, not Sade: what he is interested in are the ultimate consequences and disavowed premises of the Kantian ethical revolution. In other words, Lacan does not try to make the usual 'reductionist' point that every ethical act, as pure and disinterested as it may appear, is always grounded in some 'pathological' motivation (the agent's own long-term interest, the admiration of his peers, up to the 'negative' satisfaction provided by the suffering and extortion often demanded by ethical acts); the focus of Lacan's interest rather resides in the paradoxical reversal by means of which desire itself (i.e., acting upon one's desire, not conceding it) can no longer be grounded in any 'pathological' interests or motivations and thus meets the criteria of the Kantian ethical act, so that 'following one's desire' overlaps with 'doing one's duty'.

Far from being overrun by the later decentrement of the cognitive sciences, the Freudian decentrement is thus much more unsettling and radical than cognitivism, which remains confined within a simple naturalization: it opens up a new domain of weird 'asubjective phenomena', of appearances with no subject to whom they can appear – it is only here that the subject is 'no longer a master in his own house', in the house of his (self-)appearances themselves. Ten minutes into Hitchcock's *Vertigo*, there is the scene of Scottie encountering Madeleine for the first time. We begin with Scottie sitting at the bar counter in the front room of Ernie's, looking through a partition into a large room full of tables and guests. A long panning shot (without a cut) then takes us back and to the left, giving us an overview of the entire crowded room, the soundtrack reproducing the chatter and clatter of a busy restaurant – we should bear in mind that this, clearly, is *not* Scottie's point-of-view. All of a sudden, our (or, rather, the camera's) attention is caught by a focal point of attraction, a *fascinum* that fixes our gaze, a bright, dazzling stain that we soon identify as the naked back of a beautiful woman. The background sound is then drowned out by Bernard Hermann's passionate music, which accompanies the camera in its gradual approach to the *fascinum* – we first recognize Elster facing us, and from it we deduce that the woman must be Madeleine. After this long shot, there is a cut back to Scottie peeping at Madeleine's table from a different perspective than the previous long shot approaching her, and then another cut to Scottie's point-of-view and what he sees (Madeleine covering her back with her jacket and getting ready to leave). After Madeleine and Elster leave their table and approach Scottie on their way out, we get another famous shot. Scottie sees that the couple are getting close and, in order not to betray his mission, he looks away towards the glass across the partition of the bar, just barely peeping over his back. When Madeleine comes close to him and has to stop for a moment (while her husband is settling the bill with the waiter), we see her mysterious profile (and the profile is always mysterious – we see only one half, while the other half could be a disgusting, disfigured face, or, as a matter of fact, the 'true', common face of Judy). This fascinating shot is thus again *not* Scottie's point-of-view shot: it is only after Elster rejoins Madeleine, with the couple moving away from Scottie and approaching the exit from the restaurant, that we get, as a counter-shot to the shot of Scottie behind the bar, his point-of-view shot of Madeleine and Elster.

The ambiguity of subjective and objective is crucial here: precisely in so far as Madeleine's profile is *not* Scottie's point-of-view, the shot of her profile is *totally* subjectivized, depicting, in a way, not what Scottie effectively sees, but what he imagines, that is, his hallucinatory inner vision (recall how, while we see Madeleine's profile, the red background of the restaurant wall seems to get even more intense, almost threatening to explode in red heat turning into a yellow blaze – as if his passion is directly inscribed into the background). No wonder, then, that, although Scottie does not see Madeleine's profile, he acts as if he is mysteriously captivated by it, deeply affected by it. These two excessive shots are somehow 'subjectivized', without the subject being given: it is as if they directly register the passion of an intensity that cannot be assumed by the (diegetic) subject. So, what we get in these two shots, which are subjectivized without being attributed to a subject, is precisely the *pure, pre-subjective phenomenon*. Is the profile of Madeleine not such a pure appearance, permeated with an excessive libidinal investment – in a way, precisely *too 'subjective'*, too intense, to be assumed by the subject? Or, to put it in Lacan's terms, this shot of the profile of Madeleine appears on the Other Scene, inaccessible to the subject precisely in so far as it is located in its very core.

And even the twentieth-century evolution of 'hard' sciences generated the same paradox: in quantum physics, the 'appearance' (perception) of a particle determines its reality. The very emergence of 'hard reality' out of fluctuation through the collapse of wave-function is the outcome of observation, i.e., of the intervention of consciousness. Consciousness is thus not the domain of potentiality, multiple options, etc., opposed to hard single reality – instead, reality *previous* to its perception is fluid, multiple, open, and conscious perception reduces this spectral, pre-ontological, multiplicity to one ontologically fully constituted reality. This opens up the way that quantum physics conceives of the relationship between particles and their interactions: in an initial moment, it appears as if first (ontologically, at least) there are particles interacting in the mode of waves, oscillations, etc.; then, in a second moment, we are forced to enact a radical shift of perspective – the primordial ontological fact is the waves themselves (trajectories, oscillations), and particles are nothing but the nodal points in which different waves intersect.

Consequently, quantum physics confronts us with the gap between the Real and reality at its most radical: what we get in it is the mathematized Real of formulas that cannot be translated into ontologically consistent reality, or, to put it in Kantian terms, they remain pure concepts that cannot be 'schematized', translated or transposed into objects of experience. This is also how, after the crisis of the 1920s, quantum physics in practice resolved the crisis of its ontological interpretation: by renouncing the very effort to provide such an interpretation – quantum physics is scientific formalization at its most radical, formalization without interpretation. Is it then not accurate to say that quantum physics involves a kind of reversal of the Kantian transcendental ontology?[12] In Kant, we have access to ordinary experiential reality, but the moment we try to apply our transcendental categories to the noumenal Real itself, we get involved in contradictions; in quantum physics, it is the noumenal Real that can be grasped and formulated in a consistent theory, while the moment we try to translate this theory into the terms of our experience of phenomenal reality, we get caught up in senseless contradictions (time runs backwards, the same object is in two places simultaneously, an entity is a particle and a wave, etc.). (However, it can still be claimed that these contradictions only emerge when we try to transpose the 'Real' of the quantum processes into our experiential reality – in itself, this reality remains the same as before, a consistent realm with which we are well acquainted.)

So not only is appearance inherent to reality; what we get beyond this is a weird split in appearance itself, an unheard-of mode designating 'the way things really appear to us', as opposed to both their reality and their (direct) appearance. This shift from the split between appearance and reality to the split inherent to appearance itself, between 'true' and 'false' appearance, is to be linked to its obverse, to a split inherent to reality itself. If, then, there is appearance (as distinct from reality) because there is a (logically) prior split inherent to reality itself, is it also that 'reality' itself is ultimately nothing but a (self-)split of appearance (the 'parallax' thesis)?

There are three main attitudes one can adopt towards this breakthrough. The first is simply to insist on radical naturalism whatever the price, heroically to pursue the logic of the scientific 'disenchantment of reality' whatever the cost, i.e., even if the very fundamental coordinates of our horizon of meaningful experience are shattered. (In cognitive sciences, Patricia and Paul Churchland have most radically opted for this attitude.) The second option is the attempt at some kind of New Age 'synthesis' between the scientific Truth and the premodern world of Meaning: the claim is that new scientific results themselves (say, quantum physics) compel us to abandon materialism and point towards some new (gnostic or Eastern) spirituality. The third option is that of a neo-Kantian state philosophy whose exemplary instance today is Habermas. It is a rather sad spectacle to see Habermas trying to control the explosive results of biogenetics, to curtail their philosophical consequences – his entire effort betrays the fear that something would effectively happen, that a new dimension of the 'human' would emerge, that the old image of human dignity and autonomy would not survive unscathed. The very *excessiveness* of these reactions is symptomatic here, like the ridiculous overreaction to Peter Sloterdijk's Elmau speech on Heidegger and biogenetics, discerning echoes of Nazi eugenics in the (quite reasonable) proposal that biogenetics compels us to formulate new rules of ethics. What this attitude towards scientific progress amounts to is a kind of 'temptation of (resisting) temptation': the temptation to be resisted is precisely the pseudo-ethical attitude of presenting scientific exploration as a temptation that can lead us into 'going too far' – entering the forbidden territory (of biogenetic manipulations, etc.) and thus endangering the very core of our humanity.

The latest ethical 'crisis' apropos of biogenetics effectively created the need for what one is fully justified in calling a 'state philosophy': a philosophy that would, on the one hand, condone scientific research and technical process, and, on the other hand, contain its full socio-symbolic impact, i.e., prevent it from posing a threat to the existing theologico-ethical constellation. No wonder those who come closest to meeting these demands are neo-Kantians: Kant himself was focused on the problem of how, while fully taking into account Newtonian science, to guarantee that there is a space of ethical responsibility exempted from the reach of science – i.e., as Kant himself put it, he limited the scope of knowledge to create the space for faith and morality. And are today's state philosophers not facing the same task? Is their effort not focused on how, through different versions of transcendental reflection, to restrict science to its preordained horizon of meaning and thus to denounce as 'illegitimate' its consequences for the ethico-religious sphere? It is interesting to note how, although Sloterdijk was the target of a violent Habermasian attack, his proposed solution, a 'humanist' synthesis of the new scientific Truth and the old horizon of Meaning, although much more refined and ironically-sceptical than the Habermasian 'state philosophy', is ultimately separated from it by an almost invisible frontier (more precisely, it seems to persist in the ambiguity between the Habermasian compromise and the New Age obscurantist synthesis). According to Sloterdijk, 'humanism' always involves such a reconciliation, a bridge between the New and the Old: when scientific results undermine the old universe of meaning, one should find a way to reintegrate them into the universe of Meaning, or, rather, to expand metaphorically the old universe of Meaning so that it can 'cover' also new scientific propositions. If we fail in this mediating task, we remain stuck in the brutal choice: either a reactionary refusal to accept scientific results, or the shattering loss of the very domain of Meaning. Today, we confront the same challenge: 'Mathematicians will have to become poets, cyberneticists philosophers of religion, [medical] doctors composers, information-workers shamans.'[13] Is this solution, however, not that of *obscurantism* in the precise sense of the attempt to keep meaning and truth harnessed together?

> The simplest definition of God and of religion lies in the idea that truth and meaning are one and the same thing. The death of God is the end of the idea that posits truth and meaning as the same thing. And I would add that the death of Communism also implies the separation between meaning and truth as far as history is concerned. 'The meaning of history' has two meanings: on the one hand, 'orientation', history goes somewhere; and then history has a meaning, which is the history of human emancipation by way of the proletariat, etc. In fact, the entire age of Communism was a period where the conviction that it was possible to make correct political decisions; we were, at that moment, driven by the meaning of history . . . Then the death of Communism becomes the second death of God but in the territory of history. There is a connection between the two events and the consequence is, so to speak, that we should be aware that to produce truthful effects that are primarily local (be they psychoanalytical, scientific, etc.) is always an effect of local truth, never of global truth . . . Today we may call 'obscurantism' the intention of keeping them harnessed together – meaning and truth.[14]

Badiou is here correct in emphasizing the gap between meaning and truth – i.e., the non-hermeneutic status of truth – as the minimal difference that separates religious idealism from materialism. This is also the difference between Freud and Jung: while Jung remains within the horizon of meaning, Freudian interpretation aims at articulating a truth which is no longer grounded in meaning. Badiou is also correct in formulating the ultimate alternative that confronts us today, when the impossibility of the conjunction of meaning and truth is imposed on us: either we endorse the 'postmodern' stance and renounce the dimension of truth altogether, constraining ourselves to the interplay of multiple meanings, or we engage in the effort to discern a dimension of truth outside meaning – i.e., in brief, the dimension of truth as *Real*.

However, what remains false is the parallel between the death of God and the death of Communism, implicitly referring to the old boring anti-Communist cliché that Communism is a 'secular religion'; and linked to this falsity is also the all too hasty acceptance of the 'postmodern' notion that, in today's politics, we are limited to 'local' truths, because, without a grounding in global meaning, it is no longer possible to formulate an all-encompassing truth. The fact that renders this conclusion problematic is the very fact of capitalist globalization – what is capitalist globalization? Capitalism is the first socio-economic order which *de-totalizes meaning*: it is not global at the level of meaning (there is no global 'capitalist world view', no 'capitalist civilization' proper – the fundamental lesson of globalization is precisely that capitalism can accommodate itself to all civilizations, from Christian to Hindu and Buddhist); its global dimension can only be formulated at the level of truth-without-meaning, as the 'Real' of the global market mechanism. Consequently, in so far as capitalism already enacts the rupture between meaning and truth, it can be opposed at two levels: either at the level of meaning (conservative reactions to re-enframe capitalism within some social field of meaning, to contain its self-propelling movement within the confines of a system of shared 'values' that cement a 'community' in its 'organic unity'), or to question the Real of capitalism with regard to its truth-outside-meaning (what, basically, Marx did). Of course, the predominant religious strategy today is that of trying to contain the scientific Real within the confines of meaning – it is as an answer to the scientific Real (materialized in biogenetic threats) that religion is finding its new *raison d'être*:

Far from being effaced by science, religion, and even the syndicate of religions, in the process of formation, is progressing every day.

Lacan said that ecumenism was for the poor of spirit. There is a marvellous agreement on these questions between the secular and all the religious authorities, in which they tell themselves they should agree somewhere in order to make echoes equally marvellous, even saying that finally the secular is a religion like the others. We see this because it is revealed in effect that the discourse of science has partly connected with the death drive. Religion is planted in the position of the unconditional defence of the living, of life in mankind, as guardian of life, making life an absolute. And that extends to the protection of human nature . . . This is what gives a future to religion through meaning, namely by erecting barriers – to cloning, to the exploitation of human cells – and to inscribe science in a tempered progress. We see a marvellous effort, a new youthful vigour of religion in its effort to flood the Real with meaning.[15]

This simple, but salient, diagnosis ends up in a surprising paraphrase of Heidegger, defining the analyst as the 'shepherd of the Real'. However, it leaves some key questions open. Is the death drive for which science stands, which it mobilizes in its activity, not simultaneously an *excess of obscene life*, of life as Real, exempted from and external to meaning (life that we find embodied in Kafka's 'odradek' as well as in the 'alien' from the film of the same name)? One should not forget that death drive is a Freudian name for immortality, for a pressure, a compulsion, which insists beyond death (and let us also not forget that immortality is also implicitly promised by science). One should therefore also assert a gap between life and meaning, homologous to that between truth and meaning – life and meaning in no way fully overlap. Furthermore, can all religious experiences and practices themselves effectively be contained within the dimension of the conjunction of truth and meaning? Does not Judaism, with its imposition of a traumatic Law, point towards a dimension of truth outside meaning (which is why Judaism is the mortal enemy of any Gnostic obscurantism)? And does not, at a different level, the same go for St Paul himself? This is why it is wrong to oppose the Christian god of Love to the Jewish god of cruel justice: excessive cruelty is the necessary obverse of Christian Love, and, again, the relationship between these two is one of parallax: there is no 'substantial' difference between the god of Love and god of excessive-arbitrary cruelty – it is one and the same god who appears in a different light only due to a parallactic shift of our perspective.

Notes

1   Martin Heidegger, *Identity and Difference*, trans. Joan Stambaugh, London, Harper and Row, 1969, p. 72.

2   For instance, Jacques Derrida, *Foi et Savoir, suivi de 'Le Siècle et le Pardon'*, Paris, Éditions du Seuil, 2000. [eds]

3   For instance, Sigmund Freud, 'Delusions and dreams in Jensen's *Gradiva*', in *The Penguin Freud Library, 14: Art and Literature*, ed. and trans. James Strachey, Harmondsworth, Penguin, 1985, pp. 66–87. [eds]

4   I rely here on conversations with Alain Badiou.

5   Jacques Lacan, *The Seminar of Jacques Lacan XX: On Feminine Sexuality, the Limits of Love and Knowledge (Encore), 1972–73*, ed. Jacques-Alain Miller, trans. Bruce Fink, New York and London, W. W. Norton, 1998, pp. 66–71. [eds]

6   See Carl Zimmer's concise report, 'The ultimate remote control', in *Newsweek*, 14 June 2004, p. 73.

7   Daniel C. Dennett, *Consciousness Explained*, Harmondsworth, Penguin, 1991, p. 397. [eds]

8   Jean Laplanche, *Vie et mort en psychanalyse*, Paris, Flammarion, 1989, p. 58.

9   Karl Marx, *Capital: A Critique of Political Economy, Volume 1*, trans. Ben Fowkes, London, Penguin/New Left Review, 1976, p. 163.

10 Karl Marx, 'Towards a critique of Hegel's philosophy of right: introduction', in *Early Texts*, ed. and trans. David McLellan, Oxford, Basil Blackwell, 1971, p. 115.

11 David Chalmers, *The Conscious Mind: In Search of a Fundamental Theory*, Oxford, Oxford University Press, 1997, p. 13. [eds]

12 I rely here on unpublished texts by Adrian Johnston.

13 Peter Sloterdijk, *Nicht gerettet*, Frankfurt, Suhrkamp Verlag, 2001, p. 365.

14 'A conversation with Alain Badiou', *lacanian ink* 23, 2004, pp. 100–1.

15 Jacques-Alain Miller, 'Religion, psychoanalysis', *lacanian ink* 23, 2004, pp. 18–19.

Glossary

As noted in the first volume of Žižek's *Selected Writings*, this Glossary could be only a momentary *capitonnage* of Žižek's theoretical system. There are any number of other entries we could have chosen and any number of other passages from Žižek's texts we could have included under any entry. This is evident in those entries that are also to be found in the first volume, but which return here in different circumstances and with different meanings. At the same time, what is attempted to be brought out is the real conceptual rigour that characterizes Žižek's choice of terms: the work they do to organize and hold together the extremely disparate material he covers in his writing. Indeed, in some ways – this is what we attempt to show here by means of the cross-references under every entry – we would even claim that each of these entries is the 'same' entry: that each is as it were a synonym of that *universal exception* (and its covering over) that is the subject of Žižek's work in this volume. Finally, it might be noted that a number of proper names, both here and in the first volume, are listed as concepts. This is true: proper names do the work of concepts in Žižek's system, but this is also to say that these concepts for their part are proper names. When they are used correctly – and this can only be demonstrated ironically in this Glossary, through its very failure – it is always in a singular and event-like way, beyond the reach of any classification.

ACT/ORGANIZATION (see also **REAL, REVOLUTION, THINKING, VIOLENCE**)

The act is bound by a paradox, which is to say it is always divided from itself. On the one hand, it is necessary to act prematurely, without objective justification: 'Like the Lacanian analyst, a political agent has to commit acts that can only be authorized by themselves, for which there is no external guarantee' (54). On the other hand, a simple acting-out or *passage à l'acte* merely reproduces the ideological coordinates in which it takes place: 'If, today, one follows a direct call to act, this act will not be performed in an empty space – it will be an act within the hegemonic ideological coordinates' (238). What is the difference between these two conceptions? How to distinguish a genuine from a false act? In fact, we cannot do so in advance – it is for this reason that an act is always premature – but only by what occurs afterwards. As Žižek says: 'It is *only* this reference to what happens *after* the revolution, the proverbial "morning after", that allows us to distinguish between libertarian pathetic outbursts and true revolutionary upheavals' (50). That is, it is only in retrospect that objective reasons for the act exist, after the revolution has organized and stabilized itself. But there is a further point here: the ultimate act of any revolution is its imposing of a new order. And it is for this reason that the 'instrumentalization' of the revolution is not to be understood as its sublation or compromise, but as part of the revolution itself, for the revolution does not exist *until after it*: '[Revolution] begins with the gesture of radical negativity . . . There then follows a second stage, the invention of a new life – not only the construction of a new social reality within which our utopian dreams would be realized, but the (re)construction of these dreams themselves' (50).

ANTAGONISM (see also **CLASS STRUGGLE, COMMUNISM, REAL, UNIVERSAL EXCEPTION**)

Antagonism is inherent to the social field. As such, the social can only be constructed around its own constitutive void. For Žižek, the essential fantasy is that the social can be rendered as whole, that any antagonism is merely contingent or tied to some particular element: 'The elementary image of the social fantasy is that of a *social body*, through which one eludes the impossible, the antagonism around which the social field is structured' (89). And this denial can take several forms. In fascist ideology, this antagonism is displaced on to an apparently external obstacle, whose removal would restore an imaginary wholeness. (We have a more contemporary version of this in the now-popular idea of the 'clash of civilizations', which reduces the internal limits of capitalism to an 'us' versus 'them' opposition [278]). In postmodern identity politics, the antagonism that is inherent to the 'all' of the social is dispersed into the multitude of local struggles: 'Postmoderns, of course, will calmly reply that antagonisms are radical only so long as society is still – anachronistically – perceived as a totality' (35). What Žižek himself proposes might, at first, appear similar to this strategy of local struggle: 'Therein resides one of the tasks of the "postmodern" criticism of ideology: to designate those elements within an existing social order that – in the guise of "fiction", that is, of the "utopian" narratives of possible but failed alternative histories – point towards its antagonistic character and thus "estrange" us from the self-evidence of its established identity' (18). However, the crucial difference is that for Žižek this particular thing or event is not an exception to the Universal but *is* the Universal; it does not reveal the failure or impossibility of the Universal, but precisely invokes the Universal as the incessant attempt to take into account that antagonism that makes it possible: '[This paradox] can only be conceived of if *the antagonism is inherent to universality itself*, that is, if universality itself is split into the "false" concrete universality that legitimizes the existing division of the Whole into functional parts and the impossible/Real demand of "abstract" universality' (178).

APPEARANCE (see also *COINCIDENTIA OPPOSITORUM,* INFINITE JUDGEMENT, MARX/ALTHUSSER/BADIOU, PARALLAX VIEW, TRUTH, UNIVERSAL EXCEPTION)

One of Žižek's great Hegelian themes is his emphasis on the importance of appearance. Indeed, underpinning his entire argument is an inversion of the usual relationship between appearance and what lies behind it. It is not for Žižek a matter of revealing a deeper, material basis for surface, ideal phenomena, but rather of tracing material processes back to their ideal origins. This is consistent not only with the move from energetic industrial production to our own virtual, frictionless capitalism, in which 'the image does not represent the product, but, rather, the product represents the image' (238). It is also part of Žižek's long-running emphasis, derived from Althusser, on the symbolic efficiency of appearances: '[Althusser's] theory of ideological state apparatuses assigned the crucial role in the reproduction of an ideology to "external" rituals and practices with regard to which "inner" beliefs and convictions are strictly secondary' (17). It is the belief that appearances are not important – that it is a matter of the convictions underlying them – that Žižek describes as *cynicism*, the prevailing ideology of contemporary society. It is even, in another way, appearance that is lost with the current emphasis on simulation: 'Crucial here is the distinction between appearance and the postmodern notion of the simulacrum as that which is no longer clearly distinguishable from the Real . . . what gets lost in today's plague of simulations is not the firm, true, non-simulated Real, but *appearance itself*' (19). However, if there is nothing outside of appearance – this is how Žižek differs from that previous notion of cause or exception that might be thought to mark materialism – appearance is nonetheless 'not-all'. Appearance is always split precisely by what ensures that all is appearance. What occasionally shines through appearance is not some deeper cause that is solid and permanent, but something more fleeting and fragile – which can occur at any time and place – a kind of *universal exception*. As Žižek writes: 'It is this dimension of appearance that transubstantiates a piece of reality into something that, for a brief moment, illuminates the suprasensible eternity that is missing in the logic of the simulacrum . . . "the Suprasensible is appearance qua appearance" does not simply mean that the suprasensible is not a positive entity *beyond* the phenomenon, but rather points to the inherent power of negativity, which makes appearance "merely an appearance"' (192).

CAPITALISM (see also FETISH, IDEOLOGY, INHERENT TRANSGRESSION)

In a profound formula, Žižek will often speak of capitalism in terms of the Lacanian category of the Real (216–17, 348). By this he means that, in the same way as we cannot avoid the Real, so capitalism today is unavoidable. It represents the totality of our situation, the 'untranscendable horizon' of all particular instances: 'Today, we can easily imagine the extinction of the human race, but it is impossible to imagine a radical change of the social system – even if life on earth disappears, capitalism will somehow remain intact' (149). It is certainly the case that all *partial* attempts to overcome capitalism are doomed in advance: 'the history of capitalism is a long history of the way that the predominant ideologico-political framework was able to accommodate – and soften the subversive edge of – the movements and demands that seemed to threaten its very survival' (106). Accordingly,

Žižek rejects every attempt to alleviate its injustices, all forms of humanitarian intervention, up to and including such organizations as the Zapatistas in Chiapas and Médecins sans frontières. He even rejects such powerful single-issue parties as the Greens, which necessarily remain ineffective in so far as they are not organized in terms of some universal struggle. And yet, if these resistances are only the 'inherent transgression' of capitalism, allowing it to continue, they might also be understood as a kind of 'infinite judgement' upon it, that 'antagonism' outside of which it is not possible. As Žižek will say of another series of political movements, this time conceived of in terms of the Universal: 'It is too simple to conceive of these movements as the last embodiments of the millenarian radicalism that structures the social space as the exclusive antagonism between "us" and "them", allowing for no possible forms of mediation . . . Khmer Rouge and the Senderistas as the "infinite judgement" on late capitalism are, therefore, in Hegelese, an integral part of its notion: if one wants to constitute capitalism as a world system, one must take into account its inherent negation, "fundamentalism", as well as its absolute negation – the infinite judgement on it' (23).

CAPITONNAGE (see also **LOGIC OF EXCEPTION**)
This concept, derived from Ernesto Laclau's analysis of ideological hegemony, continues to be used throughout the later Žižek, despite the increasing distance he adopts toward Laclau's work. To recapitulate what is meant by hegemony: 'the Universal acquires concrete existence when some particular content begins to function as its stand-in . . . The fact that this link between the Universal and the particular content that acts as its stand-in is *contingent* means precisely that it is the outcome of a *political* struggle for ideological hegemony' (152). This notion of *capitonnage*, the idea that the meaning of political terms is not given in themselves but according to how they are organized within an overall configuration, allows Žižek to argue against any essential meaning to these terms, to insist that they are always contingent, open to dispute. Thus, on the one hand, he can say: 'Fascism was not characterized simply by a series of features like economic corporatism, populism, xenophobic racism, militarism and so on, for these could also be included in other ideological configurations; what made these features "fascist" was their specific articulation within an overall political

project' (40–1). And, on the other: 'I find [Havel's] idea of civil society doubly problematic. First, the opposition between State and civil society works *against* as well as *for* liberty and democracy . . . These [conservative cases] are authentic expressions of civil society – "civil society" designates the terrain of open struggle, the terrain in which antagonisms can articulate themselves, without any guarantee that the "progressive" side will win' (145). Indeed, Žižek will speak elsewhere of the way that the ideological meaning of such things as homosexuality, bodily discipline and even Islamic fundamentalism is also not fixed but open to ideological negotiation.

CLASS STRUGGLE (see also **ANTAGONISM, COMMUNISM, INFINITE JUDGEMENT, UNIVERSAL EXCEPTION**)

We might ask: where is class struggle? What is the continued relevance of the notion of class struggle? In fact, the existence of class struggle is denied by both the Right and the Left today. As Žižek admits: 'Of course, even to mention terms like "class" or "labour" is enough to invite the reproach of "economic essentialism" from the postmodernists of the Third Way. My first reaction to the charge is: *why not?*' (35). And yet, if Žižek does assert the existence of class struggle – and this is perhaps his difference from Stalinism – it is not as some ontological, actually existing social reality, involving some specifiable group of people. On the one hand, Žižek asserts that – and he fully accepts the comparison often made between Marxism and religion – anyone can be touched by class struggle (199). And, on the other hand, class is not something that can ever be fully embodied, and thus ever entirely resolved, because 'class' is another name for the excess, the inherent division of each particular from itself. 'We could say that class struggle functions in a strict sense as the "object" of *Capital*, that which *cannot* become the "positive object of research" and that which necessarily *falls* outside and thus makes of the totality of the three books of *Capital* [and we might say of Capital itself] a "not-all"' (82). Class, we might say, is Real not Symbolic. Like the Real of the unconscious in psychoanalysis, there is nothing outside of it; it already takes its own denial or resistance into account. And this is to say that it is *self-relating*. Any pronouncement on class applies before all else to itself, is subject to the very procedure it sets out. And, indeed, class does return today, whether it be in the sweatshops of the Third World, making consumer goods for the First (36), or in the heart of Hollywood, in those moments when the villain shows his secret factory to James Bond before killing him (37).

COINCIDENTIA OPPOSITORUM (see also **APPEARANCE, INFINITE JUDGEMENT, MESSAGE IN REVERSE, PARALLAX VIEW, THIRD WAY, YUGOSLAVIA**)

Žižek notes throughout his writings a strange coming together of opposites, things somehow engendering their own contradiction. From the side of capitalism: 'What defines postmodern post-politics is thus the secret solidarity between its Janus faces: on the one hand, the replacement of politics proper by depoliticized, so-called humanitarian operations . . .; on the other hand, the violent emergence of depoliticized pure evil in the guise of excessive ethnic or religious fundamentalist violence' (193–4). From the side of Communism: 'To put it in the terms of the speculative coincidence of the opposites, or of the 'infinite judgement' in which the highest coincides with the lowest . . . "Arise, you prisoners of work!", is granted a deeper ironic meaning: the ultimate "truth" of the pathetic original meaning of these words ("Resist, break the chains that constrain you and reach for freedom!") turns out to be its literal meaning, the call to tired workers, "Get up, slaves, and start working for us, the Party *nomenklatura!*"' (102). And Žižek's point – this is the *coincidentoria oppositorum* that defines the Real – is that we must refuse both of these alternatives. We cannot choose one in an unmediated way, but must insist that both in their very opposition are the truth – a truth that is always split, partial, 'not-all'. In fact, more than this, in a properly Hegelian dialectical process, one of the opposites is also the medium through which this opposition occurs, is not merely one of the species but also the genus the species have in common. This is how a proper 'universality' works, as not only what is specifically opposed to what is but as the very form or possibility of this opposition itself: 'It is far more productive, theoretically as well as politically – because it opens up the way for the "progressive" subversion of hegemony – to perform the opposite operation of *identifying universality with the point of exclusion* . . . In a hierarchically structured society, the measure of its true universality resides in the way its parts relate to those "at the bottom", excluded by and from all others' (179).

COMMUNISM (see also ANTAGONISM, CLASS STRUGGLE, INHUMAN, REVOLUTION)

In the wake of the 'failure' of Really Existing Socialism, it is easy to condemn Communism, along with fascism, as one of the twentieth century's great disasters. However, Žižek insists against such a response that would make Stalinism and Nazism equivalent, which is precisely a way of depoliticizing both, of failing to think their historical and organizational specificity. For him, we *have* to make a distinction between them, declare one worse than the other: 'It is here that one has to make the choice: the "pure" liberal stance of equidistance towards leftist and rightist "totalitarianism" (they are both dead, based on intolerance towards political and other differences, the rejection of democratic and humanist values, etc.) is *a priori* false – one *has* to take a side and proclaim one fundamentally "worse" than the other' (126). But in what would this distinction lie? What is the difference between them? In fact, for all of their shared fate, the two régimes are fundamentally opposed. In fascism, the inherent antagonism of the social is projected outwards on to some external, contingent agent; in Communism, the social itself is structured by those repeated, failed attempts internally to grasp its own principle, that of the revolutionary vocation of the proletariat as incarnated in the Party: 'In the case of race [in Nazism], we are dealing with a positive naturalized element (the presupposed organic unity of Society is perturbed by the intrusion of a foreign body), while class antagonism [in Communism] is absolutely inherent to and constitutive of the social field – Fascism thus obfuscates antagonism, translating it into a conflict between positive opposed terms' (127). However, if there is an error with Stalinism, it is the belief that – very close to Nazism – this internal principle can be objectively represented, its truth spoken of in some neutral disengaged way: '[In Stalinism] the Party functions as the miraculous immediate incarnation of an objective, neutral Knowledge, which in turn serves as a point of reference to legitimate the activity of the Party' (67). Nevertheless, for all of its mistakes, Communism, even in its Stalinist version, remains for Žižek a model of the materialization of the revolutionary impulse and its life-transforming possibilities: 'As Alain Badiou pointed out, in spite of its horrors and failures, Really Existing Socialism was the only political force that – for some decades, at least – seemed to pose a serious threat to the global rule of capitalism, genuinely scaring its representatives, driving them into paranoiac reaction. But now that, today, capitalism defines and structures the totality of human civilization, every "Communist" territory was and is – again, in spite of its horrors and failures – a kind of "liberated territory", as Fredric Jameson put it' (46).

DEMOCRACY (see also LOGIC OF EXCEPTION, UNIVERSAL EXCEPTION)

Žižek's position on democracy is complex and changing. At times, following the work of the French political theorist Étienne Balibar, he concedes the liberatory potential of democracy and, indeed, its efficacy as a way of thinking the 'universal exception', the fact that political space is permanently open to what can be given no place within it. As he asks: '"What is politics proper?" It is a phenomenon that appeared for the first time in ancient Greece when the members of the *demos* (those with no firmly determined place in the hierarchical social edifice) presented themselves as the representatives, the stand-ins, for the whole of society, for the true universality' (183). However, Žižek can also condemn contemporary versions of democracy for forgetting this absolute limit – the fact that no political system can constitute an 'all' – or for trying to reduce this limit to a simple 'other': 'The problem with liberal democracy is that – for structural reasons – it cannot be universalized *a priori*. Hegel said that the moment of victory of a political force is the very moment of its splitting: the triumphant liberal-democratic "new world order" is more and more marked by a frontier separating its "inside" from its "outside"' (21). This is why Žižek can on occasions advocate the suppression or even overthrow of democracy, a refusal to follow its rules, because democracy itself is merely a contingent form of political organization: 'At this point, it is crucial to avoid the "democratic" trap. Many 'radical' leftists accept the legalistic logic of "transcendental guarantee": they refer to "democracy" as the ultimate guarantee of those who are aware that there is no guarantee . . . The only adequate position is the one advocated already by Lukács in *History and Class Consciousness*: democratic struggle should not be fetishized; it is merely one of many forms of struggle, and its choice should be determined by a global strategic assessment of circumstances, not by its ostensibly superior intrinsic value' (54). And yet at other moments he can also see the signs of 'another' democracy emerging from within the cracks of global capitalism: 'direct democracy is not only still alive in many places (like *favelas*), it is even being "reinvented" and given a new impetus by the rise of "post-industrial" digital culture – do the descriptions of new "tribal" communities of computer-hackers not often evoke the logic of "council-democracy"?' (52).

FAILURE (see also INFINITE JUDGEMENT)

It is a fundamental lesson of Hegelian dialectics that we are aware of failure only from within a horizon that already admits success, that the acknowledgment of failure already is a form of success. Žižek will make this point with regard to the great 'failures' of the twentieth century: 'Most of today's claims that the twentieth century was the most catastrophic in human history, the lowest point of nihilism, a situation of extreme danger, etc., forget the elementary lesson of dialectics: the twentieth century appears as such because the criteria themselves changed – today, we simply have much higher standards of what constitutes a violation of human rights, and so on. The fact that the situation *appears* catastrophic is thus in itself a positive sign, a sign of (some kind of) progress' (42–3). This will allow Žižek to argue of Communism, for example, that although it is judged a failure it also allowed the space from which this verdict could be rendered: 'What anti-Communist dissidents as a rule tend to overlook is that the very space from which they themselves criticized and denounced the everyday misery of the régimes *was opened and sustained by the Communist breakthrough, by its attempt to escape the logic of Capital*' (46). Indeed, Žižek will even go on to assert something like this of Stalinism, which arguably embodied the very worst extremes of Really Existing Socialism: 'Even the most "totalitarian" Stalinist ideology is radically ambiguous. While the universe of Stalinist politics was undoubtedly one of hypocrisy and arbitrary terror, in the late 1930s the great Soviet films (say, the Gorky trilogy) epitomized authentic solidarity for audiences across Europe' (146). This last example points towards the most important aspect of this notion of failure as success: that every phenomenon is in a way self-splitting, opens up room for its own critique. The dialectical conversion of failure into success does not ever come to an end, but rather suggests a kind of 'infinite judgement'.

FETISH (see also **CAPITALISM, IDEOLOGY, LOGIC OF EXCEPTION**)

The fetish, within the Freudian psychoanalytic tradition, is the denial of that lack necessary for a universal symbolic order: 'the *castrative* dimension of the phallic signifier is disavowed with the fetish, the "nothing" that necessarily accompanies its "all", the radical heterogeneity of this element relative to the *universality* that it is meant to incarnate' (7). Žižek will emphasize two things in particular with regard to this fetish: the first is that it is not a subjective illusion but is embodied in material practices, and for this reason it works despite – or, indeed, through – our apparent distance from it (the problem of 'cynicism' in contemporary societies). Thus it is not a matter of us directly believing in the magical properties of something like money, but rather of us behaving in our social interactions *as though* we do: 'the fetishist illusion resides in our real social life, not in our perception of it – a bourgeois subject knows very well that there is nothing magic about money, that money is just an object which stands for a set of social relations, but he nevertheless *acts* in real life as if he believed that money is a magical thing' (254–5). The second is that we believe, not directly, but only through another (again, the question of cynicism). One distinctively modern form this takes is what Žižek calls 'interpassive leftism', in which the Western (often academic) Left idealizes the lives of people under Communism as embodying their own inner beliefs: 'what these leftists displace on to the Other is not a specific kind of activity, but their passive authentic experience. They allow themselves to pursue their well-paid academic careers in the West, while using an idealized Other (like Cuba, Nicaragua, Tito's Yugoslavia) as the stuff of their ideological fantasy: they dream through the Other, and rage against it if it in any way disturbs their complacency' (45).

IDEOLOGY (see also **CAPITALISM, FETISH, INHERENT TRANSGRESSION, MESSAGE IN REVERSE**)

As Žižek insists, 'ideology is always self-referential, that is, it always defines itself through some distance towards an Other dismissed and denounced as "ideological"' (162). This is why he is able to condemn, on the political Right or Centre, humanitarian interventions in such places as Kosovo or even Rwanda, which understand themselves as strictly non-ideological or depoliticized (219–20). It is also why, on the Left, he is able to condemn Westerners for criticizing Eastern Europe's move to capitalism instead of remaining true to some notion of socialism after the fall of Communism: 'There are few things more worthy of contempt, few attitudes more *ideological* (if this word has any meaning today, it should be applied here), than a tenured Western academic leftist arrogantly dismissing (or, even worse, 'understanding' in a patronizing way) an Eastern European from a Communist country who longs for Western liberal democracy and some consumer goods' (43). And indeed it is something like this 'interpassivity' that characterizes ideology today: while the other is condemned for an excess of belief, our supposedly 'non-ideological' stance is only possible because they believe in our place. That is, even in our personal relationship to ideology, our stance is characterized by a certain distance. As embodied in concrete social practices, it does not matter whether we actually believe – our belief is already assumed by the big Other: '[Althusser's] theory of ideological state apparatuses assigned the crucial role in the reproduction of an ideology to "external" rituals and practices with regard to which "inner" beliefs and convictions are strictly secondary' (17). This is why the true 'anti-ideological' attitude is not at all to adopt a critical attitude towards ideology, but to seek to do away with any such distance. This is what Žižek sees at stake in those naïve, 'sincere' believers in Communism, who were in fact intolerable for the régime (17), in Václav Havel's notion of 'living in truth' (141) and in the Slovenian rock-performance group Laibach (65). The distinction might be made in this regard between so-called 'reality' TV shows, in which 'real people' falsely play themselves (275), and something like the 1920 restaging of the 1917 October Revolution, in which the participants, simply by playing their assigned roles, did away with any distance between them and the new social order (48–9, 130).

INFINITE JUDGEMENT (see also **APPEARANCE,** *COINCIDENTIA OPPOSITORUM,* **FAILURE, INHERENT TRANSGRESSION, LOGIC OF EXCEPTION, MESSAGE IN REVERSE, REVOLUTION, THIRD WAY, TRUTH, UNIVERSAL EXCEPTION, YUGOSLAVIA**)
Žižek provocatively refers to the 'infinite judgement' that 'asserts the speculative identity of these "useless" and "excessive" outbursts of violence that display nothing but a naked ("non-sublimated") hatred of Otherness, with the post-political multiculturalist universe of tolerance for difference in which no one is excluded' (214). What he means more

generally by this is the Hegelian idea that every proper notion is 'self-relating', comes about only by standing in for its opposite. And Žižek uses this idea not only to speak of the way that certain processes when pushed beyond a certain limit begin to produce the opposite effects from those intended – as above, multiculturalist universalism leads to particularist violence, global capitalism leads to the impoverishment of the workers – but of the way that, from the beginning, these processes are possible only because of their opposite. To put this otherwise, every proper notion is subject to the universal law it proposes. There is no exception to universality, not even that place from where it is enunciated: a true universality is one in which he who proposes it is necessarily in breach of the law put forward. Hence, as Žižek can say of the recent American invasion of Iraq: *'The problem with the United States today is not that it represents a new global Empire, but that it does not, i.e., that, while pretending to be Imperial, it continues to act as a Nation-State, ruthlessly pursuing its own interests'* (303 n. 5). On the other hand, a 'good' example of this infinite judgement in action is Freud's analysis in *Moses and Monotheism*, in which he applies the Enlightenment gesture of psychoanalysis to his own Jewish identity: 'One has to gather the strength to repeat the exemplary heroic gesture of Freud who answered the threat of Fascist anti-Semitism by targeting Jews themselves and depriving them of their founding father: *Moses and Monotheism* is Freud's answer to Nazism' (19).

INHERENT TRANSGRESSION (see also CAPITALISM, IDEOLOGY, INFINITE JUDGEMENT, LOGIC OF EXCEPTION)

Inherent transgression is that operation by which an ideology captures us not directly but only through its apparent overturning or opposite: 'The deepest identification that holds a community together is not so much an identification with the Law that regulates its "normal" everyday rhythms, but rather identification with the specific form of transgression of the Law, of its suspension (in psychoanalytic terms, with the specific form of *enjoyment*)' (28). The idea derives from the Russian literary theorist Mikhail Bakhtin and his understanding of the way societies required periodic fêtes and festivals, the upending of social conventions – that is, instituted days in which the usual social roles were reversed – although, as Žižek argues, Bakhtin's mistake was to present only an 'idealized' version of these transgressions (64).

However, this idea is also consistent with Žižek's own understanding of the way ideology works today through our distance from it – our 'interpassive' belief through another, our apparent scepticism towards society's prevailing values. Some examples of this less 'idealized' form of inherent transgression that Žižek points to throughout his work include such things as the 'lynching parties' of the Deep South, where the white population was held together by their shared but denied complicity; the famous 'Code Red' of the film *A Few Good Men*, which permits certain 'illegal' actions in particular circumstances (63); and even the small acts of dishonesty and compromise that Havel sees as contributing to the hold of Communism in his famous essay 'The Power of the powerless' (8). The important ambiguity here – perhaps left slightly unexplored by Žižek – is the way that, if this 'inherent transgression' means that there is no way out of the system, that every transgression is recuperated, it also means that the Law is 'not-all', that it can work only through its other. As Žižek asks: 'Where does this splitting of Law into the written public Law and its underside, the "unwritten", obscene secret code, come from? The answer is from the incomplete, "not-all" character of public Law itself: explicit, public rules do not suffice, so they must be supplemented by a clandestine, "unwritten" code aimed at those who, although they violate no public rules, maintain a kind of inner distance and do not truly identify with *l'ésprit du corps*' (63–4). In this regard, the notion of inherent transgression is also caught up in the relationship between the 'masculine' logic of a universal proved by an exception and a 'feminine' universality as itself exception.

INHUMAN (see also **COMMUNISM, REVOLUTION**)
There is a productive version of anti-humanism that runs throughout Žižek's work – which must be seen as opposed to the false empathy and feeling of others' pain of both Third Way politics and Peter Singer and Richard Rorty's versions of ethical pragmatism – but it must be understood very carefully. Take, for example, Žižek's treatment of Lenin's letter to Gorky, written before the revolution in 1913. Lenin repeatedly expresses concerns over Gorky's health. Why? Because, to Lenin's way of thinking, it was the failing of Gorky's health that explained his ideological deviations. For Lenin, the true revolutionary overcomes his body, or more precisely, it is cast aside as unimportant in the revolutionary cause: 'the spirit of a true Communist cannot deviate,

because this spirit is immediately the self-awareness of historical necessity. Consequently, the only thing that can disturb or introduce disorder and deviation is his body – this fragile materiality serving to support another body, the sublime body, "made of a special stuff"' (69). We could perhaps compare this 'different fabric' to the Lacanian notion of the subject ($), which is a kind of non-pathological excess over and against its physical incarnation. This is why Žižek emphasizes throughout his work recent advances in genetics and the discovery of the human genome (337–8). The genome, like the revolutionary cause, simply uses the human body for its own impersonal ends. And yet, paradoxically – this is also Lacan's point regarding the subject, following Descartes – this genome is very close to what one might mean by the 'soul': it is what necessarily remains excessive within human experience, separating us from ourselves. In this regard, it might be compared as well to the Freudian death drive, that which takes us beyond ourselves and leaves us 'between two deaths'.

LOGIC OF EXCEPTION (see also CAPITONNAGE, DEMOCRACY, FETISH, INFINITE JUDGEMENT, INHERENT TRANSGRESSION, UNIVERSAL EXCEPTION)

Close to the notion of 'inherent transgression' is what we might call the 'logic of exception'. Instances of this discussed in Žižek's work include Western societies' 'outsourcing' of both their working classes and the torture required for the 'war against terrorism'; America's refusal to allow its citizens to be tried before the Tribunal at the Hague, while insisting that other countries do; and wealthy countries insisting on trade reforms in the Third World, while failing to enact these same measures themselves (296–7). In each case what we are speaking about is an apparently universal principle being enunciated, but that place from where it is enunciated somehow being excluded or exempted. Žižek writes of this empty place that allows the making-equivalent of all others within multiculturalism: 'that of a *symptom*. When one is dealing with a universal structuring principle, one always automatically assumes that – in principle, precisely – it is possible to apply this principle to all of its potential elements, and that the empirical non-realization of the principle is merely a matter of contingent circumstances. A symptom . . . is an element that . . . *must* remain an exception, that is, the point of suspension of the universal principle: if the universal principle were to apply also to this point, the universal system itself would disintegrate . . . the properly capitalist utopia is that, through appropriate measures (for progressive liberals, affirmative action; for conservatives, a return to self-reliance and family values), this "exception" could be – in the long term and in principle, at least – abolished' (171). As Žižek suggests here – and this point is perhaps too little understood – it would never be a matter of entirely doing away with the exception. The 'universal exception' is not simply opposed to the logic of the exception, nor really some principle outside of it. Rather, it is the logic of exception endlessly applied to itself, where each time we find the exception that allows the exception to be stated and reveal that any stated universality is only another exception. This 'opposition' can be seen in the distinction Žižek makes between 'globalization' and 'universalization'. 'Globalization' remains a universality defined by an exception (whether it be the exclusion of the working class, the Third World or 'fundamentalist' ethnic or religious minorities), while 'universalization', although always defined by an exception, is also an attempt to think that for which this exception stands in: 'Here one should oppose *globalization* to *universalization*: globalization . . . is precisely the name for the emerging post-political logic that progressively precludes the dimension of universality at work in politicization proper. The paradox is that there is no *universal* proper without the process of political litigation of the part of no-part, of an out-of-joint entity presenting/manifesting itself as the stand-in for the universal' (193).

LUKÁCS/ADORNO/BRECHT (see also **MARX/ALTHUSSER/ BADIOU, STALINISM**)
What does this trilogy of authors have in common? What does putting them together like this allow us to think? What is at stake in each of them is a certain disavowed relationship to Stalinism. Žižek emphasizes this several times with regard to Adorno: '"Stalinism" was a traumatic topic on which the Frankfurt School *had* to remain silent – silence was the only way for its members to retain their underlying solidarity with Western liberal democracy, without losing their mask of radical leftism' (143). (And Žižek will go on to speak of the way that the Frankfurt School precisely served as support for the régime in the ex-Yugoslavia.) With regard to Brecht, Žižek will on the one hand

approve of his support for the East German government's violent suppression of the workers' strikes of 1953, which proved to him the 'authenticity' of its revolutionary determination. On the other hand, he will also remark that Brecht's gesture was disingenuous: 'as soon as the situation got really serious and the socialist system was effectively threatened, [Brecht] publicly supported the system' (44). Finally, the same ambivalence can also be seen with regard to Žižek's attitude towards Lukács. On the one hand, he seeks to redeem the early Lukács (of, for instance, *History and Class Consciousness*) from the charge of being 'a determinist "Hegelian" Marxist' (106). On the other hand, he does acknowledge that this ambiguous relation to Stalinism can be seen in the later Lukács who, 'in the gesture of a personal Thermidor withdrew and turned to the more specialized areas of Marxist aesthetics and literary theory, justifying his public support of Stalinist politics in the terms of the Hegelian critique of the Beautiful Soul' (98).

MARX/ALTHUSSER/BADIOU (see also APPEARANCE, LUKÁCS/ADORNO/BRECHT)

This conjunction of names allows us to address something surprising, which is often overlooked in Žižek's work: that for Žižek a properly materialist analysis is not a matter of looking for some 'deeper' cause, of explaining apparently superficial cultural phenomena through a more profound socio-economic (or, in Žižek's case, psychoanalytic) explanation. Indeed, if anything, the opposite is the case. The radical insight of analysis is that the truth lies in *appearance*, that it is a matter of getting rid of the idea of some deeper cause, something behind the surface in which the answer is to be found (if there is a missing figure in Žižek's list of references, it is perhaps Nietzsche). As Žižek writes apropos of Marx, for example: 'Marx long ago emphasized that the critical test of any historico-materialist analysis is not its ability to reduce ideological or political phenomena to their "actual" economic foundations, but to cover the same path in the opposite direction – that is, to show why these material interests articulate themselves in just such an ideal form' (39). This can be seen in such things as Žižek's emphasis (against Marx himself, it must be admitted) that the fetish reaches its highest form when it is dematerialized (231, 276); his argument, derived from Althusser, that the power of ideological state apparatuses lies in their subjects' external behaviour and not their internal beliefs (17); and in his understanding, indebted to Badiou, of the revolutionary Event as an inherently fragile, fleeting circumstance, which exists only for those who are faithful to it (199). In all of this, Žižek seeks to break with any notion of a 'conspiracy' behind things, of some secret agent pulling the strings. A proper critique of ideology must first of all forego any such transferential relationship to the big Other. In this sense, the position of the materialist thinker is akin to that of the analyst (or the saint): they grasp a world in which actions are underwritten only by themselves, in which an act only retrospectively leads to its cause.

MESSAGE IN REVERSE (see also *COLNCIDENTLA OPPOSITORUM*, IDEOLOGY, INFINITE JUDGEMENT)

Žižek takes the well-known Lacanian dictum of 'the speaker gets back from the addressee his own message in its true, inverted form' and applies it to a number of specific situations. As part of the 'coincidence of opposites' that he sees characterizing contemporary society, he will speak of the way that, for example, the violent skinhead repeats the clichés explaining his actions back to the sociologist, who in turn 'receives his own message in its inverted, true form' (216). More generally, in the election of Jörg Haider's Freedom Party in Austria the false multicultural tolerance of something like Tony Blair's Third Way 'gets its own message back in inverted form' (41). In a more extended development, Žižek will speak – following the French political theorist Jacques Rancière – of the way that, having mailed off their excess, useless 'human rights' to the poor and oppressed, thus depoliticizing their struggles and rendering them helpless, this letter returns in the guise of a series of intractable dilemmas for the West in its 'humanitarian interventions' (221–2). Žižek's point in all of this – this is the 'lesson' of Lacan's original treatment of the theme – is that our actions inevitably lead to unforeseen consequences that are in fact their true meaning. We cannot deny these consequences, for – in a manner akin to Hegelian 'infinite judgement' – we must see that they apply to us, that we are ultimately responsible for them. As Žižek writes: 'In this precise sense, the dissolution of transference designates the moment when the arrow of the question that the analysand pointed at the analyst turns back toward the analysand himself' (66).

PARALLAX VIEW (see also APPEARANCE, *COINCIDENTIA OPPOSITORUM*)

In a world of dialectical negativity, in which we cannot grasp anything without also grasping its opposite, the correct mode of perception is the 'parallax view'. This term, originally taken from the Japanese philosopher Kojin Karatani, but having precedents in Adorno, indicates an attempt to keep both alternatives in mind at once. The truth is not to be found in either one of them, but only in their impossible simultaneity. Žižek can evoke this 'parallax view' in amusing ways: in his essay on Bill Gates, for example, he speaks of the way that, just as with those postcards that when tilted a certain way reveal a naked woman beneath her clothes, by looking at the Microsoft boss awry we can see a 'sinister and threatening dimension' (233). More substantially, Žižek characterizes the relationship between politics and economics, not only in Communism but also in capitalism, as being like that famous optical trick of 'two faces or a vase': 'one sees either two faces or a vase, never both of them – in other words, one has to make a choice . . . if, for Lacan, there is no sexual relationship, then, for Marxism proper, there is no relationship between economy and politics, no "metalanguage" enabling us to grasp both two levels from the same neutral standpoint, although – or, rather, *because* – these two levels are inextricably intertwined' (247). Or, with regard to the alternative between 'terrorism' and the 'war on terrorism' proposed after 11 September: 'The WTC attacks confront us again with the necessity of resisting the temptation of a double blackmail . . . the only solution is to reject this very opposition and to adopt both positions simultaneously, which can only be done if one resorts to the dialectical category of *totality*' (282). The difficult aspect of this parallax view – and the true Hegelian lesson implicit in it – is that it is ultimately not a question of looking for some deeper commonality beneath these alternatives, or of somehow mediating between them. The truth lies not in any resolution of the split, but in this split itself: 'If, then, there is appearance (as distinct from reality) because there is a (logically) prior split inherent to reality itself, is it also that "reality" itself is ultimately nothing but a (self-)split of appearance (the "parallax" thesis)?' (345).

REAL (see also **ACT/ORGANIZATION, ANTAGONISM, REVOLUTION, VIOLENCE**)

Žižek cites French philosopher Alain Badiou's diagnosis of a certain '"passion for the Real [*la passion du réel*]" as the key feature of the twentieth century: in contrast to the utopian or "scientific" projects and ideals, and plans about the future, of the nineteenth century, this century aimed at delivering the thing itself, at directly realizing the longed-for New Order' (267). Examples of this 'passion for the Real' that Žižek provides in his work include the celebration of face-to-face trench warfare in World War I, the perverse universe of Stalinism and even crashing the airplanes into the World Trade Center. However, this 'passion for the Real' and its attempt to 'directly realize' the Thing itself is more ambiguous that it appears. Although Žižek approves of the Real of social revolution, arguing that any genuine challenge to the social order is impossible without it, it is also not sufficient – or, more precisely, this Real can be understood in two different ways. Either this 'passion for the Real' becomes a form of passing enthusiasm, which ends up as merely a 'pure semblance of political theatre', or it is formalized in a political organization that attempts to remain faithful to it. These – as both violence and organization – are the two sides of the Real Žižek speaks of throughout: 'In Lacanian theory, the Real has two principal sides. One is the Real as a remainder that is impossible to symbolize, a scrap, the refuse of the symbolic, a hole in the Other . . .; the other is the Real as writing, construct, number and mathème'. He then goes on to say: 'These two sides perfectly correspond to the opposition fascism/Stalinism' (5). Indeed, we could even say that fascism is either one of these sides as such, while Leninism–Stalinism is the necessary simultaneity of both.

REVOLUTION (see also **ACT/ORGANIZATION, COMMUNISM, INFINITE JUDGEMENT, INHUMAN, REAL, STALINISM, THINKING, VIOLENCE**)

Today, in our liberal democracies, the very possibility of revolution seems unthinkable: we can have the endless critique or questioning of the system, but nothing is fundamentally changed. As Žižek writes: 'what is problematic with this position of depoliticizing the revolt is that it precludes any actual radical political change: the existing political régime is never effectively undermined or overturned, just endlessly "questioned"' (123 n. 32). However, revolution proper is never simply this overturning or doing away with the existing order, which we might associate with a period of revolutionary enthusiasm or even violence (although this too is necessary). Something else is required that is more difficult to grasp: 'In this suspension of goal-orientated instrumental activity, we effectively get a kind of Bataillean "unrestrained expenditure" . . . [t]he pious desire to deprive the revolution of this excess is simply the desire to have a revolution without revolution. However, this "unrestrained expenditure" is not enough: in a revolution proper, such a display of what Hegel would have called "abstract negativity" merely, as it were, wipes the slate clean for the second act, the imposition of a New Order' (130). But what exactly is meant by revolution as at once the wiping of the slate clean for a new order ('abstract negativity') and the imposition of a new order (what we might call, following Hegel, the 'negation of negation')? Perhaps Žižek's ultimate example of revolution, which occurs several times in this volume, is paradoxically the *restaging* of the 1917 October Revolution in Russia some three years afterwards as a kind of theatrical event (48–9, 130). What this restaging suggests for Žižek is revolution as the constant wiping of the slate clean in an 'infinite judgement' that keeps on applying the lessons of the revolution to itself. The bureaucratic implementation of the revolution is not simply the following of some pre-established plan but a radical questioning of the revolution's own assumptions, the field in which the original decision took place. 'And this brings us to the key question: how are we to construct a social space within which revolution can stabilize itself? Perhaps, one of the options is to pursue the trend of self-organized collectives in areas outside the Law. Arguably the greatest literary monument to such a utopia comes from an unexpected source – Mario Vargas Llosa's *The War of the End of the World*, a novel about Canudos, an outlaw community deep in the Brazilian backlands, which was home to prostitutes, freaks, beggars, bandits and the most wretched of the poor. Canudos . . . was a utopian space without money, property, taxes and marriage' (51). We could even paraphrase Žižek by saying that the desire for Leninist revolution without its corresponding Stalinist bureaucracy is the desire for 'revolution without revolution'.

STALINISM (see also **LUKÀCS/ADORNO/BRECHT, REVOLUTION, VIOLENCE**)

Žižek repeats it several times: Stalinism is neither a contingent deviation of Leninism, having nothing essentially to do with it, nor its logical outcome, the only way it could have turned out. As he writes: 'One should oppose both temptations: the Trotskyite notion that Stalinism was ultimately a contingent deviation, as well as the notion that the Communist project is, in its very core, totalitarian' (128); or elsewhere: 'the great task today is to think the necessity of the passage from Leninism to Stalinism without denying the tremendous emancipatory potential of the Event of October' (99). If we can say this, Stalinism represents the 'infinite judgement' of Leninism, the application of its own logic to itself through the necessity of organization. Stalinism thus embodies the inherent *risk* of Leninism in having to turn its original revolutionary enthusiasm into an ongoing political organization. It is in this sense that Žižek can approve of the violence of Stalinism: it proves that it was serious about the desire to achieve revolution. This is even why he can note with approval that the régime changed its mind three times over its alliances during World War II: it again demonstrated that something 'authentic' was going on. Along the lines of Žižek's remarks on revolution, we might say that Stalinism was precisely the necessary 'second stage' of Leninism: the 'imposition of a New Order' (130). But, if there is a 'mistake in Stalinism', it is that it sees this second stage as separate from the first. If Leninism is always in a sense 'subjective', 'performative', Stalinism believes it can become 'objective', necessary: 'the Kautskyist–Stalinist Party addresses the proletariat from a position of "objective" knowledge intended to supplement the proletarian subjective (self-)experience of suffering and exploitation, i.e., the split here is the split between proletarian "spontaneous" subjective self-experience and objective knowledge about one's social situation, while, in an authentic Leninist Party, the split is thoroughly subjective, i.e., the Party addresses the proletariat from a radically subjective, engaged position of the lack that prevents the proletarians from achieving their "proper place" in the social edifice' (111). That is, although Stalinism should occupy the position of the Analyst vis-à-vis Leninism, it in fact seeks to occupy that of the University: 'Stalinist discourse presents a neutral-objective knowledge as its agent, while the repressed truth of this knowledge remains S_1, the performative of the master' (76).

THINKING (see also **ACT/ORGANIZATION, REVOLUTION**)
An unexpected strain of Žižek's work, at odds with the cliché of him endlessly throwing off wild revolutionary schemes, is his continued emphasis on the power of *thinking*. To this extent, as he himself says of Freud and Lacan, Žižek remains faithful to the Enlightenment: 'the leftist Enlightenment is defined by the wager that culture can serve as an efficient answer to the gun: the outburst of raw violence is a kind of *passage à l'acte* rooted in the subject's ignorance – as such, it can be counteracted by the struggle whose main form is *reflective knowledge*' (179–80). This 'reflective' thinking is to be opposed in the first instance to the desire to act immediately, which merely reproduces the existing coordinates and perpetuates what it is opposed to, functioning as its 'inherent transgression': 'I am therefore tempted to reverse Marx's thesis 11: the first task today is precisely *not* to succumb to the temptation to act, to intervene directly and change things . . . but to question the hegemonic ideological coordinates. If, today, one follows a direct call to act, this act will not be performed in an empty space – it will be an act *within* the hegemonic ideological coordinates' (238). But in fact Žižek's ultimate point – in the 'coincidence of opposites' that marks his work – is that thinking is *already* a revolutionary act, or more exactly that the discipline of thinking is like the organization that is the true form of revolution: 'Lukács advocates the dialectical unity/mediation of theory and practice, in which even the utmost contemplative stance is eminently "practical" (in the sense of being embedded in the totality of social [re]production and thus expressing a certain "practical" stance of how to survive within this totality), and, on the other hand, even the most "practical" stance implies a certain "theoretical" framework; it materializes a set of implicit ideological propositions' (113).

THIRD WAY (see also *COINCIDENTIA OPPOSITORUM*, **INFINITE JUDGEMENT**)
What is Žižek's objection to the Third Way (that form of modern democratic politics that seeks to find a middle path between the alternatives of socialism and capitalism, and exemplified by such governments as those of Blair in Britain, Schröder in Germany and Clinton in the United States)? It is that it seeks to deny the fundamental antagonism that characterizes the social, believing that capitalism can

one day be rendered harmonious and unified, or more simply that there is no alternative to capitalism: 'The idea of a "third way" emerged at the very moment when, at least in the West, all other alternatives, from old-style conservativism to radical social democracy, crumbled in the face of the triumphant onslaught of global capitalism and its notion of liberal democracy. The true message of the notion of the Third Way is that there is no "second way", no alternative to global capitalism, so that, in a kind of mocking pseudo-Hegelian 'negation of negation', the Third Way brings us back to the first and only way. Is this not global capitalism with a human face?' (149). If put into these terms, not only would it be a matter of avoiding the 'blackmail' of the existing alternatives to capitalism, but also of rejecting any 'third' choice between these alternatives and capitalism. Indeed, the true lesson of Hegelian dialectics is that the very attempt to create a universal necessarily brings about an exception, and this is the case with the Third Way. For what characterizes the period of its emergence in the 1990s after the collapse of Communism is a series of nationalist racisms and religious fundamentalisms, which must be understood as the exact equivalent of its false multicultural inclusiveness: 'The "disappearance" of the working class then fatally unleashes its reappearance in the guise of aggressive nativism. Liberals and populists meet on common ground; all they talk about is identity. Is not Haider himself the best Hegelian example of the "speculative identity" of the tolerant multiculturalist and the postmodern racist?' (40). In fact, in just that kind of 'infinite judgement' that Žižek often speaks of, there was a real 'third way' that emerged at the time of Communism, a brief 'vanishing mediator' that was swept away either by the drive towards capitalism or the revival of nationalism: '*Neues Forum* consisted of groups of passionate intellectuals who took socialism seriously and were prepared to put everything at stake in order to destroy the compromised system and replace it with a utopian "third way" beyond capitalism and "Really Existing Socialism"' (17).

TRUTH (see also **APPEARANCE, INFINITE JUDGEMENT, UNIVERSAL EXCEPTION**)

Žižek throughout his writings asserts the possibility of Truth. This is against what he sees as both the postmodern relativization of Truth and the vulgar materialist attempt to reduce Truth to an effect of its socio-historical determinants. As he says of the former: 'We live in a "postmodern" era in which truth-claims as such are dismissed as expressions of hidden power mechanisms . . . The very question, "Is it true?", apropos of some statement is supplanted by another question: "Under what power conditions can this statement be uttered?" What we get, instead of universal truth, is a multitude of perspectives, or, as it is fashionable to put it today, "narratives"' (240). As he says of the latter: 'Lukács' point is precisely to undermine this false alternative of historicist relativism (there is no neutral knowledge of "objective reality", since all knowledge is biased, embedded in a specific "social context") and the distinction between the socio-historical conditions and the inherent truth-value of a body of knowledge (even if a certain theory emerged within a specific social context, this context provides only external conditions, which in no way diminish or undermine the "objective truth" of its propositions . . .)' (115). However, if Žižek does assert a kind of Truth, it is not so much 'objective' as 'subjective', does not so much speak of the world from somewhere outside of it, introducing a split between it and the world, as from within it, introducing a split between the world and itself. To put this another way, the Truth in Žižek is always *engaged*. It does not erect a division between the Universal and the Exception that speaks of it, but seeks to cross all boundaries in ceaselessly turning upon itself: 'Lenin's wager – today, in our era of postmodern relativism, more actual than ever – is that universal truth and partisanship, the gesture of taking sides, are not only not mutually exclusive, but condition each other: in a concrete situation, its *universal* truth can only be articulated from a thoroughly *partisan* position – truth is by definition one-sided' (245). This particular, engaged Truth is to be seen in such things as the great emancipatory movements led by Gandhi and Martin Luther King (148, 222–3), in de Gaulle's appeal to the 'French people' from exile during World War II (198–9) and elsewhere in the identification with Jews (or Palestinians).

UNIVERSAL EXCEPTION (see also ANTAGONISM, APPEARANCE, CLASS STRUGGLE, DEMOCRACY, INFINITE JUDGEMENT, LOGIC OF EXCEPTION, TRUTH)

Žižek outlines the process involved in Hegelian dialectics, which is not at all a final 'synthesis' of differences, but an ongoing process of continuing to fold the result over on to itself, attempting to find within each universality the exception that makes it possible: 'each genus has only one species, the other species is the paradoxical negative of the genus itself. Just as in the instance of the "limit case" of the logic of the signifier, the All is divided into its Part and a remainder that is not nothing but a paradoxical, impossible, contradictory entity' (77). Žižek then goes on to draw a distinction between this proper Hegelian conception and its Stalinist perversion: 'Unlike the Hegelian division, however, instead of *including* through its specification/determination, the genus *excludes* its own absence and "negativity"' (78). But all of this needs to be read very carefully. Two points in particular are worth noting: first, that this logic of exception is only the 'limit case' of the usual logic of the universal proved through exception; second, that this 'universal exception' is to be attained only through a process of inclusion (of showing each time how the universal is only an exception) and not exclusion (of holding on to an exception from which the universal is stated). Accordingly, when Žižek says that the universal exception is the bringing-together of the universal and the exception, of directly embodying the universal in the exception, this is to be understood as a goal to be aimed at rather than something to be directly accomplished: 'Politics proper thus always involves a kind of short-circuit between the universal and the particular; it involves the paradox of a singular that appears as a stand-in for the universal . . . This *singulier universel* is a group that, although without any fixed place in the social edifice . . . presents itself as the immediate embodiment of *society as such*, in its universality' (183–4). Žižek provides a number of examples of this universal exception throughout his work: the networks of the new virtual technologies (236); the proletariat within Marxist theory (101–2); the Palestinians in the West Bank and slum-dwellers across the globe (225 n. 25). However, as Žižek equally insists, each of these is also *not* it, their exceptional character is not some inherent property – as he says, for example, of the proletariat: 'the overlapping of the Universal and the Particular in the proletariat does not stand for their immediate identity . . .: the universal revolutionary potential is rather "inscribed into the very being of the proletariat" as its inherent radical split' (111). Nevertheless, this failure does not have the logic of the Hegelian 'bad infinity' or 'inherent transgression'. He is not simply against the American attempt to inaugurate world democracy, beginning with Iraq. Instead, his point is that the United States should be subject to the very universality it appeals to, that there is precisely *no* exception to this rule of democracy: 'In Hegelese, *the existence of the true Universal* (as opposed to the false concrete universality of the all-encompassing global Order of Being) *is that of an endless and incessantly divisive struggle*; it is ultimately the division between the two notions (and material practices) of universality' (199).

VIOLENCE (see also ACT/ORGANIZATION, REAL, REVOLUTION, STALINISM)

Žižek follows the French political theorist Étienne Balibar's critique of 'standard Hegelian-Marxism' for its 'conversion-theory' of violence: the fact that violence must necessarily be sublated in the political process, eventually to be seen only as a momentary stage within an overall 'rational' progress. And yet, read carefully, neither Žižek nor Balibar proposes a direct, unmediated, unsublimated violence as opposed to this. Rather, the theoretical task is always double: 'According to Balibar, for necessarily structural reasons, Marxism is unable to conceive of an excess of violence that cannot be integrated into the narrative of historical progress . . . The task then becomes double: to deploy a theory of historical violence as something that cannot be mastered, instrumentalized by any political agent, which threatens to engulf this very agent in a self-destructive cycle, and – the other side of the same task – to pose the question of how to "civilize" revolution, of how to make the revolutionary process itself a "civilizing" force' (213–14). To put this another way, on the one hand, violence is necessary as a sign of the commitment to seizing and maintaining political power: 'Violence is the necessary supplement to power' (217). On the other hand, violence without organization is not enough; it can in fact be the very way *not* to do something, a surface action that hides a true passivity: '[fascist violence] is a violence whose aim is to prevent the true change' (218) – and perhaps the same criticism might apply not only to the violence of the Islamic fundamentalists but also to that of the American invasion of Iraq.

YUGOSLAVIA (see also *COINCIDENTIA OPPOSITORUM*, INFINITE JUDGEMENT)

The first question to ask – in so far as it is not merely the name for a once-existing nation-state, but a kind of ideological fantasy – is where exactly *is* Yugoslavia? Throughout his work, Žižek is eager to dispel the fantasy that constructs the Balkans in terms of its identification either with *Mitteleuropa* or with the undifferentiated 'Slavic hordes'. It is a fantasy shared both by those within the old Yugoslavia and by the West itself. For the former, their assertion of long-standing national identity is false, nothing but a response to present-day political exigencies: 'In this sense, the tale of ethnic roots is a long way from being the "myth of origins": what is "national heritage" if not a kind of ideological fossil created retroactively by the ruling ideology in order to blur its present antagonism?' (30) And for the West too, this image of ancient ethnic quarrels is a self-serving illusion: 'What [films like Emir Kusturica's *Underground*] offer to the Western liberal gaze is precisely what this gaze wants to see in the Balkan War – the spectacle of a timeless, incomprehensible, mythical cycle of passions, in contrast to decadent and anaemic Western life' (163). For Žižek, the proper point to be made is that these two fantasies are self-sustaining: the Yugoslavian resort to national identity is staged for and only possible under the Western gaze. As he concludes: 'So the lesson is that the alternative between the New World Order and the neo-racist nationalism opposing it is a false one: these are the two sides of the same coin – the New World Order itself breeds the monstrosities that it fights' (266).

Index